LE GRAND
TOUR

...ON A BIKE CALLED WANDA

ANDREW P. SYKES

CyclingEurope.org
CYCLING | TRAVEL | ADVENTURE | PODCAST

Le Grand Tour
on a Bike Called Wanda

CyclingEurope.org

ISBN: 978-1-3999-8525-3

*To everyone who likes to ride a bicycle
and occasionally gets lost*

Also by the author

*Crossing Europe on a Bike Called Reggie
Along the Med on a Bike Called Reggie
Spain to Norway on a Bike Called Reggie*

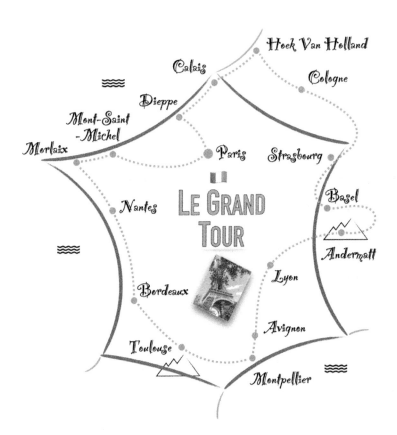

Hoek Van Holland

Calais

Cologne

Dieppe

Mont-Saint
-Michel

Morlaix

Paris

Strasbourg

**LE GRAND
TOUR**

Basel

Nantes

Andermatt

Bordeaux

Lyon

Avignon

Toulouse

Montpellier

Contents

Prologue	7
Part 1: The North Sea Cycle Route / La Vélomaritime	9
Part 2: L'Avenue Verte	45
Part 3: La Véloscénie	65
Part 4: La Vélomaritime (Again...)	95
Part 5: La Vélodyssée / EuroVelo 1	125
Part 6: Le Canal Des 2 Mers À Vélo	163
Part 7: La ViaRhôna / EuroVelo 17	221
Part 8: The Rhine Cycle Route / EuroVelo 15	297
Epilogue	367
Acknowledgements	371
About the author	373

Tout pour les yeux semble si près et pour les jambes si loin.

Everything for the eyes seems so close and for the legs so far away.

Jean-Luc Parant

(As painted on the towpath of the
Canal de la Garonne near Auvillar, France)

Prologue

It was a breezy morning on July 3rd at the Hook of Holland. I had been looking for an iconic signpost and had just found it. As the crow flew it was only 5km from where my ferry had docked on the southern side of the Nieuwe Waterweg, one of the many rivers that carve their paths across the Rhine-Meuse Delta en route to the North Sea. However, thanks to the idiosyncratic geography of Rotterdam Harbour (and a somewhat inconveniently closed bridge) the cycle from the ferry had stretched to over 30km.

The signpost was not quite vertical. It leaned a few degrees towards the south-west. I stood beside it and paused for a few moments to reflect.

Much had happened in the seven years since completing my cycle from the southernmost point of Europe at Tarifa in Spain to its most northerly point at Nordkapp in Norway.

As one adventure finished, another was about to begin.

It was with these words that I concluded my account of that journey in the book *Spain to Norway on a Bike Called Reggie*. The adventure that "was about to begin" was a return to Yorkshire after 25 years of living in London, then France and then Berkshire.

As for my next long-distance *cycling* adventure, that had been delayed by global events beyond my control. Grand plans had been formulated and shelved. However, I had not been prevented from finding a new cycling companion: Wanda, my Koga WorldTraveller bicycle. Reggie had been retired to the cellar.

The blue panels at the top of the wonky sign at the Hook of Holland pointed in the direction of far-flung locations: Cape Town – 6,645km, Shanghai 8,934km, St. Petersburg – 1,831km… My destination was somewhat closer to hand. I was already standing there.

The plan was to follow the Dutch, Belgian and French coasts as far as Dieppe. I would then cycle south to Paris before continuing west to the Mont-Saint-Michel. After passing through Brittany, I would travel along the west coast of France in the direction of La Rochelle and Bordeaux, before heading east along the canals of Midi-Pyrénées to Toulouse and then Sète on the Mediterranean coast. Here I would begin the long trek back to the Hook of Holland following the Rhône to Lyon and into Switzerland, over the Alps via the Furka Pass before a long journey north beside the Rhine.

My return ferry was booked for the evening of Saturday 3rd September. It was a non-negotiable deadline as I needed to be back at work in the classroom on Monday 5th September. I had exactly two months to complete my quest.

But was such a trip feasible in just 62 days?

If I remained loyal to the routes I intended to follow (a mixture of EuroVelos and branded national routes such as the Avenue Verte to Paris and the Vélodyssée in the west of France), I estimated the journey would be one of around 5,500km. Assuming a non-cycling day every week, that would require an average daily cycle in excess of 100km. I had achieved this in 2013 on a two-month cycle along the Mediterranean coast from Greece to Portugal, but it had left me bereft of energy in the final weeks of the trip as I wilted under the heat of the Andalusian sun. Nearly ten years later I was sceptical that I would be able to repeat the feat. So I decided that during my journey, I would allow myself to take a maximum of ten trains a maximum of 100km each. This could bring the estimated distance down to 4,500km, a more manageable average of around 80km per day.

———

I looked up at the sign. Its south-westerly lean was a subtle nudge suggesting I should get a move on. Perhaps you are thinking the same.

PART ONE:

The North Sea Cycle Route / La Vélomaritime

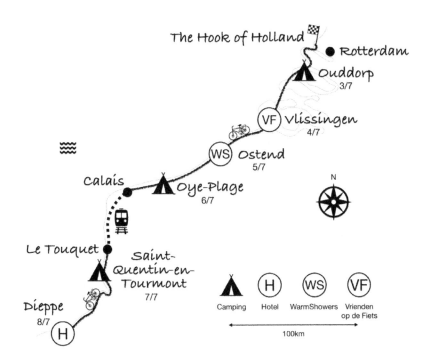

Day One: The Hook of Holland to Ouddorp (73km)
Sunday 3rd July

It was almost precisely midday when I set off along the 5,500km loop that, if all went to plan, would see me return to The Hook of Holland in two months. I was fully expecting to retrace my route back to the small ferry at Maassluis where I planned to cross - again - the Nieuwe Waterweg to Rozenburg on the southern side of the estuary. It would be a 15km cycle through familiar territory and, as Wanda's robust touring tyres rolled over the rough concrete of the wide path beside the water, I began to contemplate what was to come over the next few weeks. The known knowns, the known unknowns and the unknown unknowns.

Very little of my journey was planned in detail. I knew that to give myself a fighting chance of returning to the wonky signpost and back to Britain in time for the start of the new school year on September 5th, I needed to be in certain places at certain times. Somewhere in the north-western corner of France by mid-July, in south-western France by early August and in the Alps within a couple of weeks of my ferry leaving Rotterdam on September 3rd. Everything was very "ish".

That said, I *had* planned the first three nights of accommodation. I had booked a campsite a few kilometres to the west of the Dutch town of Ouddorp, a second night at a Vrienden op de Fiets (I will explain later) house in the port of Vlissingen and a third at a co-housing project near Ostend arranged via the accommodation sharing website Warmshowers. Lack of concern as to where I would sleep on those first three nights would, I thought, give me the mental space to reacquaint myself with the itinerant life of a cycle tourist. This always took time, and I was fully prepared to feel out of my comfort zone for the first few days - perhaps even the first week - of the trip. Even the most experienced cycle tourists need a few days to readjust and feel comfortable not just on the saddle but in their skin. For many onlookers what we do is at best mildly curious, at worst plain weird. Overcoming that feeling of being different can take time.

My internal musings were interrupted after only 3km of cycling when I arrived at the Hook of Holland Berghaven, or harbour. The cycle path descended a little to follow the edge of a small port. Half a dozen metal jetties were floating on the water and next to the path opposite one of the jetties was the sign for *knooppunt* number 94. I had been initiated into the delights of *knooppunten* during my 2015 cycle across Europe whilst travelling through Belgium. The numbered-node network was ubiquitous across the Netherlands and Belgium and facilitated (almost) idiot-proof route finding for travellers on foot or by bike. Cyclists could often be seen consulting a list of numbers taped to their handlebars, each number guiding them to the next node of the network. At node 94 in the harbour, I noticed the arrows for nodes 55 and 57 pointed out across the water. *Had the knooppunt network been extended to embrace the needs of wild swimmers?* Not yet. The map on the adjacent noticeboard confirmed what I was desperately hoping: there was a ferry that could take me across the water at this point of the estuary rather than having to retrace my route back to the ferry at Maassluis. But there was no ferry floating on the water nor queue of expectant people beside the jetty, and it *was* Sunday. I loitered for a few minutes searching for definitive proof - in both the real and online worlds - that I was not waiting for a ferry that would ultimately never arrive. I struggled to find a sign or a timetable that would give me any hint of confidence I was not just wasting my time.

I then noticed movement on a nearby lifeboat and went through the superfluous motions of asking the man - who was busy tidying some ropes ready for the next rescue - if he spoke English. He did: he was Dutch. I enquired tentatively about the ferry.

"Yes, of course it operates on a Sunday," he replied. "It's mainly for tourists and cyclists so it's the busiest time of the week."

Despite the lack of evidence of it being the ferry's "busiest time of the week", I took the man at his word and waited. After a few minutes, a couple with their bikes arrived at the jetty and repeated my motions of looking puzzled before approaching me to ask what the situation was. I took heart in the fact that these Dutch cyclists were as bemused as I had been. It was not me being a stupid foreigner.

Shortly before 1 pm, the ferry arrived. It resembled a small fishing boat, was freshly painted in blue and white and sported a large canopy over much of its deck to protect its passengers - and their bicycles - from the elements.

As we bumped our way through the choppy waters of Rotterdam port, tall stacks of shipping containers towering ominously over the small vessel in almost all directions, I chatted to the captain. His white shirt matched the colour of his hair and his resplendent, well-maintained moustache. He explained that the boat dated from 1958 but had only recently been donated to the Port of Rotterdam by the authorities in Amsterdam where it had plied its trade ferrying pedestrians along the canals. However, for a vessel that was rapidly approaching retirement age, it was looking just as sharp as its captain and a perfect example of recycling, Dutch style.

Despite its brutal ugliness, it was difficult not to be impressed by the sprawling Port of Rotterdam, Europe's largest and, on a global level, only beaten in terms of trade by those of Singapore and Shanghai. It took 50 minutes for the ferry to arrive at its destination. This was the FutureLand visitor centre, a complex of buildings dedicated to explaining how the port will develop in years to come by continuing to devour large sections of the sea. Perhaps, I reflected, it might one day extend as far as the beaches of Norfolk and form a land bridge to the UK. If that meant I would not have to endure the dreadful live music on board P&O's *Pride of Rotterdam* ferry at some point in the future, I would happily volunteer my labour and start shovelling earth.

Once back on dry (albeit probably reclaimed) land I set off along the coast in the direction of Ouddorp and the campsite. My hopes of seeing anything other than the sprawl of industry along this stretch of the North Sea were minimal. Initially, I was not disappointed as the beautifully maintained bike path mirrored the direction of the almost deserted dual carriageway to my left. Electricity pylons stood defiantly beyond the road as did railway lines, more cranes and, in the distance, cylindrical oil storage containers with shallow turreted roofs. They may have been painted to camouflage them against the grey sky, but such was their size, no one was being fooled.

Then something strange happened. Within a matter of minutes, the port and all its peripheral infrastructure disappeared as I was plunged into a very different landscape of immaculate suburbia. Smart, detached properties - one or two were even thatched - vied for position between the trees and shrubs of a very affluent neighbourhood. I initially assumed this was where the great and the good of Rotterdam society came to spend their weekends. On reflection, it was more likely a visible display of the high standard of living enjoyed by most Dutch people. It never ceases to amaze me just how much Britain has to learn from places such as the Netherlands when it comes to providing a quality of life not only for a minority of its population but for the vast majority. A cycle through most European countries - and certainly through those of our near neighbours in the north of the continent - brings home the depressing reality that Britain is a very different, unequal place. It was such a shame that since my last long European escapade, we had chosen to isolate ourselves politically from our continental cousins.

More changes were afoot as I continued along the Kustroute, the local name for what, on a European level, is known as the EuroVelo 12 or North Sea Cycle Route. I would continue to follow route 12 as far as Calais in France, at which point it would board a ferry and sail off in the direction of Kent. The Kustroute would take me across four fingers of land - one in South Holland and three in Zeeland - before handing me over to the Belgians. Of the five bodies of water that separated these four tentacles, two were crossed by boat, two by long dams and one by a long dam followed by a short dam. (Still with me?) If you like your engineering big, this is the place to come as much of the Netherlands is one big science project. This was especially the case in the south-western corner of the country.

The facts are astonishing. About a fifth of the total land mass of the Netherlands has been reclaimed from the sea by the building of dikes, or *dijken* or levees or dams. I will settle for the latter. If these dams were suddenly removed, Amsterdam would be completely submerged, and Rotterdam would become an offshore island destination. The youngest Dutch province, Flevoland, was almost all reclaimed from the Zuiderzee (remember that from your 1980s geography textbook?) - the southern sea - in the 1950s and what was left of the Zuiderzee is now a freshwater lake called the IJsselmeer.

Here in the south, the fingers of land across which I was cycling would have been somewhat daintier and none would have had a land bridge to the mainland were it not for the Delta Works series of dams. There was a dozen of them in total and crossing all of them would have been a long cycle tour in itself. In 1994 the American Society of Civil Engineering listed the Delta Works as one of their Seven Wonders of the Modern World stating, "The North Sea Protection Works exemplifies the ability of humanity to exist side-by-side with the forces of nature".

To get as far as Ouddorp and my campsite, this bit of humanity on a bicycle needed to cross the first of my four dams: the Haringvlietdam. As you might expect, the Dutch had afforded cyclists much more than a painted line on the road. We had our own two-way segregated lane and the only force of nature I had to contend with was that of the wind which was doing its best to toss me over the edge of the dam and into the lake on my left. It was not difficult to see why the concept of the windmill had taken off in such a big way in these parts.

There was a particularly stunning example of one such windmill as I passed through the outskirts of the village of Goedereede. It stood, motionless, at the far end of a busy field of allotments which was dominated by a pleasingly chaotic display of red, orange and yellow wildflowers alongside more disciplined rows of vegetables. On a day that had already exposed me to many of the delights of the Dutch nation, this scene was perhaps the finest and I paused to appreciate it in all its glory.

Less glorious was campsite number one of the trip. Camping Zuidhoek was situated near a busy road which, although hidden by the trees that surrounded my allocated plot in the corner of a small field, was clearly audible. The welcome was friendly enough but when I returned to the reception to pay the €11.50 I owed, I was not able to use my debit card. Not having passed a machine during the day, cash was not an option either. I eventually managed to pay using an international bank transfer via the banking app on my phone. It seemed somewhat laborious for a tenner's worth of accommodation.

"Do you sell bread?" I enquired before processing my online payment. "I couldn't find a shop open in the town."

The owner paused before replying.

"They're a bit religious in Ouddorp," she said but held back on the details. I could only assume the local hardliners would come marching down the road in hooded cloaks and torch the place if rumour got around she was engaging in commercial activity on the Sabbath.

However, it was not all bad news.

"Would you like a beer? No charge."

I returned to my pitch, beer in hand, to toast a successful day on the cycle paths of the Netherlands. A group of elderly friends were enjoying an evening meal in their corner of the field and I cracked open the can of Heineken in mine. I noticed it was alcohol-free. The local brethren would have been delighted. Their box of matches could be saved for another day.

Day Two: Ouddorp to Vlissingen (64km)
Monday 4th July

When I set off to cycle across Europe in 2010 - my first long trip on a bike - my kit was pretty standard. I had some clothes, some camping equipment (including a tent of course) and an assortment of items that I thought I may have needed but ultimately never used. A washing line, for example. On subsequent journeys either in the UK or on the continent, my list of kit had gradually shifted in the direction of things I *would* need rather than things I *might* need. I had come to the happy conclusion that when cycling in Europe you are rarely very far from a well-stocked shop that can sell you the item you discovered was essential during the trip but which you never thought once about packing in your panniers.

However, there is one list of kit that has lengthened with every trip I have embarked upon: the tech list. On that first trip, I had an iPhone 4 and an extra battery pack. I did not record my route digitally: I just had a Spot device that I never really figured out how to use. Its main purpose was to provide me with a button to press to call the emergency services should I need them. Thankfully I never did. I also had a basic cycling computer that registered the number of kilometres travelled. That was it. The phone was sufficient to take a few photos and, when I could latch onto a decent Internet connection, upload them to my website along with a bit of carefully crafted prose.

Twelve years later my desire to speak to the world as I travelled had evolved somewhat and so had my list of technical requirements. The iPhone 13 was the hub of my broadcasting unit on two wheels. This included a microphone and an iPad (to record and edit episodes of The Cycling Europe Podcast), a GoPro Hero 10 camera and a DJI Mini 2 drone. These, along with the iPhone, allowed me to record video in 4K/UHD quality for daily short films uploaded to YouTube as well as for a series of longer films that I planned to put together once I arrived back home.[1] Everything needed to be kept charged so I had a stock of extra batteries for the GoPro and drone. And then there were the cables and adaptors - over a dozen of them in total. Having been focussed on simply getting to the Hook of Holland and then the campsite on day one, it was not until the morning of July 4th - day two - that much of the technology got its first outing.

About 3km from the gates of Camping Zuidhoek I noticed a large block of concrete beside the cycle path attached to which was an information

---

[1] You can watch all the films by visiting YouTube.com/@CyclingEuropeYouTube

panel dominated by a star-shaped diagram. *A Napoleonic fort?* The text revealed a much more recent story: the Tobruk Bunker. It was a recently uncovered remnant of the German Atlantic Wall fortifications that ran from Norway to the south of France dating back to 1943. According to the panel the bunker took its name from a town in Libya where the Italian army had built similar fortifications. The design had been copied by the Nazis, but they had kept the original name.

The fortifications would, I thought, look their best from the air so I reached into my front-right pannier and, for the first time on continental soil, prepared to launch the drone. I had purchased it the previous year and the learning curve had been a steep one. Within minutes of its first flight - rather short sightedly in my front room at home - it had crashed (or, rather, I had crashed it) into a lamp and I was required to replace two of the rotors. Things went much better when I stuck to flying it outside and over the months leading up to the cycle, I had gradually become more competent in piloting the contraption.

When folded up it was no bigger than the palm of my hand and very light - under 250 grams - but capable of reaching a (legal) height of over 100 metres and travelling at astonishing speed. The controller was bigger and much heavier with two joysticks. One controlled vertical and spin movement, and one controlled movement forward, back, left and right. Not so much patting your head and rubbing your stomach at the same time, more patting your head, rubbing your stomach and doing an Irish jig while coping with increasing levels of stress when you realised you could no longer see the drone's grey body against the grey sky. We now wonder why cigarettes were ever allowed to go on sale. Give it 30 years and we will be saying the same thing about drones.

Alas, the Tobruk Bunker fortifications looked more impressive on the information board than they did from 50 metres in the air, so I turned the drone to the south and flew it in the direction of the next of my Delta Works dams: the Browersdam. From the perspective of the drone's camera (transmitted live to my phone which was clamped into the controller), I could see the dam snaking first right then left as it linked two fingers of Dutch reclaimed land. On the North Sea side of the dam, there was a large sandy beach. This was heavy engineering with a softer edge, literally.

I packed up the drone and headed off in the direction of the beach. There was little traffic on the road, which was strange for early Monday morning, but I was not complaining. Indeed, when I started my journey along the ridge of the dam itself, I could not see anyone: not walking, not cycling not driving.

What the dam lacked in height - it was only 15 metres above sea level at its highest point - it made up for in width. Between the lake and the beach, there was plenty of room to squeeze in two roads, a cycle lane and a single-track railway. Most of the 150 metres were made up of a grassy incline to my left and a gentle concrete incline to my right. I fought the temptation to swerve away from the rusty red surface of the cycle path and weave up and down the vast expanse of concrete. If I had been 12 years old again, I would certainly have done so.

But still so few people. The reason why became apparent about halfway across the dam where I chose to ignore the four signs telling me that in another 1.4km, the route was blocked because of the "Concert at Sea". I wrongly surmised that these signs were leftovers from a weekend event and had yet to be taken down on Monday morning. I dearly wanted to keep cycling along the top of the dam on my pristine cycle lane overlooking the gloriously flat and seemingly endless landscape. It was also a factor that in my slightly elevated position I was being pushed south by a stiff breeze from the north. We cyclists often ignore "road closed" signs because we normally get away with it but on this occasion, I should have paused for thought. These were "road closed" signs on a cycle lane. And this was the Netherlands, a country where stuff is done properly, for a reason.

1.4km later, when the cycle route was indeed blocked by the security fences of the concert, I was obliged to turn around and battle the fierce wind. It was a calf-straining reminder to do as I was told.

I spent the next couple of hours crossing the third of the four fingers of land south of Rotterdam. An abundance of wildflowers welcomed me as I started to make up my own inland route rather than stick to the Kustroute / EuroVelo 12 which more slavishly followed the coast. I was keen to make distance in these first few days, but occasionally my route and the official one would coalesce, especially when crossing the dams. After pausing for a sandwich in a supermarket café in the town of Haamstede (it was more Waitrose than Aldi, but then again even the Aldis in the Netherlands were more Waitrose than you would imagine) I approached the final two dams.

The first - the Oosterscheldekering - was a storm surge barrier and was probably uppermost in the minds of the American Society of Civil Engineering when they listed the Delta Works as one of their Seven Wonders of the Modern World. Much narrower than the Browersdam, no one was packing up after a concert here. The description of the Oosterscheldekering (Eastern Scheldt Barrier) on the Ministry of Infrastructure and Water Management's website pulled no punches:

"It has 65 colossal pillars, separated by sluice gates that are roughly 42m wide and 6 to 12m high, each weighing between 260 and 480 tonnes. It is designed to withstand a flood that is statistically unlikely to occur more than once in 4,000 years."

Sadly, in recent years this kind of statistic has had to be revised because of climate change but such is the grandeur of this structure, I feel that the Dutch will be sleeping easily in their beds for a while yet.

The final dam of my cycle along the Dutch coast, the Veerse Gatdam, came and went without me realising that it was indeed a dam. Much smaller in scale than any of its cousins further north, it did a commendable job of masquerading as a long dune. Now on my final finger of land, I was aiming to get to the southern port of Vlissingen by the end of the day. With only 20km to cycle after I arrived on the central peninsula of Zeeland, I could sit back and take things easy.

The Kustroute continued to maintain its intimate relationship with the sea whereas I wanted to visit the city of Middelburg, the capital of the province of Zeeland. Branching away from the Kustroute, I followed signs for Middelburg and by early afternoon I was standing before the splendid Gothic glory of the Middelburg Stadhuis, or town hall. A friend had recommended that I visit Middelburg and here I was at not yet 2 pm with only a short cycle along the canal to get me to Vlissingen. Excellent! Well, kind of…

Although I had only been on the road for two days, I was feeling rather lethargic. Perhaps it was the sun, perhaps it was the battle against the wind earlier in the day, perhaps it was me only slowing acclimatising back into the life of a cycle tourist. At least I knew it could not have been the non-alcoholic beer from the previous evening.

There was a busy bric-a-brac market taking place in the large square in front of the town hall and I pushed Wanda around the stalls eyeing up a few items. Aside from its array of antiques, the city itself was impressive. In its day - around the time of the Dutch East India Company which did much of its business there in the 17th and 18th centuries - Middelburg was one of the most important cities in the Netherlands. Before the arrival of the Luftwaffe in 1940, the city was second only to Amsterdam in the number of historic buildings it boasted. To a casual observer (that would be me), it appeared that the Second World War bombers had missed their targets as it remained an exceptionally pleasant place around which to saunter on an early July afternoon.

As fatigue set in, my sauntering took me to a local park. The young guy running the Smulhoekje fast food kiosk took time out of his busy schedule of chatting up the girls from the secondary school across the road to serve me a tray of French fries and mayonnaise. I was happy watching the world go by and significantly overstayed my welcome at one of the tables behind the kiosk. Not that anyone minded. Middelburg was a relaxed, feel-free-to-overstay-your-welcome kind of place.

My remaining mission for the day was to cycle along the canal to Vlissingen where I had arranged to stay at the Vrienden op de Fiets house. Having heard about "Friends on Bicycles" some years earlier, I was keen to try out the system when in the Netherlands and had signed up for the scheme before leaving home. This had cost me €10 and to reserve my night of accommodation in Vlissingen at the home of Froukje and Paul I had paid €22.50.

Before investigating the Vrienden op de Fiets option I had looked on Warmshowers (the touring cyclists' accommodation sharing website that I had been using since that first cycle to southern Italy in 2010) and had approached a woman who also lived in Vlissingen. However, she had rejected me because she believed me to be a "digital nomad" instructing me, rather curtly, to read her online profile which stated clearly "We do not want to host influencers or the like".

I did not consider myself to be a "digital nomad" or an "influencer" or indeed "the like". For me, a digital nomad was a person who continued to work whilst travelling. I was a secondary school teacher of French. Yes, I was blogging and making videos as I travelled but not to the detriment of the experience and I was always careful to socialise with the people I was staying with. I would never hide away in the evening simply to satisfy the needs of Instagram or YouTube. That was not my style.

I put all that down to experience and was happy to have found my alternative Vlissingen host in Froukje (a nurse) and her partner Paul (a former national backgammon champion). I easily located their house near the harbour and Froukje was sitting on her doorstep. I was not quite sure of the formalities with Vrienden op de Fiets. Was it more like a bed and breakfast (where you were left to your own devices) or more like Warmshowers (where usually you were not)?

I introduced myself but my initial impression of Froukje was that she was a little frosty. In my notebook, I used the word "prickly". The house she shared with Paul was part of an old convent and she explained that the garden at the rear of the property - the former convent garden - was a shared space. It all seemed very Dutch. (Hardly surprising, as it was.) Her backyard was tightly packed with ground-level wooden beds in which she grew a wide range of vegetables. It boded well for a nutritious evening meal, which was included in the price.

The room I was staying in was in the attic of the house and was stuffed full of books. They were arranged by colour. At the top the spines were white but as I scanned towards the floor they transitioned into yellow then green then blue and finally red. It was all very Instagram-friendly so I quickly snapped a picture. The Warmshowers woman who had rejected me would not have approved. Another shelf boasted a creditable collection of cycle touring books and included works by Bella Bathurst, Tim Moore and Nicholas Crane but not, alas, Andrew P. Sykes. Again, I smiled as I thought of the Warmshowers woman: she would have turned away all three authors!

After taking a shower I went back downstairs and was promptly press-ganged into shelling peas. This was more like Warmshowers than a B&B and I for one was delighted. There was another Vrienden op de Fiets guest who had now arrived. Hendrik was Dutch and on a short tour from his home in the east of the country, but we all conversed happily in English while continuing to help prepare the evening meal. Many shelled peas later we sat down for the meal and the conversation turned to Vrienden op de Fiets.

"I'm using it for every day of my trip," explained Hendrik.

"Do you use Warmshowers?" I asked, but he did not.

It was at this point that Froukje joined in.

"Do you realise you contacted me on Warmshowers before Vrienden op de Fiets?" she enquired.

"I did?"

Day Three: Vlissingen to Ostend (63km)
Tuesday 5th July

By that point in the evening, having helped prepare the meal, eaten my share of it and, over several glasses of red wine, engaged in a wide-ranging conversation with my new Dutch friends, I had established my credentials as a good guest and certainly no "digital nomad". It was only much later in the evening when I repaired to my room in the attic that I managed to suppress a deep desire to sleep to finish editing and upload the first of a series of podcasts I was planning to publish during the trip.[2] My initial suspicions that Froukje might be rather standoffish had been entirely misplaced: both she and Paul had been exceptional hosts.

Indeed, the following morning before leaving via the shared garden behind her house, Froukje posed for a photograph with a smile beaming across her face. She was not the only one in a good mood. Although only a couple of days old, my trip was going well and I was already looking forward to country number two, Belgium. The plan was to take a ferry across the estuary to the south of Vlissingen to Breskens and follow the coast in a south-westerly direction. The journey would be roughly one-third in the Netherlands and two-thirds in Belgium, as far as the southern outskirts of Ostend and my first Warmshowers host.

The ferry took just 20 minutes. It weaved a path between ships heading out to sea, piled high with containers painted from a pallet of varying - but admittedly rather dull - colours. I wondered what ephemera of life were hidden inside their echoey interiors. Barbecue sets, plastic toys, pens, pencils, rubbers… perhaps with a few high-end cars thrown in for good measure. The transient utility of the items being carried - even the cars - seemed totally at odds with the effort required to construct ships so large and the logistics demanded to move them around the globe. In contrast, here I was with my bicycle - one of the simplest forms of transportation - and just a few essential chattels. I preferred it my way.

According to the CIA World Factbook, Belgium has a coastline of 66.5km and a population of 11.9 million. Metropolitan France, in comparison, has a coastline of 3,427km and a population of 68.3 million. The French have nearly eight times as much personal coastline to their name (albeit just 48mm each) compared to the Belgians (a measly 6mm

---

[2] Episode 052 of The Cycling Europe Podcast. Visit CyclingEurope.org/Podcast.

each).[3] Had I reflected upon these statistics at the time, I might not have had the image in my mind of remote Belle Époque villages sprinkled spartanly amongst the Belgian dunes. With so many people clamouring for so little coastline, it was inevitably going to be a crowded place.

That said, the first third of my journey along the coast of the Netherlands was giving me little reason to doubt such delusions. In Breskens I picked up the Kustroute and would follow it for most of the day. The coastal path took me past a splendid black and white striped lighthouse standing proud and erect against a backdrop of wispy clouds and beside long, sandy beaches only interrupted by the occasional beach bar or restaurant. Small groups of lethargic horses plodded slowly over the sand, their riders seemingly content with the complete lack of urgency in their pace. And then, within sight of the border, a small seating area was surrounded by a semi-circle of haiku, Japanese three-line poems penned in the hope of evoking images of the natural world. They were written in Dutch, so I pointed the camera of my phone at several of them and asked Google to translate. Japanese poems written in Dutch being translated into English by an algorithm. What could possibly go wrong?

One of the haiku was written by the former Belgian prime minister, Herman Van Rompuy[4]:

> *fietsend langs de dijk*
> *zicht op de eeuwige zee*
> *dromend en denkend*

> cycling along the dike
> view of the eternal sea
> dreaming and thinking

That seemed to work OK.

I was, inevitably, reminded of my abandoned journey which should have seen me cycle the length of Japan. I would keep cycling along the dikes, looking out over the sea, dreaming and thinking of adventures yet to come.

---

[3] If you were wondering... Canada has the longest coastline in the world - 202,080km - and each of their 38.2 million citizens has a whopping 5.3m metres upon which to sunbathe. It might, however, be a bit chilly.

[4] After his short stint as Belgian prime minister, Herman Van Rompuy went on to become the President of the European Council. He was famously described by Nigel Farage - who at the time was an MEP - as having "all the charisma of a damp rag and the appearance of a low-grade bank clerk". It is not recorded what Farage thought of Herman's haiku.

An algorithm-translated Haiku seemed to summarise that sentiment more efficiently and poetically than prose ever could.

Much of the area was protected for the benefit of the littoral wildlife, no more so than the Zwin mudflats, salt marches and dunes that straddled the border. The information board claimed it to be an "international airport for birds" on their migratory journeys across Europe and I was instructed to keep an eye out for storks, curlews, oystercatchers, redshanks, geese, egrets, gulls and "numerous species of ducks". I think at this point they had run out of space on the board.

The border itself - my first since setting off from the Hook of Holland - was marked not with a sign but a cattle grid. Aside from the array of birds, the Zwin was also home to dune-nibbling sheep and cattle, and it seemed that whoever was in charge wanted them to stay on the Belgian side of the border. On this particular Tuesday in July, however, they were nowhere to be seen. The only nibbling to be spotted was that of a small group of hungry cyclists who were indulging in an early picnic beside the gravel path.

The natural park extended to the eastern suburbs of the comically named town of Knokke Heist and it was to here where the Belgians had come to find their 6mm of beach. That said, the first to plant their tricolours in the sand appeared to have claimed rather more than their fair share. As I cycled into the centre of the town, large, whitewashed mansions dominated the tree-lined avenues. It was only when I was within a few hundred metres of the sea that apartment blocks began to appear, as they would with increasing frequency until I crossed my next border into France the following day.

Much of the Kustroute on this first of my two days in Belgian was set back a little from the sea. I was obliged to negotiate the busy industrial port of Zeebrugge (in almost every way a far cry from its inland cousin Bruges) but the towns of Blankenberge and De Haan were much more pleasant. The final part of the day, as I approached Ostend, was the most delightful. I had been gradually edging back to the coast since leaving De Haan. Then, somewhat abruptly, the path took a sharp right turn, passed over a dune and down a very steep incline towards an immaculate sandy beach. It came complete with turquoise-roofed beach huts and a parking lot for small yachts mounted on trolleys ready to be wheeled out into the sea. The path from here to Ostend harbour ran beside the sand and, under a deep blue sky it was a wonderfully relaxing way to while away the late afternoon.

In a small café beside the beach where I had stopped for a coffee, I leafed through a large format book of old black and white images. On August 4th, 1945 - a few months after the end of the war - an American military plane had flown the length of the Belgian coast and had taken a series of 80 photographs. They had only recently been rediscovered in the US National

Archives in Maryland and had been published in the book that was subtitled "*de zomer van de vrijheid*" - "the summer of freedom" - in reference to the newly liberated status of the country. The photographs included those taken of Ostend, which had been very badly damaged, but other areas appeared to be in very good shape after so many years of war. VRT (the Flemish public service broadcaster), reported that the long-hidden photographs showed that "...much of the coast had few if any scars from the war and while along the coast east of Ostend, the occasional villa had been burned down by the Germans, the area west of Ostend was almost completely unscathed".

So, although what I was discovering was far from the Belle Époque quaintness I had imagined, neither was it the brutal landscape that it might have been had it been flattened in the 1940s. That was excellent news for my onward journey.

My second ferry of the day allowed me to access the centre of Ostend without being forced to take a long detour around the harbour. However, I was not at the end of the cycling day just yet. My Warmshowers host, Bram, lived a few kilometres to the south of the city.

Before arriving at the home of any Warmshowers host, there was always a sense of heading into the unknown. Almost all my Warmshowers encounters over the years have been positive ones. Indeed, some of my most memorable evenings whilst travelling have been spent with Warmshowers hosts. Every host was different and each of them had a unique approach when it came to accommodating their guests.

What Bram alluded to in his online profile, however, was something very different:

> "Staying with us means you stay in a co-housing [scheme] and can use the common facilities, which means you are rather independent. In our project, there are 18 houses so you might meet different people. In general, the common facilities are not used intensively, so you can expect to have a lot of space for yourself. Maybe some children will come and play in the playing room or [if] you happen to stay when we have dinner together... you will probably be invited to join... When you stay with us you can pitch your tent in the garden, or you could sleep in the guest rooms if they are available... We do not expect you to entertain us nor will we entertain you during your stay. But we like to get to know you so we might invite you... [to] walk around the garden or whatever suits... your schedule and mood."

Perhaps Bram had worked as an advertising copywriter. It sounded wonderful.

The complex of buildings that formed the co-housing project was on the southern edge of the suburbs of Ostend but apart from an old brick barn that had been renovated only recently, there was not a great deal visible from the road. The large doors of the barn were open - perhaps permanently - and the gap in the wall had been glazed allowing me to peer through. It was, I guessed, one of the communal areas of the project with large tables and a kitchen to one side. I pushed Wanda around the side of the barn and found a quadrangle, of sorts. Perpendicular to the renovated building were at least three modern buildings each housing a short terrace of homes. Beyond these buildings was farmland. There were, however, no people.

After a moment or two of tentative standing around, a woman appeared. I explained why I was there and whom I had come to meet. Within a few minutes, I was being welcomed by Bram, a biologist in his 30s, and being given a guided tour. It turned out that he was one of the lead people in creating the co-housing project which housed around 70 people. Although each house was self-contained, shared facilities allowed the group to combine their resources. This was a particular advantage when it came to looking after the many young children who, instead of being carted off every day to childcare facilities elsewhere, were all looked after within the project. The room where I would be staying in the barn was one of two available to be used by any visitor and the kitchen that I had spotted from outside was regularly put into service for communal meals. Such a meal was on the agenda for that evening and, after having showered and changed I joined some of the community who were sharing homemade pizza and beer. On that marvellously warm evening in July, there was a wonderful village atmosphere, and I could not help but wonder why, in the 21st century, most people had shunned this convivial way of living. 200 years ago, it would have been the norm.

I spent much of the time chatting with a retired firefighter called Michel. He shared one of the houses with his wife, a teacher, and over several hours it was fascinating to learn about how the group of people had come together and how they had made such a success of the endeavour. It was also interesting to hear his views on the deteriorating political situation back home in the UK as Boris Johnson's premiership seemed to be moving inexorably towards the edge of a cliff. It was being widely reported on the continent and Michel did not hold back.

"He's a joke," he said, somewhat pitifully.

In 10 Downing Street
A dishonest man is shamed
And prepares to go

(Inspired by Herman Van Rompuy, Belgium's haiku-writing former PM.)

Day Four: Ostend to Oye-Plage (94km)
Wednesday 6th July

For the first time since leaving the Hook of Holland, I was cycling into the unknown. Well, kind of. I had planned my first three nights of accommodation. When I woke up at the co-housing project near Ostend it was with the task of having to find somewhere to sleep that evening still on the to-do list. The vague plan for the day was to cycle along what remained of the Belgian coast even though "what remained" was half of the country's coastline. I would then cross the border into France and head for Dunkirk where I would take the first of my ten trains and make a little more progress south. I was hoping to be in the Boulogne-sur-Mer area by the end of the day, preferably back in the tent on a campsite.

At 7.30 am, the co-housing project was even quieter than it had been when I had arrived the previous afternoon. I packed my panniers and, somewhat pointlessly, crept downstairs. I had been the only person sleeping in the barn that night and the communal area on the ground floor was empty. I wrote a short thank-you note on the blackboard in the corner of the room, wheeled Wanda into the cool morning air and set off back into the centre of Ostend. I was excited by the prospect of arriving in France later in the day. It was, after all, the predominant country of this jaunt around Europe and would be my home for at least the next month before I cycled over the border into Switzerland in the direction of the Alps.

However, I still had 30km of Belgium to cycle before I could start celebrating my arrival in country number three. Breakfast of coffee, *croissant* and *pain au chocolat* was consumed somewhat inelegantly in a large square overlooked by the delicate towers of the Church of Saint Peter and Saint Paul close to the harbour in Ostend. As I ate, flakes of pastry crumbled onto the ground around me attracting most of Belgium's ravenous population of pigeons. I scoffed what I had managed to retain in my hands and made a swift exit in the direction of the promenade.

The coastline was more built up than it had been after crossing over the border from the Netherlands. Not that this made for unpleasant cycling: far from it. In most seaside towns the motorised traffic had been shunted inland by at least one-block-of-flats worth of land. What I assumed to have once been the coastal road had been transformed into a wide active travel paradise with plenty of space for pedestrians, cyclists, café terraces and the forecourts of shops that hired out vibrantly painted four-wheeled pedal-powered karts. These contraptions could seat an entire family and there seemed to be an unwritten rule that the member of the family who possessed the lowest level of driving skill should be in charge of the steering wheel. For anyone on a cycling mission to get to the French border in one piece - that would be me - they made for potentially treacherous adversaries but, mercifully, I survived.

It was another warm, sunny day with only a gentle breeze blowing in from the sea. Maps and signposts were redundant: all I needed to do was keep the water on my right and continue pedalling. Perhaps anticipating that your average cyclist would not be challenged in any meaningful way along their user-friendly coast, the Belgian authorities had gone out of their way to keep travellers' minds amused with... art.

In Ostend there was an impressive installation of truck-sized crumpled metal containers painted bright orange and titled "Rock Strangers" through which I had to weave. Further out of town was a precariously balanced pile of stone cushions in the sea. The gulls seemed to appreciate the platform they had been given as it allowed them to eye up effortlessly their breakfast-in-waiting swimming out in the water. In Middelkerke a "*Walk of Fame de la BD*" was on display at various points along the seafront. BD - *bandes dessinées* or comic strips - are not just for the kids in Belgium: they are seriously big business. Tintin, The Smurfs, Gaston Lagaffe and Lucky Luke all hail from these parts. And then on the sand at Sint-Idesbald, the rear panels of many of the otherwise unremarkable white beach huts had been commandeered to create space for a diverse range of abstract paintings and photographs inspired by the surrealist artist Paul Delvaux. It was only upon arrival in my final Belgian town, De Panne, where the art reverted to the traditional with a bronze statue of King Leopold I under a protective triumphal arch. On a cultural level, it had been an exhausting ride.

My mind had so far been exercised much more than my body, but things were about to revert to type. At De Panne the cycle path ventured 3km inland - my greatest incursion into the country since my arrival the previous day - and I was directed to cycle beside a canal before being sent back in the direction of the coast along the Franco-Belgium border. It was a little unnerving not having the security blanket of the sea to my right and suddenly I was plunged back into a world where I had to make an effort to work out where I was going.

Not totally confident I had not taken a wrong turning at some point, I was relieved and disappointed in equal measure to arrive at a junction where the EuroVelo sign announced simply "Finish". Relieved to know that I was still on the route but disappointed that the sign was so adamant in its message. I knew that the EuroVelo route - at this point it was both number 4 and number 12 - would continue, but perhaps it would no longer be signposted as such.

I glanced around for clues but as soon as I saw the blue sign marking the border with France, I set aside my concerns for the cycle route and wandered over to take a photo. *Je suis arrivé...*

In recent years the French have done a remarkable job in creating a network of branded cycle routes and, over the next few weeks, I would be following several of them. Sometimes just in part: for others in their entirety. Some followed EuroVelo routes: others existed independently of the European-wide network. Their names took inspiration from their locations or the delights that they could offer the cycle tourist. The Vélomaritime was beside the sea. The Véloscénie suggested something very scenic. The Vélodyssée along the west coast of France would indeed be an odyssey if you chose to cycle it from one end to the other. Each route came with signage, maps that could usually be picked up for free in tourist offices and good online support via dedicated websites. If I were ever to get lost, it would be entirely my fault.

First up was the eastern segment of the Vélomaritime from the border with Belgium to Dieppe but after having taken my photo of the sign welcoming me to France, I looked around in vain for any other signs pointing me in the direction of a cycle route. I was still a couple of kilometres inland but the compass on my handlebar confirmed that the road I was standing beside was heading in a westerly direction, so I mounted Wanda and set off.

After a few minutes, I noticed a concrete path to my right. *Could it be a cycle route? Could it be the Vélomaritime, the EuroVelo 4? Why were they being so discrete about the whole thing?* It was frustrating being able to see it but not cycle onto it because of fences and buildings being in the way. Eventually, a short access path appeared and I moved away from the road to investigate. Stretching out in both directions I could see a *baguette*-straight concrete path. It was unmistakably a disused railway line repurposed for the likes of me to cycle along. Just no signs telling me as much.

Confirmation that I was on the right track - literally - came about five minutes later when a slight kink in the path required a short shimmy to the right. According to the sign, this was indeed the Vélomaritime / EuroVelo 4 and the EuroVelo 12 to boot. Marvellous!

The railway line had only closed in 2003 but before that it was, to say the very least, one of France's quieter routes. There used to be just two return trains on Sundays in July and August according to the information board beside the disused station at Zuydcoote. The writer of the sign - clearly a fan of the line - did not miss the opportunity of pointing out that to travel by train the 17km from Dunkirk to De Panne in Belgium would now take five hours as opposed to 45 minutes back in 1875. I was beginning to wonder if it might take me even longer if there was much more faffing around with the route. In the Netherlands and Belgium - two of the world's most cycle-friendly countries - navigation had been almost too easy. A return to the normality of travelling in most other places by bike was proving to be a tad frustrating. However, things were now looking up and by mid-afternoon, I was in the centre of Dunkirk, the end of my cycling day.

Markus Stitz, the German-born but Edinburgh-based bikepacker whom I had come to know a little in recent years, had been following my journey via social media. When he noticed that I was in the Dunkirk area, he put me in touch with a friend of his who in turn had generously offered me the opportunity of pitching my tent in his garden, even though he would not be at the property. It would have been a great solution. But my arrival in Dunkirk was earlier than I had anticipated so I thanked him and declined the offer opting instead to head for the station and jump on that train to Boulogne.

As I entered the modern building of the Gare de Dunkerque the first thing I noticed was a woman speaking in a very animated fashion on her phone. Such was the volume of her voice and the manner in which she was spitting the words down the phone, it was almost impossible to ignore her. I could not quite catch the thread of her anguish, but she was clearly having a bad day. Mine was about to edge in a similar direction.

I glanced up at the information screens to find a train that was heading along the coast in the direction of Calais and then Boulogne. One word was repeated next to almost every train: *suprimé*. Cancelled. *Merde!* The woman on her phone had just discovered the news about the nationwide rail strike as well. Perhaps her options were limited. With it being relatively early in the day, I could at least continue cycling, find a campsite nearer to Calais and then, hopefully, take a train the following morning to advance my journey along the coast.

It was, however, destined to be one of those afternoons when small inconveniences combine to darken the mood disproportionately. The blue sky from earlier had now all but disappeared, the wind was picking up and trying its best to blow me back in the direction of Belgium and signage for the Vélomaritime had all but evaporated. *Was I following it or not?* It was difficult to tell. And my energy levels were plummeting fast.

I crawled into pretty Gravelines, a fortified town complete with a star-shaped moat and thick defensive walls with one objective in mind: food. The local Spar supermarket came to my rescue and I spent a good hour lazing on the steps of the *mairie* taking alternate bites from an over-sized *baguette* and a delicious camembert cheese. It is difficult to beat the rush of calorific satisfaction that such a combination can offer, and it would not be the last time that this unedifying energy-replenishing scenario would be acted out in the coming weeks.

I still had to find accommodation for the evening and was beginning to regret not having stayed in Dunkirk and made use of the offer of the garden from Markus Stitz's friend. It was, however, too late to change my mind. An online search suggested a campsite near the village of Oye-Plage, which was only another 5km down the road. With the wind continuing to blow, it felt more like ten.

Camping Les Tamaris was a simple place populated mainly with caravans that looked as though they were permanent fixtures. A few camper vans filled the vacant spaces in-between. The small reception was, however, shut. Hand-written instructions on the door directed me to a nearby house where a woman welcomed me and told me to meet her back at the campsite in a few minutes. It was all a bit John Le Carré and to add an extra twist to the tale, when I met her back at the reception, she had changed gender and looked considerably older. I paid my €8, pitched the tent and headed off for a shower.

Despite its name, Oye-Plage was a good distance from any beach. I had not seen the sea all day. So much for it being the maritime cycle route, in this part of France at least. On the positive side, I was no longer hungry after the *baguette*-camembert feast from earlier in the afternoon, but I did fancy a beer. Options in Oye-Plage were limited to one bar, curiously named Le J'Anserien.[5] To me, this sounded like "*j'en sais rien*", an expression used to deny all knowledge of something, which only added to the feeling that George Smiley might be found lurking around the next corner.

From the outside, the bar exuded all the rustic French charm of a service station on the M1, so I chose to buy my beer at the supermarket a little further down the road before heading back to the campsite to drink it in the tent. It was developing into quite a cool evening as I drained the deliciously sweet Vieux Lille cherry beer from the bottles. I could not help but conclude that the day had turned out to be a rather muted, downbeat start to my

---

[5] It turns out that an Ansérien is the name of someone who hails from Oye-Plage. All French towns and cities have an associated noun to describe the people who live there. Usually they are obvious - un Parisien for example - but some are less so. Here in Oye-Plage it was a classic example of the latter. The person running the bar had clearly decided to exploit the sound of the word Ansérien by adding the "J'" or "I" and in the process create an amusing name.

adventures in France. As one group of politicians once said, things could only get better. And on the subject of politicians...

Day Five: Oye-Plage to Saint-Quentin-en-Tourmont (91km + Train) Thursday 7th July

I admit it. I am just like most other British tourists heading into France: far too keen to escape the northern corner - the Pas de Calais - in search of more exotic destinations further south. It is, however, an eagerness that is not justified. The coastline south of Calais can be spectacular: much less built up in comparison to its English sister coastline 35km to the north. Cap Gris Nez - Grey Nose Cape - is perhaps the highlight with its high cliffs and lighthouse surveying the expansive beaches below. Further inland you do not have to travel far from the ferry terminals to arrive at historic towns such as Saint-Omer and Arras and, of course, the battlefield at Agincourt. The area offers so much more than booze-cruise supermarkets on the outskirts of Calais.

I know all this as, over many years of being a French teacher, I have escorted large groups of 12-year-olds on many day trips to the area. In one particularly memorable year, I visited three times in one week and nearly managed to leave the grandson of a famous TV chef in the pedestrian precinct of Boulogne-sur-Mer.[6]

So, if there were to be one section of my Grand Tour of Europe that truly merited taking a train because of previous visits to the area, this was the standout example. Having failed in my first attempt to catch the train from Dunkirk to Boulogne on the previous day, I was determined that militant French train drivers would not prevent me from doing so again. A glance at the SNCF app on my phone suggested that strikes were not continuing into a second day, so things were looking up on that score.

The sky was overcast as I left the campsite at Oye-Plage. It seemed likely that at some point it would rain, perhaps heavily, but on the positive side, the wind was blowing from the north. The route followed a series of narrow farm tracks which, although open to motorised traffic, were extremely quiet. I fell into conversation with a Belgian cyclist called Denis who was heading in the same direction as me. He had taken a few days to cycle along the coast before looping back towards Belgium and he provided me with my first opportunity of the trip to have an extended conversation in French. After all those years of absence from France, it was good to know that my

---

[6] In my defence, his small group of ten students was being looked after by a maths teacher with a remarkable inability to count beyond single figures. It was only when I was keeping up the rear of the group of 40 students as we ambled along the harbour back to our coach that, to keep my mind occupied, I counted the children again. After about four attempts of only getting as far as 39, I suspected something might be amiss.

language skills could still *couper la moutarde* (as I am pretty sure they do not say in French).

The news from home was the continued instability in the higher echelons of British power and, echoing Michel's thoughts at the co-housing project near Ostend, Denis did not hold back in his criticism of the British Prime Minister, Boris Johnson:

"*C'est un idiot,*" he laughed. It was a sentiment with which it was difficult to disagree.

Politicians are often viewed very differently abroad to how they are perceived in their own countries. It is fair to say that removed from the harsh realities of the day-to-day lives of the people they govern, many benefit from a more positive international reputation compared to their domestic one. It would be no understatement to say that Margaret Thatcher was a divisive British leader. However, on the international scene (where they knew little about the Poll Tax), she was often seen as a figure of strength willing to stand up and fight for her values. When Jacinda Ardern announced her resignation as the Prime Minister of New Zealand in 2023, she was recognised around the world as one of the preeminent politicians of her day, breaking new ground for women in politics. At home, her popularity was plummeting fast due to pressing domestic issues and she was facing imminent electoral defeat.

Alas in recent years in both the United States and Britain we have seen two politicians who have been ridiculed on the international stage and their reputations around the world have been even worse than their reputations at home. These two politicians are, of course, Donald Trump and Boris Johnson. I will leave the former for others to comment upon but as my Prime Minister during the summer of 2022, Boris Johnson does merit a moment of my time. I never voted for the man nor his party, but he was the head of the government of the United Kingdom. However, as a citizen of the UK, I bore collective responsibility for putting him into power. It is the British system that has infantilised politics to the extent that it has become akin to a reality TV programme. It is the British system that elevated Johnson to levels of stardom because of his bumptiously idiosyncratic personality. It is the British system that elects politicians on the basis of divisive and archaic 19th-century rules rather than a more sensible, collaborative approach to modern democracy.[7]

---

[7] According to The Electoral Reform Society, "The UK is unique among European countries in terms of its electoral system – and not in a good way. It is the only country with a parliamentary system that uses the outdated, one-person-takes-all first-past-the-post system".

To have travelled around Europe and to have had intelligent conversations with my fellow Europeans about the merits (or lack thereof) of our respective leaders is one of the many aspects of foreign travel that I enjoy. To be met with the almost universal assumption that my Prime Minister is indeed a "joke", or an "idiot" is somewhat frustrating, especially when I agree wholeheartedly with their opinion. He represents me and I want to be represented by someone who has at least a few redeeming features. Johnson had none.

As we cycled in the direction of Calais my political discussion with Denis did not last long and, as only an embarrassed British person could do, I started talking about the weather instead. Boris would, however, be back.

After the Aéroport du Grand Calais, the Vélomaritime began to follow the Canal de Marck and within half an hour I had dismounted from Wanda and was admiring the top-heavy glory that is the bell tower of the *hôtel de ville* in central Calais. In a town that was almost completely destroyed during World War II, it is extraordinary to think that it survived unscathed.

It was still only 9.30 and my train to Le Touquet was not until much later in the morning. To pass the time, I set off on a short tour of the town to take in the not-unattractive (but not-quite-attractive) rebuilding that had taken place since 1945. One of the main streets leading into the Place d'Armes had been festooned from one end to the other with a dense flying carpet of colourful strips of cloth. It had the dual impact of making the 1950s streetscape a little prettier and of deadening the urban sound.

In the square itself, I found cyclists, both human and plastic. The former had presumably just cycled off the ferries from England and were embarking upon their own tours of France or the wider continent. I wondered if any were planning anything as audacious as me. I acknowledged a few of my two-wheeled colleagues with a discrete nod of the head but we chose not to engage in conversation. I thought back to my first morning in Rotterdam. I would not have appreciated meeting anyone who wanted to bang on about their grand cycling plans and here in Calais, I did not fancy being that barroom bore.

As for the plastic cyclists, they were painted in bright primary colours and on their bikes, cycling yet motionless, at one end of the square. It was easier to work out why they were here. On a temporary billboard was the stylised image of a male cyclist wearing just a pair of swimming shorts, his skin burnt red from the midpoint of both his biceps and his thighs as far as his hands and his feet respectively. But this comical cartoon figure was not just any cyclist. He was a Tour de France cyclist and the lower part of the billboard declared:

"ARRIVÉ DU TOUR DE FRANCE 2022"

That had been only two days previously on the 5th of July and it had been stage 4 of the annual race, the first in metropolitan France after having kicked off with three days of cycling around Denmark. The stage had taken them from Dunkirk to Calais on an inland route of some 172km. By comparison, my more coastal route between the two had amounted to just 55km. As my journey progressed, it would prove to be only the first of my missed encounters with *Le Tour*.

Back at the train station near the *hôtel de ville*, I placed Wanda about halfway along the platform and prepared myself to dash in one direction or the other depending upon where the bike carriage of the train was located. I had some experience of travelling with my bike on a train on the continent during previous trips, especially that first adventure with Wanda in the innocent pre-COVID summer of 2019. After cycling from Santander to Coimbra in Portugal, I train-hopped back to the ferry in northern Spain. It had gone rather well. The secret, my friends, is to stay well clear of fast trains. Regional trains are the way to go. In Spain it had been the RENFE Media-Distancia trains: here in France it would be the Transport Express Régional trains of the SNCF, and I was about to jump on my first.[8]

As the train approached, I prepared myself to move. *Left? Right? One carriage? Two carriages?* ("*Move away old woman with stick! Bike coming through!*") However, in a moment of gloriously unplanned coordinated colocation, as the screeches from the brakes faded into the Calais ether, I found Wanda and myself standing directly opposite the door of the bicycle carriage. Marvellous! That never happens on the Trans Pennine Express from Huddersfield to Leeds.

I had never previously visited Le Touquet, or, to give it its full name, Le Touquet-Paris-Plage. For some reason, I had always associated the town with the English. It turns out that association should have been with a fellow Yorkshireman. It was the successive attempts of Parisian lawyer Alphonse Daloz and the Leeds-born entertainment entrepreneur Sir John Whitley who made Le Touquet what it is today. Or, rather, what it was like before the war.

---

[8] Transport Express Régional, or TER trains are those on the SNCF network that are most amenable when it comes to travelling with a bike. As the name suggests, they operate on a regional level, administered by the regional governments of France. No charge is made for travelling with a bicycle, but reservations are required. This can be done via the SNCF app which is available in English. Sorry to be the bearer of bad news but all that time that you spent practising the ticking-buying dialogue in your French lessons at school is now redundant.

In 1837 Daloz bought the Domaine du Touquet, started planting trees to stabilise the dunes and invited his mates up from the capital to do a spot of hunting. He subsequently started building the resort of Paris-Plage - Paris Beach - to attract Parisians who were *not* his mates but who, presumably, could pay him good money to enjoy a few days on the coast.

After Daloz's death, both Le Touquet and Paris-Plage were purchased by Whitely (can you see what's coming?) and he created... Le Touquet-Paris-Plage. He then started encouraging the *British* to visit and pay *him* good money for the privilege. Many would subsequently turn up including the future Edward VIII, Noel Coward and P.G. Wodehouse who was captured here by the Nazis in 1940.

Despite the best efforts of Allied bombers and the Germans, who were under orders to mine the town as they evacuated it in the final days of the war, much of the Belle-Époque splendour of Le Touquet - rather miraculously - survives to this day.[9] Great mansions lurk behind the manicured hedges, nestled into the undulating dune-inspired landscape. It is not difficult to imagine Edward, Noel or P.G. scuttling from one 1930s society party to the next, sipping champagne and generally having a jolly good time.

I was about to join them - 90 years late to the party - as I made my way through the pretty suburbs of the town. One eye was on the opulent houses, one eye was on my phone as Boris Johnson stepped out onto Downing Street...

> "Good afternoon everybody. It is now clearly the will of the parliamentary Conservative Party that there should be... a new Prime Minister... It is painful... but as we've seen at Westminster, the herd is powerful and when the herd moves, it moves and... no one is remotely indispensable. And our brilliant and Darwinian system will produce another leader equally committed to taking this country forward..."

I pulled on my brakes and looked up. Before me was the five-star Art Deco splendour of Le Touquet's Le Westminster Hotel. I smiled. The man was going and what better place to mark his imminent departure than here? By the time I stepped back on British soil in early September, he would be packing his bags and a replacement would be preparing to move into

---

[9] After the town was liberated, Le Touquet was described as France's most heavily mined town. An astonishing 92,745 mines and explosive devices were discovered and made safe.

Downing Street. Surely he - or she - would restore our country's standing on the international stage. No?

The seafront of Le Touquet was, admittedly, more Brutal Époque than Belle Époque, and the part of town that had suffered the most during the war. I paused to reflect on a momentous afternoon but was soon drawn back into the realities of life and the fact that I still had no accommodation sorted for that evening. But it was only just after 2 pm. Something would turn up.

In theory, I was now heading due south. In practice, the route resembled a distressed snake contorting itself first one way and then the other. Following the signs for the Vélomaritime, I was kept inland by a few kilometres, with good reason: the dunes and the beaches to the west would have provided a formidable obstacle for anybody apart from the most experienced off-road mountain bikers. I did manage to see the sea again, in Berck, by deviating a little from the route and was rewarded with a fine display of colourful ribbons attached to long ropes and flying high in the sky courtesy of the strengthening wind. Just as it had been in Le Touquet earlier in the afternoon, the view out to sea was in stark contrast to the view of the concrete apartment blocks on shore.

Back inland good provision had been made for cyclists with segregated paths beside the busier roads. Another lurch towards the sea at Fort-Mahon-Plage did not present me with any accommodation options and the issue was increasingly playing on my mind. I was not used to cycling so late in the day - it was now nearly 6 pm - without a good idea as to where I would be sleeping that evening.

Yet again the route turned inland but the only campsites I passed were the gigantic places that were not designed for solo travellers on a budget. Although I accepted that the average campsite spend would vary according to location and facilities, my financial comfort zone was somewhere between €10 and €15. Any hint that I would have to pay significantly more would just encourage me to keep pedalling until the point where I was falling off the bike with exhaustion. And today, that was still some distance away.

At this juncture in proceedings, may I draw your attention to the dictionary definition of a campsite. It is "a place used for camping". So what is "camping"? It is, "the activity of spending a holiday living in a tent". A tent. Have you got that?

Close to Monchaux I found a campsite: Camping de la Motte. Fantastic. The reception was closed so I headed to the bar:

"*Bonjour. Je cherche un camping pour ce soir. C'est possible?*"

"*Caravane? Camping car?*" asked the woman serving drinks.

"*Non. Une tente.*"

"*Une tente?*"

The disdain with which she looked at me made me feel as though it was me who was breaking with the long-established conventions of the whole camping thing. I successfully fought the urge to embark upon a semantic argument in French over the misuse of the word and, somewhat grumpily, I cycled on.

10km later I finally found a campsite that did have the audacity to accept people who wanted to camp in a tent: Camping Espace Vert des Tremières. It was a cracker.

Day Six: Saint-Quentin-en-Tourmont to Dieppe (96km)
Friday 8th July

I was finally getting into my stride and the experience of grabbing victory from the jaws of campsite defeat the previous evening provided a timely reminder that things always seemed to work out for the best. Eventually. Usually...

As far as I could see, I was the only person waking up in a tent at Camping Espace Vert des Tremières. However, at 7 am, the partially wooded area where I had pitched my Hubba Hubba tent was very noisy. Not with any human sound but with a wonderful symphony from an orchestra of birds. It was very pleasantly deafening and, for a good few minutes, I remained horizontal and listened.

When I poked my head out of the tent, sunlight flooded in. I always tried to position the door of the tent so that it would be facing the sunrise. Sometimes this worked, sometimes it did not, my efforts thwarted by a mountain or a building or the weather or, admittedly, my inability to work out from which direction the sun would appear. On this morning, however, it had worked a treat, the sun edging up over the horizon between two wooden-clad static caravans and directly in line with the flap of the tent.

The sky was an endless ocean of blue and there was no wind to speak of, so I reached for the drone and launched it into the sky. The views from 100 metres were even more stunning than those from the door of my tent with the morning mist lingering over the muted green and brown tapestry of fields that stretched out in all directions. This was a day that had been invented for leisurely cycle touring so I quickly packed away my things and headed off in the direction of the Baie de Somme.

I was planning to continue cycling along the Vélomaritime / EuroVelo 4 as far as Dieppe, the point at which I would turn south along the Avenue Verte in the direction of Paris. This latter route had dominated my thoughts for this portion of my Grand Tour so I had few, if any, preconceptions about what I might encounter on today's cycle. "Follow the coast as far as Dieppe" had probably been my mental note with no thought given as to what that might entail. And perhaps that lack of forethought only added to the sheer delight of the day that was about to unfold.

Within half an hour of leaving the campsite, I had arrived at the bay. What I discovered was far removed from the images usually associated with the word Somme. The notorious 1916 battle had been fought out some 100km inland to the east of Amiens. What did link the battle and the coast was the River Somme from which the French *département* took its name and which had its mouth at the bay. Here on the coast, I discovered a serene natural landscape dotted sporadically with villages and small towns that were in perfect harmony with their surroundings.

My first stop was in the coastal town of Le Crotoy where I satisfied my need for a pastry-laden breakfast at perhaps the most visually stunning *boulangerie* I have ever had the pleasure to frequent. It was straight from the notebooks of Elizabeth David. I was also able to stock up on fruit at the busy open-air market beside the bay. The best views across the Baie de Somme were from the grassy area below the rocket-like turret of Les Tourelles, a hotel with an envious position overlooking the water. In the far distance, I could just about make out the lighthouse at the Pointe du Hourdel, 4km across the bay. The route of the Vélomaritime would insist - with good reason - that I travel some 25km around the 3,000 hectares of natural reserve to arrive there on a bicycle.

Most of the route from Le Crotoy to Saint-Valery-sur-Somme on the southern edge of the bay was along a busy road. However, the cycle path was segregated and, on such a nice day, the regular rush of cars and lorries was only a minor inconvenience. Indeed, their occupants could easily be pitied for missing out on the opportunity to appreciate the views at a much more amenable speed.

To reach the lighthouse at the Pointe de Hourdel, the Vélomaritime took me north and, as I approached the lighthouse, slightly east. Such is the nature of a bay where straight-line routes are the preserve of birds and those with a boat. It took most of the morning to cycle to the *pointe* and admire the view back towards Le Crotoy. Although on a macro level, my progress along the long loop of my tour around Europe had been minimal, it was a sacrifice that had been well worth making.

I took more than just a few moments to pause and reflect upon nothing in particular, aside from the fact that it was all going marvellously well. Then I pointed Wanda west and set off again along a shallow coastal curve that would eventually leave me cycling towards the south. Until relatively recently the path that I was following had been a road called La Route Blanche. In 2008 the authorities had seen sense and closed it to all but sedate forms of travel arguing - quite understandably - that the combustion engine was completely at odds with maintaining the natural environment. I could not have agreed more.

Shortly after setting off again, I passed a sign for the curiously named Brighton-les-Pins. This was another holiday resort financed originally by British investors (a safe manufacturer, a barrister, and an "adventurer and gold miner") but it had fared less well than Le Touquet. The grand plans of the speculators were thwarted by a combination of two world wars and shifting sands. The latter, somewhat inconveniently for a coastal resort, moved the shore a kilometre away from the balconies of the swanky hotel that they had built. A policy of destruction by retreating German soldiers finished the place off in the final months of World War II.

I cycled through the coastal town of Cayeux-sur-Mer, ignoring the no cycling signs to investigate the wooden boardwalk on the beach. It gave access to long strings of huts painted in dark pastel shades of blue, green and yellow. Had it been 7 pm and not 1 pm I might have been tempted to try a few door handles to see if any of the huts could accommodate me - illicitly - for the evening. Facing west, their sunset views must surely have been memorable. My timing was not good, but it did at least save me from the risk of arrest for breaking and entering (and sleeping).

After Cayeux the route plunged inland along a series of farm tracks and paths, climbing steadily and linking a succession of rural towns and villages before again joining the sea at Mers-les-Bains. Upon arrival on the edge of the town, the minor exertions required during the ascent were rewarded with a view across the rooftops, with white cliffs visible in the far distance. I guessed, correctly, that more climbing was to come. Yet the most rewarding visual treat was not to be found from this lofty position beside the Église Saint-Martin but when I returned to sea level and approached the southern edge of the town. Here was a parade of colourful timber-framed four-storey villas looking out over the sea. After disappointment in Belgium, I had found my first Belle-Époque town.

Mers-les-Bains was my final destination in Somme before I entered Seine-Maritime. I know nothing of the rivalry between these two French *départements* but there did seem to be a curious no man's land separating the two. Mers-les-Bains ended rather abruptly after the villas, immediately followed by nothing. Then came a slightly isolated train station and two harbour gates across which I pushed Wanda into the town of Le Tréport, my first in the Seine-Maritime *département*. Perhaps it was not so much a departmental rivalry but more a regional rivalry as I had now arrived in one of the most iconic of France: Normandy. Or, as we English should surely call it, home.[10]

---

[10] As ever, it appears that scientific progress has now disproved this facile assumption. According to an article in *The Guardian* in 2015, research by Professor Sir Peter Donnelly, formerly of Oxford University's Wellcome Trust Centre for Human Genetics, found that "...people living in southern and central England today typically share about 40% of their DNA with the French, 11% with the Danes and 9% with the Belgians... The French contribution was not linked to the Norman invasion of 1066, however, but a previously unknown wave of migration to Britain some time after the end of the last Ice Age nearly 10,000 years ago."

There was now a series of short climbs to tackle. The first was to the top of the cliffs above Le Tréport. These were the cliffs that I had seen earlier from a distance and which now provided me with a mirror-image view back to the white cliffs of Mers-les-Bains. This was followed by a shorter climb a few kilometres before Criel-sur-Mer and finally, a longer, more gradual climb as I was edging towards the end of the cycling day. It was at the foot of the second climb that I found what I had been looking for ever since leaving the campsite that morning: a cycling sign that told me how far I was from Dieppe. 27km. This was a psychologically important moment of the trip. Dieppe marked the point in my mind when I would have escaped the clutches of the familiar. I could finally begin to get excited.

Once again I had been pushed slightly inland, the route continuing to guide me under the cloudless sky that had barely changed since I had emerged from the tent that morning and beside vast fields of yellow crops. Since the border with Belgium, the Vélomaritime had co-existed with the EuroVelo 4, or the Central Europe Route. After starting in Brittany, it followed the northern coasts of France and Belgium before crossing Germany, Czechia and Poland, completing its journey in Kyiv in Ukraine. It seemed unlikely that there would have been many people in the summer of 2022 who had ambitions of setting off along the EuroVelo 4 with any intention of making it as far as the Ukrainian capital. The Russian invasion was now in its sixth month and the lives of millions of people in the east of the continent had been shattered by the crazy decisions of a bunch of demagogues in Moscow. Perhaps if Putin had ever taken the time to get on a bicycle and travel along the EuroVelo 4, he would have had the opportunity to visit some of the people who had been impacted by his actions, and things might have been different. But he had not, and they were not. In Normandy, towards the western extremity of the EuroVelo 4, the blue sky and yellow fields created an almost perfect Ukrainian flag, the dots of the poppies a reminder of the senseless shedding of blood. I would return to the EuroVelo 4 upon arrival at Mont-Saint-Michel.

———

Three things were on my mind as I approached the port of Dieppe: accommodation, food and clean clothes. My desire for all three was high but, after nearly a week on the road, I was most looking forward to having freshly laundered clothes. Accommodation was easy to sort out. After spending an average of only €10 per night to this point (assisted to some extent by the free Warmshowers accommodation in Ostend), I felt more comfortable about splashing out on a hotel. It was with this in mind that I booked two nights at the Ibis Budget in central Dieppe.

The ease with which I was able to book hotel accommodation within a matter of seconds via my phone was a delight. More often than not, a sense of anxiety about where I would end up pitching the tent would grow inside me, very gradually, from early afternoon. The reality is that long trips such as this would not be possible - for me at least - were it not for the relative cheapness of the nights on a campsite. That said, I would like to think that if I were ever to be in the position of affording to stay every night in a hotel, I would still opt for the tent on a regular basis. For me, cycle touring has always been synonymous with cycle-camping: it is part of the package and to eliminate it from the equation altogether would be detrimental to the experience. I do, however, reserve the right to one day change my mind in my arthritically challenged dotage.

Within an hour of checking into the hotel opposite the Parc François Mitterrand, I was watching my clothes being tossed around the washing machine in the Lav-O-Clair launderette. Joy! I could glory in wearing clothes that were not damp or sticky or (more usually) both, at least for a few hours. I celebrated by heading off on a stroll beside the harbour, sinking a small beer at Le Balto Bar-Tabac and then taking up evening residence on the terrace of a restaurant called Le Sully overlooking the water.

I have never felt at ease eating alone in a restaurant. Channelling my inner Bill Bryson (who always does a commendable job of turning up as a stranger in the towns he visits and getting merrily sloshed) I consumed more alcohol than was appropriate for effective cycle touring and tucked into a starter of smoked salmon and herring on a bed of new potatoes. Delicious! As was the faux filet with Roquefort sauce and the plateau of cheeses. The accommodation budget was not the only one being stretched. However, I reasoned (to the extent that I could reason under the influence) that I had successfully completed nearly a week on the cycle paths of Europe and would be able to sleep off my excesses in the morning at the start of my first day of rest.

PART TWO:

L'Avenue Verte

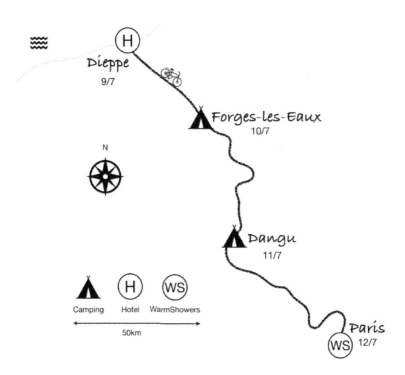

Day Seven: Dieppe
Saturday 9th July

My body clock had not signed up to the day-off-cycling deal. I woke at my usual time - around 6 am - and instead of doing what I should have done - turn over and close my eyes - I got up and headed out to explore Dieppe. It was Saturday and the town was predictably quiet at such an ungodly hour. Even the fishing boats that were lined up against the harbour wall were bereft of life despite the working lives of fishermen being governed more by tides than time.

My local - Le Balto Bar-Tabac - was, however, open for business. I ordered a small black coffee and, for a few minutes, watched the world go by despite there being few comings and goings to observe. The excesses of the previous night were not yet being felt. I knew they would - probably mid-afternoon - when a deep desire to do nothing but sit down and close my eyes would overcome any enthusiasm for making the most of my first day off. I had a few hours to play with, but the clock was ticking…

Although my non-cycling days were not generally planned, I envisaged that they would happen roughly once a week. Dieppe was unique in that it was always part of the plan. Reason one: I had never visited the town before. Reason two: I knew I would arrive here after about a week of cycling. Reason three: I needed time to study the map of the onward journey along the Avenue Verte to Paris. All these reasons were predictable and together they provided a compelling argument for taking a break from cycling. Future days off were much less predictable. Places such as Paris or Mont-Saint-Michel or Bordeaux or Toulouse were all on the list of possibles, but I would leave the final decision until shortly before arrival.

Coffee consumed, I retraced my steps from the previous evening around the harbour passing Le Sully restaurant and in the direction of the mouth of the harbour. Aside from the *château*, which was sitting above the western edge of the old town, and Les Tourelles, the one remaining gate to the town, much of what had been built in the 15th century had been destroyed. Not by war, but by modernisers during the 19th century. There is a debate to be had as to whether it is such modernisers or the military who have wreaked the most architectural havoc in Europe over the centuries. We tend to blame the wars of the 20th century for the architectural ills of 21st-century Europe (I've already mentioned them several times in this book and we have barely started), but in Dieppe it did seem that the actions of the generals resulted merely in tinkering around the edges.

Not that Dieppe has not played its part in the annals of conflict. The Dieppe Raid - codenamed Operation Jubilee - of August 1942 is regarded as a tragic military blunder. It was part of a series of raids whose main purpose was to test the coastal defences of the Germans. 6,000 soldiers - most of them Canadians - set off from England to seize the harbour. Despite the support of tanks, eight destroyers offshore and RAF fighter cover, after seven hours, nearly 3,500 men remained on the beach either dead or as prisoners.

Several memorials to the lost soldiers had been erected beside the beach. My suffering because of the previous night's overindulgences was somewhat insignificant in comparison. I paused to read the citations on each memorial and tried to imagine what scenes might have played out on the wide pebble beach between the path where I was standing and the sea.

Further wanderings took me to the *château-musée* where I spent much of my time hovering beside a group of English-speaking and very studious Wikipedia writers. Their t-shirts and name badges were the not-so-subtle giveaways. They listened attentively to their guide whilst photographing anything that did not move. It being a museum, that was almost everything. However, with fatigue beginning to rear its ugly head I decided to make my way back to the hotel via the tourist office.

Outside the *château*, I spent some time chatting to two cycle tourists from Normandy. They were nearing the end of their own grand tour of France - they had been at it for several months - and they explained how they had been wild camping most nights. This is a concept that I have never embraced. The availability of cheap campsites made my long trip affordable. For many, however, it was the ability to find a quiet corner of a field or a cave or a hidden patch of rough ground that made such a long trip feasible. Perhaps if my teacher's pension does not live up to expectations, I might have to join them one day.

The tourist office was not far from the hotel, and it was able to provide me with a map for the Avenue Verte cycle route as hoped. Once back at the Ibis Budget, I spread it out on the double bed and started to plan.

I sincerely hope that, in the ever-expanding digital realm, the paper map lives on. I embraced my online mapping just as much as the next cyclist and was already happily using websites and apps such as OpenStreetMap, Cyclemeter and, of course, Google Maps to help me navigate from one place to the next. Yet nothing beats a good old paper map. For this trip, I would be relying on two maps. Firstly, a national map of France from the French national mapping agency, IGN. It was map number 924 and it went by the name of Voies Vertes et Véloroutes de France (Greenways and Cycle Routes of France). I had purchased a copy before setting off. Secondly, I was using local maps. I tried to pick them up in tourist offices and they were almost always given away for free. They gave me an overview of the route I was following. Both were clamped to my handlebars, although I tended to rely more on the local maps whilst cycling.

With the light fading outside, I struggled to keep my eyes open as the previous night's excesses not only caught up with me but went zooming off down the fast lane of time. My eyes may have been shutting but I mustered sufficient energy to examine the maps and formulate a plan that would see me arrive in Paris before the national holiday on July 14th.

Cycling from London to Paris has long been a popular cycle route, often adopted by those wishing to raise money for charity. The traditional London to Paris route - from London Bridge to Notre Dame cathedral - followed Watling Street (the old Roman road otherwise known as - somewhat less poetically - the A2) to Dover and then the Route Nationale 1 (RN1) to Paris. However, in our car-ravaged 21st century, if you are hoping for a leisurely cycle between the two capitals, it is a route best avoided. That said, it is possible to follow a series of National Cycle Network routes out of London and across Kent. Upon arrival in France, follow the general direction of the RN1 to Paris making use of a mixture of quiet roads, greenways and towpaths. In his Cicerone guidebook[11], Mike Wells refers to this as "the classic route".

The origins of the Avenue Verte go back to 2003 when the Seine-Maritime *département* in France opened a greenway that followed part of the former Dieppe to Paris railway line. By 2009 they had persuaded five other French *départements* and, on the other side of the channel, East Sussex Council to join them in an initiative to open a traffic-free route from Paris to London in time for the 2012 Olympics. Although at the time of opening much of the route was not traffic-free, by 2022, almost all the French section was. Good news for me as I prepared to set off south from Dieppe.

I would break the Dieppe to Paris section of the Avenue Verte into three stages. On the first day, I would cycle as far as a town called Forges-les-Eaux where there was a campsite. On the second day, I had a choice as shortly after Gournay-en-Bray the route split into two. I could either head east to Beauvais and then loop back in the direction of central Paris via Chantilly on a route that seemed similar to the classic London to Paris cycle, or I could continue south towards the valley of the Seine. If I chose this

---

[11] *Cycling London to Paris 'A Trail of Two Cities': The classic Dover/Calais route and the Avenue Verte*, Cicerone Press

latter option, there was a campsite at Dangu. This would leave a longer third day - probably over 100km - to get to central Paris via Clergy.

Accommodation in Paris was a slight concern. I had contacted a Vrienden op de Fiets member who lived near the centre of Paris, but I had yet to receive a reply.[12] Warmshowers was an option but in tourist hotspots such as Paris, it was always a bit hit-and-miss as the competition for beds in spare rooms was fierce, especially in high season. Back in 2015 when I had cycled through Paris en route to northern Norway, I had stayed at the campsite next to the Bois de Boulogne. This was an option once again, but I was conscious that with Bastille Day fast approaching, it may already be fully booked. In typical man style, I chose to ignore all these accommodation issues and would worry about them when they started to scream at me three days down the line.

With the planning complete, I did what I really should have done some 16 hours earlier. I turned over, closed my eyes and slept.

---

[12] Although the Dutch organisation operates primarily in the Netherlands, the network does extend further afield, with accommodation offered around the world, often by Dutch nationals who happen to be living abroad.

Day Eight: Dieppe to Forges-Les-Eaux (57km)
Sunday 10th July

At 8 am on a Sunday, the centre of Dieppe was predictably quiet. Correction: deserted. It was even quieter than it had been at 7 am on Saturday. I ambled my way through the pedestrianised old town on a familiar route that I had taken the previous day when the streets had been packed with locals and tourists hopping from one market stall to the next. There was now no trace of the market, and the locals and tourists were still in their beds. They were missing a treat as, again, the sky was cloudless, and the temperature was slowly edging its way through the Goldilocks zone from being not too cold to not too hot. It was, however, beginning to be reported that temperatures across Europe were on the rise and were predicted to break records within the next week. In preparation, I had purchased a wide-brimmed hat from the market in Dieppe and every square centimetre of bare flesh was daubed with factor 50 sun protection cream. Such was the increasingly serious nature of the warnings that I was a little nervous about what was to come. It was strange to feel that cycling in this part of Europe should come with a health warning.

The first section of the Avenue Verte followed a disused railway line and, as envisaged, I found my first sign for the route very close to the train station just to the south of the centre of Dieppe. Examining the map that I had been given at the tourist office, almost all the route to my planned destination - Forges-les-Eaux - was marked in green indicating that this was 100% bona fide *voie verte* or greenway. There was a train station marked at Serqueux, close to Forges-les-Eaux, and then the distinctive black line of a railway that had not been abandoned heading in the direction of Paris. If ever there was a day to revel in cycling along a French *voie verte*, it looked as though this would be it.

Initially, the path of the Avenue Verte followed a route that was just beside the old train tracks. I knew this as the tracks were still there, often behind a metal fence, gradually rusting away, evidence that trains had not trundled down the line for quite some time. To my left, on the side of another metal fence was a large field of allotments and it was here that I noticed the first human life of the day with a few gardeners pottering around, examining, clipping and watering their vegetables. On the cycle track, however, I had yet to encounter another soul, either on a bicycle or not.

The rusting railway line disappeared when I entered what I assumed to be an area formerly occupied by a quarry. On one side there were great piles of ground rock, on the other, a patchwork of small lakes. I guessed that these had their origins in the holes created when digging for stone. Now they were home to more leisurely pursuits such as camping, fishing and birdwatching. It was only after a few shimmies to the left and to the right and after crossing a short bridge at right angles to the path that I recognised the distinctive slow sweep of what used to be the railway line to Paris. It would be a path that I would follow until the trains reclaimed the route shortly before I arrived at my destination in Forges-les-Eaux.

If you were to write a short checklist of attributes that a good quality cycle route should have, it would look something like this:

- segregated from things that might kill you,
- a good quality surface that is pothole-free,
- bespoke signage that is clear, regular and informative and
- maintained to a high standard, not left to decay once the fanfare of the opening ceremony was over.

Governments across the globe spend hundreds of billions of dollars, euros, pounds... in making sure that the motorways under their jurisdiction adhere to every bullet point on such a list. It is, alas, rare (outside the Netherlands of course) to be able to tick off all four of these fundamental yet entirely achievable bullet points when it comes to a greenway. Indeed, thinking about my local greenway near Halifax in West Yorkshire - the 15km Calder Valley Greenway / Hebble Trail from Hebden Bridge to Halifax - I can tick off... None. Zero. Nowt.

May I now introduce the 40km of the Avenue Verte from Dieppe to Forges-les-Eaux? Never in my years of being a cycle tourist had I encountered such a monumentally wonderful cycle route. *Segregated? Tick. Quality surface? Tick. Bespoke signage? Tick. Maintained? Tick.* But the ticking did not stop there.

Many of the disused railway stations along the route had been repurposed for the benefit of greenway users. This is not unusual and quite a common feature of disused railways. However, the one at Saint-Aubin-le-Cauf elevated the genre to a whole new level. A fully functioning bicycle service station had been installed where you could clean your bike, pump up your tyres and use a range of basic tools to sort out any mechanical woes. There was also a water tap to top up your bottles and electricity available for those on eBikes. Admittedly at 9.30 on this Sunday morning the place was closed (and, according to a sign, you had to buy tokens to operate the water and air machines from the local town hall which might have been problematic on the Sabbath) but I refuse to quibble. This was high-end cycle infrastructure. Close to Mesnières-en-Bray (more of that in a moment) was a well-chosen patch of ground beside the *voie verte* which had been set aside for use as a basic camping spot. There was even a small wooden shed containing a shower and toilet. I could have kicked myself for arriving at 11 am rather than 7 pm, the time after which the pitching of tents was permitted.

Perhaps the crowning glory of this stretch of the Avenue Verte had nothing to do with the cycle planners and everything to do with the combined efforts of Mother Nature and the local population down the centuries. The countryside through which the old railway line cut was Normandy at its finest with pretty villages complete with pointy church spires, timber-framed barns and houses nestling serenely in the undulating landscape of maturing crops.

Could things possibly get any better? Well, yes, they could.

I had noted the sign for a *château* at Mesnières-en-Bray and the small picture on my map showed a pretty turreted building sitting at the end of a short avenue of stunted shrubs. I was not quite expecting the other end of the line of shrubs to be within metres of the cycle path. But it was. The stunning building was a few steps further along the architectural scale of glory than the picture on my map had suggested. I pushed Wanda towards the gates of the *château*, still somewhat taken aback by the proximity of a railway line to such a jewel of the French Renaissance. Clearly planning permission was less of an obsession back in the glory days of the ever-expanding French train network.

The surprises kept coming. Two cyclists - one male, one female - were standing with their backs to me staring through the metal bars of the large ornate gate. On the back of the man's cycling shirt was the familiar yellow serifed Y of the Tour de Yorkshire, the legacy cycling event held annually since the *Grand Départ* of the Tour de France had visited my home county in 2014 (until being scuppered by a combination of mismanagement and a global pandemic).

"Are you from Yorkshire?" I asked.

They were and they introduced themselves as Ian and Marjorie from Rotherham. They were staying at a nearby campsite with their camper van and cycling whenever they could.

At this point, Marjorie paused, looked me up and down and glanced at Wanda who was resting on her stand a few metres away.

"Are you Andrew Sykes?" she enquired.

This was turning out to be a very memorable day indeed. Not only was I travelling along a wonderful cycle route in a bucolic part of France but, after 12 years of toil maintaining a website, writing books, giving talks and making podcasts… I had finally been recognised by a stranger on the streets of a foreign country. Fame at last. Another tick. Perhaps I should stop now and return home in triumph.[13]

It was with a certain sense of reserved contentment - that feeling you get after having finished your first beer - that I climbed the hill away from the Avenue Verte in the direction of the centre of Forges-les-Eaux and Camping de la Minière. It was still only 3 pm and the distance cycled had been a modest 57km but to continue would risk not finding a suitable place to stay as well as potentially tainting the experience of the day's cycle. I suspected that from here to Paris, however wonderful sections of the route might be, it was unlikely that the Avenue Verte would be so enduringly glorious as it had been today. Quit while you are ahead, happy and famous.

---

[13] For the pedants... Yes, back in book 3 - *Spain to Norway* - I do recount being recognised by a chap called Steve at a supermarket near the Norwegian border in Sweden. Steve, however, had been primed to look out for me by the person he had stayed with and with whom I was planning to stay with myself in Trondheim further north. Another Steve also recognised me in Glasgow in 2021, but this encounter in France was the first time on foreign soil. (As well as being the first time I had been recognised by someone who was not called Steve...)

Day Nine: Forges-Les-Eaux to Dangu (77km)
Monday 11th July

The straight green line on my map from Dieppe to Forges-les-Eaux and the smooth incline on the route profile from sea level to around 200m that my tracking app had generated were both hallmarks of a disused railway line. Between Forges-les-Eaux and Gisors, the line turned red indicating a "shared cycle route". It was as straight as a spiral staircase as the Avenue Verte negotiated its way along the valley of the Epte repeatedly crossing both the river and the still-functioning railway. I had discounted heading east towards Beauvais because the route south via Dangu was a much more direct way of getting into central Paris. I could at least look forward to a return to a segregated, smooth and straight greenway in the final few kilometres of the day after Gisors.

I could not remember when I last woke up to anything other than a blue sky and there was no surprise waiting for me as I crawled from the tent at Camping de la Minière. The pitch that I had been allocated - number 82 - was in the campsite equivalent of a suburban cul-de-sac. Another seven pitches were arranged beside a tarmac path that looped back on itself around a well-established small copse of trees. In true suburban style, the pitches were separated from each other by tall privet hedges but below the tree was a picnic bench and it was here that some neighbourly fraternisation could take place.

The elderly couple in the camper van at number 83 kept themselves to themselves but the French woman at number 84 had been keen to talk as I prepared my evening meal of pasta, pesto, bread and cheese. She was cycling with her husband and two young children, but I got the distinct impression that she was desperate for a chat with somebody - anybody - she was not related to.

"Have you used HomeCamper?" she enquired in French.

I had not but she went on to tell me how it worked, even though from its English name, I had a pretty good idea.

"It's great. You can camp in people's gardens. We've used it a lot since we set off at the start of the month."

She went on to explain that there was a website and that hundreds of locations were available. It sounded like the camping world's answer to Airbnb. I made a mental note but forgot to write down any details before the conversation moved on to more pressing matters such as how desperate she was to leave her husband, dump the kids in foster care and go live on a tropical island in the Pacific with a chap she had met on Tinder.

It was thus fortuitous that within a couple of kilometres of leaving the campsite on the morning of the 11th of July, my eye caught sight of a homemade poster pinned to a pole. Next to simplistic rural clip art and a cartoon image of a bicycle, was written the following:

Accueil Vélo
Camping chez l'habitant en toile de tente ou en Van
Réservation sur HomeCamper.fr

How strange that a concept that until the previous evening I had never heard of should have been referenced twice within 12 hours. This was not just the obsession of a woman in an unhappy marriage but something that was perhaps more widespread. On those occasions when no campsite could be found, this might provide the solution. I took a photo of the sign and continued pedalling.

Although no longer following a *voie verte*, in fairness to the Avenue Verte cycle route planning committee, they had done a remarkable job in ticking most of the boxes I had spent the previous day ticking myself. Although I was cycling on the road for almost all the route to Gisors, these were the famed roads of rural France that linked village to village to small town to village. Cars were far outnumbered by farm vehicles that passed me noisily but with utter respect and I was left to take in the glory of the Norman countryside, its flora and its fauna in relative peace. A succession of multi-barrelled place names came and went: Dampierre-en-Bray, Cuy-Saint-Fiacre, Saint-Germer-de-Fly, Bazincourt-sur-Epte… They put the simplicity of the likes of Haussez, Ménerval and the somewhat prosaic Neuf-Marché - Newmarket - to shame. Only my destination - Dangu - was as linguistically curious as it was brief.

The one thing I *could* find to complain about - and I was not particularly looking - was the fact that this was my least favourite day of the week to be travelling in France. It was a Monday. I grew up in a country that has moved gradually but seemingly inexorably in the direction of the American dream of everything being open and available 24/7. *How has France consistently and successfully resisted such radical change?* No one would argue that 21st-century France is anything other than a modern, progressive and very successful nation. Yet it has managed to retain this status by holding onto aspects of life that countries elsewhere - especially those in the Anglo-Saxon world - have ditched with distasteful enthusiasm. Including the sanctity of Monday. I could cope with Sunday by stocking up on a Saturday, but Monday always seemed to arrive with the thought of "Oh yeah, it's Monday. Bugger."

You will always be able to buy a *croissant* on a Monday and if you needed one, there would be a doctor or a dentist or a pharmacy open for business. It is just that you might have to walk - or in my case cycle - a bit further to locate one. It is less of an issue in the big towns and cities where you will easily discover a large supermarket that will furnish all your needs, but in rural Normandy, from the perspective of this British national, it was proving frustrating.

I had managed to buy breakfast from a *boulangerie* in the high street of Forges-les-Eaux. It had been the only establishment open. However, by mid-morning, I was on the lookout for a top-up. So, when I stumbled upon the suitably themed Café Vélo Jaune - the Yellow Bicycle Café - in Dampierre-en-Bray, could I have found a more suitable place to sink my teeth into a calorific Gallic *gâteau*? Alas not. The Café Vélo Jaune was closed, as it was every Monday. I cycled on, mouth salivating, stomach grumbling.

In Cuy-Saint-Fiacre, a small village with an envious collection of civic amenities including an ornate town hall, church (Norman, pointy steeple…), school and community hall all within a few *baguette* lengths of each other, there was a farm shop. Perfect! Well, on days other than today. It was, you guessed, closed. Edible salvation finally came in the town of Gournay-en-Bray where I managed to buy a sandwich in the somewhat surprising hustle and bustle of the main square. Were they expecting me? Or perhaps they had not got the memo about Mondays in the post. (It was, after all, Monday...)

As I continued my cycle around France, that Monday morning feeling of having to try a little bit harder to keep myself fed and watered would return each week. But if it were a sign that the country was not yet ready to hurtle into the arms of commercial totalitarianism, so be it.

Just to the south of Gournay-en-Bray, a defunct branch line split away from the railway that I had been shadowing and, on occasions, crossing all morning. For a few kilometres, I was back on a fully paid-up member of the *voie verte* network of France. It was this greenway that, had I chosen to continue cycling along it, would have taken me in the direction of Beauvais and then Clermont before looping back towards Paris from the north-east. However, I had chosen to cycle in the alternative direction of Gisors on the more direct route to Paris so after around 4km, I turned right to Saint-Germer-de-Fly, a small village with a phenomenally large parish church. It had once been a Benedictine Abbey but had hit hard times during the French Revolution and the people in the village have not been wanting for Sunday-morning legroom ever since. Its main attraction for me was not its size but its temperature. I parked Wanda beside the door, wandered inside and was immediately welcomed by a wall of gothic air-conditioning.

Outside in the heat and back on the bike, I noticed that the cycling signs were somewhat older than they had been up until this point. It made me wonder if the route to Beauvais was a newer version of the Avenue Verte - a preferred route even - and that I was now following something that had fallen from favour. Further suspicions were aroused when, shortly after passing through Neuf-Marché (a village that, for the record, had no visible market, old or new but then again it was a Monday...) I paused next to a "*Route Barrée*" sign. Was this just for motorised vehicles? Or bicycles as well? Another sign announced "*à 5km*" but I was not willing to risk cycling 5km only to have to turn around and retrace my steps if whatever obstacle it happened to be was indeed a barrier to bikes as well as cars. A third sign pointed in the direction of a deviation which took me back over the railway line again before joining a long, straight road beside the River Epte.

Arriving in the town of Sérifontaine and assuming that I had now passed the obstacle on the Avenue Verte, I crossed back over the railway line and the river to rejoin the cycle route. The diversion had, at least, sent me in the direction of a small Carrefour supermarket that did have the temerity to open on a Monday afternoon, so I used the opportunity of filling up on essentials for the next 24 hours.

More triple-barrelled place names came and went before I arrived in Gisors, a historic town on the very edge of the Duchy of Normandy. To ram home its Norman credentials, a fortified motte and bailey castle stood proud on a mound above the town. It was in the park between the keep and the walls where I paused to escape from the heat of the day under the branches of a parched tree. I was not the only one beginning to suffer from the lack of moisture.

> "From Gisors towards Giverny and the Seine, this route in the bucolic Epte Valley, former border between the Kingdom of France and Normandy the source of inspiration for numerous impressionist painters... is part of the Avenue Verte from Paris to London."

It was with these words that I was welcomed onto the Voie Verte de la Vallée de l'Epte, a 28km greenway that would not only complete today's cycle but also form the start of tomorrow's. It was an easy 5km to the point where I diverted away from the disused railway to the small town of Dangu, my final destination.

Camping de l'Aulnaie was beside a lake and for a modest €11 I was instructed to erect the tent on a small peninsula that jutted out into the water. Mindful of the heat and a forecast that suggested temperatures would not fall much below 20°c, for the first time of the trip, I left the outer skin of the tent in its bag. Tonight it would be just the fine mesh of the inner tent that would seal me off from the elements (or any of my fellow campers who happened to be passing).

After I ate, with a mist of insects beginning to descend upon the surface of the lake, I retreated inside the tent and my mind turned to Paris. There was no response yet from Vrienden op de Fiets, but I had received a message via Warmshowers from my potential Parisian host. His name was Mizu, and it was a "yes". For the first time, I read through his online profile in detail:

> "Please respect my rules... use SIGNAL... don't call my mobile... this is not a restaurant... food must be vegetarian and organic... no alcohol... do not feed the iniquitous and deadly industrial lobby by buying junk food... No coffee... No television... There is an organ with two keyboards, 56 notes and 30 pedals."

Oh dear... It might well be a healthy and worthy night in Paris, but it might also be a loud one. What *had* I let myself in for?

Day Ten: Dangu to Paris (101km)
Tuesday 12th July

"Where are you from?" asked the elderly gentleman standing at the bar of Le Gladiateur in the centre of Dangu. His English was precise and he spoke with authority. It was 8 am and I had just ordered my morning coffee. On the pavement outside was a striking wooden sculpture of a horse rearing up on its hind legs. Inside, the bar was still quiet and the *serveuse* was setting out the tables when not attending to the needs of her two customers.

"England," I replied.

"Ah! There are two connections between Dangu and England," explained the silver-haired gentleman.

"In 1865 Gladiateur was the first foreign horse to win the English Triple Crown - the 2,000 Guineas, the Derby and the St Leger."

As he spoke, he pointed to a photograph on the wall. Gladiateur had been bred in the town by the local count, Frédéric Lagrange.

"And the second connection?" I enquired.

"My name is Reynier Pozzo di Borgo and in 1944 Montgomery asked my grandfather - Le Duc Pozzo di Borgo - if he could park his tanks on the lawns of the family *château*."

It turned out that my well-spoken coffee companion was the current duke. His family - who were originally from Corsica - had purchased the *château* in the late 19th century when it was situated on the outskirts of Paris. It had once been the residence of none other than Madame de Pompadour, mistress to Louis XV, but that had not prevented them from dismantling it, putting it on a train and moving the whole thing to Dangu. The Rolling Stones had stayed there during preparations for their 1990 European tour and Dave Stewart from the Eurythmics had been married there.

"Perhaps next time I'm in Dangu I'll ask if I can pitch my tent on the grounds of your *château*," I suggested.

The duke pointed at a set of ornate gates on the opposite side of the road.

"I now live in the gatehouse," he explained, laughing.

It turned out that the family had sold the *château* and it was now run as a hotel. Perhaps the current owners would not be so keen on seeing my tent on the lawn after all.

I cycled down the hill in the direction of the *voie verte*, rejoining the route that I had left the previous evening about a kilometre further south, next to the disused Dangu railway station. It was presumably here where Madame de Pompadour's *château* had been unloaded. It gave a whole new meaning to the expression "moving house". I hoped that Mick Jagger and Dave Stewart appreciated all the effort involved.

The plan was to retrace the path of the deconstructed *château*, in reverse, all the way to Paris. I had estimated a distance of around 100km so it would be a significantly longer ride than the previous two days of cycling along the Avenue Verte. It would also, I assumed, require me to pay more attention to the route I was taking. My first day had been almost too easy: the unnecessarily well-signposted disused railway line from Dieppe to Forges-les-Eaux. Although the second day had been a mixture of greenways and on-road, I had been following the River Epte. When I had not been able to see the river, I could usually see the railway line which shadowed its course as far as Gisors.

Today was going to be different. A continuation of the *voie verte* to Bray-et-Lû and thereafter a mixture of on-road cycling and segregated paths to Maisons-Laffitte. As the crow flew, that was about 20km from the centre of Paris but thereafter the Avenue Verte began to follow the elongated meanders of the Seine on a route that could easily double the flight of the crow. Oh, to have the power of flight...

For the first 15km, however, I could forget about all that. The Voie Verte de la Vallée de l'Epte was doing a fine job in making the start of the day a very pleasant one indeed. It had all the positive attributes of the greenway south of Dieppe with two added extras: it was heading ever-so-slightly downhill and provided significantly more protection from the sun courtesy of the abundance of trees.

I arrived in Bray-et-Lû in fine form, ready for the rigours of an increasingly suburban cycle into the French capital. Before leaving the confines of the disused railway line, I found an information board with a large map of my onward route as far as a place called Cergy, not too far from Maisons-Laffitte. It came complete with a tantalising description:

> "We invite you to discover in the heart of the Vexin... a collection of bells towers and prestigious *châteaux*... forests, agricultural plains, quarries and riverbanks..."

That did not sound very suburban at all. Perhaps I had been a little hasty in my assumptions about today's route.

The next three hours were spent cycling across the Parc Natural Régional du Vexin français. The Vexin français - so called to distinguish it from the Vexin normand on the western side of the River Epte - sits to the north of the River Seine. It is a 71,000-hectare chalk plateau that rises above the surrounding land by some 100m. This was immediately evident as the gradient reversed from almost imperceptible downhill along the *voie verte* to steady climbing in the 10km before I arrived in the village of Maudétour-en-Vexin. By this point I had indeed discovered much of what the information board had promised: an imposing *château* near Chaussy, an abundance of farmland and even the odd bell tower. Presumably, the forests, quarries and riverbanks were still to come.

There was a second *château* in the village of Maudétour itself. Just like Madame Pompadour's former residence in Dangu, this *château* had also been reborn as a luxury hotel to accommodate the needs of the idle rich of the 21st century (as opposed to the very idle rich of the 17th century). However, the view from behind the ornate main gate (the nearest this peasant could get) suggested that only half of the *château* had ever been built. Either that or some disaster had befallen the northern wing. Perhaps it too had been sold off to the highest bidder, dismantled and transported elsewhere. Until that is, the new owner realised that it would be far easier to get some local builders in to finish off the job. Who knows?

More farmland came and went and although I was rarely afforded the opportunity to cycle through it, there was clearly a lot of forest, especially to the south between the Avenue Verte and the Seine. The increasingly predominant crop was sunflowers, their heads drooping slightly under the weight of their seeds. They were now at the point where the sun had done its work and they seemed desperate for the bees to take their pollen, the birds to eat their seeds or a farmer to decapitate them and turn them into a tub of Flora. But as of yet, no semi-detached houses, tree-lined cul-de-sacs, excruciatingly polite dinner parties or seething resentment of the people next door. Suburbia had yet to be reached.

Signs for Paris had been a common feature of the Avenue Verte waymarkers since leaving the *voie verte* earlier in the day but none of them had given any indication as to how many of the estimated 100km there remained between me and Notre Dame Cathedral. Suburbia did finally kick in at Cergy, a very modern town on the north-western edge of the Parisian transport network. I made the most of its well-stocked fruit and veg shop opposite the train station to indulge in a colourful and healthy lunch of avocado, banana and peach.

Thereafter, route-finding became increasingly difficult. The signs for the Avenue Verte that I had been following since leaving Dieppe now had to fight for my attention beside all the other distractions of the urban world. In Jouy-le-Moutier - just a few kilometres after Cergy - I was, however, delighted to find not only a cycling sign for Paris but one that told me how far I still had to cycle: 30km. I had not yet arrived in Maisons-Laffitte, the town that was about 20km from the centre of Paris, so clearly my initial estimate had been far too pessimistic. I had arranged to meet my Warmshowers host Mizu at 6 pm and with much of the afternoon still to come, time would not be an issue. My ability to follow the prescribed route, might. The organ recital could still be in jeopardy.

I was now cycling beside the River Oise, which had meandered its way towards me from the north. It would be a brief relationship - just 5km - and we were only shoulder partners until its bigger sibling - the Seine - arrived on the scene at the confluence of the two. I paused for a few minutes to watch the barges plod slowly upstream before crossing the river for the first time just to the north of the Forêt domaniale de Saint-Germain.

The signposts directed me first along the edge of the forest - a perilously narrow track with a high metal fence on my left and perhaps France's longest bramble bush on my right - before I plunged into the depths of the forest itself. So much for having arrived in suburbia. This clump of oak trees spread out over 35 square kilometres of prime Parisian real estate. As I cycled along the rough tracks from one nodal point to the next it was not difficult to imagine King Louis and Madame de Pompadour galloping past on their horses, obscured not only by time but by the dense arboreal landscape that surrounded me.

I re-emerged into the real world at the end of a wide boulevard that led me in the direction of the impressive and perfectly symmetrical Château de Maisons. Once I had cycled around its perimeter, I turned to appreciate the front elevation of the building and was impressed to see how those in charge had embraced the concept of allowing the garden to grow wild. After having seen so many manicured gardens in recent days it was wonderfully liberating to see such a radical approach being adopted. And it worked perfectly. It somehow gave the *château* an air of fading decadence. Miss Havisham would have loved it.

I crossed the Seine for a second time shortly after the *château* and, after taking a few moments to consider my options, decided to deviate away from the route of the Avenue Verte. I was now eager to arrive at my destination and by cutting across one of the wide meanders of the river I could save perhaps an hour of cycling. However, by the time I crossed the Seine for the third time over the Pont de Bezons, I was questioning whether it had been a wise decision. I might have saved time, but it had been 30 minutes of dodging traffic and negotiating junctions. I resolved that after this point I would stick to following the signs.

To begin with, this was not a problem as the Avenue Verte continued to follow the south bank of the river but then I was directed into an industrial suburb where I was often cycling blind. I scoured the urban environment for signs and whenever I spotted the familiar compass logo of the Avenue

Verte I would jump (internally) for joy but then they would disappear again and my heart would begin to sink.

My penultimate crossing of the Seine was at Saint-Denis where the route followed a canal and passed the national stadium. At one point a dishevelled man raised a stick that he was carrying and pretended to throw it, spear-like, in the direction of my wheels. Had he done so, that might have been it for my Grand Tour, but he held back and snarled. It was confirmation that I had now passed through genteel suburbia and had arrived in the inner city.

I continued to follow the canal until prevented from doing so by barriers blocking the path. An event was being prepared - presumably to coincide with the 14th of July which was now only a day away - and I all but gave up hope of sticking to the official route. The compass on my handlebars was again pressed into action and I headed south on any road that I was allowed to cycle along. Not easy when so many of the streets were one-way but eventually I turned onto the Boulevard de Sebastopol and within a few minutes, I was able to glimpse the twin towers of the Cathédrale de Notre Dame.

Crossing the Seine for the final time, I arrived on the Île de la Cité, passed the Palais de Justice and turned left beside the Préfecture de Police before emerging into the large square in front of the cathedral. Point zero for all the roads in France. But not for me. My journey had still barely begun.

———

It was on the dot of 6 pm when I found the entrance to the building containing my Warmshowers host's flat in a back street in the Marais district, a few blocks to the north of the cathedral. Echoing around my mind were the details set out in Mizu's online profile: "Don't call my mobile… not a restaurant…vegetarian… organic… no coffee… no television… two-keyboard organ…". The lock was operated remotely without exchange of words and I squeezed myself and Wanda into the narrow corridor. Leaving the bicycle on the ground floor, I climbed the wooden stairs to the first floor where my host had his flat, knocked on the door and waited. A few moments later a middle-aged man appeared and we exchanged introductions…

Le Grand Tour

PART THREE:

La Véloscénie

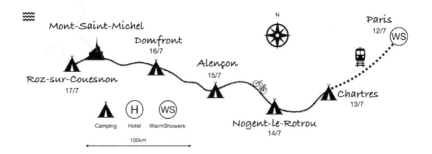

Day Eleven: Paris to Chartres (Train)
Wednesday 13th July

I warmed rapidly to Mizu. It would have been difficult to find a kinder, more gentle man in the 4th arrondissement of Paris. His apartment was tiny consisting of a multi-purpose sitting room with a sofa bed behind a curtain, one bedroom, a minuscule galley kitchen and a bathroom tucked behind the entrance door. Mizu was a man with values - this had been evident from what I had read on his Warmshowers profile - but he was not ready to ram them down my throat, or anyone else's. As opposed to many (including, on occasions, yours truly) he lived his values. He went everywhere by bike or on foot, bought local produce from local shops and did all that he could to minimise his negative impact on the environment. He led by example. How many of us can honestly say that? To a greater or lesser extent, we are all hypocrites. I extol the virtues of cycling but am happy to jump into my car to drive to the shop for a bottle of wine, even though it would only take me ten minutes to cycle there. When Mizu is no more, the planet will be a little less rich and certainly a little less protected.

After sharing several glasses of filtered water, Mizu offered to take me on a short tour of the Marais district, an area of Paris that has been his home for 30 years. The Marais - it means swamp - is to Paris what Soho is to London, without the seedy bits. (For those you need to head north to Pigalle.) And just like Soho, long-term residents of the Marais have seen many changes in recent decades as property prices have soared and gentrification been rampant. However, when Baron Haussmann was busy redesigning Paris in the 19th century, much of the Marais remained untouched. This is reflected in today's narrow streets, occasional turreted *hôtels particuliers*[14], remnants of the original walls of the city and even an old foundry chimney hidden at the back of a swish Japanese fashion outlet. Mizu took great pride and delight in pointing out all these delights. Perhaps in these glimpses of the past, he saw a reflection of his own spirit, one member of a dwindling band of Parisians holding out against the inevitable tide of modernity.

As Mizu headed back to his flat, I continued my stroll. Where better to be a *flâneur* than in the city for which the word was invented? And what better

---

[14] If you turn up at a *hôtel particulier* in the hope of finding a room for the night you will probably get short shrift from the owner. The term refers to a large, often detached property in a town or city which was originally a private residence. The French prime minister's official residence is the Hôtel Matignon for example. You will not find it on Booking.com.

time to be doing it than a late evening in the warmth of the summer? My day ended in a small bar called La Tartine on the rue de Rivoli with me paying far too much for a couple of draft beers which in some corners of France might only have cost €2 each. As I sipped my expensive refreshments, I plotted my escape west...

———

Mizu had made it clear that if I wanted to stay for a second night in his flat, I was more than welcome to do so. I was tempted, especially as I had never experienced the 14th of July celebrations in Paris first-hand. But of all the places on my Grand Tour, Paris was the one that I knew best having visited on many occasions since hitchhiking there as a university student in the late 1980s. Yet it was more current events that were beginning to play on my mind. In the vague plan of my cycle, I had envisaged arriving in the north-west of France in the middle of July. I was nowhere near the north-west of France and it was already July 13th. I needed to move on.

Day ten of the trip would ultimately involve very little cycling. Having cycled through the northern suburbs of Paris the previous afternoon, I was not at all enthused by the prospect of pedalling through the western suburbs the following day. Instead, I whipped out my SNCF app and booked the second of my ten trains. My chosen departure - the 15:06 from Paris Montparnasse - would deposit me in Chartres about an hour later. Crucially, by taking me a smidgeon under 100km, my self-imposed distance rule would not be broken. Chartres was one of the first major towns on the Véloscénie cycle route which would eventually take me as far as the Mont-Saint-Michel. Much to my delight it was also home to a *camping municipal*.

My mid-afternoon departure from Paris would allow me a little time to complete a few urgent tasks in the capital. Chief amongst these were my attempts to bring the ongoing saga with the GoPro camera (which had now entered the realms of something that Kafka might have written) to a close. The problem was so obviously the camera itself, not the battery, and my discussions with several GoPro customer service centres around the globe were becoming a little tiresome. We had gone a little beyond the "Have you switched it on and off?" / "Is the software up to date?" stages, but not by far. The anonymous GoPro operatives now wanted me to try a new battery (to prove me wrong and them right) but because I had no fixed address, this was proving to be problematic to say the least. One of their agents in the Far East even suggested that a new battery be sent to her aunt who happened to live in the Parisian suburbs. I declined the offer and resolved to find one myself.

After traipsing around central Paris on an unsuccessful hunt, I decided to head a couple of kilometres south to the Latin Quarter. Mizu had recommended a shop called Au Vieux Campeur. Its reputation did seem to give hope that this might not be a forlorn quest. Perhaps they would come up with the goods, literally.

Au Vieux Campeur is a French institution. Set up in the early part of the Nazi occupation of Paris in the 1940s by the then chief scout of France, Roger de Rorthays de Saint-Hilaire, it still resides in rue des Écoles near the Sorbonne. After over 80 years in business, many of the neighbouring shop units now house specialist departments catering for those who seek pleasure in the outdoors. A small village of some 25 Au Vieux Campeur outlets can all be found within a few hundred metres of each other. Surely one of these would be able to solve my GoPro gripes. After more wanderings following a map provided by one of the shops, on the corner of the rue du Sommerard and the rue Jean de Beauvais, I finally found what I was looking for: the technology department.

Battery purchased I stood outside on the pavement and loaded it into the camera. I was hoping to be proved wrong... but I was not. The camera continued to shut down almost immediately after having been switched on. Its technological tantrums were continuing and another phone call to the Far East would be needed.

However, all was not lost. *Au contraire*. Another Au Vieux Campeur shop was able to furnish me with a good quality, wide-brimmed sun hat. It replaced the cheap one bought from a market stall in Dieppe which had already started falling apart. I was also able to double my limited stock of just two t-shirts. The novelty of pulling on sweat-dampened clothing every morning was beginning to wear thin. With extreme heat warnings continuing to lead the news bulletins, my ability to perspire when cycling was only going to increase.

Via a modest detour to take in the Eiffel Tower, I arrived at the Gare Montparnasse shortly after 2 pm and was delighted to spot my first sign for the Véloscénie on the road leading down to the façade of the station. The route had started near Notre Dame and continued south through the suburbs before sweeping west through large swathes of forest in the direction of Chartres. This would be the section of the Véloscénie that I would see from the comfort of a railway carriage. I was not alone in letting the train take the strain through the French capital in search of greener and more pleasant pastures elsewhere. Fighting for space in the storage section of the train were bikes of all shapes and sizes. They were leaning against each other blocking the path for any passenger who might want to make a swift exit, but the conductor was not fazed. He had clearly experienced worse.

However, with Wanda next to the window, I did hope that all the other cyclists would be alighting before Chartres. If they were not, it might take some time to extricate her from the tangled web of steel and rubber currently sitting between her and the door of the train.

I had managed to pick up a brochure about the Véloscénie earlier in the day. In contrast to the map I had been given for the Avenue Verte in Dieppe, which was more map than brochure, this was definitely more brochure than map. The 450km route had been condensed to fit on a side and a half of folded A4. But the potential stopping points were clearly marked and, with much of the line from Paris to Mont-Saint-Michel being marked in green - *voies cyclables* - I guessed that route-finding over the coming days would be no more challenging than it had been along the Avenue Verte. The route was subtitled as "*l'itineraire de grand spectacle*" which sounded promising, although I did wonder to what extent this description played heavily on its two iconic endpoints of Paris and the Mont-Saint-Michel.

As the TER train trundled through the increasingly green landscape, I tried to work out a series of overnight stops and circled three intermediate destinations after Chartres: Nongent-le-Rotrou, Alençon and Domfront-en-Poiraie. All of these had municipal campsites nearby, as did Chartres, so I was looking forward to not just good quality camping over the next few days but also cheap camping. Indeed an online contact, David Naylor, had wholeheartedly recommended the campsite at Domfront.

Planning done I looked up to discover that most of my fellow cyclists on the train had now bailed out leaving a path through which I could wheel my own bike. It had been a fruitful (if admittedly effortless) start to my journey along the Véloscénie.

Camping de Chartres was on the opposite side of the town to the train station, but I managed to skirt around the centre and its most famous attraction - the cathedral - to erect my tent in good time and settle in for the evening. I would return in the morning to have a poke around Chartres' gothic masterpiece before setting off west. The campsite was a gem set in a wooded area beside the River Eure and I paid just €12 for the pleasure. My only complaint was that I had arrived a few days too early to appreciate a cycling-themed film courtesy of "Cinécyclo", a touring event that was also following the route of the Véloscénie in the second half of July.

As had been the case two days earlier in Dangu, only the inner tent was needed, the hot day morphing slowly into a very, very warm night. The only risk might be if the heat provoked a thunderstorm, but I was willing to take the risk. And I was not alone: several other cyclists were dotted around the large free camping area[15] and many of them had also chosen to sleep with only the interior single skin mesh protecting them from any rain that might fall.

The evening was spent relaxing, catching up on admin and, when I summoned up the effort required, editing and publishing the latest episode of the podcast. It covered my journey through Belgium, along the coast into France and then the Avenue Verte to Paris.[16] Aside from a record of what I had achieved so far, the cutting, pasting, clipping and cropping gave me time to reflect upon what had, so far, been a very successful cycle tour.

But I did need to be in Brittany by the end of the weekend to keep alive my chances of returning to Rotterdam and the Hook of Holland on time. It was now Wednesday so I had four full days of cycling ahead of me on a route that looked relatively flat. My main concern was with the heat. The temperatures in Spain were already hitting 44°c and that hot air mass was heading north. Météo-France, the French national weather agency, was predicting similar temperatures in France by the weekend. One British newspaper was proclaiming that the "hottest day ever" was nearly upon us with its headline "Red Alert". There was seemingly no escape to be had across Western Europe. Was it a wise time to be doing anything, let alone cycling hundreds of kilometres on a fully laden touring bike?

---

[15] The expression "free camping" has caused confusion when I have used it in previous books. It does not mean that you do not have to pay. It refers to a plot of land on a campsite which is set aside for those travelling without a motor vehicle - often people on bikes - and which has not been split up into pitches. It is, by far, a more preferable option encouraging fraternisation between like-minded campers if they want it, but also isolation if they prefer it that way.

[16] The links to Episode 053 of The Cycling Europe Podcast can be found at CyclingEurope.org/Podcast.

Day Twelve: Chartres to Nongent-le-Rotrou (79km)
Thursday 14th July

Even in a country that is not lacking for picturesque towns, Chartres must surely be towards the top of the list. As the sun had set, I flew the drone from the campsite and caught some stunning glimpses of the cathedral, towering above everything in its midst. Now I was seeing it from close quarters, craning my neck to examine its asymmetrical twin towers from the square beneath its 13th-century rose window of the last judgement. If the son of God himself had descended from those central panes of glass and delivered that final judgement, it would not have been a bad place to hear what he had to say, good or bad.

It was not, alas, a great place to take a photograph. Such was the grandeur of the building, and such was the relatively small size of the square, squeezing everything in - even with the wide-angle lens of my phone - was proving tricky so I headed inside to try my luck from within. Although it was not yet 9 o'clock, the contrast between the heat outside and the cool inside was stark. There was every reason to linger, and I took my time strolling across the polished stone floors from one medieval masterpiece to the next. The stand-out attraction was a choir screen, 7-metres high and 100-metres long depicting the life of Christ in 40 sculpted scenes. Its detail was astonishing and recent renovation work had returned it to the day it had been chiselled in the early 16th century. We think we live in an advanced age where we can see inside the human brain, observe storms on distant stars and communicate instantaneously with the other side of the planet. When it comes to the fundamental skill of making something beautiful with our hands, however, have we really progressed?

For a non-believer, this was destined to be a surprisingly religious day as, over the next eight hours, I would seek sanctuary in no less than four churches. If each chapter of this book were to be sponsored (and I am open to offers…), day twelve would be snapped up by the Catholic Church within seconds. Although nothing quite matched the Cathedral of Our Lady of Chartres, each establishment had its attractions and chief amongst these was an escape from the relentless heat outside on the Véloscénie.

As I finally started to make my way out of town, I spotted several distinctive yellow and blue seashell signs. I became familiar with these waymarkers in 2015 as I cycled from Tarifa in Spain to Nordkapp in Norway, especially after my route ran alongside that of the Camino de Santiago in northern Spain. As far as Trondheim in Norway I followed, on and off, the pilgrimage route of Saint James. In cycling circles, this is the

EuroVelo 3, but it chooses not to pass through Chartres and takes a more southerly, less direct route via Tours and Orléans beside the Loire before turning north in the direction of Paris. For the walkers, however, the pull of Chartres is strong and the first 35km of my route as far as Illiers-Combray would be shared with those travelling on foot. That said, after a few easily identifiable pilgrims in Chartres with their backpacks, sticks and seashells hanging from their backpacks, there were few hikers to be seen outside of town.

For the first hour or so of the morning, I cycled in the vague direction of the River Eure as far as Thivars. Although the path I adopted was an official deviation away from the promised segregated cycleway, it did keep me on quiet roads. Shortly after Thivars, I took my second pitstop courtesy of the Catholic Church in a small, simple chapel at Meslay-le-Grenet, its main attraction being a series of painted frescos from the 15th century depicting "*la danse macabre*". I hoped it was not a bad omen as temperatures continued to rise by the day.

Thereafter it was an almost straight line in the direction of my lunch at Illiers-Combray. The final section would have been on a busy road had it not been for the kind people at the European Union who had financed 40% of the construction of a segregated cycle path as far as the outskirts of town. This was celebrated by a phenomenally large sign, the cost of which, I reflected, might have financed a few more metres of cycle track. That said, one of the reasons why so many people voted to take the UK out of the EU was because they were not aware of the important role the organisation was playing in our lives. At least on the continent, the authorities have never been shy to extol the virtues of how contributions to "Brussels" are being spent. If we had adopted such an enlightened approach in Britain things might have been different. When we return to the European fold - as one day we surely will - let us celebrate what the EU is doing with a few more signs. It will mean that our cycle paths are a couple of metres shorter than they might otherwise be, but I can live with that.

I had few expectations of Illiers-Combray. In fact, until that morning I had never heard of the place. However, I was getting hungry and, this being the 14th of July, I had not passed any shops that were open. I was hopeful that I might be able to locate some edible sustenance in the centre of the town, even if it might mean pilfering the communion wafers in the local church. Fortunately for the parish priest, the man running the Epicérie de Combray opposite the Église Saint-Jacques had cast aside his republicanism for the day and was open for business. I purchased a packet of fake Pringles, some fruit cake and a can of Coke and went to sit on the bench beside the church to scoff them. But I was not alone...

Next to me was a boy - perhaps ten years old - with an oversized bow tie. He was staring earnestly into the distance, in the vague direction of the *épicerie*, perhaps wondering whether to purchase his own tube of knock-off crisps. He was motionless. On the floor beside the bench was a brass plaque:

P'tit Loup
Marcel Proust enfant à Illiers-Combray
1871-1922
Auteur de "A la recherche du temps perdu"

My route into the noble profession of being a teacher of French was a non-standard one and I never benefitted from a higher education in French. I mastered the lingo on the mean streets of, err… Tours, the gentile French city in the Loire Valley where I worked teaching English during much of the 1990s. I do not claim to have read any of the works of Marcel Proust, but he is revered as one of France's greatest writers. His series of novels - *À la recherche du temps perdu* (in English, *In Search of Lost Time*) - lean heavily upon his childhood recollections of time spent in Illiers. In his books, he refers to the town as Combray.

This is all very fascinating but nowhere near as fascinating as the fact that until 1971 Illiers-Combray was simply Illiers. To mark the centenary of Proust's birth, the town decided to change its name to Illiers-Combray. 50 years on and the move still seems to be a touchy subject between *Islériens* (the inhabitants of Illiers / Illiers-Combray) and *Proustiens* (the fans of Marcel). The newspaper *La Croix* reported in 2018 that the local Proust museum was lacking investment and the people running it were often seen as "intellectual Parisian snobs"! Perhaps, however, the installation of the little boy with the bow tie in 2020 and the recent renovation of the museum were positive signs of a more pro-Proust future for the town. Even if the man himself described (fictional) Combray as "a little sad".[17]

For a place to sit and have lunch on a hot afternoon in July, it worked for me and for the third time in the day, I headed inside the local church to cool

---

[17] In 2017 letters came to light showing that Proust paid for positive reviews of his first volume in the *À la recherche du temps perdu* series to appear on the front page of newspapers. *The Guardian* reported that "The novelist wrote the notices himself and sent them to be typed up by his publisher 'so there is no trace of my handwriting' to distance himself 'absolutely from the money that will change hands'… Proust's desperation for publicity was partly because he was having to pay for the book's publication himself, experts said. A string of publishing houses had turned it down before… Bernard Grasset [took] it in 1913 – but only if the author paid all the costs." No comment.

down. I was rewarded with an astonishing wooden roof that pre-dated the great writer by several centuries. If Proust is not your thing but fancy ceilings are, it is worthy of a minor diversion. You will not be disappointed. Shortly after leaving Illiers-Combray, I entered the Parc Naturel Régional du Perche. Over the next 24 hours, the Véloscénie would take a diagonal route across its "forests, hills and pastoral landscape'", or so the brochure that I picked up in church number four in Frazé promised. This one had no grandeur, no scary frescos or colourful ceiling but on a day when the chief attraction was the ecclesiastical air-conditioning, it was just as welcome as the previous three.

The Perche is an area of land sandwiched between the honeypot destinations of Normandy and the Loire Valley and with gentle inclines, arresting open countryside and quiet country lanes, it made for almost perfect cycling. For this section of its route, the Véloscénie was 100% on-road. However, when those roads are single-track rural affairs with most of the traffic made up of tractors in no rush to get anywhere fast, who needs a disused railway track or a canal towpath? It was a joy. Cycle touring as it should be. No complications. No fuss. No bother. Pretty things to look at. Pretty places in which to pause and take a breath. Pretty well most of the time. Tick, tick, tick. (Tick, tick, tick.) The wind was a minor distraction, blustering from the west, but it did at least keep the perspiration at bay. Every twist and turn of the Véloscénie was clearly signposted. In the village of La Gaudine, a local resident had even been kind enough to erect a homemade sign - presumably for the benefit of cyclists - with a picture of the Mont-Saint-Michel and a distance: 253km. As I was within 15km of my destination, this would mean another 240km spread over three days, which seemed eminently doable. It had been a good day to be on the bike.

I arrived in Nogent-le-Rotrou at around 5 pm. It was an unremarkable place with no obvious connections to literary greatness. All the shops were, of course, closed. This would need to be an evening when I would have to cook for myself. I might even have to forgo my daily baguette ration as everyone - even the bakers - appeared to be at home celebrating being French.

I located the Camping Municipal des Viennes on Google Maps - it was on the western side of town adjacent to the open-air swimming pool - and within a few minutes I could see the entrance. But there was something not quite right. When approaching most campsites there are tell-tale hints that you are indeed about to arrive at a campsite: signs, tents, motorhomes... people. Camping Municipal des Viennes appeared to have adopted a somewhat radical approach to camping by dispensing with all of them. I dismounted from the bike. All I could hear were the screams of children emanating from the swimming pool, which I could not see but which was obviously somewhere close. The gravel path guided me beside what looked like a small water treatment plant on my right and a large field on my left. And then I saw it. A tent. But just the one, in the distance beside the river. I kept pushing. There was no obvious – or unobvious - campsite reception. There *was* a wash block, albeit a deserted one. The grass around me had been cut and the wash block was in operation. A light could be seen inside. But no people. I then noticed a laminated sign:

Le Camping des Viennes est désormais réservé uniquement
aux randonneurs et cyclistes avec tentes.

The campsite was open, but only to walkers and cyclists with a tent. A second sign with prices explained that someone would come to collect money *"regulièrement"*.

Over the years I have experienced many different approaches to camping. Some campsites try too hard to be like hotels (individual toilets in Spain for example), and some campsites are on the map and listed online but have vanished on the ground (often in Italy…). But this was something new. A campsite that had, to all intents and purposes, closed but was hanging on in there - just - for the benefit of people who were not in a position to drive 20km down the road to the next site. How commendable. Perhaps the pandemic had been the final straw but whatever the reason, it was gratifying to know that the local authorities recognised the utility of the facility to the likes of me. Whoever had made that decision, *merci*.

Beyond the wash block were several pitches separated by hedges as well as some cages for locking bikes. There was a family who had erected their large tepee-style tent at the end of the row and by the time I had put up my own tent and eaten, three other cyclists had arrived. After locking their bikes in the cages, they presumably returned to the town centre in search of food. I got chatting with the family in the tepee. They were also cycling along the Véloscénie but in the opposite direction to me, back to their home in Paris. Later in the evening, two teenagers turned up to collect the fees for the tourist office, or so they claimed.

That said, it was all slightly eerie and had I been camping alone that evening, I might have been tempted to take myself back into town in search of alternative accommodation. If, as the years go by, the Camping Municipal des Viennes remains closed to all but walkers and cyclists and the interest of the local council wanes, the place could gradually descend into a dystopian outpost along the route to Mont-Saint-Michel. The presence of others gave me confidence that I would not end up listed on the

Wikipedia page of people murdered in creepy abandoned camping grounds. But when you turn up? Who knows?

Day Thirteen: Nongent–le–Rotrou to Alençon (93km)
Friday 15th July

The first of my four days cycling along the Véloscénie had been almost all on road. That was about to change as the remaining three days to Mont-Saint-Michel promised lots and lots of disused railways. We now think of France as one of the more enlightened countries when it comes to travelling by train. The high-speed TGVs whizz passengers around France at speeds in excess of 300 kilometres per hour and they have been doing so since 1981 on an ever-expanding network of dedicated high-speed lines. According to the International Union of Railways, France boasts a network of over 29,000km. The UK, with a similar population but roughly half the land mass, has just 16,000km. There are over 4,000 people per kilometre of railway in Britain. In France, the number is a mere 2,400. That might explain why you struggle to get a seat on the 4.50 from Paddington. It can be murder being a commuter in the UK.

Yet this was not always the case. In the early 19th century, the French were slow to get out of the train shed never mind speed along the lines. By 1842, Britain had six times as much railway as France and it was only in the second half of the century that the French started to play catch up. But when they did, there was seemingly no stopping them as by 1938 the network had expanded to nearly 43,000km. The pre-war map of French railway lines resembled a poorly maintained piece of porcelain.

Post-war, the network has thinned out somewhat. Not great for French railway fans but wonderful if you happen to be into your long-distance cycle touring. I had been making use of disused railway lines since crossing the border into France from Belgium (and would continue to use them regularly until the end of my Grand Tour). However, it would be over the next couple of weeks in the north-west of France that I would benefit the most from the decision to ditch the trains. Thanks to the closure of the railway line from Alençon to Condé-sur-Huisne in the 1980s, today would mostly be spent pedalling along embankments and hurtling through cuttings.

There was little hurtling being done by anyone at Camping des Viennes in Nogent-le-Rotrou at 7 am. The slightly eerie atmosphere of the previous evening as the light had dimmed and the silence descended had been replaced with birdsong: the twit-twoo of a pair of owls and the on-off chit-chat of humans, preparing their breakfasts and packing away their tents. It is difficult to do dystopia when the warm rays of the morning sun are flickering through the branches of a row of tall poplar trees and the only things to be heard are calm, quiet and entirely natural.

On the neighbouring pitch, each member of the French family in the tepee had an allocated task to complete making their morning routine of eating and preparing to move on a wonderful logistical spectacle. I had witnessed this familial piece of theatre many times over the years and on this occasion the son, who was perhaps 10 years old, was diligently cleaning the bikes. I joked that he should consider giving Wanda the once over with his bucket of water and sponge but rather than smiling and making a smart comment (as I was expecting), he said he would love to. I quickly backtracked leaving him a little bemused as to why I had asked in the first place. Perhaps dark sarcasm in the classroom has never been a feature of French schools.

With my destination of Alençon firmly in mind and, courtesy of a diversion back into the centre of town, a fast-food breakfast resting in my stomach, I set off. Between Chartres and Mont-Saint-Michel, there was only one town that I had previously heard of and that was Alençon. I estimated the day would be one of around 100km and after Sablons-sur-Huisne it promised to be traffic-free cycling because of the disused railway. However, I had noticed on my map that there was a *musée du vélo* - a bicycle museum - to the east of Alençon so I was planning to branch away from the old railway about 15km before it finished to pay it a visit.

To start the day a short *voie verte* escorted me out of town beside the River Huisne. Having only just been constructed it came complete with the obligatory over-size information hoarding telling me that, in this case, the town of Nogent-le-Rotrou was "investing to improve the quality of my life". Well, the bit that I lived as I cycled the 1,650 metres of its length. Thereafter, the quality of my life did not degenerate to any great extent as the roads along which I was travelling were quiet affairs through the pretty countryside. Only upon arrival in Sablons-sur-Huisne itself did I feel the joy of my existence start ebbing slightly away when I struggled to find the start of the disused railway.

After a few head-scratching minutes, normal service was resumed when I found a sign for the *voie verte*. Why I had thought the disused railway line would be anywhere other than near the stretch of track that still had trains running along it was a mystery that did not escape me. I shrugged my shoulders in true Gallic fashion and kept cycling.

It was immediately apparent that the Voie Verte Alençon - Condé-sur-Huisne was perhaps a little more established than the previous disused railways that I had followed. The signs were a somewhat dated and often askew, the track firmly embedded after years of feet and tyres pounding across it and many of the abandoned stations remained as closed as the day they waved off their final train in the 1980s.

A large blue sign welcomed me to the first section of the route as far as Corbon and it described the Huisne Valley and especially one of its residents - the Percheron horse - in poetic terms:

> *"Mais l'enfant du pays, c'est le cheval percheron: sa puissance est tranquille, son regard est franc, ses formes sont rondes et généreuses, à l'image des collines du Perche..."*

Quiet power? Frank look? Round and generous forms? I would feel very much at home.

I later noted on my daily write-up of events that the day had felt very much like a spinning class. Long, continuous stretches of cycling with just enough of an incline to require effort. The river could be glimpsed just beyond the trees which provided a welcome level of protection from the glare of the sun. In many places, their canopies had joined and I was left to cycle through a delightful green tunnel of vegetation.

Until it all stopped rather abruptly at a junction with the D272.

I pulled on the brakes and ground to a halt. Opposite me on the other side of the quiet road, the greenway appeared to continue but there was a no-entry sign under which was written "*sauf piétons*" - "except pedestrians". The path seemed to be a shadow of its former self, slightly weedier suggesting that not many pedestrians and few cyclists ventured any further. The cycling signs for the Véloscénie indicated a diversion to the left with my destination of Alençon being listed as 39.5km in that direction. A second destination, Mortagne-au-Perche was listed as being just 2km away. It was lunchtime and that would make a good place to pause for a bite to eat and drink. I was hungry and especially thirsty as there had not been anywhere to refill my bottles in the 45km since leaving Nogent. This frustration with dehydration was getting to the point of being annoying so the news that I would only have to cycle a couple of kilometres to quench my thirst was welcome.

Had I *not* known this, the sign beside the entrance to a house adjacent to the truncated *voie verte* might have been taken somewhat differently. Securely pinned to a painted blue board behind a thick sheet of laminated plastic (this had not been put there on a whim) was a sign in three languages:

> *NOUS NE SERVONS PAS D'EAU*
> WE DO NOT SERVE WATER
> *WIR SERVIEREN KEIN WASSER*

MERCI DE VOTRE COMPRÉHENSION

To ram home the fact that the residents were not going to provide anyone with water from their taps, the background image depicted a stainless-steel tap from which a torrent of water was flowing.

"See this refreshing clean water oozing abundantly from the tap? Well, you can't have it, not from here. Clear off!" shouted the voices in my mind.

I wondered if the residents had also been instrumental in the closure to cyclists of the old railway line beside their house. Was this an example of French anti-cycling nimbyism? (Or, as I am pretty sure they do not say, *pas dans ma cour arrière*[18].) As a fully paid-up member of the human race, I am just as susceptible as the next man or woman when it comes to taking a dislike to the actions of other, more annoying members of my species. However, it takes a special kind of person to elevate that animosity to the point of designing a colourful poster in three languages, laminating it, attaching it to a board, nailing it to a post and painting the whole thing blue. Impressive!

With the dwindling energy of a man crawling across a parched desert, I climbed the hill to the centre of Mortagne-au-Perche, stopped at the first shop I could find, bought a large bottle of water and sat down to guzzle.

The spinning class continued into the afternoon. The only thing to have changed was the gradient which had modified its direction and was now almost imperceptibly downhill. Had I not been able to see it on my GPS tracking app, it would have gone unnoticed. What was not going to be ignored, however, was the *musée du vélo* in the small town of Villeneuve-en-Perseigne. It would mean abandoning the traffic-free greenway for the final 15km of the day, but so be it. It was never going to be an option to shun the opportunity of visiting a bicycle museum if I was travelling in the vicinity of one. I just hoped it would be open.[19]

At 3.30 pm, after a few kilometres back on the road, I arrived in Villeneuve and was standing in front of the large sign that announced I had indeed found the museum:

Le Musée du Vélo "La Belle Echappée"
Espace Muséographique Régional
L'Histoire Du Cyclisme

---

[18] "Not in my back yard."

[19] I have been cycling in the vicinity of bicycle museums twice before: once in the west of France in 2015 and once in Wales in 2020. On both occasions they were closed. Third time lucky...

With such an elongated name it was a wonder there was any room left for the exhibits, but it was at least open. That said, I appeared to be the only one who knew as, aside from a woman sitting behind the desk at the far end of the entrance hall, I was alone.

The bicycle-themed collection housed in the large wooden shed in front of me had been curated over many years by a resident of Villeneuve-en-Perseigne, Ivan Bonduelle. In 2018, it was purchased by the local authorities and Ivan's museum continued to tell the story of the bicycle, with a particular focus on the Tour de France. I dare say many personal collections across the world have ended up in refuse skips on the road once their owners have found them too unwieldy or have moved into a long-term plot beside the church. But this was France, and this was cycling. If ever there was a collection that would be saved for the nation it was that of Monsieur Bonduelle. The skips were never in with a chance.

The entrance hall resembled a school gymnasium but with the exercise equipment replaced by bicycles from the mid-19th century to the present day. On the wall to my right were photographs of all the winners of the Tour de France since its inception in 1903, including the seven-time "winner" Lance Armstrong. *Should I break the bad news?* I made no comment. But this was just the hors d'oeuvre. By paying €6 I could enter the inner sanctum of the museum, concealed behind a heavy door and a black curtain. I had the distinct impression that I had been transported back to Paris and was about to enter one of those late-night establishments on the Boulevard de Clichy in Pigalle...

"It's a bit dark because the electrician has not arrived yet to mend the lights," apologised the woman behind the counter.

As I pushed back the curtain I was engulfed by the sound of accordions and could just about make out the naked frames... of old bicycles.

The first examples were from 1888 and 1892 and, over the next 30 minutes, I took a slow wander around the dimly lit museum. Le Tour de France featured heavily with all the period items carefully labelled, perhaps in the words of Monsieur Bonduelle himself. A soundtrack of archive recordings that slowly drifted from one event to the next escorted me as I walked.

"Elle set polulaire sur toute la France: la bicyclette Christophe..."
Wonder Dunlop... Vélo Alcyon... les poupées tricolors... le vélo de replacement de Jean Robic... les années Anquetilles... Merckx: le champion des champions... le retour des français: Hinault, Fignon... Induráin: cinq années de suite... Le Tour Féminin... Maillots des champions..."

The story of Le Tour finished somewhat conveniently in the late 1990s with the display of a Tour de France-themed ashtray. There was only a passing mention of Armstrong but nothing so unequivocal that it had resulted in his photograph being prised from the wall in the foyer.

I thanked the woman at the reception desk and wandered back towards the entrance, passing beneath the portrait of the doper-in-chief. It seemed that in this forgotten corner of France, his cycling crimes were beginning to be pardoned.

Day Fourteen: Alençon to Domfront (73km)
Saturday 16th July

I had been making good use of the network of French municipal campsites since leaving Paris. Chartres had an excellent one. Nogent-le-Rotrou had one too, just. And I woke up on day 14 of the trip at a third, on the outskirts of Alençon.

Camping Guéramé was, however, looking a little tired. Some areas had been cordoned off, the tennis court did not appear to have seen much action since Henri Leconte was strutting his stuff and the echoey communal area was frequented only by a small group of teenagers and me. We were all desperate to find a Wi-Fi signal, but the router was not having a good day and the trickle of data being supplied was reflected in the glumness of the young faces on the other side of the room. What could be worse than having to spend the summer with your parents on a campsite in northern France and not be able to tell your mates on Snapchat just how dreadful it was? My concerns were more existential. Was the French municipal campsite in gradual and inexorable decline?

In a rather nice coincidence, the word "*camping*" began to appear in the French press in the summer of 1903, the very same summer that the Tour de France was taking place for the first time. Writing in the newspaper *L'Auto* - the newspaper that organised that first Tour de France - the French writer and journalist Octave Uzanne put the origins of the phenomenon that is camping firmly in the hands of not just the British, but British cyclists:

> "The English have a genius for organising things in the open air. For a long time now, the love of camping out... has become very popular in the United Kingdom... English cycle tourists are becoming more and more the 'Robin Woods' of the highways. The hostel cannot be enough for them because those thirsty for fresh air cannot lodge in hotel rooms... They always want to camp in the open air and not lock themselves inside where they feel as though they are starting to suffocate. There has been for some time in London an association of cyclists who love camping. It already has more than 250 members."

That association was the Association of Cycle Campers, now known as the Camping and Caravanning Club. Its founder, Thomas Hiram Holding is recognised as being the inventor of camping as we experience it today.

However, just as they did with the railways, the French were left to play catch-up when it came to their enthusiasm for camping. It was the introduction of paid holidays in 1936 that was the catalyst for it to take off in a big way. In the short period before the Second World War, the *camping municipal* was born, and it continued to flourish once the fighting was over.

But 80 years since they were first conceived, were my suspicions about the slow decline of the humble *camping municipal* well placed? According to a 2019 report in the French regional newspaper *Ouest France*, municipal campsites account for around a quarter of all campsites in France. However, as local authorities have faced funding cuts and invested less and less in their facilities, council-owned and run campsites are increasingly seen as a source of expense rather than income. When sites are sold off to the private sector this is, according to the newspaper, usually accompanied by a desire to move them upmarket with the new owners wanting to transform them from 2-star to 5-star sites. Small, simple and cheap no longer seems to be the *plat du jour*.

It was with a certain glumness that I made my way back towards the Véloscénie via a lazy half-hour sipping coffee and watching the world go by next to the Saturday morning market in the centre of Alençon. I listened attentively to the conversations at the nearby tables trying to fill in the gaps in my knowledge. *How do those old chaps know each other? Do they always come here on a Saturday morning? Why is that woman alone? What is she thinking? Is she wondering what I am doing and where I am going?* Some of my fellow cyclists from the campsite could be seen across the square and I nodded in acknowledgement, but we did not speak. We had exhausted our lines of conversation the previous evening.

As campsites went, Camping Guéramé had been a little on the disappointing side but that could not be said of the town of Alençon itself. With a deep blue sky hovering above the ornate stone buildings, timber-framed houses and colourful market, this was very reminiscent of southern France. It was strange to think that I was only around 100km from the north coast and the English Channel. This feeling of being much further away from home than I actually was would develop as the theme of the day.

For the first time since leaving Chartres, I had a decision to make regarding the route. The choice was between a more southerly path "*par la voie verte*" - 50km and "easy", or "*par Carrouges*" - 49km and "challenging". On the information board just outside Alençon where I needed to make the decision, the former was described as "the safe and family-friendly option". It would take me in the direction of (but not up) the Mont des Avaloirs, the highest point in north-western France at 416m. The latter was "definitely the most challenging part of the Véloscénie route". This did not frighten me, but it was going to be another very hot day and when the option was to travel along a disused railway line, it was difficult to summon up the enthusiasm to opt in for a strenuous day on the bike.

The reverse side of the information board provided an excessively detailed history of the railway linking Alençon with Domfront, so I feel obliged to pass on a brief summary. It had been a very slow decline: passenger traffic stopped in 1938 although the location of a fertiliser factory along the route about 20km to the west of Alençon kept the trains running until 2008. By that point, the speed of the two trains per month was limited to just 10 kilometres per hour due to the poor state of the track. Even with four panniers and a tent, that was a speed that I would have no difficulty in smashing, and I did.

Once I had finished absorbing all the information (I did think some kind of certificate of achievement was in order, but the local mayor never turned up to congratulate me), I set off along the greenway and, courtesy of a sign, was immediately reminded that I had 159km to cycle to Mont-Saint-Michel. This was good news. I had split the trip from Chartres into four cycles of approximately 80km each and here was another sign confirming that my back-of-a-Gitanes-packet plan was continuing to work well.

Over the next four hours, I sweated my way up and then down the railway track. Although never quite reaching the dizzy heights of 400m, I did pedal my way to a respectable 300m and could see the Mont des Avaloirs to my left. It was very much more a hill than a mountain but with it being the highest point in north-western France, credit where credit is due. Let us not get sizeist about this. Of greater note was the wider landscape that surrounded me: attractive fields dusted with yellow flowers and vast expanses of barley, swaying like a drunkard, nearing its point of harvest.

A few kilometres short of Bagnoles-de-l'Orne the *voie verte* finished and I was flung onto the road, but not for long. It was a short climb along mainly quiet lanes to Bagnoles and I was fully expecting to fly through the centre of the town before heading for my campsite at Domfront. I had earlier felt transported (several weeks too early) to the south of France when sipping my coffee in the main square of Alençon. My virtual journey was about to head west, into the Pyrenees.

The first clues were the signs for thermal baths and an excessive number of medical facilities for such an out-of-the-way place in southern Normandy. Then a large and ornate redbrick hotel rising to five storeys. The "Hôtel des Thermes". A lake was signposted and then a narrow building beside the road came into view, complete with a wizard's hat of a roof. Further along the slight incline, I arrived at the lake around which were arranged a mixture of manicured gardens and more fancy buildings from the Belle Époque. This was Normandy's very own spa town, but it was all very reminiscent of those that I had previously visited in the foothills of the Pyrenees. The only thing missing was a backdrop of mountains. How charmingly unexpected. A little discombobulated by what I had stumbled upon, I turned to my guidebook for assistance:

> "The quaint spa town of Bagnoles-de-l'Orne is quite unlike anywhere else in this part of the world, attracting the moneyed sick and convalescent from all over France to its thermal baths…"

It was indeed unlike anything I was expecting on a cycle through Normandy. The writers of the Rough Guide had summed it up perfectly.

I stood for some time taking in the view whilst eating a banana. I felt somewhat out of place. My healthy pleasures - cycling and eating impromptu fruit on the street - were in stark contrast to the healthy pleasures of those surrounding me behind the glass panes of the spas and treatment emporiums, being massaged, pampered, fed and watered in five-star luxury. I could, however, see the attractions, especially in such a charming town as Bagnoles-de-l'Orne.

Leaving Bagnoles I was almost immediately transported from the south-west of France to the north-east and the Ardennes. Tall trees surrounded me as I cycled along the military-straight roads and tracks of the local *forêt domaniale* for the next 10km. It was a tortuous trudge through a seemingly endless landscape of wood and greenery and, following the signs for the Véloscénie, after I left the road, a rather disconcerting one along a narrow path. Earlier in the day a large black boar had scuttled across the route just a few metres in front of the bike on the disused railway line. If that were to happen now, I would surely be in cardiac arrest. After several kilometres with not one reassuring sign to confirm that I was indeed still heading in the direction of Domfront (and no phone signal to check online), I was increasingly fighting the urge to turn around and head back to the safety of the passing cars. But I persisted and, eventually, was reacquainted with the road on the edge of the forest. I would, after all, not be appearing on the local news that evening as a missing person in the Forêt Domaniale des Andaines.

It was a much more relaxing few kilometres at the end of the day downhill in the direction of Domfront-en-Poiraie and my fourth consecutive night in a *camping municipal*. Were my suspicions regarding their slow fall from grace about to be confirmed? As the route of the Véloscénie headed up another hill into the centre of Domfront, I switched on Google and followed its directions to the campsite. This avoided the climb and guided me through pretty suburbs and past one of France's many Colléges Jacques Prévert. There can surely be no other poet in history with more educational establishments to his name than good old Jacques.[20]

At the entrance to Camping Municipal Champ Passais, things were looking hopeful. As noted earlier, my online contact David Naylor (more of David later in the story) had described it as a "gem of a campsite". The flags of France, the European Union, Germany and Britain were hoisted high above the gate, and they were not in tatters as was so often the case elsewhere. The reception was housed in a smart building just below me. I pushed Wanda through the gate, stood her outside the building and entered.

"*Bonjour.*"

"*Bonjour.*"

"*Je peux rester au camping ce soir?*"

"Are you English?"

"Yes."

"We can talk in English then. I'm English. I've lived here for 20 years."

"That will be… €4."

"€4?"

"€4"

"Four Euros? *Quatre Euros?*"

I had reverted to French lest, in her 20 years in the country, she was no longer able to distinguish the word "four" from "fourteen" or perhaps even "forty". She handed me the receipt and it confirmed what I could hardly believe. One person, one bicycle, one tent… €4.

The good news did not stop there. The facilities were excellent. There was a large free camping area for people travelling without a motorised vehicle and a convivial communal area complete with armchairs, a microwave and functioning Wi-Fi. (Those grumpy teenagers would be delighted.) All for €4. Yes, four Euros.

Once the tent had been erected and I had showered, I headed up the hill into the centre of the old town to celebrate my good fortune. An hour later I had managed to spend three times as much on beer as my one night of accommodation had cost me back at the campsite. I sat back in my chair on

---

[20] Jacques Prévert is the poet who wrote the wonderful *Déjeuner du Matin*. If you happen to be learning French at the moment, look it up as it is a great way to see the *passé composé* in action: regular verbs, irregular verbs, verbs with *avoir*, verbs with *être*… there's even a reflexive in there. *Formidable!*

the terrace of the Bar Normand and smiled. Reports of the demise of the French *camping municipal* had been much exaggerated. Especially by me.

Day Fifteen: Domfront to Roz-Sur-Couesnon (83km)
Sunday 17th July

Perhaps the price was a key influence but on reflection, the greatest pull of Camping Municipal Champ Passais was the fact that it was a bloody good campsite in a bloody good location. As a result of all these factors combined, it was a popular place with cycle tourists and walkers. In the words of Kevin Costner, "If you build it, they will come" and here in this field of (camping) dreams, they had, and people did.

When I emerged from the tent on Sunday morning there were more than a dozen tents in the free camping area and perhaps as many as 20 people milling around, eating breakfast, packing up or just lazing on the ground. Swap the modern bikes for those to be found in the *musée du vélo* in Alençon and take away the colourful high-tech fabric of the tents (and the phones, the plastic utensils, the PVC panniers, the gas canisters...) and the scene was reminiscent of how those pioneering British cycle tourists of the early 20th century might have spent an early Sunday morning. Thomas Hiram Holding would be doing a celebratory jig in his grave if he knew that his invention was still going strong after all these years.

The start of my third week on the road would coincide with my final day on the Véloscénie. It had been a festival of not just municipal campsites but also of disused railway lines and that was not about to change on the final stretch of the route as far as Mont-Saint-Michel. Indeed, so much of the previous few days had been spent on the railway lines that I was now looking forward to a different kind of cycling when I rejoined the Vélomaritime (EuroVelo 4) after the mount. Variety is the spice of life, but I had not benefitted from much of it in recent days. Yet these were minor grumbles. After breakfast in Domfront and a leisurely wander around its crumbling cliff-top castle, I looked forward to a downhill ride in the direction of the coast, despite much of it being along another stretch of disused railway.[21]

Many of the overnight campers from the campsite in Domfront were also cycling west. For the first few hours of the day, I overtook many familiar faces who in turn overtook me, some on several occasions as we chose to pause our journeys at different times and in different places. It was nice to

---

[21] The Vélomaritime would join the Véloscénie about 30km into my ride just to the south of Mortain and for the remaining 50km of the cycle I would be following both routes at the same time. The Vélomaritime is, on occasions, not very maritime at all and that is certainly the case after it passes through Cherbourg and heads south in the direction of Saint-Lô and Vire at which point it is more than 50km from the coast.

spend a little time with some of them and they all shared my opinion about how wonderful the campsite had been. It was not just a case of me being a skinflint.

Since leaving Rotterdam two weeks earlier, it had yet to rain on Wanda and me and it was obvious that little rain had fallen along the Véloscénie as the path was excessively dry. As I cycled, I was continuously kicking up a small cloud of dust, as were all of the other cyclists along the route. Everything exposed to the elements - including much of me at the end of each cycling day - was covered in a layer of powdery grime. The dryness was exacerbated by the heat and the lack of cloud cover which might have otherwise kept a check on the temperatures. At their daily peak, they had been steadily climbing through the 20s and into the 30s as the days went by.

The situation had arisen because of an anticyclone creeping slowly over western Europe from the Atlantic and a depression moving in from the south bringing hot air from Africa. With the jet stream sitting somewhere over the northern portion of the British Isles, Météo France (the national weather agency) likened the situation to France being in a cooking pot, heated from below, lid firmly closed, and the contents simmering nicely. Nobody likes stew in the middle of summer but along with all the other cyclists out there on the *voies vertes* of France, I was one of the vegetables, albeit a rather dry one. When I looked at my weather app for the temperature for Mont-Saint-Michel for the following day, it was predicted to reach 43°c. And that was in the shade. I was now cycling for my eighth successive day. A day of rest was overdue and tomorrow seemed an opportune moment to take one as cycling conditions would be hostile. On a more positive note, I would be cooked to perfection. *Délicieux!*

At least the old railway line afforded shade courtesy of the abundance of trees that had grown alongside it so, for much of the time, I was protected from the direct rays of the sun. The hat that I had purchased back in Paris had served me well since leaving the capital and I was regularly covering exposed skin with factor 50 sun protection cream. I was drinking as much water as I could although finding places to fill up my bottles was not always easy. The railway line skirted around the edges of towns and villages, and it was not always obvious when this was happening because of the thick wall of trees beside me. With it being Sunday in France, places to buy bottles of water were limited. I knew this would be the case, especially in the afternoon. So, at the halfway point of my cycle, as the clock was approaching midday, I ventured away from the route and into the centre of the small town of Saint-Hilaire-du-Harcouët. I was in luck. The local

Carrefour supermarket was open until midday and I was able to stock up on provisions - including water - to see me through the afternoon.

One of the beauties of my Koga WorldTraveller bicycle was its combination of Rohloff hub gears and Gates carbon belt drive. They had not come cheap but on the cycling journeys I had embarked upon since becoming Wanda's owner, they had been worth every penny of the investment. From the perspective of a cyclist who does not have a great ability, inclination or indeed interest in getting my hands dirty and fiddling with the bike when it goes wrong, I considered the hub gears and carbon belt combination to be a maintenance-free option. Well, almost.

The Rohloff Speedhub is a marvel of modern engineering and I first fell in love with it at a cycle show many years ago when preparing to purchase my first touring bike, the Ridgeback Panorama also known as Reggie. It was never either a practical or financial option at the time to have one fitted to that bike, but on the Rohloff stand at the cycle show, there was a Speedhub on display. It had been cut in two to show a cross-section that revealed a tightly packed arrangement of cogs, big and small, fat and thin, neatly arranged around a central axle. There was barely any free space. I stood and stared and dreamed of the day a Rohloff hub would be mine.

The company is, as you might have guessed, German, but its origins are relatively recent compared to other giants of Teutonic engineering. It was set up in 1986 by Barbara and Bernhard Rohloff and the first Speedhub was sold in 1998. By 2020 the company had produced over 300,000 Speedhubs but the factory still only employed around 50 people. This may be a small giant but a giant nevertheless. It is said that a Rohloff should last for a minimum of 100,000km but there are many examples of cyclists who have ridden their Speedhub well beyond this, err... milestone.

As for the Gates carbon belt, that is a marvel of American engineering and has its origins at the other end of the 20th century. Charles C. Gates set up his company in Denver in 1911 and made his first belt drive shortly thereafter but it was not until the 1980s that Gates entered the bicycle market. The technology was not new having been honed on motor vehicles in the preceding decades and the belts are "composed of a weather-resistant polyurethane exterior [and] feature strong, stretch-free carbon fibre tensile cords" according to the Gates website. They can operate effectively in temperatures ranging from -53°c to +85°c which was good news for me as I continued to cycle into the eye of the heatwave.

So why only "almost" maintenance-free? Well, the Rohloff hub requires an oil change every 5,000km but it is, apparently, an easy job. The long-distance cyclist Alee Denham claims to be able to do this in 15 minutes. If I were to try, I suspect it would take a little longer. As for the Gates belt, the recommendation is that you apply nothing more than silicon lubricant. However, I had yet to find a can of silicon lubricant which was small enough to take with me on a long cycle. As I was approaching Mont-Saint-Michel, in the dry, dusty conditions of the disused railway, the Gates Drive was squeaking to the point of it becoming a cry of agony. The solution - albeit only a short-lived one in the conditions - was to keep the belt wet. With water not being readily available on this particular Sunday morning in France, I would need to ignore the cries until I could drench Wanda at the campsite later in the day.

The tree-covered railway ended abruptly, and somewhat comically, about 10km to the east of Mont-Saint-Michel. At one point in its history, the railway had continued over the River Sélune to join up with the line heading north in the direction of Caen and Cherbourg. I knew this as in front of me was a rusting square tunnel made from cast iron girders that was supported by three stone pillars, two on either side of the river and the third in the water. I could not access it as the path fell quickly away to the level of the river and a fence was blocking access. It was a bridge to nowhere, standing forlornly in haughty isolation as a monument to the effort required to bring the trains to this corner of France.

The sun was now at its highest and strongest. Not the best time to be moving away from the shady protection of the trees but I had little choice. For the next few kilometres, I followed the meandering path of the ever-widening river as it made its way towards oceanic freedom. However, it was not until the river had melted imperceptibly into the sea and I had turned to head west along the coast that I could see what I had been looking forward to seeing since leaving Paris: the Mont-Saint-Michel.

From a distance of 7km, the cluster of distant buildings appeared to be floating upon the field of corn that was located between me and the sea, isolated, cut off, untouchable even. The sign for the Véloscénie said 19km to get to the mount. *Really? What kind of tortuous route did they have in mind?* Even Google suggested that I need only cycle about ten. Another sign warned me of the dangers of crossing the bay: drowning, getting stuck in the sand, getting cut off, storms, fog... ("Welcome to Mont-Saint-Michel!") Surely Google was not expecting me to head out to sea. In the end, by sometimes following the Véloscénie but often not, I arrived at the monument after having cycled a smidgen over 10km.

Since my last visit to Mont-Saint-Michel - back in the winter of 2013 on a school exchange trip - significant investment had been made to the infrastructure allowing permanent access to the mount. The causeway had been rebuilt and a park-and-ride scheme now transported visitors on a fleet of push-me-pull-me shuttle buses. Why, I wondered, had the concept of a bus that did not need to turn around when it arrived at its destination never caught on elsewhere? Not that this was relevant to me. I clattered my way over the wooden planks of the causeway and after about 10 minutes I arrived at the foot of the mount.

My arrival - on a very warm Sunday afternoon in the middle of summer - coincided with the arrival of several thousand other people. I locked Wanda in the designated bike storage area and wandered up the hill via a side entrance. My enthusiasm was waning, to say the least. It had already been dented by having cycled 80km, the vibrations of the rickety walkway, the sun, the wind, mild dehydration and a deep desire to adopt a horizontal position and do very little for an extended period. My fellow tourists were not helping, sitting down wherever there was shade. This was often on flights of steps and a pitifully slow one-way system had been created. I trudged halfway to the top of the mound before giving up. Where were the French riot police when you needed them to clear the streets of your pesky fellow humans?

For me, Mont-Saint-Michel had never been a visitor attraction, not on this trip anyway. It had always been an oversized waymarker, keeping my mind focussed upon a medium-term objective. In that respect it had served its purpose well. In all other respects I was delighted to escape the place and find somewhere to hide from the arriving heat storm.

Le Grand Tour

PART FOUR:

La Vélomaritime (Again...)

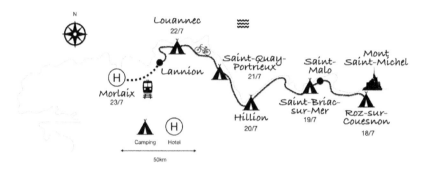

Day Sixteen: Roz-Sur-Couesnon
Monday 18th July

I had found a campsite just over the regional border some 10km to the south-west of Mont-Saint-Michel. I was now in Brittany, and it would be my home for the next ten days as I continued my cycle west and then south across this far-flung corner of France. Usually an area famed for its subdued temperatures and abundant rainfall, there was no escape from the *canicule*, even here. Temperatures were about to hit the low forties, but I was grateful to have found a campsite that had gone out of its way to welcome cyclists and attend to their particular needs, especially when the weather took a turn for the worse.

Camping Les Couesnons was located on the southern edge of the vast area of reclaimed land across which I had cycled the previous evening. Behind the campsite was a steep hill that must once have been the coast, the village of Roz-sur-Couesnon at the top of the hill a former coastal town. A small area of the campsite had been set aside for the exclusive use of those travelling by bicycle or on foot and a large three-sided shed had been erected for our use. The intention was, presumably, to give shelter from the rain but on this occasion, it afforded a cool escape from the hostile rays of the sun. Tables and chairs had been set up inside the shed and plugs were provided to replenish electronic devices. It was a simple and cheap facility but offered a welcome layer of luxury to the humble walker or cyclist. To make things even better, I had managed to erect my tent in a fortuitous position. When the sun began to rise on the morning of July 18th, I remained in the shed's shadow for a while longer than my fellow cycle campers and I was able to take my time before emerging from within.

I envisaged that I would not be alone in deciding to opt out of cycling on this day that promised to break climatic records, but by mid-morning I was the only person left in the dedicated cyclist-walker patch of the campsite. Perhaps their schedules were not as flexible as mine. At this relatively early stage of my two-month journey, time was only a minor concern. I had now cycled over 1,000 of the anticipated 4,500km since leaving Rotterdam and was at the start of my third week in the saddle. The rough calculations bouncing around my mind pointed in the direction of me having completed just under a quarter of the distance in just under a quarter of the available time. One day here or there would make no difference in my great scheme, not yet anyway. That would inevitably change, but it was not a worry for Monday 18th July.

Monday, however, was. Monday! Another working week was starting and with it the national French struggle to find somewhere to buy stuff. With the temperature still climbing I could not muster any enthusiasm for travelling far on the bike, but nearby Roz-sur-Couesnon did - according to the woman in charge at the campsite - have a small shop that had the nerve to break with tradition and open. It required a steep climb up a switchback road to get there but the cycle was mercifully short and it was not long before I was standing inside Le Bist' Roz marvelling at just how limited the range of goods on offer was.

In fairness to the establishment, it was not so much a shop as a bar which had branched out into other areas of commerce in a quest to satisfy the needs of locals and tourists alike. Tobacconist, post office, newsagent, games room, lottery ticket seller... and *épicerie*. The sign outside even promised weekend concerts. Presumably only the location of the village church - immediately opposite on the other side of the street - prevented them from offering baptisms, weddings and funerals. However, the Venn diagram of what I needed to buy and what was being sold consisted of two non-overlapping circles so I decided to splash out and, later in the day, I ate at the campsite restaurant instead.

What Roz-sur-Couesnon lacked in opportunities to go on a spending spree it certainly made up for in its views, or rather, one view in particular. On the northern edge of the village, behind the local town hall and at the point where the hill fell rapidly away in the direction of the campsite, was a park. I wheeled Wanda towards its furthest wall and there before me, spread out across a panorama of more than 180 degrees, was the vast plain over which I had cycled the previous evening. It was a detailed patchwork of small fields, woods and lakes all arranged within a complex interlocking grid of irrigation channels. In the far distance was the Mont-Saint-Michel. It made for an inspiring place to do a little planning for my onward journey through Brittany, west along the Vélomaritime to Morlaix. It was there where I hoped to join the Vélodyssée and start pedalling south in the direction of Bordeaux.

My average distance cycled since leaving Rotterdam had now climbed to 80km per day. This had been the target before setting off and if I were to maintain this distance, it would suggest a journey of five days to Morlaix. However, since leaving Rotterdam there had been few hills to climb. That, I suspected, was about to change so was I being overambitious in aiming to cycle 80km per day in Brittany? Day one to Saint-Malo or thereabouts? Day two to Saint-Brieuc? Day three to Perros-Guirec? Those latter cycles would both be well over 80km. There was, however, a train from Saint-Brieuc to Morlaix which would be around 100km - my self-imposed train distance limit - but hang on! A train? Through Brittany? What a wasted opportunity that would be.

Another factor to consider was the location of a branch of the FNAC, the French multimedia store, in Dinard. The Vélomaritime did not pass through Dinard but if I wanted to replace the malfunctioning GoPro camera, according to their website, the Dinard FNAC had one in stock. It was a deviation worth considering. It would, potentially, also be a shortcut as the official route of the Vélomaritime headed south from Saint-Malo along the banks of the Rance Estuary. A visit to Dinard would require me to cross the river further north. But was that feasible? Just as they had been doing since I first set off on a long continental cycle back in 2010, my attempts at short-term planning were simply throwing up more questions than answers.

I continued to drink in the stunning view from my lofty position above the plain to Mont-Saint-Michel and cracked on with editing the next episode of The Cycling Europe Podcast.[22] In doing so I was reminded as to just how little I had known about the Véloscénie when setting off from Paris. Of all the unknowns, the unknown unknowns were, it seemed, the most appealing and long may that continue. I would figure out the answers to my questions about crossing the estuary to Dinard in the morning.

Upon my return to the campsite, I fell into conversation with a French cyclist who had arrived in my absence. He had been travelling from the west along the Vélomaritime from Saint-Brieuc and was about to return to Paris on the train.

"It's not so hilly. It lasts five or ten minutes and goes up perhaps 100 metres," he explained, "but between here and Saint-Malo there are not many trees along the route which is not great when it's so hot and sunny."

Perhaps my greatest challenge would not be the hills after all but continue to be the weather conditions. I reached somewhat reluctantly for my phone to check the forecast and was in for a shock. The temperature for Tuesday was about to plummet by well over 10°c to just 29°c. I might even need a jumper. At least on Tuesday, the shops would have reopened and I would be able to buy one.

---

[22]   The links to Episode 054 of The Cycling Europe Podcast can be found at CyclingEurope.org/Podcast.

Day Seventeen: Roz-Sur-Couesnon to Saint-Briac-Sur-Mer (72km) Tuesday 19th July

Things were indeed changing and it was not just the temperature.

The first line of article 2 of the French Constitution states that "*La langue de la République est le français*"[23]. In the late 1990s, France's highest court declared that the nascent European Charter on Regional and Minority Languages violated the constitution. The then-French president, Jacques Chirac, refused to sanction any amendments to the text. *The Guardian* newspaper quoted one of his aides as saying, "The President does not wish to take the initiative for a revision of the constitution that would violate the basic principles of our republic".

When I lived in France during the 1990s, this was big news. Article 1 of the French constitution kicks off as follows: "*La France est une République indivisible, laïque, démocratique et sociale*"[24]. That word "*indivisible*" - handily an exact cognate in English and French - is defined as "unable to be divided or separated". Combined with the first line of article 2, it is why the French courts - and Chirac - could not bring themselves to ratify the treaty on regional languages that would have helped promote France's minority languages including its most high-profile regional language, Breton.

All rather ironic as, over the next week or so, I would have to remind myself repeatedly that I was indeed cycling through France, not simply the independent republic of Brittany. It was not just the language. It was the topography, the coastline, the music, the food, the castles, the ancient megaliths, the at times mysterious feel of the place... The efforts of Chirac and the judges to maintain *une nation indivisible* were, it seemed, floundering somewhat here in the north-west. It was France, but not as I knew it. Even the quintessentially French game of boules was played differently here *en Bretagne*.

Once covered by impenetrable forest, the Celts arrived in the 6th century BC then, five hundred years later, the Romans. They stuck around for another 500 years before scuttling back to Rome encouraging even more Celts to arrive from Britain and Ireland. It was not until 1491 that Brittany became part of France following the marriage of Charles VIII to Anne de Bretagne. Move forward another 500 years and there's no great clamour for Breton independence. In a 2013 survey, fewer than 20% wanted that, but

---

[23] "The language of the Republic is French."

[24] "France is an indivisible, secular, democratic and social Republic."

the region has done a remarkable job in becoming a very distinctive part of France, notwithstanding what the politicians and bureaucrats in Paris might desire. From the perspective of someone who had just spent many days cycling along rather similar disused railway lines, I was fertile territory when it came to welcoming a bit of variety into my life. It was about to be thrown in my direction on a scale that I had yet to encounter since stepping off the ferry in the Netherlands. Bring it on!

The route of the Vélomaritime was handily located near the campsite, just a couple of minutes ride north across the irrigated plain. The first half hour of the day was spent cycling beside the long lines of crops in the fields, the sun rising gradually behind me and a slight morning breeze pushing me ever-so-gently to the west. Rabbits bobbed their way across my path, hopping slowly away from what they presumably judged to be an unwelcome but probably innocuous visitor on their patch. Their pauses and stares suggested that they had greater concerns in life other than a man on a bicycle. The dusty lanes were otherwise deserted until the Vélomaritime rejoined the coast - and civilisation - near the tiny steep-roofed Chapelle Sainte-Anne-de-la-Grève. With only a few short-lived incursions inland, there it would stay until it arrived in Morlaix.

This poetic vision of cycle touring in France was about to be interrupted by the practicalities of life on the road. In Le Vivier-sur-Mer I paused to pay a visit to the post office where I was able to return the malfunctioning GoPro camera to the UK. I took the opportunity of including a handful of other small items in the box. This included my watch. In the heat, it had become an uncomfortable inconvenience and my eagerness to dispatch it with the camera was a sign, perhaps, that I was beginning to live according to the natural rhythms of the day rather than the entirely man-made time. My phone, clamped during the day to my handlebars, would of course keep me updated on this score. It is a shame that modern smartphones do not have an option to turn off time. How liberating might that be? Until that is, I next decided to take one of my trains.

At the positive end of the spectrum of simple things in life that bring you joy, I became very excited when, just outside Saint-Benoît-des-Ondes, I spotted a jet wash. This was my opportunity to rid Wanda and everything she was carrying of the layers of dust that had been building up gradually ever since leaving Dieppe as I had trundled along the increasingly dry disused railway lines. As with all foreign "laundrettes", it took some time to read the instructions and figure out which slots to drop my coins into and which buttons to push. However, once I mastered the technology, I stripped Wanda of everything that could be removed - she blushed ever-so-slightly as a result - and set to work. It was a glorious few minutes of seeing the muck of northern and central France wash effortlessly away. So pleased was I with my efforts that I even turned the lance towards the panniers. For the first time on the trip, I was about to find out if they were actually waterproof. The high-pressure water transformed them from grimy grey back to the inky black with which they had left the factory. The topographical charts of this corner of Brittany would now have to be resurveyed as the average height of Saint-Benoît-des-Ondes had just increased markedly courtesy of Wanda's clean and the muck that had been deposited on the ground. It was a price worth paying: she looked fantastic.

Cycling an unblemished bicycle was a novelty and I felt slightly conspicuous as I descended towards the beach to the east of the fortified city of Sant-Malo. Would anyone believe that I had been on the road for over two weeks and cycled over 1,000km? Even my clothes - which had been put through the washing machine back at Camping Les Couesnons - were clinging to their freshness. I readied myself to big up my credentials as an adventurer should anyone ask.

The mighty walls of Saint-Malo could be seen from quite a distance. They protruded into the sea like the stern of an old battleship, a turreted building within the city's thick walls forming the bridge, a high steeple its mast. These walls had been deterring invaders since the 14th century but their architects had not envisaged aerial warfare and it was in 1944 that the city's greatest challenge arrived in the form of Allied bombardment from the skies. When the fighting was over, 80% of the *intra-muros* area had been destroyed. Reconstruction started in earnest in 1947 and was to continue for the next 25 years: 2022 marked not just the 75th anniversary of the start of the rebuilding process but the 50th anniversary of its completion. The Saint-Vincent cathedral spire that I had seen from afar had been the finishing touch.

My arrival in Saint-Malo was via the eastern Porte Saint-Vincent and to commemorate the anniversaries, there was a display of photographs comparing the pre-war city with the immediate post-war city and today. 20th-century reconstruction has taken many forms. Munich was rebuilt so meticulously that you need to look very carefully indeed to find the clues that much of it was destroyed during the war. On the other hand the French city of Royan - that I was due to revisit en route to Bordeaux - is a physical homage to concrete. Some love it, others loathe it. Many cities in Britain are a botched mishmash of styles that are testament to the lack of a coherent plan and poor-quality post-war design and construction.

Here in Saint-Malo, however, it was different. From a distance, you see an ancient city but up close the reconstruction has been carried out without slavishly copying what came before. The buildings are solid and well-built but there's nothing inferior about them whatsoever. They respect the historic character of the city but are in no way a second-rate pastiche. It is, nearly 80 years after much of it was destroyed, a remarkable place to visit.

After spending far too long looking at the photographs on display I remembered that the real thing was only a few metres away so I pushed Wanda through the gate and went for a stroll inside the walls. It was at this point that something rather wonderful happened. Something which, had I known about it earlier in the day, might have saved me a few euros back at the jet wash. For the first time since arriving on the continent, it started to rain. Lovely, globules of the wet stuff. Such was the novelty that I slowed my pace as the bike bounced over the cobbles. Perhaps Brittany had not received the pan-European heatwave memo. It was such a joy to be drenched by something other than perspiration. It did not last long and by the time I had made it to the bric-a-brac market on the western side of the city walls just a few puddles remained in evidence of this rare phenomenon of the summer of 2022. Blue sky and fluffy white clouds had returned but while it lasted the rain was simply wonderful.

I had taken a few moments whilst in Saint-Malo to try and find somewhere to stay that evening, but without much luck. For reasons that have been lost in the mists of time, the campsites to the west of Saint-Malo that I was finding online were not ticking my boxes. I then remembered HomeCamper, the network of people willing to rent out space in their gardens that I had been told about way back in Forges-les-Eaux as I cycled along the Avenue Verte to Paris. Might this be a good time to give it a go? I went online, registered and started searching.

Within a matter of minutes, I had found a potential host for the evening. Her name was Joëlle and she lived a couple of kilometres from a coastal town called Saint-Briac-sur-Mer. The website description could have passed for that of a fully-fledged campsite, not just an empty patch of ground that the enterprising owner wanted to exploit. I was promised toilets, shower, picnic tables… and should my life take an unexpectedly dramatic turn in the next few hours, even a playground for my children. It was described as "quiet, shaded and wooded". This was ticking lots of those boxes and at only €13, I was willing to take the risk. I plugged in my details, touched the "request to book" button and waited.

Within minutes an email arrived: "You will be very welcome". Accommodation sorted.

The only problem I had was the route of the Vélomaritime. It now headed due south along the eastern bank of the Rance Estuary. This was all rather inconvenient as Joëlle and her garden were only about 10km to the west of Saint-Malo. Following the official route would mean cycling south and then back north along the opposite bank of the river on a round trip of about 50km. The solution appeared to be a bridge that crossed the estuary and linked Saint-Malo with the town of Dinard. Visiting Dinard would also help solve my GoPro problem. *But why did the cycle route avoid it?*

The reason became abundantly clear as I approached the bridge on a dual carriageway that masqueraded as a motorway. Everything about it shouted *autoroute* without officially being an *autoroute*. When I arrived at the bridge, I realised that it was in fact a tidal barrage - the first in the world to produce electricity apparently - not dissimilar to the dams I had cycled across back in the Netherlands. But here no effort whatsoever had been made to accommodate cyclists. I was an unwelcome visitor albeit one they had not yet erected the signs to ban from being there. Rather than cross the barrage beside the high-speed cars on very narrow lanes, I dismounted and walked along the thin pedestrian walkway beside the road. There was not much room and I was required to negotiate several small flights of steps as well as many groups of disgruntled pedestrians coming in the opposite direction.

At the far end of the barrage, I could see a much longer flight of steps allowing those on foot to access the headland but it was never going to be an option to climb those with Wanda in tow. I would have to return to the road that was an *autoroute* in all but name. After waiting for a hydraulic bridge to be lifted and then lowered to allow a couple of small yachts to pass upstream, I took a deep breath and rejoined the traffic. Not an easy task as the queue that had built up during the passage of the boats was significant. Eventually, a small gap appeared between the cars so I edged the bike back onto the carriageway and set off along the road and around the corner. It was, without question, the most perilous 50 metres of cycling since leaving Hull.

Mercifully it did not last long as I was soon able to access a slip road that was closed to cars but which gave access to the suburbs of Dinard at the top of the cliff. It was a blessed relief, to say the least, and I was annoyed by my stupidity of not having investigated more carefully how I would get to the HomeCamper garden when I booked it. All rather exasperating. Even more so when, later that evening, it was pointed out on social media that I could have taken a small ferry from Saint-Malo to Dinard. I made a point of kicking myself brutally.

If I was an adventurer in need of a holiday after my experiences crossing the estuary, I had come to the right place. Dinard had been the French retreat of a young T.E. Lawrence who came here in the early 20th century and did some cycle touring! (I wonder if he was ever a member of Thomas Hiram Holding's Association of Cycle Campers.) This surprising news was announced to me via an information board as I made my way into the centre of the pleasantly sedate town. The local council had seen fit to dedicate a walk to their adopted local hero. Perhaps after my adventurous journey from Saint-Malo to Dinard, they might one day dedicate a walk to me. It might require someone of David Lean's stature to make a film about me first, but you never know. The Barrage Over The River Rance?

I idled my way through the centre of Dinard. It was not difficult to understand why T.E. Lawrence had come here to spend his downtime when not doing all the exciting stuff. The place whispered, "slow down". Although it was now late afternoon, I did just that, pausing at a local bike shop where, after asking if I could borrow a hand pump for my tyres, a whole team of mechanics surrounded Wanda and pumped up her tyres. It was akin to watching a crack Formula 1 team in action, without all the noise. Nice town, nice people, nice hard tyres.

I found the FNAC a few kilometres out of town, purchased the camera and looked forward to having a more positive experience with it than I had done with the one that was now winging its way back to the UK. A further 5km cycling west in the direction of Saint-Briac-sur-Mer brought me to the HomeCamper location of Joëlle. Her house - a large, detached bungalow - was set back from the road and, as I started to cycle along the length of the drive, I was welcomed by a large brown dog barking loudly and running quickly in my direction. There was nobody around and I was in the early stages of seeing my life pass before my eyes (I got as far as the late 70s...) when a loud shriek came from within the building. The dog stopped dead in its tracks, as did I. This never happened at a *camping municipal*.

With the beast subdued, Joëlle then appeared. She was a woman in her 60s who sported a welcoming smile. The mutt sloped off looking a little disgruntled that it had not been able to sink its teeth into my increasingly toned thighs. To one side of her house was not so much a garden as a large field of perhaps a couple of hectares. A small number of cars were dotted across the grass and a few tents erected. She showed me around the back of the bungalow where, just as promised, there was a sink, toilet and a couple of makeshift showers. Joëlle explained that, along with her husband, she once farmed the land but since the creation of HomeCamper they had turned it into a campsite, of sorts. It was easy to see the attraction. A quick mental calculation would suggest that in the summer season, she could earn a decent income by renting the space out to the likes of me. Perhaps €50 a night if tonight's campers were anything to go by? Far more profitable, I guessed, than growing spuds and flogging them down at the local market.

Day Eighteen: Saint-Briac-Sur-Mer to Hillion (80km)
Wednesday 20th July

The cycling challenges had so far been much more horizontal than vertical. That said, even the distances I had been cycling each day were not about to break any records. My daily average was still hovering around the 80km target I had set myself before setting off. I had only once cycled more than 100km in a day, on the 101km journey into central Paris. Vertically, after an initial week that barely lifted me out of the flood plain in the Netherlands and Belgium, the number of metres climbed had, until this point, been ridiculously modest. And those climbs were rather tame affairs as I chuffed my way along the disused railway lines into Paris and then towards Mont-Saint-Michel. Long, gradual ascents and long, gradual descents which often went unnoticed until I happened to glance at the GPS track in the evening.

However, things were about to change and today would be the first when I was challenged in any meaningful vertical way. As I set off from Joëlle's field on the morning of July 20th, ahead of me was over 500 metres of climbing. Not in itself too much to worry about but bearing in mind that it would be six hours of constant ups and downs, enough to make the heart sink just a little if I had been aware of it in advance. I was not, so I set off with a smile.

In the centre of Saint-Briac-sur-Mer - a couple of kilometres west of where I had camped - I had reason to continue smiling as there was not one, not two but three *boulangeries* all within a few metres of each other. I was spoilt for choice when it came to buying my now regular breakfast of *croissant* and *pain au chocolat*. The terrace of the local café was already very busy with punters doing exactly what I was doing: sitting, relaxing and sipping strong black coffee. French tricolour bunting - presumably left over from the July 14th celebrations - had been strung between many of the buildings and was fluttering in the breeze. There was every reason to outstay my welcome, and I did, not leaving until past 10 am. For me, this was ridiculously late. Was I procrastinating? Perhaps my subconscious mind had figured out the GPS route profile before my GPS device had even plotted it.

Unlike the previous day, I was starting my cycle some way from the route of the Vélomaritime. Yesterday, it had headed south along the Rance Estuary whereas I had cycled west to Dinard. Today it would not be until I had cycled over 10km before our respective paths met. This inevitably resulted in some frustrating on-road cycling as I attempted to work out exactly where I was going. To make matters even more exasperating, I had run out of data on my phone. Uploading pictures, videos and podcasts had taken a heavy toll on my roaming allowance of 25GB and I had yet to figure out how to buy more data. That was a problem perhaps for a lazy evening on a campsite. The more immediate problem was not having access to Google Maps or the cycling layer of OpenStreetMap. I had been using the latter website increasingly since the start of the trip. It was the easiest way I had found to locate and follow the various routes I was using and to be suddenly divorced from it was a difficult separation with which to cope. To add a third level of frustration to my morning, I had yet to find a paper map for the Vélomaritime. I had not spotted a tourist office where I could sweet talk an assistant into giving me one for free, as I had done for the Avenue Verte and Véloscénie.

Salvation came on the D768 halfway between the villages of Beaussais and Trégan when I finally spotted the familiar lighthouse motif of the Vélomaritime on a signpost leading into a side road. I was back on track, literally. It was a small victory but one that soothed my mind. For the remainder of the morning, in the absence of any other means of finding my way, it was back to the age-old method of following the arrows and it seemed to work just fine.

It was a different sign that caught my eye as I was approaching Matignon. Under a familiar red-bordered metal panel announcing that I was about to enter the town was a second board:

Site Historique
Grimaldi De Monaco

The ruling family of Monaco? Here in Brittany? It seemed somewhat incongruous that they should be linked with a small town at the opposite end of France, about as far as you could get from their palaces on the Mediterranean. Very intriguing.

As were the barriers blocking the road to motorised traffic. Something was taking place in the centre of Matignon and within a few moments all became apparent. It was market day and my arrival at lunchtime was very well timed. It was a popular market (was it the royal connection?) with the streets leading into the central square lined with stalls selling the usually high-quality French fare that back in Britain was normally reserved for the food halls of Harrods. To add to the atmosphere, a couple of old boys were knocking out acoustic tunes on their guitars beside the fountain. I watched and listened as I nibbled my way through a lunch harvested from some of the stalls. Who needs the Internet when you can walk into a town in Brittany and be fed and entertained like this?

However, I was still on the lookout for a map. The *office de tourisme* was handily located adjacent to the fountain so I stepped inside. The woman behind the desk jumped as the automatic bell that I had activated rang out. I suspected that most of her usual customers had been enticed away by the market and perhaps a Lycra-clad cyclist entering her establishment was a shock to the system.

"Do you have a map for the Vélomaritime?" I enquired, in French.

"I don't have them for all the way to Morlaix, but nearly," she replied. *Them? How many were there?* She proceeded to get down on her knees and start rummaging in a cupboard. After a few minutes, I had not one but five detailed maps in my hand covering the route of the Vélomaritime along the entirety of its journey through the Côtes d'Armor *département*. I would be lost no more.

I decided to move the conversation in the direction of the Grimaldi family. I hoped she would not have to crouch down to search another cupboard for the answer and that there was not a set of five leaflets explaining the royal association.

"The connection is very old... 17 something... The Sire Goyon de Matignon married the daughter of the Grimaldis and became the Prince of Monaco, Jacques I... Prince Albert is a descendant and he has visited!"

And so he had, back in 2012. Among his (many) other titles, he is the current Sire de Matignon. If nothing else, his visit would have saved him a trip to Harrods, as long as it was market day.

I had been in Brittany for three days but I had yet to get up close and personal with one of its key attractions: its coast. Yes, I had seen it over there on the right, I had cycled beside its beaches and even crossed one of its estuaries. But where was this rugged, gnarled coastline that I had always conjured up in my mind when I thought of Brittany? It was about to appear in welcome and spectacular fashion at Cap Fréhel.

José was from Portugal and he was only the second cyclist I had cycled with since Rotterdam. We tourers are a diverse bunch: we travel at different speeds and we pause our journeys as our whims see fit. Without making an effort to plan it, it is quite rare to fall into conversation with someone who is not only travelling in the same direction as you but also at the same pace. Added to this is the risk that the person you have met may feel the need to cut short the encounter to catch their breath, eat, drink, take a photograph or, admittedly, get rid of you.

I cycled beside José for about 10km as we both followed the Vélomaritime from Matignon to Cap Fréhel. José was in his early 30s and was taking a commendably laid-back approach to cycling back home. After several months working in restaurants and bars in Switzerland and then

Amsterdam, he had decided to head south on a second-hand bike that he had bought cheaply in the Netherlands. It dated from 1988 which made it several years older than its new owner. He was travelling with gear that he had managed to cobble together from eBay or friends. He talked about a vague timescale of returning to Portugal by mid-September but he was travelling without strict deadlines in place and if it took him longer, so be it.

This was an approach towards which I had become increasingly envious over the years. My trips had always been defined in advance with time scales that usually fitted around a requirement to get back to work. Even when this had not been the case on my cycle to Nordkapp in northern Norway in 2015, I had managed to manufacture a deadline - the last opportunity to see the midnight sun on July 28th - to keep me pedalling with at least a modicum of urgency.[25] But by setting myself a series of inflexible parameters, was I missing a trick? Return to the Hook of Holland by September 3rd and only ten trains of a maximum of 100km each? It was encounters with people like José that had me reflecting seriously upon my choices. *What was I trying to prove? And to whom was I trying to prove it? Would my journey be any the less enjoyable if I were to liberate myself and just ride with a vague destination in mind?* If time became an issue, I could jump on a train when it became apparent that I needed to be somewhere else, such as back at work. Perhaps I should not make life so difficult for myself. At times I needed to be a bit more José.

After cycling beside the Baie de la Fresnaye for a couple of kilometres, the route took us inland and across a headland that marked its most northerly point - the cape itself - with a lighthouse. This was by far the most remote part of Brittany that I had so far visited and we followed a rough, stony track that scratched its path through a heather-strewn landscape of purple, dark green and brown until we arrived again at the sea. Here the high cliffs faced west and looking north the coastline cut an imposing jagged course of granite, the only manmade features being those of the coastal path and the lighthouse in the far distance.

It was here, as I was staring at the natural wonder before me, that José disappeared. To catch his breath? To eat? To drink? To take a photograph? Or perhaps to get rid of me? I am guessing he arrived safely at his destination at some point in the September of that year, but who knows? He may still be out there, taking his time, following his whims, eschewing any kind of urgency on his journey home to Portugal. I do hope so.

---

[25] I did make it to Nordkapp in time to see the midnight sun on the last possible day of 2015. It was a fitting way to end the journey.

A man with a definite mission in mind was Cyril, a former sailor in the French navy, from Toulon in the south of France. Along with his girlfriend, he had set up a gazebo on an off-road section of the Vélomaritime a few kilometres south of Cap Fréhel. On the side of the gazebo was written "*les cyclos sont nos héros!*" - "cyclists are our heroes!" - and, as I was a cyclist and always up for a bit of adulation, I stopped for a chat.

"We are building an association to promote cycle-tourism in France," he explained. "We have a solar-powered photo booth to give a souvenir picture to cycle tourists."

When I glanced inside the gazebo, I could see that he had set up a camera and printer connected to a large solar panel fixed to a bike trailer. Posing for a picture were a young family of four and their bicycles. Behind them was the wall of the gazebo upon which had been written, many times, "*Souriez, vous pédalez!*" or "Smile, you're pedalling!".

"We want to encourage and promote social relationships when you are cycling. You are free when you are riding a bicycle: you can smell the air, see people and very easily speak to them without any barriers. We also think that cycle tourism, with its small impact on the environment, could be one of the solutions to climate change."

Europe had just experienced one of its hottest days on record. Wildfires were raging in the south of France and the Vélodyssée south of Royan had been closed because it passed through the affected forests. Cyril's initiative was well-timed. But was it well placed along the route of the Vélomaritime? Surely he was preaching to the already converted minds of people such as José and me.

I had my picture taken but refrained from suggesting that we each pick up a leg of the gazebo and plonk it beside the nearby road. It was there where the car drivers were happily making their way to Cap Fréhel and its lighthouse in their carbon-emitting vehicles. It is a difficult task, but when it comes to climate change, it is the unconverted who need to hear the preachers preach. Cyril was a skilled preacher but were the cyclists along the Vélomaritime his best congregation?

My two interesting encounters had provided me with much upon which I could ponder as I continued my journey south-west in the direction of Saint-Brieuc. I still had no fixed point in mind for the end of the day and I was not too concerned. Perhaps the influence of José was already kicking in. I knew that campsites were strewn along the entirety of the Breton coast including two just a few kilometres from the small town of Yffiniac. Perhaps one of those would accommodate me overnight.

It was almost inevitable that I would encounter more disused railway lines in Brittany and that was the case as I cycled towards Yffiniac. Although the

Vélomaritime vaguely followed the route of the old railway from Matignon to Yffiniac - it was only in operation for a short period between 1924 and 1948 - visual evidence of it doing so was thin on the ground. Perhaps a piece of civil engineering that had been abandoned before it could celebrate its 25th birthday was easy to erase. Or rather most of it. As it passed along the coast, long *passerelles* were required to lift the line above the soggy landscape and two of these structures were still in use ensuring that I too was able to keep my feet dry. They were not inconsequential structures. The Passerelle de la Côtière extended over 150 metres. It had been built from reinforced concrete, manufactured offsite and "assembled in the manner of Meccano". Yet as with most *baguette*-straight constructions of this type, travelling over them was rarely the best place from which to appreciate their architectural glory.

Not so, the Viaduc des Pont-Neufs further along the line near Coëtmieux. Here, the engineers had foreseen my inquisitive arrival a century in advance and had kindly built their stunningly elegant bridge along a curve 30 metres above the ground allowing me to pause and admire it even from the cycle track. After a long day in the saddle, it was much appreciated, even if it too resembled something that might have been inspired by a box of Meccano.

Shortly after the bridge I deviated away from the Vélomaritime in the direction of the two campsites. The first - the Camping Village Nature d'O - was clearly preparing itself for the arrival of the Mad Max film crew. A collection of ramshackle buildings sat beside a dusty, refuse-strewn open area. Although a few rebellious patches of grass were growing, in no way did they mask the unkempt nature of the place. I started a conversation with the young lad running the campsite. However, when he was momentarily called away to deal with a group of Germans who were having comical issues reversing their caravan, I seized the opportunity. I made a swift escape back up the hill and along the coast to the second site, Camping Bellevue Mer. This was much more my kind of place. Until that is, the woman in the reception building told me that they were full. Envisaging a return to the Thunderdome down the road I put on my most disappointed, disillusioned look. I may even have wiped a fake tear from my eye. It worked. I was squeezed into a tiny plot between pitches 24 and 9b with a fabulous view overlooking the sea. Just as they had promised in their name.

Day Nineteen: Hillion to Saint-Quay-Portrieux (50km)
Thursday 21st July

Upon arrival at Camping Bellevue Mer, the wind had been blowing as it had rarely blown before on the trip. I had just about managed to erect the tent but boiling water for my gourmet meal of pasta and pesto on a small gas burner had been almost as comical as watching the Germans park their caravan. I did eventually eat and, despite the wind buffeting everything that was willing to flap (on a campsite the list is long), I did grab a few hours of sleep. However, I was barely rested and crawled from the tent in somewhat of a daze. At least the wind had all but disappeared and my ability to brew my morning coffee was somewhat greater than it had been to heat the pasta. I needed it, especially as the small town of Hillion had broken recklessly with French tradition and seen fit not to open a *boulangerie*, or so it seemed. For a place its size, it boasted an admirable range of amenities: town hall, bank, butchers and even an *"atelier des rêves"* that sold clothes, bags and cushions… but the dreams did not extend to selling anything I could eat for breakfast. No *croissant* or *pain au chocolat*. Somewhat grumpily, I cycled on.

My troubles were soothed by a calming early morning chat with a birdwatcher who was peering through his binoculars beside the Baie de Saint-Brieuc. The salt meadows of the bay were, he explained, the perfect feeding ground for many migratory species who paused their journeys here for a month or two en route to or from Africa. It was good to hear that at least some living creatures were able to find a decent breakfast in these parts although I may have turned up my nose at the worms upon which they were feasting. However, he explained that he was not having much luck with his ornithology on this particular morning. I could only imagine that many of the birds had taken advantage of the previous evening's high winds and continued their migrations north.

Calorific salvation came in Saint-Brieuc itself but I had to earn it as the climb into the centre of the town was an arduous one. When I turned around at its summit I noted that the sign claimed the gradient to be a mere 10%. Nonsense. It was one thing being forced to take on such a hill, another thing altogether not to be rewarded with a sign that you could photograph and post to social media to boast about your preternatural level of fitness.

Saint-Brieuc announced itself in three languages: French, Breton (Sant-Brieg) and Gallo (Saint-Berieu). This was a level of linguistic diversity that would have had Jacques Chirac turning in his grave. After several days of cycling in Brittany, I had become accustomed to the bilingual signs, but this was the first time I had noticed the third language - Gallo - in action. According to the Ofis Publik Ar Brezhoneg - the Public Office of Breton - the origins of the Breton language lie in the British Isles. However, it was not the *first* wave of migration in the 6th century BC which brought the language to the continent but the *second* in the 5th and 6th centuries AD. It has now been spoken in Brittany for over 1,500 years but today only around 225,000 people use it on a daily basis. Five million people live in the historical region of Brittany[26] making Breton a minority language spoken by just 4.5% of the population. UNESCO includes the language in its Atlas of the World's Languages in Danger (of which there are some 2,500) at the level of "severely endangered". Fellow Celtic language Welsh, in comparison, is merely "vulnerable" although, at the other end of the scale, Cornish is "critically endangered", only one step away from being "extinct".

The situation with Breton is hardly surprising when you bear in mind that the French state banned the teaching of the language until 1951. Even then, it was not until parents set up bilingual *diwan* (the word means "seed" in Breton) schools in the late 1970s that the language started to be taught formally. State schools came on board in the early 1980s with the introduction of bilingual Breton streams and finally, the private Catholic schools caught up in 1990. The result is that today 20,000 students in Brittany attend bilingual schools and a further 13,000 learn the language as part of their curriculum. And in a nod to modernity, Wikipedia hosts 70,000 articles in the Breton language. Google, however, has yet to adopt Breton as one of its Google Translate languages even though it does include Scottish Gaelic (60,000 speakers) and Sanskrit (20,000 speakers).

Unsurprisingly, the Gallo language is also listed in the UNESCO atlas, also at the level of "severely endangered". But surprisingly (to me at least), for a language that I had never previously heard of, it is spoken by around 200,000 people in historical Brittany, albeit across a broad swathe of the region that does not include Finistère. According to the Institut du Galo, it is the Romance language of Brittany. However, as with its distant linguistic cousin Breton, the French Revolution of 1789 did it no favours whatsoever. The new folk in charge of the Republic considered regional languages as

---

[26] This is distinct from the modern region of Brittany which is made up of the *départements* of Côtes-d'Armor (where I was cycling at this point of my Grand Tour), Finistère to the west, Ille-et-Vilaine to the east and Morbihan to the south. Historical Brittany also includes the *département* of Loire-Atlantique, south of Morbihan which is now part of the Pays de la Loire region.

an impediment as they strove for *égalité* across the nation. It is now taught as an optional subject in secondary schools but its profile is much lower than that of Breton. Visiting Brittany today it is hard to miss Breton. It is easy to miss Gallo, and I nearly did.

Saint-Brieuc had a refreshing rough-around-the-edges feel to it. The grey sky helped create an atmosphere of normality in the place. I had mentioned that I would be passing through the town to a French person a few days earlier and when I asked them what it was like, they responded by saying, rather prosaically, *"c'est une grande ville"* - "it's a big town". I was a little puzzled at the time by their lack of enthusiasm for the place. It was, after all, the biggest settlement between Saint-Malo and Brest along a very tourist-friendly stretch of coastline. But having now arrived, I could understand what they meant. It *was* just a big town. From the saddle of a casual observer on a bicycle who just happened to be passing through, grabbing a bite to eat and watching the world go by from a bench at the top of the high street, that seemed to sum it up perfectly. It was gritty, scruffy and a notch further along the graffiti scale than most French towns... but after so many pristine towns and villages, I quite liked that. Perhaps as an increasingly gritty and scruffy cyclist, I blended in quite well.

North of Saint-Brieuc there was more early-20th-century railway architecture to admire courtesy of the Viaduc du Parfond de Gouët. This elegant two-tiered structure with its 13 graceful arches spanned the 120-metre-wide Gouët Valley at a height of over 30 metres. It too had been part of the same relatively short-lived coastal network of narrow-gauge railways of which I had seen remnants the previous day. However, the information board beside *this* viaduct elevated the structure to an altogether new level. It explained that "these works of art allowed the small Côtes-du-Nord train to follow the winding and steep coast without getting too out of breath." Having just descended from Saint-Brieuc back to the coast and having climbed again to reach the viaduct, this comment was not lost on me. It must once have been a spectacular ride on the train looking down along the coastal valleys and the seaside villages. I could only rue the fact that since its closure in 1957, only short sections of the route remained in place. Modernity had rubbed most of the line from the map, leaving me and the other Vélomaritime cyclists to put in the effort and get out of breath in a way that the trains were never obliged to do.

The up-and-down nature of the day was set to continue. It was perhaps this energy-sapping topography, combined with a severe lack of sleep that was always going to make this one of the shorter cycling days of the trip. After yet another steepish climb out of Binic-Étables-sur-Mer, I was on the lookout for somewhere to camp for the evening. I had already pinpointed a site near Saint-Quay-Portrieux. I had even gone to the bother of calling them to reserve a pitch in advance so as to avoid the situation from the previous evening. That said, if I had passed the gates of any suitable establishment at any time after about 3 pm I would have pulled on the brakes and booked in. Some days you need to read your body and give in. Cycle touring is not a sport for superheroes, even if cycle tourists are capable of achieving a very occasional super-heroic endeavour. Such feats are always scattered sparingly amongst the far more frequent days when you cannot be bothered to go any further.

The final 10km of the day were relatively urban, the towns strewn along the coast having crashed into each other at slow speed over the decades. I did not happen to pass a suitable-looking alternative campsite in those final few kilometres of the day so I finally ground to a halt, somewhat fatigued, outside Camping Bellevue. This was the site I had called earlier in the day. It shared its name with the campsite from the previous evening. I wondered if it too lived up to its name by offering a cracking vista from my tent. I was not about to be disappointed.

The chap running the place was an energetic man in his 50s. He gave every impression of once having done something that required a high level of fitness in a location where the sun always shone: fireman on the Côte d'Azur perhaps or personal bodyguard to one of the Grimaldis. That kind of thing. Whatever it had been, he was now running a campsite in Brittany and, after having checked in at the reception, he escorted me on his bike to the northern edge of the site. It was here, in long almost parallel terraces that the land fell gradually away in the direction of rocky outcrops where the sea gently crashed into the land. It was indeed a *belle vue*.

I quickly worked out that, due to the craggy nature of the coast, this section of the campsite was facing due east. Although there would be no sunset to view that evening, come the morning the sunrise would be a spectacular one, especially viewed from my slightly elevated terrace on the hill. I had been using my drone-mounted camera to good effect in recent days, increasingly confident about not crashing it into any inconveniently placed tree or person. The viaduct earlier in the day, for example, had provided me with some remarkably cinematic footage of me cycling over the bridge as the camera gently climbed into the sky. It was the kind of shot where you would expect the credits to start scrolling up the screen. However, one bit of filming that I had not yet managed to put in the can was a sunrise. Here at Camping Bellevue, I had the perfect opportunity. I just needed to be up before the sun and for the weather to play ball. Never before had I regretted so much my decision to leave my folding camping chair at home. Lights? Camera?

Day Twenty: Saint-Quay-Portrieux to Louannec (72km)
Friday 22nd July

I did not quite manage to beat the sun but not long after sunrise, I was out of the tent with the drone. It was still well before 7 am and I was conscious that the hum of the DJI Mini 2 might disturb other campers, but it was a risk worth taking. The sky was far from cloudless but neither was the sun completely hidden behind a bank of clouds. Crucially there was barely a whisper of wind. Conditions for filming were good. I found a bare patch of ground near the tent where there was no grass to interfere with the rotor blades of the drone. I waited for the required number of GPS signals to be detected and selected "take off" on the screen of my phone, which was clamped into the control unit. The buzz of the blades kicked in and the drone was launched. Aside from a couple of seagulls perched on a nearby building calling "ha-ha-ha" to each other, all was quiet at Camping Bellevue.

Action!

I flew the drone above the terraces of the campsite towards the rocks and out over the sea. The sun was reflecting off the gentle waves and, for a couple of minutes, I piloted the craft slowly over the water and then back to shore, filming as I went. This was working well. The view from the camera - sent live to the screen of my phone - was just what I had been hoping for.

Much to their oblivious delight, I seemed to have managed the whole operation without disturbing any of my fellow campers. Again, only the gulls could be heard, "ha-ha-ha", perhaps a little more loudly than before.

It was easy to lose sight of the drone as its grey body often matched the colour of clouds in the sky, so it was no surprise to look up from the screen and not be able to spot it immediately. However, I did see something. One of the gulls. It had now taken flight and it seemed a little… agitated. Its "ha-ha-ha" sounds were becoming increasingly loud and frantic and it was flying somewhat erratically in the sky. I then spotted the drone, hovering just a few metres away from the gull. Panic set in. I was witnessing the start of a full-blown dogfight. War had been declared… by a seagull!

Trying to stay calm, I channelled all my piloting skills in an attempt to get the device back on the ground. Flying the drone towards me required simultaneous movement both horizontally and vertically and this was never an easy manoeuvre even at the best of times. It was certainly not one of those. With the gull showing an ever-increasing amount of anger, flapping its wings and darting back and forth near the drone, I managed to bring it towards the ground, passing it over a small red tent a few metres from my own. As I did so, the gull swooped in and fired high-velocity bird crap in the direction of the drone, missing it and hitting the red tent. The drone was, however, now on the ground. Surely the gull would no longer be concerned. Wishful thinking. It was coming back for a second run at its target.

I grabbed the drone and dived back into my tent but I had been spotted by the gull. It continued to swoop low over the tent but without anything specific to aim at, refrained from firing its liquid missiles. After a few minutes, the attacks stopped but when I dared stick my head out of the tent I could see the gull back on the ridge tiles of its building giving me hard stares and continuing to squawk.

Elephants are famous for never forgetting and goldfish for never remembering. Where did my gull sit on the great scale of memory? I sat in the tent and waited.

The previous summer, at the end of a cycle along the Outer Hebrides in Scotland, I had woken to find the tent - that had been pitched beside a remote beach - was surrounded at close quarters by a herd of big black cattle. On that occasion, I threw everything into the panniers as quickly as I could, ripped the pegs out of the ground, screwed the tent into a ball and scarpered to safety behind a nearby metal fence. Although the cows had been mercifully disinterested in me, they could, at any moment, have trampled the tent with me inside it. Here it was different. I was safe in the tent, but as soon as I exited, the bird might attack.

After 10 minutes I made a tentative move to leave the tent but immediately heard an angry squawk and quickly retreated. Imprisoned inside, I set about packing up my things.

It took about half an hour for the gull to lose interest. It was still perched on the building as I pushed Wanda back up the path away from my now-empty pitch on the terrace. It had been a frightening experience but my lesson had been learnt. Over the coming weeks, I was always very careful never to launch the drone if I thought there was even the slightest risk of disturbing local wildlife, especially birds. In Brittany, they were only seagulls. In the Alps, they might well be eagles.

Near the top of the hill, I turned for a final time to gaze down across the terraces. A young woman had now emerged from the red tent. She was looking puzzled at the large white splatters on its roof. Lest she also turn violent, I set off cycling.

It was destined to be a tough day on the bike with the route bouncing repeatedly between sea level and 100 metres as I made my way along the Vélomaritime. A cold westerly wind blew for much of the time which added an extra level of challenge to proceedings and did nothing to help me recover from the fatigue I had been feeling for several days now. Indeed in my notes, I officially designated Friday 22nd July as a Mercedes day. This reference related to an encounter that I had had on the 2015 pan-European Spain to Norway trip with an octogenarian Dutchman named Paul near Seville. Reflecting upon his many years of cycle touring, he offered his advice:

"Remember that there will always be Mercedes days," he explained.

"What's a Mercedes day?" I enquired.

"It's a day when it's probably raining, perhaps cold, the scenery is not that inspiring and you tell yourself you'd rather be somewhere else."

"So, why a Mercedes day?"

"Because it's when you wonder why you didn't buy an air-conditioned Mercedes instead. I've never bought one because I know that the next day will always be so much better."

However, of all my days in Brittany, it was today which would turn out to be the most quintessentially Breton. I was, on reflection, perhaps a little too eager to designate it as a full-blown Mercedes day. The cycling may have been tough but in most other respects I was well-catered for. The area was rich in culture, history and natural beauty and I did take time to pause, investigate and explore. I suspected that my growing level of tiredness had a large part to play in disproportionately skewing my opinion because it was, without a doubt, one of the more interesting days of the entire Grand Tour.

Despite the wind, by mid-morning, I was making reasonable progress and was north of a town called Plouha, about 15km into the cycling day. It could get confusing with the names as so many of them started with Plo or Ple or Plu. Perhaps this was why I was paying particular attention to the signs I was passing and why I also kept noticing the ones referencing "*la maison d'Alphonse*". I noted them as a curiosity (the world would be somewhat cluttered if we all put up signs telling people where we lived) but thought nothing of it. I then arrived at a quiet countryside junction and read the following:

Ici fut
La maison d'Alphonse

"Here was the house of Alphonse". Mmm… I had inadvertently stumbled upon Alphonse's house and now felt duty-bound to find out a little more about the chap. *Who was he? And why did his house merit a sign? (And, come to think of it, if it merited a sign, why had it been knocked down?)* Below the sign was another making reference to the "*réseau Shelburn*", the "Shelburn network". That sounded more British than French or Breton. On the opposite side of the road next to a modern corrugated farm building was a short section of wall. A stone had been added to the wall and the inscription told me that in 1943 *la Maison d'Alphonse* had been the home to Jean and Marie Gicquel. Presumably, the wall was all that was left of the house. There were more details given on a small monument and an information board beside the wall.

During the Second World War, many Allied soldiers and airmen found themselves stranded in enemy territory on the continent. Several escape lines were set up and operated by helpers who sheltered, fed, nursed and guided the servicemen to safety. This was usually in the form of a boat that could repatriate them back to the UK. One of these lines was codenamed Shelburn and its purpose was to move men from Paris to a beach - codenamed Plage Bonaparte - less than a kilometre away from where I was standing. It seems remarkable bearing in mind that the country was occupied by the Nazis at the time, but the soldiers and airmen were put on the train in Paris to travel to Saint-Brieuc. From there they either caught the narrow-gauge *petit train* that operated along the coast (the bridges of which I had been making use of myself in recent days) or they were moved in a gas van to *la maison d'Alphonse*. It was the last safe house before the escapers made their way in darkness down the steep cliffs to the beach. During its period of operation from January to July 1944, 135 men were brought here and successfully transported back to Britain in eight escape operations.

The final operation nearly ended in disaster when a group of drunk German soldiers knocked on the door of the safe house with five British and American servicemen inside. Jean Gicquel slammed the door in their faces and the escapers managed to hide in the attic, but one of the drunk soldiers ended up shooting one of his colleagues in the groin in the ensuing confusion. The Allied servicemen were never found but the incident was reported to the Gestapo who returned the following day and razed *la maison d'Alphonse* to the ground. By that point, realising that the house had been compromised, all the occupants had left and the five British and American soldiers were successfully taken to the beach on the night of the 25th of July.

So who was Alphonse? It seems that too was just another codename, used by the BBC to alert the helpers that a boat had arrived to collect the escapers: "*Bonjour aux amis de la maison d'Alphonse. Le chapeau de Napoléon est à la Plage Bonaparte*"[27] were the words used in broadcasts. My questions had been answered.

After a steep climb out of a pristine coastal town called Bréhec, I could see the beaches from which the servicemen had been evacuated. How different my journey from Paris had been compared to theirs. It was here, reflecting on the adventures of a bygone era, overlooking the land and sea, that I first noticed how reminiscent the area was of the south-west of England. The rocky outcrops, the white beaches, the steep hills, the fields of blue hydrangeas... Even most of the buildings would not have looked out of place if they could have been transported to the other side of the English Channel and rebuilt. Brittany, as one of the Celtic nations, may be an entirely human construct, but the first migrants arriving from the British Isles all those centuries ago must surely have found familiarity in their new home. From what I could see, with their independent spirits, their stories of clandestine escapades and their feelings of being at the ends of the earth - Cornwall has Land's End, Brittany has Finistère[28] - they continue to develop along similar parallel tracks to this day. Brittany was most definitely growing on me.

Its hills, however, were not. The ascents and descents were relentless, the cold wind continued to blow and the pretty towns and villages came and went. Past the derelict Abbaye de Beauport, through the busy Port de Paimpol, along the half-timbered lanes of Tréguier and across the suspended Passerelle Saint-François. It was a great day of cycling in almost all respects aside from the cycling itself. That was becoming an increasingly arduous grind, not made any easier by the poor state of many of the paths and quiet roads that the Vélomaritime followed.

I had identified a campsite just short of tourist hotspot Perros-Guirec - the Camping Municipal de Louannec - as a potential place to stay overnight but was anxious that it might be a busy place. I tried ringing in advance on several occasions during the afternoon but each time the recorded message told me to wait before cutting off the call about a minute later. It was frustrating, to say the least.

Back on the cycle track and with my energy waning as each hill appeared I *did* manage to take a few shortcuts along the route. A day that I had estimated would be around 80km finally finished after 72 but whether my

---

[27] "Hello friends of Alphonse's house. Napoléon's hat is at Bonaparte Beach."
[28] Literally, "end of earth"

estimate had been inaccurate or whether my shortcutting had been successful, I was not able to say.

At least the welcome at Camping Municipal de Louannec was warm. As I had predicted, it was worryingly busy but I was allocated a small corner pitch that was permanently reserved for cycle tourists at the end of one of the long rows of tents and caravans. Although the price was municipal, the aspirations of the campsite were anything but. It had a whole host of noise-inducing attractions. Great if you were a seven-year-old boy with a barrel full of energy to expend until you conked out at 10 pm. Not-so-great if you were a middle-aged man who had just had a tough day on his bicycle. I did not grin but had to bear it, cooking up a predictable pasta-based meal on my gas burner and knocking back a few cans of lager.

It was at this point that the family on the other side of the hedge, whose camper van was parked within metres of my tent decided to unleash their young children upon the ears of their fellow campers. The baby's crying through an open window of the van was particularly painful, stretching out late into the evening.

What had Paul said when explaining his Mercedes days? "I know that the next day will always be so much better." I bloody well hoped so.

Day Twenty-One: Louannec to Morlaix (36km + Train)
Saturday 23rd July

My night of sleep had been a difficult one what with the late-evening noises ringing in my ears and the hard ground punishing the rest of my body. Even a Therm-a-rest mat has its limits in softening an unforgiving surface. At 8.30 I was standing next to the refuse and recycling bins outside the campsite entrance contemplating my lot in life trying desperately to make the positives outweigh the negatives. And they did, by far.

Yes, I was tired, several of my bright red and (rather sexy) lightweight Hubba-Hubba tent pegs were now bent and I had a big hole in one of my sandals after using its sole to try and force the pegs into the ground. However, the wind was nowhere near as strong as it had been on the previous day, and blue sky dominated at least one half of the sky. I had sorted out two nights of accommodation in my next destination of Morlaix and had a comparatively leisurely cycling day ahead of me.

I knew this as the route profile on the Vélomaritime website was somewhat more cycling-friendly than it had been for Friday's ride. In addition, I had decided that I would take the third of my ten trains, from the town of Lannion to Morlaix itself. Lannion was only around 10km from my starting point near Louannec. However, the route I would be following to get there was along the other three sides of a diamond-shaped path that followed the Côte de Granit Rose, or the Pink Granite Coast. It promised to be a visual treat. If that was indeed to be my reward, I was perfectly happy cycling the extra 30km that would be required to see it.

Fifteen minutes later, after having skirted around the corner of the bay, I was sitting perusing my map whilst sipping a strong black coffee on the terrace of the Café du Port in Perros-Gueric. I tried to hide the fact that I was feasting on the *croissants* I had purchased from the *boulangerie* around the corner. I think I got away with it despite evidence of the crime attracting many of the local pigeons to my table.

 Most of my upcoming cycle appeared to be on the road, initially heading north-west in the direction of Tourony, then south-west to Trébeurden before making its final ninety-degree turn towards the south-east and Lannion. This small area of Brittany stuck out into the sea. It would be a stretch to call it a peninsula but it was a part of the coast where the narrow gauge Côtes du Nord trains had never ventured and as a result, my cycle would be devoid of disused railway lines.

Adopting the roads as it did, the route was set back slightly from the sea, often through wooded areas or gently undulating suburbia where it was difficult to judge where I was or how far I had travelled. But then I would descend slightly and find myself confronted with a picture-postcard view of a coastal village or an otherworldly beach. This was especially the case as I approached Tourony, but before I could explore, I noticed some familiar faces.

For several days now I had seen, from a distance, three young men on bikes. They had been at both the municipal campsite in Louannec on the previous evening and Camping Bellevue the night before that. I had also seen them on the road several times but up until this point we had only exchanged an occasional nod of acknowledgement. However, as they were standing beside a stone bridge spanning the estuary at Tourony, I introduced myself, eager to find out how their Breton cycling trip was going.

"We are Fabian, Julian and Guillaume," explained Fabian in confident English. "We started in Saint-Jacut-de-la-Mer and we are following the coast until... we are fed up," he added, laughing.

The trio had been taking a couple of weeks every summer for the past few years to go on a cycling adventure somewhere in north-west France. They had all met in La Rochelle as students but were now dispersed across France. This seemed like a good way of maintaining friendship.

"The coast is wonderful but it's going up and down and up and down. It was difficult to begin with but it's getting better. We're starting to like going up and down."

It was gratifying to discover that I was not alone in finding the going tough in Brittany, but I had not quite reached the same level of appreciation for the hills as the French threesome. They too were heading for Morlaix but would not arrive there until Sunday. I kept quiet about my plans to abandon the route in Lannion in preference for the train. It was a sign, perhaps, that I was still not completely at ease with my decision to include the railway journeys. I never felt entirely comfortable telling people about them and rarely did, even though I knew that they were playing an essential role in me getting back to Rotterdam in time for the ferry home at the start of September.

Shortly after saying goodbye to Fabian and his friends, the route turned inland again only to reappear a few minutes later at a beach, the Plage de Tourony, home to some of the most curious rocks that I have ever had the pleasure to encounter. Strip away the people sitting on the bench to my left, the small yachts bobbing on the turquoise water before me and the follyesque turreted buildings on the far shore and I could have been persuaded that I had cycled into an extra-terrestrial episode of Star Trek from the 1960s. If Captain James T. Kirk himself had wandered onto the sand from behind one of the many large boulders strewn across the beach,

I would not have been in the least bit surprised. (And it had nothing to do with me being accustomed to seeing men in tight Lycra.)

It is here, in the area around Ploumanac'h, that the Côte de Granit Rose gets its name and where you will find "rock formations and sands in hues seldom found elsewhere"[29] (outside of an episode of Star Trek...). I was lucky to arrive at a moment when the tide was out revealing the geology of the small crescent bay at its best. Admittedly the pink hues were a little less than vibrant under a cloudy sky but that did not prevent it from displaying its mystical charms to all who chose to stand and stare.

The geology dates back some 300 million years to a time when great mountain ranges covered the area that we now know as Brittany. Hot magma was injected into this thick crust creating chambers of molten rock deep below the surface. Over time, erosion wore down the 5km-high mountains to the level at which we see the land today and, in places such as Ploumanac'h, the exposed and now-cooled chambers of granite. This granite has, in turn, been eroded by the air and the sea to form the distinctive rounded lumps of rock that lounge around on the shore like motionless flabby walruses. It is the kind of place that puts the paltry human time frame into perspective. The environment all around had its origins millions of years before even the dinosaurs and its destiny will be written hundreds of millions of years in the future. A place to feel insignificant in the presence of greater powers. Beam me up Scotty.

Much of the rest of the cycling day was run-of-the-Breton-mill in comparison to what I had just seen but not without its charms and curiosities. Le Menhir de Saint Uzec, an intricately carved standing stone dating back over four thousand years. The panoramic views of the port and coast from the hillside at Trébeurden. And a large pan of *moules au cidre Breton* at a riverside shack in Lannion. I washed them down with a celebratory beer to mark the end of the cycling day. The emphasis was, of course, on cycling as it was only mid-afternoon and I still had most of my journey to Morlaix to complete, albeit by train.

There was no conveniently timed direct train to Morlaix so I had to change in Plouaret. The modern TER trains were exactly the same as the one that I had caught from Calais to Le Touquet earlier in the trip (although different from the older rolling stock used on the Chartres line out of the capital). These were by far the easiest to use from the perspective of a cyclist with step-free access and hectares of space inside to store the bike. It was normally possible simply to rest Wanda on her stands, one supporting the back wheel, one the front. However, hooks were provided towards the

---

[29] *The Daily Telegraph*: Ploumanac'h, France - Secret Seaside, 28th May 2014

ceiling for anyone feeling brave enough to launch their bicycle into the air and attempt a coupling of wheel rim and hook. I was not and, over the coming weeks would only be required to do so once. (More of that later.) All the formalities were dealt with via the SNCF app on my phone, including the bike reservation. By this stage of the trip I was beginning to dream of the day when back home in the UK, the train network is again unified under one livery, one company and one mobile phone app. Perhaps they could call it... British something. British Rail perhaps?

As noted earlier, Saint-Brieuc had been described as "*une grande ville*", the implication being that it was nothing special. Morlaix, however, had been described to me by several people as a gem of a town and I was looking forward to not just arriving there later in the day but taking time to explore the place on Sunday. There was evidently much to see and do in Morlaix but having seen it in the tourist literature and repeatedly every time I had searched Morlaix online, one image dominated in my mind: its two-tiered railway viaduct. It was from the window of the train as it slowly edged its way along the viaduct's second tier some 60 metres above the town that I was afforded my first glimpse of the place that would be my home for the next 36 hours. It was an impressive view with the port area and river snaking its way north along the steep-sided valley to my right and the imposing *hôtel de ville* and the town of Morlaix on my left towards the south. It seemed like I had chosen well in deciding to take a day off in Morlaix.

The combined soporific effects of mussels cooked in cider, a beer and the gentle repetitive rocking of the trains since leaving Lannion did not have me in the mood for doing anything in the least bit strenuous upon arrival in Morlaix. I need not have worried as to access the town centre and my hotel near the port required only the gentle release of Wanda's brakes. Gravity did the rest, transporting me effortlessly down the hill from the elevated train station in no time whatsoever. Who needs teleportation when the laws of physics work just fine?

PART FIVE:

La Vélodyssée / EuroVelo 1

Day Twenty-Two: Morlaix
Sunday 24th July

I had now arrived at the western extremity of my Grand Tour of Europe. From this point onwards all of my route in France would be heading south, east or north. I was probably a little behind schedule but with the flatlands of western France ahead of me, I would no doubt make up time along the Vélodyssée in the coming days. I had history with the Vélodyssée dating back to 2015 when I had cycled the southern portion of the route from Bayonne, near the Spanish border, to La Rochelle. This had been roughly half of the route's length. On this occasion I would be attacking from the north, cycling from Morlaix but with the same destination - La Rochelle - in mind. Once in La Rochelle, I planned to take a train to Royan before jumping back on the bike and continuing beside the Gironde Estuary to Bordeaux. It seemed to make eminent sense to travel by train along the stretch of the Vélodyssée that I had previously cycled, albeit in the opposite direction. If I could be in Bordeaux by the start of August - just over a week away - that would put my Grand Tour firmly back on track. The chances of me turning up at school in time to teach my first lesson of the academic year would be good.

My non-cycling day in Morlaix was destined to be the usual eclectic blend of the functional and the enjoyable combined with a modicum of planning. The latter had already been done to a greater extent in my head in recent days but I was keen to get hold of a regional map for the Vélodyssée. If my experiences from 2015 were anything to go by, the route - also part of the pan-European EuroVelo 1 from Portugal to the northern tip of Norway - was a flagship for the French cycling routes. My memories were of it being predominantly off-road and extremely well-signposted. I saw no reason to doubt that this would also be the case north of La Rochelle. What I did know of this northern section was that it initially followed abandoned railway lines before linking up with the Nantes-Brest Canal as far as Nantes. Thereafter it was mainly coastal. Despite this knowledge, I still wanted the security blanket of a physical map. Amongst their many benefits, paper maps tended not to auto-lock after 30 seconds or require a daily recharge.

It was Sunday morning and I wandered back in the direction of the town centre, passing under the tall arches of the viaduct as I walked. Beside the viaduct was a small building whose steep roof dominated its structure to the extent that it was more roof than anything else. That aside, it was home to several colourful tiled panels showing local scenes of the port and the nearby coast. One of the panels was somewhat more striking than the others. It was made up of around 100 tiles and was titled "*Vue aerienne de Morlaix*". According to the Roman numerals in the corner, it had been put there in 1952 but despite its age, the colours were just as vibrant as the day the jigsaw of tiles had been pieced together. The aerial painting of the town that it provided was perfect for planning my wanderings. As I had seen from the train on the previous afternoon, the bulk of the town lay to the south of the viaduct. The street pattern suggested medieval origins, as did the tightly packed timber-framed houses. I suspected that the view from on high had barely changed since the artist had finished his work more than 70 years ago.

Towards the top of the panel was the crest of the town under which was written the town's motto:

"*S'ils te mordent, mords les*"[30].

"If they bite you, bite them". It did seem a somewhat aggressive message to adopt for an inspirational town motto. As is often the case, the finger of blame needed to be pointed at... the English. In 1522, at the behest of Henry VIII, Thomas Howard, the Duke of Norfolk, was laying waste to many settlements along the coasts of Normandy and Brittany. On June 2nd 1522, it was the turn of Morlaix. Much of the town was burned to the ground and a number of its richest residents were seized and subsequently taken back to England and held for ransom. The trading fortunes of Morlaix were severely damaged and, despite a rearguard action against the English, nothing could compensate for what had been lost. The motto was subsequently adopted: if they - the English that is - bite you, bite them back. I had better watch my step.

There were plenty of steps to watch to access the lower level of the railway viaduct, which served as a pedestrian walkway between the two sides of the valley. It was an astonishing construction that dominated the whole area. The statistics spoke for themselves: 292 metres long, 2,000 workers required to build it, 11,000 tonnes of granite (no shortage of that around here), 74,000 tonnes of sand, earth and gravel, 2,500 cubic metres of wood and 43 tonnes of iron. Yet it took just two years to build and trains were running along the upper tier within a couple of months of its completion on November 22nd 1863. It even came in more or less on budget. It was the kind of 19th-century urban construction that would nowadays struggle to be given planning permission (let alone get built) but

---

[30] Whoever came up with the motto was a master of their art: "*mords les*" is identical to "Morlaix" when pronounced in French.

which today, 160 years after it opened, has come to define the town. Here was a railway bridge that should never be handed over to the cyclists for one of their greenways. With it continuing to be a key piece of the Paris-Brest TGV infrastructure, it seems unlikely that it ever will.

One great advantage of there being such a monumental structure in the centre of a town or city is that it was difficult to get lost. The Viaduc de Morlaix was not quite as omnipresent as the Parthenon is in Athens (if you get lost in Athens you really do have directional issues), but it was never more than a few metres stroll from being visible. From the terrace of the nearby Café du Commerce, the viaduct could not be missed. If only I could say the same thing for me. Despite being ignored at length by the waiter - when I did manage to grab his attention he sarcastically admonished me for not having the courtesy of saying *"bonjour"* - I eventually managed to indulge in my regular morning coffee. Perhaps, on reflection, he was still aggrieved by the events of 1522 and was merely fulfilling his civic duty of biting back. I then started to wander.

As I did, I began to notice the large paintings that adorned some of the gable ends of buildings. This was street graffiti, but not as I knew it. Some of the images were approaching a photo-realistic level of detail. They had been executed by someone other than a bored teenager with time on their hands, a few cans of spray paint and no energy to climb the hill to find a suitable train to use as a canvas. Some portrayed human figures, others animals and some were abstract. Perhaps planning regulations in Morlaix were not so strict after all. There was a seaman with his pipe and beard, every strand of hair visible in high definition. There was a portrait of a young woman dressed in traditional Breton costume, her head and body sliced carefully to fit on the uprights of a long flight of steps. And then there was a girl, kneeling inside a house-sized blue bottle along with a rolled-up piece of paper. She was writing in her notebook. A message in a bottle? If so, what was the message?

Somewhat easier to fathom was the *Journée Bretonne* that was taking place in Place Allende. The clues were more obvious: the live music being played on the accordion and (what appeared to be) bagpipes and a display of traditional dancing. The women in their long black shirts, crimson shawls and simple white hats were folding large linen sheets rhythmically. Yes, it is possible, although the display *was* pushing the limits of acceptable 21st-century gender stereotyping. The men in their blue over-shirts and black hats were dancing a jig beside them, trying to avoid doing any housework. If I was in any doubt, a sign on a nearby crash barrier told me all I needed to know which was that I had stumbled upon a rather charming festival of all things Breton. At the point when the women started to encourage audience participation in the dancing and the folding, I could feel my enthusiasm for the Breton-inspired sights and sounds of the square beginning to wane. I gently sauntered off, back under the viaduct and in the direction of the port.

En route, I found the tourist office so I popped in to find some maps, with limited success. There did not appear to be an overview map of the Vélodyssée in its entirety but I was given a detailed map of cycling routes in the Finistère *département*. I suspected that this would only be relevant for the first day of my journey south if that, but I gratefully accepted it nevertheless. The assistant was charming in the extreme. She asked me where I was from, "*pour les statistiques*". Any French person who is incapable of immediately identifying me as being British goes to the top of the customer-service class. I took the opportunity of asking her about the street art that I had seen. It was all down to a festival that took place for the first time in 2019 and which returned after a COVID-induced hiatus in 2021 and 2022. In an uncomfortable mangling of French and English (as well as a bit of Italian), the event was known as the Morlaix Arts Tour and described as "*le festival graffiti et street-art incontournable en Bretagne*". Come on Morlaix! Whatever happened to biting back, even if it is only linguistically?

I was dispatched with a recommendation to visit *la manufacture des tabacs* - the former tobacco factory - on the opposite side of the port and I duly trotted off as instructed. It was only a short walk from the tourist office and very close to the Hôtel du Port where I was staying. This 18th-century building dedicated to the development of serious long-term lung diseases is now, as surely every tobacco factory around the world will one day become, an arts centre. On this particular Sunday afternoon, it was almost deserted and lacked any kind of atmosphere. However, that did not stop me from seeking out the bar and indulging in a late-afternoon beer. Here at least, there was no risk of inadvertently being press-ganged into folding the local bedsheets.

Day Twenty-Three: Morlaix to Gouarec (98km)
Monday 25th July

My first morning on the Vélodyssée promised to be a damp one. Water dripped from the skylight window of my room in the attic of the hotel. Yet, as ever, I was eager to get back on the bike after our 36-hour separation. Wanda had spent her weekend in the basement of the hotel and a little part of me envied her ability to do absolutely nothing over an extended period. After a day of wandering around Morlaix, I was hardly rested. However, with the prospect of some less hilly days ahead of me, I summoned up sufficient energy to pick up my panniers, head back down the flights of stairs, clip them onto the bike and set off back into the centre of town.

The plan was to cycle the relatively short distance - around 50km - to the railway town of Carhaix-Plouguer where I had identified a *camping municipal* before joining the nearby Nantes-Brest Canal the following morning. I returned to the Place Allende (where council workers were clearing up the detritus of the Breton festival from the previous afternoon) to find breakfast and to re-find the sign for the Vélodyssée that I had spotted during my earlier wanderings. This was not, of course, the starting point of the Vélodyssée. That was further north in Roscoff. For the sake of ticking the box to say that I had completed the entire route, it would have been nice to cycle to the port on the northern coast, but it would have been a round trip of another 60km. This was sufficient incentive to have me thinking again. If nothing else, my decision gave me a reason to return one day to Morlaix and get that box ticked.

The signs directed me south along the valley before instructing me to climb a steep hill which gave access to the disused railway line that I would be following to Carhaix. In 1879 the French government declared that it was their ambition that nobody should live more than half a day's bike ride from their nearest station and, as a result, ordered the construction of new railway lines. The Compagnie des Chemins de Fer de l'Ouest set about building five new lines in Brittany. All of these lines met in Carhaix and the first to be built was the one that I would be following from Morlaix. For reasons of cost, the network was built using a narrow gauge (as had the lines running along the north coast) but this decision lead ultimately to the network's demise as a track width of just one metre was incompatible with high-speed trains. All but one of the lines closed in 1967. Bad news for the *ferrovipathes*[31] of France but good news for me.

---

[31] Trainspotters

The engineers of the 19th century chose not to build their railway straight across the Monts d'Arrée, the mountain range of Brittany whose maximum elevation is a modest 385 metres. However, in deciding to construct one of their lines from Carhaix to Morlaix, they could not altogether avoid the influence of the hills, as I was about to discover. It was never going to be a strenuous ride but the gradual ascent during the first two hours of the cycling day was certainly noticeable.

The summit of the railway line was the location of the now abandoned Gare de Cloître-Lannéanou and I took a few minutes off the bike to wander around its relatively well-maintained empty shell. It was of the same architectural style as almost all the former train stations that I had cycled past since joining my first disused railway line south of Dieppe. They tended to have a Spanish hacienda look to them: whitewashed plaster with red brick decoration at the corners of the building and around the windows and gently sloping red-tiled roofs. Perhaps the architect had Hispanic blood flowing through his veins. Many of the stations had been repurposed as cafés, homes or - as I had seen en route to Paris - bicycle service stations, but the station at Cloître-Lannéanou had yet to find its new purpose in life. It stood respectable but forlorn. Lonely even, waiting for trains that would no longer arrive.

The descent on the southern flank of the foothills of the Monts d'Arrée was longer and more gentle but, just as they had been on the climb to Cloître-Lannéanou, the views were limited as for much of the time the route was lined by trees. This was especially the case as I cycled through the frequent railway cuttings, a feature that had been uncommon along the Avenue Verte and the Véloscénie. Then, with little warning, I would be rewarded with a short-lived view along the valley as I crossed a short bridge, only rather suddenly to enter another tunnel of green foliage.

The *voie verte* came to an end, somewhat abruptly, at the border between the *départements* of Finistère and Côtes-d'Armor where I was presented with the rare sight of a busy main road. Mercifully there was a segregated track beside the road and this guided me towards the centre of Carhaix. Despite it being just 1 pm, my cycling day was drawing to a close. Perhaps this was my opportunity to spend an afternoon doing as little as possible and benefit from some genuine rest (as opposed to a "rest" day where I spent most of the time exploring on two feet rather than two wheels).

In the suburbs of Carhaix there was a large Leclerc supermarket. The line of checkouts was on one side of a cavernous hall and it contained stacks of promotional items and garden furniture set up around a fake beach. It was always preferable to lock the bike inside rather than outside such establishments so I wheeled Wanda through the revolving doors making every effort not to spot a *"les vélos sont interdits"*[32] sign. On this score I was successful and proceeded to lock her to a handily located water pipe. A woman in a supermarket uniform watched me from a distance but I chose not to lipread her words or take any notice of her finger. *Was that a wag?* I quickly scuttled off to locate the fresh pasta and pesto aisle.

Ten minutes later (after detours via the wine and chocolate aisles) I made my way to the self-checkout section only to notice the same woman who had been trying to communicate with me earlier. She was watching guard over the self-service machines lest anyone try to sneak through a bottle of expensive Veuve Clicquot for a bottle of vin de table.

"You can't park your bike here, monsieur," she admonished me, in French.

I acknowledged her comment but continued to scan the items in my basket (hoping she would not notice the Veuve Clicquot). We both realised that the telling off was perhaps a little late in its delivery.

"Well, next time, please do not put your bike there," she continued.

"I don't think there will be a next time," I replied, smiling. She looked across at the bike and then at me before smiling back.

"Did you scan the Veuve Clicquot?"

After a quiet morning on the cycle path from Morlaix - I had passed very few people either on foot or on a bike - it had been a nice little encounter. Two strangers seeing the funny side of something that ultimately was not in the least bit important. And it was soon to be followed by another charming encounter between strangers. As I pushed Wanda back through the revolving doors I noticed an elderly couple on bikes, but not just any bikes. They were Koga bikes, the same brand as Wanda!

Koga bicycles are manufactured in the Netherlands so it came as no surprise to discover that the couple were Dutch. Hers was a Koga purchased in 2017 but his was a Koga-Miyata that he had purchased some 25 years ago. Miyata - a Japanese bicycle manufacturer - supplied all the Koga frames until 2010 and the bikes were sold under the double-barrelled brand. It was a name that I was familiar with courtesy of Mark Beaumont's first record-breaking circumnavigation of the globe in 2008. It was watching his documentary films about that journey that helped inspire me to get on my bike and head off on my first pan-European trip in 2010. Over a decade later, I was delighted to be a fully paid-up member of the Koga-owning club myself.

When the conversation turned to our respective trips I learnt they were heading north after a journey which had taken them along the Nantes-Brest

---

[32] Bicycles are forbidden.

Canal and that the previous evening they had stayed at a campsite at a place called Gouarec. They rated it highly and it got me thinking…

Did I really need an afternoon lounging around on a campsite doing nothing? Probably not. And it was still only 1.30 pm.

I paused briefly in the centre of Carhaix to admire a small section of train shed and a narrow-gauge locomotive sheltering under its glazed roof. Realising that I had had enough of the train stuff (perhaps you have too), I made my way quickly along a final stretch of disused railway in the direction of the Nantes-Brest Canal, 5km to the south. My obsession with disused railway lines was about to be exchanged for an obsession with a disused canal.

This would be the first time I would be following a canal in any meaningful way since setting off from the Hook of Holland. There had been a short stretch linking Middelburg with Vlissingen in the Netherlands and another close to the French border in Belgium but this would be my first towpath dalliance of any significance. And it had me quite excited, more for it *not* being an abandoned railway than anything else.

I accessed the Nantes-Brest Canal via a slope branching gently away from the *voie verte*. After crossing a bridge over the canal, the former railway line continued as far as Concarneau on the Atlantic coast. At the bottom of the slope I met the canal for the first time, immediately turned left under the railway bridge and started cycling along the towpath in the direction of Gouarec. After having spent so much of the previous three weeks enclosed within narrow tunnels of trees on the greenways, it was liberating to be cycling on a wide traffic-free path beside a shimmering body of water. It is said that a change is as good as a rest. I had been planning to rest all afternoon yet here I was cycling at speed beside the canal and, invigorated by the change, I was already feeling the benefits.

There were three things that I knew about the Nantes-Brest Canal. It started in Nantes. It finished in Brest and, you guessed… it was a canal. It was thus fortunate - for you just as much as me - that the local authorities in Côtes d'Armor - the *département* through which I would be spending most of my afternoon - had seen fit to invest in a series of high-quality information boards. Just not so much on the English translations:

> "55 canal locks, one *escalier d'eau* (water stairway) comprising 15 canal locks on a 2km distance, a gigantic trench dug by men labour in the hills using shovels and pickaxes to cross the canal climax (184m), a double lock in the vicinity of a listed chapel, a retaining reservoir to feed the canal…"

Once again we have the pesky English to thank for this marvel of French engineering, on this occasion for providing Napoléon with sufficient motivation to build the canal in the first place. Following a blockade of the Brittany ports by his northern neighbours (and sworn enemies) across the channel, Napoléon decided that an inland route linking the naval ports of Nantes and Brest was required. At 360km in length, it was to be the most ambitious canal project ever completed in France requiring three summits and no less than 236 locks to be constructed. That said, only 20% of the canal was entirely man-made, the rest being made up of rivers that were canalised and incorporated into its route. Nevertheless, it was a mammoth task to build such a waterway and the workforce consisted of a combination of the local population, prisoners of war, deserting soldiers and convicts from Brest. According to contemporary reports, the pay was derisory and the conditions deplorable. Although Napoléon himself died many years before its completion in 1854, for a period, it was seen as a vital asset in the development of inland Brittany, but then the railways arrived and, in the 20th century, the roads. The final nail was hammered into the coffin in the form of a hydroelectric dam which was constructed in 1930 and the canal was cut in two. Navigation between Nantes and Brest was no longer possible.

Over the next three hours, I was to climb to and then descend from the highest of those three summits. It was located near Glomel and as I cycled, lock after lock after lock, the canal ascended almost imperceptibly to a modest 184 metres. Everything was well maintained: the towpath was pristine, the locks - *écluses* in French - appeared to be fully functioning and the lock keepers' cottages - usually labelled proudly with the number of the adjacent lock - were rarely anything other than immaculate. Almost all had been converted into private canal-side homes as the lock keepers themselves had long since disappeared. Yet other than for a few canoeists in one of the canal basins, this was a canal utterly devoid of traffic.

Immediately after reaching its summit at Glomel, the canal took a sharp left turn and entered *la grande tranchée* (the big slice). It was via this channel that the 19th-century engineers linked two of the river basins through which they wanted the canal to travel and it was no easy undertaking. In June 1823 the first contingents of condemned soldiers - sentenced to forced labour for remaining loyal to Napoléon (who had died in 1821) - arrived to start digging. For the next nine years, 4,000 men toiled to cut a hole in the hill that was over 3km long, 100 metres wide and up to 23 metres deep. 3 million cubic metres of earth were removed with shovels and pickaxes. 100 of the men lost their lives during the work, mostly due to malaria.

Within 15 minutes I had cycled through the *grande tranchée* and was continuing my journey east. I was now cycling downhill in the direction of Gouarec to the canal-side Camping de Gouarec and an Englishman with a beard, a high-pitched Solex and a keen interest in cycling.

Day Twenty-Four: Gouarec to Rohan (68km)
Tuesday 26th July

A text message arrived at 8 am. I was still in the tent after yet another night of on-off sleep. It was from Tim Sanders, a friend I had met at the Cycle Touring Festival. He had recently completed a cycle in northern France himself and had been supplying me with his top - mainly camping - tips on a regular basis since I had set off from the Netherlands.

"Have you met Geoff?" asked Tim.

"Geoff? Here at Gouarec?"

"Yes. Geoff Husband who runs Breton Bikes and the campsite. He's tall, I guess in his 60s."

I had not, but then again I was still in the tent. The previous evening I had been checked in at the reception caravan by a young woman and spent the evening chatting with a couple of my fellow cycle-campers. We were all looking forward to the €4 eat-all-you-can breakfast that was promised for the following morning. We would, however, have to wait until 9 am to benefit from this not-to-be-missed Vélodyssée deal of the day. I normally liked to be up, packed and on my way by around 8 am. It seemed positively ostentatious to be lounging around at 9 am. But the breakfast's reputation had spread far and wide. Tim had referenced it, as had the Dutch couple outside the supermarket in Carhaix.

By 9 am a group of around a dozen people had gathered on the wooden decking beside the campsite's main communal building. A Volvo estate pulled up and breakfast supplies were unloaded. The car was driven by a tall man in his 60s. I guessed that this was Geoff but he was busy sorting things out so I did not interrupt him. Most of his customers were cyclists, their bikes and panniers lined up beside the decking and, after dropping our €4 into a jar, we set about devouring the impressive spread of food before us. It was a wonderful, convivial way to start the day and I could not help but wonder why the concept had not caught on elsewhere. Geoff was a man I needed to talk to - perhaps even record an interview with for the podcast - but when I turned around he was gone.

I finally set off just after 10 am. The delay to the start of my cycling day was significant but it had been worth every second: good company and great food. However, as I trundled along the road beside the campsite in the direction of the canal towpath, my internal thoughts were interrupted by the noise of an approaching engine. It was not a car, or a motorbike or even a moped. It was different. I then noticed a man approaching me at speed on a bicycle, of sorts.

"Geoff!" I shouted instinctively and he pulled up in front of me.

"I like your…"

"It's a Solex. Built in 1967."

The Solex was a peculiarly French device that never really caught on elsewhere. A sturdy bicycle with a small gasoline motor clamped above the front wheel. They went out of production in the late 1980s but Geoff's machine was still going strong and had helped break the ice. We got chatting.

"I've been running Breton Bikes for 32 years now offering cycling-camping holidays in Brittany."

"But you also run the campsite here?"

"Yes, since taking it over six years ago, we've turned it into a cyclists' campsite. Covered areas, chairs, kitchens… And of course the breakfast. We're at the crossroads of the Vélodyssée and the V6 which runs due east so we get lots of cyclists but people don't realise that there's loads of great cycling away from the canal. Get a Michelin map and go further afield!"

It struck me that Geoff was probably the person to ask about why the canal had been so empty of boat traffic.

"After the dam was constructed the canal north of Pontivy fell into disrepair… they're now renovating the locks west of the Lac de Guerlédan but you can still only travel by boat for around 15km before you start hitting low bridges."

Perhaps it would be a different story on the other side of Pontivy. I would find out later in the day. Delighted to have met a key player in the Breton bike world I set off with renewed enthusiasm for life on two wheels.

As I started to make my way east along the towpath, I noticed that the canal was getting slightly wider, certainly compared to the previous afternoon. My paper map had run out shortly after leaving Carhaix and my cycling map of France lacked the detail required for meaningful route finding. So, consulting an online map, I noticed that I was now at the western end of the Lac de Guerlédan. This was the body of water that had been created by the construction of the hydroelectric dam in 1930, as referenced by Geoff. Between this point and the town of Mûr-de-Bretagne, the Vélodyssée moved away from the route of the canal to follow a… disused railway line. There was seemingly no escape from them. Not even when following a canal!

However, just before I moved away from the confines of the towpath, there was a curious building set back slightly from the water and it had an equally curious name: l'Abbaye de Bon Repos, the Abbey of Good Rest. From a distance, it looked as though a fire had recently gutted the place but as I approached, there were no hints of a fire, just an empty, gaunt façade, its walls still standing but its windows and interior removed. This was a sinister-looking hollowed-out stately home haunted not by ghosts but by itself.

The story dated back over 800 years to the moment when, as legend would have it, the Vicomte Alain III de Rohan fell asleep after an arduous day of hunting (as you do...). As he slept, the Virgin Mary appeared to him in a dream instructing him to build upon the very spot where he was snoozing. He did just that and an abbey was founded in 1184. Courtesy of its fortuitous location - wood and water were in abundance - and the formidable farming skills of the Cistercian monks who took up residence, Alain's dream turned out to be a very profitable one. A sceptic might think he had planned the whole thing all along...

The French Revolution in 1789 was to be the abbey's undoing. The building was sold at auction, became a linen factory and subsequently a handy place in which those building the Nantes-Brest Canal could sleep after their own hard day of toil. Perhaps this was the real vision that Mary wanted to deliver: giving rest to those digging out the canal. They probably earned it more than Alain and his hunting chums. The buildings then fell dormant for over 150 years until, in 1986, two friends decided to bring it back to life as a centre for contemporary art.

From the perspective of the disused railway line that skirted around the north of the lake, rarely closer than a kilometre from its shore, views across the water were fleeting, to say the least. Had I not known it was there, the Lac de Guerlédan may well have gone unnoticed. At its eastern end, the Vélodyssée descended sharply to rejoin the towpath of the canal at a point about 500 metres from the base of the dam. It was hidden around a corner so I cycled back along the canal as far as I was allowed to have a look. It was an impressive concrete wall, but not quite the epic Hoover Dam-sized edifice I had imagined. When it comes to dams, size matters.

I had climbed to the highest of the three canal summits on the previous day and as far as Pontivy I was continuing to descend, very gradually. It made for easy cycling. The locks came and went, as did the cyclists and the occasional walker. Both groups still outnumbered the people on the water by far.

I detoured into the centre of Pontivy to grab an impromptu supermarket lunch and then it was back to the grind of the canal. *Was I bored?* Perhaps a little, but I did not have much to grumble about. Nice weather, easy cycling, pretty things to look at. It was hardly the stuff of adventure but as a middle-aged run-of-the-mill adventurer myself, it suited me fine. Bear Grylls, I am not.

After Pontivy, the canal started to climb to its second summit. This was reached at the Écluse de Kéroret - number 79 from Nantes - and continued for about 5km until the Écluse de Bel-Air, number 78. Immediately after this section of summit, the canal plunged (in canal terms...) by around 50 metres in 4km passing through more than 20 locks in the process. It was (in canal terms...) thrilling stuff.

All the excitement must have got to me. The original plan had been to continue as far as a place called Josselin. However, within half an hour of the summit, the canal passed through the centre of Rohan, home to Alain III, he of the Virgin Mary dreams. Beside a large basin, there was a campsite that looked just perfect. Busy, but perfect. After a relatively modest 68km I decided to bring the cycling day to an end, pushed Wanda through the small green gate beside the towpath and checked in.

Day Twenty-Five: Rohan to Frossay (91km + Train + 19km) Wednesday 27th July

Point-to-point I was about to embark upon the longest journey of the entire Grand Tour but I was not aware of this when I set off from Camping Le Val d'Oust. I was not aware that I would be visiting a city which would become one of the highlights of the trip. And I was not aware that my day would include a train ride and a ferry. Or indeed an end-of-day race against the clock to arrive at my destination on time. Indeed as I began to cycle leisurely along the canal that morning it was simply my intention to make progress towards my next interim destination, Nantes. Perhaps halfway if I was lucky. It was the beauty of not having a detailed plan to follow, or at least having a very laid-back attitude towards the vague plan that I did have.

That said, I cannot deny that I have a very competitive edge when it comes to being the first person to leave a campsite in the morning. During my Grand Tour, I occasionally succeeded, but more often than not I was defeated either by other cyclists who were travelling very light or by my phenomenal ability to procrastinate. In Rohan the competition was tough and it was coming from three French cyclists who had pitched their tents opposite to mine the previous evening. They were travelling independently but I had eavesdropped on their conversation. When they made reference to La Semaine Fédérale I knew that my early morning departure efforts would be in vain. These guys were hard-core.

La Semaine Fédérale Internationale de Cycletourisme (to give it its full glorious title) is an annual gathering of cycle tourists that takes place at a different location in France each year. It has been on the calendar of French cycling enthusiasts since 1927 and in 2022 the event was about to take place for the 83rd time just up the road from Rohan in the Côtes-d'Armor town of Loudéac. Organised by the Féderation Française des Sociétés de Cycletourisme (another name worthy of some kind of award but criminally abbreviated to FFVélo), over 12,000 cyclists were about to descend upon the town for a festival of cycle touring unsurpassed in terms of size anywhere else on the continent. By the sounds of things, the three chaps who were beating me hands down when it came to speed of packing were planning on being there to take part in all the fun.

Not being one for mass gatherings of anything - the modestly sized Cycle Touring Festival is at the limit of my comfort zone - I was never going to deviate from my own journey to join them in the 10km cycle to Loudéac. Yet I could not help but wonder what it must be like to witness all those thousands of cyclists heading off on their daily organised rides along the country lanes of Côtes-d'Armor. It is the kind of thing that back home in Britain would have *the Daily Mail* leader writers frothing in contempt from every orifice. "Lycra louts," they would be shouting. "How dare they infringe upon our inalienable right to drive our cars wherever we want, whenever we want?" They would then start quoting the Magna Carta in the name of freedom. It was likely that here in France, a country in which most folk adopt a more enlightened, balanced approach towards cyclists, the event would pass largely unnoticed. Aside from a small poster advertising the Semaine Fédérale in the window of the *boulangerie* in the centre of Rohan, I saw or heard no more mention of the mass gathering of cyclists a few kilometres down the road. That made me smile. It was refreshingly normal and the non-cyclists did not seem to be batting any of their French eyelids.

After the canal summits, the deep cuttings, the quick-fire appearance of locks and the drama of the high-walled dam over the previous two days, the Nantes-Brest Canal was becoming a more sober body of water. It was, perhaps, seeing its retirement up ahead and had stopped making any strenuous efforts to impress. However, it still had its looks. With a cushion of early-morning mist floating serenely upon the surface of the water, a cloudless sapphire sky above and a low sun twinkling through the leaves and branches of the trees, cycling along the smooth towpath through the centre of Rohan was a moment of utter calm and joy.

As I continued south, the lock keepers' cottages were some of the most attractive I had yet seen, their gardens and adjoining lock gates blanketed with green foliage and bright summer blooms. The gradient of the canal had seemingly all but vanished. Between Rohan and Nantes, despite there being roughly half of the canal still to travel, just 50 of its 236 locks remained. It was now a meaningful exercise to use their numbers - usually painted neatly on a sign above the door of each cottage - as a guide to gauge the distance I needed to cycle before I arrived at the Loire.

Shortly after lock number 36, the Écluse de Beaufort, the canal turned sharply to the left and I could see in the distance a substantial settlement beside the water. The densely packed buildings were falling over each other down a short incline towards the towpath and behind them was a tall church spire. It was a pretty view made even more so by the gentle curve of the canal that was beginning to lurch back towards the right. As I made my way towards the buildings, more and more of the town came into view as the curvature of the canal slowly revealed an increasingly spectacular façade of canal-side constructions. And then suddenly there it was. Almost out of nowhere. Supported by three sharply turreted towers, the imposing wall of a *château*. It dominated all the other buildings in its vicinity. I pulled on my brakes and looked up at the sign beside me:

Josselin
Petite Cité de Caractère

I had only seen it for the first time a matter of minutes before but I could already agree with the sentiment. Time to explore.

A few metres before I arrived at the wall of the canal-side castle, there was a steepish path leading into the centre of Josselin. I pushed Wanda along its length in anticipation of finding a pretty town. My level of anticipation was, however, a little off the mark. What I discovered was not just pretty... it was stunning. The narrow streets were lined with a medieval mixture of half-timbered and stone buildings with many of the timbers painted in perfectly subdued shades of green, yellow and blue. Gilding the architectural lily were zigzags of red and yellow bunting that had been hung from one side of the street to the other throughout the centre. *Why had I never heard of Josselin until yesterday?* In most countries, this "little city of character" would be a must-visit destination on most tourists' itineraries.

I made it to the gates of the *château* shortly before 11 am and sat on an adjacent bench to soak up a little of the beauty and calm atmosphere that surrounded me. Although it had only been a matter of minutes since I had arrived, my senses had been awakened. As the clock approached eleven, to add to all the visual delights, a gentle peel of bells rang out from the basilica before a soft toll sounded to mark the hour. Wonderful. Just wonderful.

My guidebook declared that the castle was the most impressive sight along the Nantes-Brest canal. From the sections of the canal that I had experienced to this point, I could not disagree. The comment did, however, suggest that the pinnacle of the canal's attractions had now been reached and over the next few hours, this was to become increasingly evident. The canal was never anything other than a joy to cycle beside but it was beginning to lose its sheen as it idled its way south towards Nantes. The attractions were, increasingly, distractions: an industrial plant here, a motorway flyover there. Although the graffiti wishing me happiness was not required ("*Je vous souhaite du bonheur*" was scrawled across one of the bridges over the canal), I was keen to move on. I was reaching peak canal, for the moment at least.

I had noted earlier that the town of Redon, a likely candidate for the next campsite, also benefited from a glowing write-up in the Rough Guide. "A wonderful mess of water and locks" according to the writers. It would be a long 60km slog before I arrived in Redon and on this occasion, I was somewhat underwhelmed. Perhaps it was the comparison with Josselin or perhaps it was my eagerness to start a new, different part of my Grand Tour. Shortly after leaving the canal in Redon, I spread my cycling map of France on the ground and began to examine it carefully.

When I had spoken to Geoff Husband beside the road leading from Camping de Gouarec the previous morning, he had suggested that I avoid the northern suburbs of Nantes. Instead, he recommended that I deviate away from the Vélodyssée to take a ferry across the Loire at a place called Couëron, some 15km to the west of the city. I could see on the map that the train line from Redon to Nantes went through Couëron and there was a train station not far from the ferry's departure point. A quick consultation on the SNCF train app on my phone confirmed that it was indeed possible to travel there, albeit on two trains rather than one. Crucially, the combined distance would not break my self-imposed rule of a maximum of 100km. *But where would I spend the night?* Scrolling through the campsite recommendations provided by Tim Sanders (who had only recently cycled along the western end of the Loire), I noted that he had spoken highly of a place called Camping du Migron. This would involve cycling a further 15km once I had disembarked from the ferry. A quick call to the campsite revealed that I did not need to reserve - there was plenty of space - but that the reception would be closing at 7 pm. The second train was scheduled to arrive in Couëron at 17:56. Calculations involving times, distances and speeds (as well as a healthy dose of good fortune with the ferry) bounced around my head. If I could catch the boat within a few minutes of arriving at Couëron station the plan would, perhaps, work. Shortly before 5 pm, following a brief visit to the local Decathlon store to stock up on camping gas, the first of my two trains pulled out of Redon station with Wanda and me on board.

With only 300 metres of Loire to cross, the journey on the Couëron-Le Pellerin ferry was never destined to be a long one. Indeed the ferry was more a short section of floating road than ferry. It plied its trade throughout the day, six times every hour: three journeys north, three journeys south. I was never at risk of missing the final departure - that would not be until later in the evening - but it would be very useful if I did not have to spend too much time hanging around on the dock. As luck would have it, after a 3km dash from Couëron station, my arrival at the end of the ramp was within seconds of the barrier being closed. My waiting time was precisely… zero.

Upon arrival on the southern bank of the Loire, I was delighted to find a sign for the Vélodyssée. Since I had left it in Redon, it had been on a 130km trip via what remained of the canal and the centre of Nantes. Now that our paths had coalesced again, I had 45 minutes to cycle the 15km to the campsite before the reception closed and I would be left to sleep on the street.

I pedalled as I had rarely pedalled before along a road that must surely be one of the longest, straightest roads in France. Had I attached aerofoils to Wanda's frame we would surely have taken flight. As I had inadvertently omitted to pack my wings, we flew along the ground instead.

Maintaining a speed of 20km/hr on a laden bike would not, under normal conditions, be easy. But fortune was with me. The route was flat and straight, there was no other traffic on the quiet road beside the Canal de la Martinière and crucially, there was barely any wind. Initially, I could power ahead at 21, 22 even 23km/hr but as the clock approached 7 pm I was flagging and my speed began to dip. I kept going, one eye on my speed, one eye on the clock. If the reception were to be closed upon my arrival, I would have missed it by minutes, perhaps even seconds.

At this point, you might be expecting me to recount a dramatic end-of-day tale. Of how I arrived at Camping du Migron as the bells of the local church were beginning to chime for 7 o'clock. Of how I was able to fling myself through the door of the reception building just as it was being slammed shut. Of me thrusting a €10 note in the direction of the campsite manager through the ever-narrowing gap between door and frame…

Alas not. Campsites rarely adhere to strict schedules. They tend to be a little more laid back in their approach and that was certainly the case at Camping du Migron. The reception doubled as the bar-restaurant and I had to smile when instead of asking for my details and my money, the receptionist/barmaid, being confronted with an exhausted man, asked first if he would like a drink. I did. At least my efforts had provided me with a good spot of speed training. What's more, they had given me an appetite for the mountain of food I proceeded to order and then devour whilst sitting outside on the terrace.

The day had seen me travel around 200km. I was now south of the Loire and a new, very different part of my Grand Tour was about to begin.

Day Twenty-Six: Frossay to La Bernerie-En-Retz (93km minus 18km[33]) Thursday 28th July

According to the European Cyclists' Federation, the EuroVelo 6 is the most popular of their routes. It starts beside the Saint-Nazaire bridge at the mouth of the Loire Estuary and finishes on the shore of the Black Sea at Constanta. Its route takes it across the entire continent of Europe passing through France, Switzerland, Germany, Austria, Slovakia, Hungary, Croatia, Serbia and Bulgaria before arriving at its destination in Romania. It is 4,448km long and follows the routes of three major European rivers: the Loire, the Rhine and the Danube. In France, the route is more widely known as La Loire à Vélo. If all were to go to plan (no spoilers here...), I would meet the EuroVelo 6 again in Switzerland when it followed the same path as the EuroVelo 15 along the border with Germany. Here in France, it was a fleeting romance that had the EuroVelo 1 and the EuroVelo 6 sharing the same path the short distance between Nantes and the coast. I suspected that many of the cyclists who had stayed on the campsite the previous night were just starting their journeys along the Loire. Perhaps some would even make it as far as Constanta. It would also be my route at the start of day 26 albeit in the opposite direction towards the Atlantic.

Although I was still travelling in historical Brittany, there was a very different feel to the land on the southern bank of the Loire. This was not altogether surprising following my train- and ferry-assisted lurch south the previous afternoon. The modest hills of Brittany had been gently disappearing ever since I joined the Nantes-Brest canal three days earlier but the landscape that now surrounded me was as flat as a French *crêpe*. There was not a breath of wind and the dappled mackerel sky seemed to have the effect of deadening the sound: a motionless shag pile carpet hovering above the land and the increasingly wide estuary. It was both slightly eerie and ever-so-slightly magical.

Following a brief pause for breakfast in the small town of Paimboeuf, I continued along the cycle route following a gravel path close to the water's edge. In the distance, I could see the Pont de Saint-Nazaire. The bridge will soon have notched up its half-century but it remains, after all those years, the longest bridge in France at 3,356 metres. From a distance it was a low strip of concrete, its supporting pillars pushing it slightly taller as it reached the middle of the estuary before again sinking towards the land to the north. As big bridges went, it was not that impressive.

---

[33] Keep reading. All will be explained...

Of far greater visual interest were the rickety wooden piers that had been built to connect the riverbank to fishing cabins on stilts located about 20 metres from the shore. Beside each hut was a large net suspended over the water. I had seen these contraptions before and had always been a little sceptical as to how much fishing was involved. A handy information board did the fishermen no favours: "As the tide rises and falls," it explained, in English, "the nets are raised and lowered scooping up plaice, sole, mullet, prawns and more". It was the marine equivalent of the pick 'n mix at Woolworths, just not so bad for your teeth. But to what extent did it exploit the skills of an experienced fisherman? I remained to be convinced.

With my mind mulling over the list of potentially nefarious activities that French fishermen might get up to in their *cabanes de pêcheurs* as they waited for the tide to turn, I was almost imperceptibly edging towards the distant long bridge and it was soon dominating my view. Perhaps my initial thoughts had been a little harsh. I could now see the twin pylons from which white cables fanned out to support the deck from above. However, the most striking design feature of the Pont de Saint-Nazaire could only be seen as I continued to cycle west. Very gradually its lateral curve was revealed: this was a cable-stayed bridge that did not just cross a river, it slithered over the estuary of the Loire and, up close, was delightfully artistic. It reminded me of the stunning - and much more modern - bridges that I had seen on my previous long trip in Europe as I cycled along the west coast of Norway. Here on the west coast of France was a bridge with which they shared some of their architectural genetic code.

The plan was not to cross the bridge myself. I had long wanted to pay a visit to the Nazi submarine pens that were located on the northern side of the estuary but that would have to wait for a future trip. Although cyclists were not banned from the bridge, the three-lane carriageway resembled an uninviting motorway and it would be an uncomfortable, potentially dangerous long slog across to the other side of the Loire. But then, just as I was about to pass under the southern edge of the bridge, I noticed a sign:

Cyclistes
Une navette gratuite vous permet de traverser
le pont de Saint-Nazaire

A free shuttle bus for cyclists who wanted to cross the bridge? A big red arrow pointed me in the direction of the departure point and I went to investigate.

Within 20 minutes I was on board, Wanda securely fastened into the multi-bike trailer behind the van, admiring the views from the deck of the bridge. It looked as though I would see those submarine pens after all. Fewer than 20 minutes after having set off I was back on the bike cycling in a very different, industrial landscape. Warehouses to my right, shipbuilding facilities to my left, freight wagons defaced with graffiti on the unkempt railway lines beside the cycle path. Then, at the farthest end of the Boulevard Paul Leferme, a looming block of concrete: La Base Sous-marine de Saint-Nazaire.

Living and working in France in the 1990s, I remember the Saint-Nazaire submarine base being featured occasionally on the television news. One memorable fact stood out in these reports: that in the post-war era, such was the impenetrable nature of what the Nazis had built that it was now simply too expensive to demolish it. Constructed in 1941 and 1942, it contains nearly half a million cubic metres of concrete. At 300 metres long, 130 metres wide and 18 metres tall, it could safely accommodate up to 28 U-boats. And they were certainly safe. The walls are 3.5 metres thick and the depth of the roof is up to 9.6 metres in places. The original roof was constructed from layers of concrete, reinforced concrete and granite but when the Allies began to drop "Grand Slam" bombs weighing up to 10 tons it was strengthened still further with external steel cross beams. It is, without any doubt, one of the most wonderfully ugly buildings in the world.

In 1994 the local council decided to redevelop the area. The building now houses a museum dedicated to life on board the pre-war luxury ocean liners which once set off from the port, a contemporary art exhibition area and a concert venue. Yet much of the 40,000 square metres of submarine pen remains as it was when the soldiers surrendered in May 1945 and I went for a long wander through much of its empty vastness. In places, the concrete had crumbled revealing the rusting steel bars encased within, but the building was otherwise in pretty good shape. Perhaps if the Nazis had gone into the business of building secure multi-storey car parks they may ultimately have been more successful.

The day had taken a rather unexpected turn seeing me travel some 18km - in the shuttle bus and then on the bike - away from the route of the Vélodyssée and then back. I had inadvertently forgotten to switch off my GPS tracker so the day's cycling statistics were destined to be somewhat skewed as a result, especially considering the minibus reached speeds of nearly 70km/h crossing the bridge. I made a mental note to strike the 18km from the record at a later date.

In contrast to the earlier trip north when I had been one of many customers, the shuttle bus on the journey south had just one passenger and one bike. I chatted to the young woman driver and she spoke about her own cycling plans to travel further afield once the summer bus service had finished at the end of the tourist season. Any cyclists who chose to visit the submarine pens in October would have to brave it with the motorised traffic.

Upon arrival back at where we had started earlier in the morning, I bumped into a family of cyclists from the Scottish Highlands: mum, dad and two primary-school-aged boys. They had been cycling around 50km per day, travelling along the Loire from Orléans and were about to head off on the train to Saint-Malo and their ferry home. It had taken them around two weeks to arrive at the Atlantic coast and they talked about how it had been such a positive experience cycling beside the Loire, camping as they went. Their tale was a testament to just how family-friendly the route had become over the years: predominantly off-road with lots of places to stay and ample opportunities to explore the pretty towns and the river's magnificent *châteaux* along the way.

My own journey would now be due south hugging the coast and continuing to follow the signs of the Vélodyssée. I was not quite sure where I would complete my cycling day but I guessed it would be somewhere near the town of Pornic. I was, of course, now heading into one of France's most popular summer holiday destinations and this was immediately obvious. Almost all of the coastline was built up, but not in a brutal way. Small summer houses and modest apartment blocks vied for position in a polite competition for space leaving plenty of unoccupied land upon which the pedestrians, cyclists and cars could mingle. It was only fleetingly picturesque but never ugly. Although the high temperatures I had encountered earlier in the month were now a distant memory, the sporadic clouds in the sky had no impact on the willingness of the holidaymakers to strip down to their speedos and bikinis and lounge on the beaches. I was amused by the name of Saint-Michel-Chef-Chef (so good they named a bit of it twice!), there were more *cabanes de pêcheurs* hiding their work-shy fishermen and they had even hoisted the Union Flag beside the French tricolour to welcome me at La Pointe-Saint-Gildas. *Had they seen me coming?*[34]

Had this been the 1950s, I might well have stumbled into Jacques Tati preparing for his next scene in Les Vacances de Monsieur Hulo: laid back, relaxed... nice. It was that kind of place.

---

[34] Alas not. The flag was beside a memorial to those who lost their lives when the RMS Lancastria - an ocean liner requisitioned by the British government during the war - was bombed and subsequently sank some 15km offshore in 1940 whilst attempting to evacuate Allied soldiers from France. Upwards of 4,000 people perished and it remains the greatest loss of life in British maritime history.

Up, that is, to a point. And that point was Pornic. But before I could get that far I was, again, struck by a sudden deep feeling of exhaustion. It seemed to happen every few days and I would struggle to maintain the motivation required to keep pedalling. Much of the fatigue was physical and could be attributed to the lack of quality sleep that I was getting after several consecutive nights in the tent. There had only been three of them since my two nights in the hotel in Morlaix but the other factor in play was that the cycling was perhaps... too easy. Moderate to strenuous cycling required regular injections of adrenaline to be fired into my biological system. When the cycling was not very taxing it was almost as if the tap had been turned off and, as a result, I was left bereft of energy. On this occasion, I resolved to call an end to the cycling day and head for the nearest campsite even though it was only around 3 pm.

That campsite happened to be the four-star Camping Eleovic about 15km west of Pornic. It was a very busy establishment but my arrival just after two other cyclists who successfully booked themselves in was a good sign.

"Yes, you can have an emplacement for the night," explained the woman at the reception desk "and it will be €53".

At this point, my adrenal glands pounced into action.

"Mmm... I just need to check something on my phone," I explained before heading swiftly back outside, mounting Wanda and heading off at speed back in the direction of the cycle route. However tired I might have felt, there were limits to what I was willing to pay and €53 was well above that threshold.

The experience had, however, re-energised me and by the time I arrived in Pornic it was with newly acquired enthusiasm for life on the road. (Perhaps popping my head into the reception of an exorbitantly priced campsite was a tactic I could employ when the next bout of fatigue hit me hard.) It was just a pity that life on the road was the main issue I had to contend with as soon as I arrived in the centre of the coastal town. I had not encountered so many people in one place since Mont-Saint-Michel and it was somewhat overwhelming. Pornic was, without any doubt, a delightful seaside town situated around an elongated bay complete with ornate turn-of-the-century buildings beside the water and a small *château* poking out from a wooded area towards the ocean. But it was excessively busy. I weaved a path through the crowds until a man in uniform started wagging his finger at me and instructed me to get off the bike and push. In fairness, this did seem like a reasonable request. A couple of teenagers on scooters were willing to have an argument with him when they too were at the sharp end of his oscillating digit but, post-Brexit, you never know what it might take to instigate deportation so I was happy to comply.

My arrival at around 4.30 pm had coincided with the annual parade of traditional boats organised by Pornic's Yacht Club Royal Old (they really need to sort out the order of those adjectives) that had kicked off only an hour earlier. Every mariner worthy of their (sea) salt seemed to be in attendance and it took some time to escape but mercifully, the pretty corniche road on the southern side of the bay was much easier to navigate. If the prospect of paying €53 to camp overnight had not woken me up, the hustle and bustle of Pornic most certainly had.

Campsite salvation arrived in the form of the comical Camping la Goelette, a further 10km along the coast from Pornic. It was a family-run affair, this particular family consisting of an elderly mother and her two middle-aged sons. They had, it seemed, spent the afternoon checking the quality of the stocks of beer in their caravan which doubled as the reception. It was much more my kind of place and was home to a few travellers in small tents. For a mere €11 I secured a pitch within a 30-second walk of the beach and it was to there that I repaired later in the evening to spend time checking the quality of my own small collection of beers.

Day Twenty-Seven: La Bernerie-En-Retz to Saint-Gilles-Croix-De-Vie (86km)
Friday 29th July

I chatted briefly with one of the two brothers at Camping la Goelette before setting off. He had offered to charge my battery packs overnight and, despite his level of inebriation the previous evening, he had managed to insert the plug successfully into the socket. He was an affable chap but he was a little bemused by what I was attempting to do over the summer. It was the standard reaction from people that I met: a mixture of admiration and pity tinged, perhaps, with a smidgen of envy. I was proud that, at my age, I was still able to take on a cycling challenge of such magnitude but was open to the opinion that others thought it was slightly crazy. Perhaps it was.

This was a flat part of France. Very flat. I was about to set off on a cycle of approaching 90km that would see me ascend a mere 22 metres and descend just 43. I was rarely more than a handful of metres from the level of the sea. I fully expected the signage of the Vélodyssée to be just as good as it had been since leaving Morlaix earlier in the week. And to avoid the end-of-day scramble for a campsite, I had identified three two-star establishments in the area of Saint-Gilles-Croix-De-Vie. I would stop at the first that looked like a decent place to spend the night. It was a day which, thanks to geography, cycling infrastructure and a modicum of forward planning, promised to be trouble-free.

For some reason, the official route of the Vélodyssée moved inland by a couple of kilometres near La Bernerie-En-Retz. I made no attempt whatsoever to find it as there was a perfectly acceptable walkway beside the beach that would take me as far as Les Moutiers-en-Retz. It was at this point that the Vélodyssée lurched back towards the sea and where our paths were destined to meet once again. I sometimes struggled to fathom the logic of cycle route planners and this was a classic example. The path that I adopted by the sea was not one - as far as I could see - along which cycling had been banned. That said, it was not yet 9 am on a cloudy Friday morning and there were few people on my chosen route. Perhaps on a sunny Sunday afternoon, the situation would be very different. Pedestrians can become somewhat disgruntled if they have to share space with a constant stream of bicycles. Perhaps I had managed to fathom the logic of the cycle planners after all.

After breakfast at a café in Les Moutiers-en-Retz, I noticed that a nearby post office was already open for business. The French have adopted an admirable approach of maintaining their post office network rather than shunting the services they offer into a windowless corner of the local branch of WHSmith. Indeed in my experience across western Europe, Britain seems to be unique in its attitude towards downgrading the local post office from being an essential public service to being an inconvenient drain on corporate profits. In most French towns and villages, La Poste (as it is now known) still occupies the same building that once housed the offices of the now defunct Postes, Télégraphes et Téléphones. This is evidenced by the initials PTT still appearing somewhere on the facade of the building. In the UK you are more likely than not to find the words "Post Office" still visible on the façade of a branch of the Slug & Lettuce (in Reading, for example) or Cashconverters (in Halifax, for example). Rare are the towns where the current post office is still in the building constructed for the post office.

I needed to pop into a branch of La Poste because I wanted to check on the delivery status of the malfunctioning GoPro camera. I had sent it back home ten days earlier but it had yet to arrive at its destination. The woman behind the counter was very helpful and she printed off a timeline of the camera's journey north:

19th July - dispatched
20th July - in transit
22nd July - arrived in the UK

That sounded positive. But there was a problem:

26th July - "the package is awaiting payment of taxes due and will be delivered once these have been paid."

Thanks to Brexit and Britain's withdrawal from the single market, the freedom of movement of my defective GoPro camera had been severely curtailed. UK Customs and Excise had impounded it at the border thinking it had been purchased on the continent and was now being imported. It had not and it was not. I later contacted home to discover that a letter had arrived demanding payment of £68.87 "import VAT" and a £12 "clearance fee". You probably did not vote for this nonsense and I certainly did not.

I do make the rather rash assumption that I mix in circles - one of which contains the people reading this - that consist entirely of people who did not vote for the idiocy of Brexit. Cyclists tend to be liberal, enlightened folk. They have embraced two wheels not because they cannot afford to buy a car (most cyclists are also car drivers) but because they recognise that it is a good thing to do: for the individual, for society and indeed for the planet.

A bit like Britain being a member of the EU. My fellow teachers are educated, rational people who are capable of looking at the evidence before them and making intelligent decisions based on the facts. They are adept at dismissing the emotional invective that often spouts from the mouths of certain politicians and certain newspapers. It seems entirely logical to me that every single teacher in the country would have thus voted to remain in the bosom of the European Union as the balance of evidence told us that we should. And then, as mentioned, there is you, the reader of this book. You may be a cyclist yourself or a teacher, or indeed both (in which case I refer you to my previous arguments). Yet it may be that whilst waiting in the queue to post your Christmas cards in WHSmith you happened to glance down into the box of bargain books and noticed this particular tome priced at just £1 (it will, inevitably, happen…). Because you have a passing interest in travel, you thought you would give it a go. You have probably had the opportunity "to pass freely without let or hindrance" across the borders of our continent. You are keen for future generations to benefit from the same freedoms to travel, and - even if you never managed to do so yourself - work and perhaps even live elsewhere in Europe. You, I assume, saw sense and voted to remain.

So in the Venn diagram of cyclists, teachers, travellers (whether they be armchair or not) and Brexit voters, in my mind at least, the circle of those that voted leave does not come close to touching the other three. It is, as I say, a rash, perhaps even dangerous assumption. But it stops my blood from boiling and does, at the very least, prevent me from knocking on your door and asking you to cough up the £80.87 that I had to pay to the UK government to get my defective GoPro camera delivered. As I have already written in this book, and in the slightly mangled words of the Terminator, when it comes to the EU, we will be back.

From outside the post office in Les Moutiers-en-Retz, I set off on my long, flat plod along the Vélodyssée. It was destined to be a gently sapping day of continuous cycling with no opportunities to sit back and allow gravity to take the strain. A day, perhaps, to dream of the distant Alps.

It was not long - just 10 or so kilometres - before I crossed the departmental border from Loire Atlantic into Vendée. Historical Brittany was, finally, behind me and it said its *au revoir* across a vast area of marshland, strewn with salt pits. In contrast, I was welcomed into Vendée by an area of reclaimed farmland before the landscape reverted to that of marsh, an uncountable number of channels and small rectangular lakes again dominating the view. Short portions of the route adopted dusty farm tracks but for most of the time it was on the road. Traffic was, however, light with fellow cyclists and slow-moving agricultural vehicles outnumbering all else by some considerable margin.

The unimaginatively named Port des Champs - Port of the Fields - served up a rainbow of colour in an otherwise subdued pallet of green and brown. The isolated settlement consisted of a long line of industrial buildings beside a channel of water but the tide was out and most of the small pleasure craft sat motionless in the mud. Each of the buildings was painted in alternate bright colours: orange, yellow, turquoise, blue... Most of them housed businesses dedicated to the cultivation of the oyster. I guessed that beneath the surface of many of the lakes I had been passing, salty Vendée Atlantique oysters were slowly growing fat in their shells. Although a traditional local industry since the 18th century, mass cultivation developed rapidly in the post-war era and farms in the Vendée *département* now produce around 8,000 tons of oysters each year. That is a lot of raw flesh to slurp from its shell.

South of La Barre-de-Monts there was an abrupt change in the landscape as I entered the Forêt Domaniale des Pays de Monts. A treeless landscape of marshland and small lakes had been my view for much of the morning: a landscape of nothing but trees would now be my view for almost all of the afternoon. The *forêt domaniale* was very much a littoral affair and stretched some 25km along the coast but was rarely wider than a couple of kilometres. The route of the Vélodyssée followed a path along the eastern edge of the forest but never did I feel that I was anywhere other than in the heart of a vast wilderness. Pine trees dominated yet, on an increasingly hot afternoon with the clouds dissolving quickly into the vastness of the sky, they offered only sporadic protection from the sun. This was a very different experience from cycling along the cool, leafy avenues of the *voies vertes* in northern France.

Many of the day's 22 metres of ascent and 43 metres of descent were to be encountered during the next 20km of cycling as the forest blanketed the undulating dunes. Although a pleasant landscape through which to cycle, it lacked visual variety. I cannot deny that I looked forward to arriving in the concrete jungle of Saint-Jean-de-Monts for no other reason than because it would give me something else to look at other than pine trees and dunes. On that score, it succeeded. When the tourist hotspot loomed into view after a short shimmy back to the coast, it gave me what I had been craving: concrete and a long sandy beach. Cyclists had been well catered for with an uninterrupted smooth cycle lane guiding me and my fellow pedallers - both on bikes and in the family-sized karts I had first encountered in Belgian - along the several kilometres of seafront. The enormous circle of a big wheel gave me something to aim at for the first half of my journey through the urban world before the appearance of more trees in the distance, beckoning me back to the forest.

South of Saint-Jean-de-Monts the *forêt domaniale* was a much more hit-and-miss affair. On this occasion, the Vélodyssée shadowed a main road for much of the time. The wilderness was still there to my right but to my left was a constant stream of vehicles. Beyond them the not-unpleasant sprawl of tourism: holiday homes, campsites, shops... At least this time I had a choice when it came to the view: trees and dunes and one side, cars and concrete on the other.

The bit of Saint-Jean-de-Monts through which I had cycled had been cut off from the centre of Saint-Jean-de-Monts by a continuing narrow band of the *forêt domaniale*. The coastal suburbs of the town had been squashed in between the sea and the trees. That was not the case with Saint-Hilaire-de-Riez - my hoped-for destination - where the town extended as far as the rocky outcrops of land that had now replaced most of the sandy beach. Indeed at this point of the coast, the land protruded noticeably into the sea to accommodate the western portion of the town. Geologically speaking, that was, of course, nonsense. The town had simply been built upon solid rock which had provided more effective resistance against the encroaching Atlantic over the millennia compared to the much less solid dunes to the north and south. It was not a case of the land moving west but the Atlantic moving east whenever it was given the opportunity.

I stuck loyally to the coastal road that overlooked the rocks and the sea. It could now not only be seen but also heard as it crashed against the shore beside me. My mind, however, was focused on locating the first of the three campsites that I had identified in the list of possibles. Camping La Padrelle was only 100 metres from the shore but it was a world away from what I was searching for. Although only a small site, it did not appear to possess so much as a blade of grass, not from what I could see from the entrance. Curiously there was an *Accueil Vélo* sign indicating that cyclists were welcome but I did wonder where they would erect their tents. With a seven-storey building blocking the view of any potential sunset, I quickly decided that this was not the place for me and cycled on.

The second of my three identified sites proved to be much more welcoming. I had to accept that along certain sections of my Grand Tour, I would be unlikely to find a quiet country campsite. The kind of place where tents outnumbered camper vans and caravans, where a large open space of land had been made available for independent travellers on foot or on a bike and where traditional folk songs were sung long into the night around a campfire.[35] I was now in the middle of one of those areas and my expectations were somewhat lower than they had been along the Véloscénie for example. Bearing this in mind, a narrow patch of water-starved grass surrounded by campervans, caravans and mobile homes was the best for which I could hope. For just €10, Camping Le Petit Pavillon was not a bad place to spend the night. Following a trip to the nearby Aldi to stock up on essentials I settled in for an evening of cheap German non-branded food and energy theft. This came courtesy of an electricity post that I could just about reach by sticking my hand through a fence. It belonged to the adjacent pitch where the long-term residents were not at home. Come the morning I was fully recharged in more ways than one.

---

[35] To be honest, I have yet to find a campsite where such singing does take place. If I did I would probably be the first to make a complaint about all the racket if it continued past 10 pm...

Day Twenty-Eight: Saint-Gilles-Croix-De-Vie to La Rochelle (140km)
Saturday 30th July

Estimating distances was always a challenge. There were various methods that I could choose to adopt and all had their failings. Perhaps the most accurate estimation of how many kilometres I needed to cycle on any particular day was the website of the route I was following. According to the Vélodyssée website, the route from Saint-Gilles-Croix-de-Vie to La Rochelle consisted of four identifiable stages that, in total, would require me to cycle a smidgen under 153km. That, however, assumed I was starting in the centre of Saint-Gilles-Croix-de-Vie (I was not: I was a few kilometres south) and that I would be loyal to the cycle route. From time to time, this was not the case as I would regularly decide to take a shortcut. Some of these were of little consequence (occasionally they turned out to be anything but shortcuts), but some were, and they reduced the cycle by a considerable distance. Official cycle route signage showing distances was also useful but suffered from the same pitfalls, but at least it was updated throughout the day.

Then there was Google Maps. Google may have transformed our lives in many ways over recent decades but the cycling option on Google Maps is very much a work-in-progress. It takes a rather idiosyncratic approach to route finding, sometimes choosing to follow cycle routes, sometimes roads (when perfectly good cycle routes are also available) and sometimes countryside tracks that are all but impossible to follow with a loaded touring bike. If anyone from Google is reading, the algorithm requires some serious work. From my campsite near Saint-Gilles-Croix-de-Vie to La Rochelle, Google estimated 121km.

Point-to-point as-the-crow-flies distances were at least 100% accurate and as long as they were considered alongside all the obvious caveats, provided the absolute minimum distance that would, in theory, have to be cycled. From my campsite to La Rochelle the straight-line distance was 80km. Admittedly, this would necessitate some open-water swimming.

The final way in which distances could be estimated was by speaking to somebody. Rarely were people able to give accurate figures, indeed more often than not no mention would be made of a number. Yet they were still of use. A typical conversation would go as follows:

"Where are you cycling?"

"Today I'm hoping to get as far as La Rochelle."

The discussion would then head in one of two directions. Either:

"OK. Have a good trip!"

Or:

"*Oh là là!* [or the equivalent expression in the local language]. La Rochelle? Today? On a bike? Good luck!"

These conversations were more useful than you might think, especially if the other person was a cyclist themself or at least looked fit enough to be cycling long distances. They could give hints as to obstacles that I might have inadvertently missed. A chronically undulating terrain, for example, although along the flat west coast of France, this did seem unlikely. It could, however, be a bridge from which cyclists had been banned but which Google had never checked out, or perhaps a deviation to the cycle route that had not been reflected either on the official cycle route website or on the signage.

The best algorithm of course is the one that we can all follow by putting the wobbly mass between our ears to work. Although I had yet to speak to anyone about cycling as far as La Rochelle, I did have the other information to work with and it told me that it would be a long day of cycling. Certainly a lot more than 80km but probably not quite 153. More than the 121 estimated by Google so somewhere in the region of 130-140km. Irrespective, it promised to be the longest day so far of the cycle. Before today I had only broken the 100km barrier once, on the journey into central Paris and even then by just 1km. It might even turn out to be the longest cycle of the entire Grand Tour.

The incentive was arriving at La Rochelle itself. I had cycled to the harbour city on my trip from Spain to Norway several years previously. On that occasion, it was a journey from the south, over two days from Royan on the northern bank of the Gironde Estuary via an overnight stop in Rochefort. This was one section of this year's trip where I had always planned on taking a train so as not to repeat that previous cycle, albeit in reverse. Cycling as far as la Rochelle today would mean that by lunchtime tomorrow - the start of week five of the journey - I would have completed my cycle along the Vélodyssée. It would also mean that I would be embarking upon the next section of my route, the Canal Des 2 Mers à Vélo[36] to Sète on the Mediterranean coast. The southernmost point of my loop around Europe - Sète - was now tantalisingly close. I might even be there by the end of the first week in August. But would that leave me enough time - just four weeks - to get back to Rotterdam by September 3rd? Perhaps not a question to worry about today, especially with at least 130km ahead of me on the west coast of France.

---

[36] The Canal of the Two Seas (Atlantic and Mediterranean) Cycle Route

In some respects, day 28 would be similar to day 27: a mixture of cycling across seemingly vast lake-strewn agricultural plains, beside forests and through urban environments. In other ways it was to be distinct: on-road sections, inland cycling - 5,6,7km from the coast - and even, in the final 30km, a return to cycling beside a canal. Yet in one way the day was very distinct and for this reason alone will last long in the memory: the first hour in the saddle south of Saint-Gilles-Croix-de-Vie. It was stunning.

When topography does you no favours - there were no mountains to feast upon in this part of France - the other aspects of geography need to put in extra effort if they are to impress. On the morning of July 30th, they were sweating their assets hard. Within a matter of minutes of leaving the campsite at 7.30, I was on a dusty path, pine trees to my right and a meadow awaiting its grazing horses to my left. In the distance a few trees softened the line between land and sky and beyond them, across the vastness of space (and a just little bit of time), the yellow globe of the sun had started to glide effortlessly across the sky. Its golden influence washed across the field, its countless rays crashing and splintering as they came into contact with the cushion of mist on the ground. Above everything and beyond a transition from orange to yellow to white was a developing blue sky, unblemished by even the bravest of clouds. It was a scene that would have had J.M.W. Turner erecting his easel and mixing his paints without a moment of hesitation. Yellow ochre, raw sienna, burnt sienna, olive green, cobalt blue… This was a scene to exhaust the palette. And aside from an invisible Joseph and me, there was not another soul to witness the early morning spectacle. Beautiful.

Around 5km into the ride, the cycle path joined the corniche road. Here I was seemingly transported 9,000km west to a scaled-down California where the waves were lapping against the rocky shore and early morning fishermen were pushing their tiny boats through the shallows towards more lucrative waters further out to sea. To my right, the narrow beach was still in shade, the sun having not yet risen above the roofs of the houses on the other side of the deserted road. The soundscape consisted delightfully and exclusively of the waves and nothing more. At times it felt as though my main obstacle would not be the number of kilometres I had to cycle but my willingness to slow down, stop and take in the views.

A few minutes before 10 am I was standing on the seafront in Les Sables-d'Olonne, another of the west coast's tourist hotspots consuming a late breakfast of coffee and *croissants*. The *boulangerie* beside the Église Notre-Dame-de-Bon-Port had been doing a roaring trade feeding locals and visitors alike and the queue had been significant but I had been happy to wait after having travelled over 30km on an empty stomach. It being the only *boulangerie* that I had passed in well over two hours I had been a ravenously captive customer.

I took the opportunity of my mid-morning pause in Les Sables-d'Olonne to do a modicum of short-term planning. I knew that the best place for me to stay in La Rochelle would be the *camping municipal*, just a short distance from the city centre. I also knew that it would be busy so I attempted to give them a call. No answer. I had more success with the train that I wanted to catch from La Rochelle to Royan although I was required to book onto a much earlier departure than I had anticipated. It was scheduled to leave at 7.53 the following morning and required a journey north to Niort where I would need to change train before descending back to the coast at Royan. Had I chosen to cycle along the Vélodyssée it would have been 140km. On the train perhaps 170km. Crucially, however, had I chosen to cycle using Google's directions it would have only been around 80km. This meant that I was still sticking to my no-train-more-than-100km rule, even if the train journey was nearer 200 than 100km. By the time I wrote the book, I reflected, I would have come up with solid reasoning to argue my case. Surely I could not be held responsible for there being no direct train along the coast from La Rochelle to Royan. Google's distance it was.

As the day progressed, marshland was an increasingly common feature of the route, as were, ironically, dry, dusty fields. The contrast between the two was stark. The wetlands to the north of Jard-sur-Mer were a pleasing hotchpotch of artificially cut, elongated lakes with erratic rounded corners that cut into the land almost as if they had been created by the Aztecs. *Was there a secret message when viewed from above?* Perhaps momentarily mesmerised by these patterns in the land, I took a wrong turn, only realising my error after several hundred metres. The extra kilometre cycled to get me back on the correct path was, I reasoned, small fry in a day that was now heading towards three figures. In many places, the track had been replaced by a supported wooden walkway above the green, soggy land. This made for a rickety ride on the bike but was fun while it lasted.

At Tranche-sur-Mer, conscious of the competition that was raging between the distance still to cycle and the time available in which to do it, I decided to take a shortcut along a main road. For around 15km I whizzed along the D46 and then the D746. It did the trick and with a speed approaching - and occasionally exceeding - 25km/h it certainly boosted my chances of arriving in good time in La Rochelle.

This had become an increasing concern as I had now managed to contact the campsite. The receptionist had been polite in the extreme but she explained that it was not possible to reserve a space. When I asked if she expected the site to be full by the time I got there she said she had no idea.

She was not even able to tell me what the campsite did when a lone cyclist arrived after the campsite had hung out the "*complet* / full" sign. It was often the case that full did not really mean full if you were travelling on a bike. The campsite management would try and squeeze you in in the knowledge that alternative options, especially late in the day, were not viable ones for people travelling under their own steam. (That said, if the worst came to the worst, La Rochelle was not lacking when it came to hotels.) My shortcut might have only sliced 5km from the overall distance but if it meant I arrived in time to secure a pitch on the site, so be it.

Further south, once I had rejoined the official route of the Vélodyssée, the landscape became much less welcoming. The path now followed dusty, at times rocky, farm tracks. The land was parched, rain not having fallen for many, many weeks. The excessively high temperatures that I had been forced to endure in Normandy may have abated but the more urgent problem in much of France was the continuing drought. A sign that I passed announcing "*sécheresse*"[37] confirmed what was evident from looking across the fields that surrounded me. It was much more reminiscent of southern Spain than western France and a chronic problem that I was to encounter over and over again as I continued my cycle through the southern and then eastern regions of the country.

Quite why the small town of Marans once needed not one but two canals to link it to ports on the coast remained a mystery at the time.[38] However, both the Canal Maritime de Marans à la Mer and the Canal de Marans à La Rochelle provided the cycle planners with a choice of towpaths along which to place their cycle route. They had gone with the latter.

The start of the first of the two canals also marked the departmental border between Vendée and Charente-Maritime. This was evidenced by a change in the cycling signage. Throughout my cycle in Vendée, the signs had adopted a slightly retro look. They were usually stuck on wooden posts and had a wooden frame whereas in Charente-Maritime the signs appeared to be brand new. I put this down to the former *département* being an enthusiastic early promoter of the Vélodyssée and the latter *département*

---

[37] Drought

[38] A mystery now solved. The canal from Marans to La Rochelle was once part of an ambitious Napoleonic project to connect La Rochelle with... Paris! The capital is 400km from La Rochelle, Marans just 20 and, not altogether unsurprisingly, it was the only section of the grandiose plan to ever see the light of day. That said, it took 70 years to build what they did build and it opened to traffic in 1884. Alas in 1868 a railway line had already opened linking Marans and La Rochelle and it proved a far more efficient method of transporting grain to the coast. The canal had been doomed even before the first boats sailed along it.

coming a little late to the party. This was also evidenced by the harsh, unforgiving and bumpy paths upon which most of the final 30km of the route were cycled. Perhaps someone in the active travel office of the Charente-Maritime Council needed to shift a bit of the budget away from nice signs in the direction of better surfaces. It was an uncomfortable, energy-sapping conclusion to the cycling day.

This final section of my journey - from Marans to La Rochelle - was also the start of La Vélo Francette, a long-distance cycling route that linked the Atlantic with Caen and the northern coast. I cycled the first third of this route back in 2015 as far as Saumur in the Loire Valley (before continuing east along the river and ultimately in the direction of Nordkapp). It is interesting to read the comments that I made about the first section of the route from La Rochelle in the book, Spain to Norway:

> "Much of the cycling was along the towpaths of canals and rough tracks, as directed by the signs of La Vélo Francette. It made for a bumpy but traffic-free ride and the advantages of the latter more than compensated for the inconveniences of the former."

Cleary as my body ages I am becoming much less willing to put up with dodgy surfaces upon which to cycle. Or perhaps it was simply a reflection of my cycle along the canal in 2015 being at the start of a day of cycling 85km and not at the very end of a day that was now approaching 140.

The odometer registered the final of those 140 kilometres as I approached the entrance to Camping Municipal Le Soleil in La Rochelle. It was a busy place but, after waiting in the queue for a few minutes, there was good news. For a very modest €6.60 I could squeeze myself into the area set aside for those travelling with a bicycle. There were plenty of us, and more would arrive throughout the evening until the *"complet / full"* sign was indeed displayed outside the entrance. The effort had been worth it. My chances of starting the cycle along the Canal Des 2 Mers à Vélo at some point the following day were all but guaranteed and I might even be in Bordeaux by early the following week. Crucially the chances of me getting to Rotterdam were still within the realms of the possible. If, that is, things continued to go to plan.

PART SIX:

Le Canal Des 2 Mers À Vélo

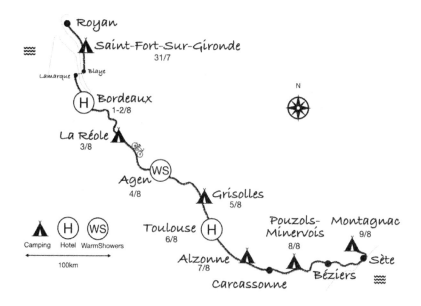

Day Twenty-Nine: La Rochelle to Saint-Fort-Sur-Gironde (Train + 39km) Sunday 31st July

Had buying a ticket for the 7.53 train been such a great idea? It did not seem that way when I finally started to gather together my things and pack up the tent at 6.20 am. 90 minutes to be off the site and standing on the platform waiting for the train. My night of sleep had been anything but. I may have snatched a few minutes here and there but the noise emanating from the nearby town centre - including, at one point, a firework display - as well as the campsite itself, kept my mind alert and slumber at bay. How can the human body not recognise that I had endured a physically draining day of cycling 140km to travel as far as La Rochelle and not shut down all but essential organs overnight as I lay in the tent? It had not helped that, in an area crowded with tents, the young couple next to me had been making good use of their own essential organs at 2 am. And again at 4.

The female half of the romantic coupling was the first person I spoke to - briefly with a croaky "*bonjour*" on my part - as she appeared from her love nest at exactly the same time that I ventured out into the open. She gave no hint of caring that the man in front of her - and presumably most of the other campers in the sea of small tents strewn across the ground nearby - had been privy to her nocturnal lovemaking. It was an admirable level of chutzpah.

I managed to pack in record-breaking time and as I wheeled Wanda in the direction of the gate it was not yet 6.45 am. Others were now beginning to emerge from their tents including an elderly German cyclist who had, for some bizarre reason, pinched my arm the previous evening to the extent that I considered it a minor assault. We had been in conversation with a younger English chap called Chris and the German man was, I think, trying to make a point about our respective ages but why this required him to almost draw blood I was not quite sure. I kept my distance lest he decide that this morning I deserved a punch in the face.

Chris was also out of his tent and we spent a few minutes rounding off the conversation we had started earlier. He had been working as an insurance underwriter in London but relocated back to his home city of Salisbury during the lockdowns. Ditching his job in finance for work with a local wildlife sanctuary, he was en route to his sister's wedding in northern Spain. He was cycling an interesting bike manufactured by an Icelandic company called Lauf. It sported a distinctive front wheel suspension system, electronic gear shifters and a bottle opener attached to the frame.[39] I took note of all three innovations, especially the third.

I had mentioned the issues with wildfires further south along the Vélodyssée and overnight he had done some research:

"You're right. There's a 20km section that's closed south of the Gironde. The roads are still open but they don't advise you to use them," he explained before adding, "but hopefully I'll be fine."

From my journey along the Vélodyssée in 2015 when I had cycled from the Spanish coast to La Rochelle, I knew that almost all of the route as far as the Gironde Estuary was forest. During a period of high temperatures and drought, it was of little surprise that the fires of summer 2022 had severely curtailed the plans of many cyclists. It would not be until the summer of 2023 that the route was repaired and fully reopened. I can only hope that Chris did indeed make it to Spain in time for his sister's wedding without singeing too much of his hair.

I was now getting used to taking my bike on the excellent TER trains. Those from La Rochelle to Niort and then Niort to Royan were identical in design to almost all the previous ones. With clearly marked carriages, step-free access from the platform, wide doors and ample bike storage space it was almost as if the train designer had given a second thought to how to make the trains suitable for use by cyclists. Not something that you could say very often, if at all, back home in the UK. Although there were hooks near the ceiling where bicycles could be hung, such was the amount of space available that these seemed to be entirely superfluous. There had been no need - or indeed instruction - to use them on any of the previous journeys. Until now.

"*Il faut accrocher vos vélos,*" ordered the guard on the first train from La Rochelle.

I did not feel as though I should start an argument. Françoise, however, was not so reluctant. She was a woman in her 60s who had travelled widely on her bike over the previous 25 years: Canada, Russia and around the Baltic as well as extensively elsewhere in Europe. She was heading north to guide a "novice friend from Paris" along the Loire à Vélo cycle route and was then planning to travel with her bicycle to meet her daughter near Lake Garda in Italy via a cycle over the Alps! She was a fascinating person to

---

[39] According to the Lauf Bicycles website, the inspiration for the unique fork design of their bikes came from "durable high-performance prosthetics" and that "the Lauf fork is a revolutionary twist on the well-known and proven 'leaf spring suspension' concept, combined with today's high-performance composite materials." The Icelandic word for leaf is *lauf*.

spend time with: strong, determined, independent and she was not going to let anything stand in her way, least of all an SNCF train conductor.

"It's ridiculous," she retorted in French upon being instructed to hang up her bike. "The train is empty. It's 8 o'clock on a Sunday morning. There are only two bicycles on the train."

She had, however, met her match in the smartly dressed train company jobsworth. He did not try to justify his instruction: he just repeated it.

"*Il faut accrocher votre vélo, madame.*"

At this point, the German cyclist from the campsite in La Rochelle might have been rolling up his sleeves readying himself for a fistfight. Françoise was more vocal in her contempt. True to my national stereotype I stood silently, tutted internally and complied, as did Françoise, eventually and under protest. At least we had bonded over a common enemy and we continued our enjoyable cycling-themed chat as far as Niort where we went our separate ways on different trains.

I eventually arrived in Royan at around 11 am having travelled south by only 60km but considerably further on the trains. Five of my ten train journeys remained. However, I did not plan on using any more of them during my cycle along the Canal des 2 Mers à Vélo cycle route. Indeed this next section of my Grand Tour would be the first that I planned to cycle in its entirety, from Royan in the west to Sète in the south. All of the routes that I had so far followed had been cycled partially (the Vélomaritime and Avenue Verte) or with at least one train taking the strain (the Véloscénie) or indeed both (the Vélodyssée).

The Canal des 2 Mers à Vélo initially followed the northern bank of the Gironde Estuary before crossing to the south at Blaye via a short ferry ride. After passing through the centre of Bordeaux, the route moved away from the River Garonne until it arrived at La Réole where it began to follow the Canal de la Garonne to Toulouse. South of *la ville rose* (so named for the pinkish colour of its buildings) the route adopted the towpath of the famous Canal du Midi. Travelling on a gently increasing easterly arc via the walled city of Carcassonne and then Béziers, its finishing point was beside the sea in Sète. If that was not a European cycling journey to whet the appetite for slow travel, nothing was.

I had never previously visited Toulouse but had heard much about its beauty and student-infused atmosphere, as well as the glory of the two canals. As I started pedalling away from the modern train station in Royan, I felt genuinely excited about the prospect of discovering pastures new. The potential achievement of cycling from the Atlantic to the Mediterranean would be the cherry on the cake.

Royan had done a good job of dressing up its otherwise bland concrete seafront for the summer months.[40] Alternate yellow and blue parasols adorned the beach and a long row of blue and white striped tents had been erected for those wishing to shelter from the sun. Or indeed the wind, which was blowing enthusiastically from the west. I soon found the first signs for the Canal des 2 Mers à Vélo and began to follow them. Although my initial ambition for this first day of cycling the route was to get as far as the ferry at Blaye - a rather over-ambitious 100km from Royan - I was soon backtracking on my promise. It was nearly midday before I really got going and I was suffering heavily from the combined effects of cycling 140km the previous day and lack of sleep the previous night. Getting as far as the ferry was never going to happen. I identified a campsite in a small village called Port Maubert, a much more reasonable 40km from Royan, and aimed for that instead. It was a good call allowing me to take my time, soak in the sights and sounds of the estuary and, if it were indeed possible, start my physical recovery whilst continuing to ride the bike slowly.

Cycling beside the Gironde Estuary was akin to travelling through an ever-changing tapestry of coastal life. The only constants were the wide expanse of muddy brown water to my right and the unblemished sky above my head. There were more *cabanes de pêcheurs* at the end of rickety wooden piers but also, in Meschers-sur-Gironde, clinging to the foot of the cliffs. Above the huts, caves had been cut into the white rock - by both nature and by man - and the scene was reminiscent of idyllic Greek islands. Aside, that is, from the colour of the sea which was as murky as anything to be found in more northerly climes. There was also a string of pretty coastal villages. The stand-out example was at Talmont-sur-Gironde where the buildings poked out into the estuary, sealed off from the land and sea by a protective fortified wall. And then, as I edged nearer to my destination, the first vineyards of the great wine region of Bordeaux and the port of Mortagne-sur-Gironde, home to dozens of modest yachts, masts twitching as their hulls bobbed on the water.

The final few kilometres of the ride were somewhat less spectacular but pretty nevertheless through parched fields of sunflowers and past occasional clusters of brown cattle. I arrived at Port Maubert near Saint-Fort-sur-Gironde in the mid-afternoon, exhausted, not by the cycle from Royan but from the cycle to La Rochelle on the previous day. It was time for a late afternoon off the bike and, after erecting the tent under some

---

[40] For the full story of the destruction of Royan during the Second World War and its subsequent rebuilding, see pages 92-94 of my previous book, *Spain to Norway on a Bike Called Reggie* (Summersdale, 2017).

handily located trees at the local campsite, I lay back on the grass and snoozed. It was a world away from the people, fireworks and rampant sex of the previous night. But the night was yet young.

Day Thirty: Saint-Fort-Sur-Gironde to Bordeaux (44km + Ferry + 42km) Monday 1st August

I thoroughly enjoy long, strenuous climbs on the bike, but they do need to be anticipated. The brain requires time to send a "brace yourself" message to the body allowing the heart, lungs and legs to start preparing themselves, imperceptibly, for what is ahead. We are not talking seconds or even minutes. These are hours, days, and perhaps even weeks of preparation. Such logic may not stand up to any kind of psychological reasoning but it is how I function. After four weeks in the saddle, I was now looking forward to the climbs of the Alps later in the month and my brain was slowly preparing the body for what was to come. On the flip side, I dislike short, sharp climbs that are unanticipated. I dislike them intensely. No, I hate them. That is not a word I use lightly. They are top of the list to be deposited in my cycling Room 101.

Alas, not one but two short, sharp, unanticipated climbs confronted me shortly after leaving Camping Port Maubert, the first from sea level to 50 metres, the second from sea level to 75 metres, both within just a few kilometres of each other. It was a cycling hell, albeit one surrounded by magical morning mists and, as I climbed, pleasingly regimented lines of vines, fat black grapes hanging from their branches. At least I had found a very pretty version of the underworld. The whole experience was made doubly exasperating as I had not reached such dizzying altitudes since the hills of Brittany and my climbing muscles seemed to be somewhat diminished. Crawling into the village of Saint-Thomas-de-Conac, I hoped to find breakfast in a *boulangerie*, but Beelzebub himself had chosen to rub salt into my wounds by bringing me to this place of torture… on a Monday. Everything was, of course, closed.

Soon, however, things were looking up significantly and the remainder of my journey - over 70 of the 80 kilometres that I would cycle - was to become one of the most enjoyable rides of the entire jaunt around Europe. It had almost everything that you might want from an excellent cycle touring day. There was ravishing scenery, variety, a favourable wind, vineyards, good signage, nice encounters along the way, quality surfaces and a cooling end-of-day beer in a favourite French city. There was even a nice ferry to break the cycle into two almost identical halves and, perhaps top of the list of delights, a launderette. You will only appreciate that reference if you have ever spent consecutive days on a bike and in a tent. I had just completed seven in a row.

The plan was to get to Bordeaux by the end of the day. I would continue to follow the route of the Canal des 2 Mers à Vélo on either side of the Gironde Estuary with the ferry taking me south at the town of Blaye. Roughly halfway to the ferry, I would also enter the *département* of Gironde. It would remain my home for at least the next three days as I intended to take a day off cycling to reacquaint myself with the eponymous city of wine.

It was the Romans who first grew vines in the region of Bordeaux on any great scale, aided by the discovery of a grape variety - Biturica - that could survive the relatively harsh winters. After the fall of the Roman Empire, viticulture passed into the hands of God. Well, kind of. The monks who looked after the land around churches and abbeys ensured the survival of the grapes. However, it was in 1152 with the marriage of Eleanor of Aquitaine to the future King of England, Henry Plantagenet, when the long-term future of Bordeaux wines was secured. The union allowed Bordeaux to establish a monopoly in selling wine to Britain. Although the monopoly may be long gone, the merchants of Bordeaux have continued to excel in flogging wine to the British - and everyone else - ever since. Even when the English and French were at each other's throats, the lure of good wine didn't prevent the customers from coming back.

According to Decanter magazine, notwithstanding recent falls in the *number* of bottles sent to the UK, the *value* of the wine sold "leapt by 31% in value to £230m [in 2021]". The country maintains its position as the third largest importer of Bordeaux wines after China and the USA. That said, home consumption of Bordeaux wine remains dominant with over half of the 559 million bottles produced in 2021 heading down the throats of the French. Or indeed foreign visitors such as me. I have always had a suspicion that the *Bordelais* keep the reasonably priced good stuff for themselves or their fellow countrymen. It would have been churlish of me not to do a little research whilst I was there and, from what I remember, my theory was not proven wrong. I think.

My cycle would see me carve a route through the heart of the wine region, Blaye & Bourg on the northern side of the Gironde before the famed vineyards of Médoc on the south. Even for non-lovers of wine, the lines of vibrant green vines that rolled across the contours of the gentle inclines of the land made for a magnificent, quintessentially French landscape through which to travel. Better still if - as they often were - the fields adjoined one of the many *châteaux* under which the wine was sitting patiently in vats, barrels and bottles awaiting its brief moment of fame as it passed from the bottle to the glass to the mouth and finally to the stomach.

By late morning I had arrived at the ramp to the ferry. It was not much more than that although the ferry itself was sizeable. It plied its trade throughout the day across the muddy brown waters of the Gironde. There was never any risk of missing it, just the minor inconvenience of being forced to wait an hour or so for the boat to return if my arrival had happened not to synchronise with the timetable. As things were, it did so it was straight on board for the 30-minute crossing. For €3.50 I could sit back and let others do the hard work, an enforced but welcome opportunity to spend some time watching the world float by alongside the scores of other passengers in their cars, motorhomes and motorbikes. I was, as far as I could see, the only passenger to be travelling by bicycle.

When I rejoined the cycle route after disembarking from the ferry, a sign beside the ramp informed me that I needed to cycle another 49km to get to Bordeaux. This matched the official distance on the Canal des 2 Mers à Vélo website but it was not long before I had shaved off several kilometres by cycling along a main, yet quiet road. The official cycle route adopted a curious course heading west by a couple of kilometres then south before returning east by another couple of kilometres. Aside from cutting down on the cycling, my one-kilometre shortcut took me via a much-needed supermarket that had the gall to open on a Monday and I duly stocked up for the afternoon. But it played on my mind that I might have missed something important, something that merited such a westward lurch. Thereafter I remained as loyal as I could to the cycle route lest I continue to feel further pangs of non-compliant cyclist anxiety.

Then again, perhaps I had made the right call. A railway line linked Bordeaux to La Pointe de Grave. It was from there where, in 2015 whilst cycling along the Vélodyssée, I had taken the ferry to Royan. The railway line cut across my 2022 cycle route several times but I had managed to avoid two of these crossings thanks to my shortcut. To the west of the town of Margaux, there was no escape. When I arrived, the level crossing barrier was down and the lights were flashing. On such a hot, sunny day that would not be a problem. Any opportunity to pause the cycling was not to be turned down. Here I had no choice and I was happy to wait.

Several minutes passed. A queue had now developed on both sides of the railway. The road was still blocked, and the warning lights continued to flash. A small car could have easily squeezed around the barrier on each side as it only stretched across one half of the road. Ten minutes… Fifteen minutes… *Would anyone risk it?* Some of the motorists were clearly considering their options having exited their cars and walked towards the barrier to peer down the one-track railway. There was no train to be seen. The flashing continued. The crossing remained closed. Of everyone in attendance, I was probably in the best position to feature on the evening news programmes by easily pushing Wanda across the track and promptly getting run over by a train. I did not risk it.

Anyway, I was too mesmerised by the car that was stationary at the front of the ever-lengthening queue on the other side of the track. A silver Citroën DS 21, circa 1970. I was momentarily transported to Paris in the 1960s and President Charles de Gaulle...

Not that I was ever there myself. But I had seen the film version of Frederick Forsyth's thriller *The Day of the Jackal* and had vivid memories of a fictional de Gaulle arriving in Paris for the 14th of July celebrations in his favourite car: a Citroën DS. In the film, he survives an assassination attempt, not because of the car but because Edward Fox chooses the wrong moment to fire his bullet, seconds before being killed in a volley of machine gun fire. The real de Gaulle, however, had good reason to rate the DS as it was instrumental in saving his life.

In 1962, as he was being driven to the airport, two cars approached the presidential motorcade and opened fire. The gunmen had not counted on the design of the car or the skill of the driver. The car was, to say the least, revolutionary: hyper-distinctive streamlined design, front-wheel drive, comfortable interior... and an iconic hydropneumatic self-levelling suspension system that made use of pressurised oil and gas on each wheel. This resulted in a very smooth ride indeed, akin to "riding on a magic carpet". Back in Paris en route to the airport, this was rather handy when the would-be assassins' bullets punctured all four of the Citroën's tyres. Although it entered into a skid, the chauffeur was able to regain control and keep driving as the suspension system kept the car level despite it having no functioning tyres. The story of de Gaulle's foiled assassination was the inspiration for Frederick Forsyth's book and the subsequent film.

The Citroën DS remains just as much an icon of 1960s France as Brigitte Bardot, Jean-Paul Belmondo or the student protests of May 1968. I am no petrol head but even I can recognise a good-looking car when I see one and the Citroën DS is certainly that. It comes as no surprise to discover that in 1999 it was placed third in a competition to recognise the Car of the Century, pipped at the post by the Model T Ford and the Austin Mini.

I was suddenly snapped out of my Citroën-induced coma of admiration by a slow whoosh of sound and metal. The train had finally arrived - one of the familiar TERs no less - and the barriers lifted. My twenty-minute wait was at an end.

Throughout the early afternoon, the environment was increasingly urban as Bordeaux approached. Planes flew above my head and a high-quality segregated cycle path next to a busy arterial road guided me through the urban sprawl. In Blanquefort, at least 400km from my interim destination on the Mediterranean coast I smiled when I passed a cycling sign for Sète. I was not lost, not yet anyway. Then, after 80km of cycling, I took a right turn and found myself cycling beside the Garonne River: I had arrived in Bordeaux.

Day Thirty-One: Bordeaux
Tuesday 2nd August

I had been looking forward to returning to Bordeaux for a long time. I had previously visited the city in August 2003, 19 years earlier, and it was a visit that had stuck in my memory. Not because of the city's architecture, history, food or wine (although all were reasons in themselves for recommending the place). Its roadworks. Yes, roadworks. Let me explain...

In June 1995, Alain Juppé was voted in as the mayor of Bordeaux. Only a month earlier he had been appointed as the Prime Minister of France by the newly elected French President, Jacques Chirac. You would think he would have been so busy in Paris that keeping an eye on what was going on in Bordeaux would have been something of a challenge. Not for Alain. He was very keen to sort out the city's transport problems and by the middle of the year 2000, spades and diggers were poised to start construction of a tramway system consisting of three lines that passed straight through the city centre. Around 25km of tramway and 50 new stations would need to be constructed.

Now if this were a city in the UK, things, I suspect, would be slightly different. In Nottingham, for example, it took over 15 years to build a tramway system of roughly the same size as that of Bordeaux's phase one. Construction of a more modest tramway system in Edinburgh started in 2008 and did not finish until 2023.

Back in Bordeaux, Alain Juppé decided that rather than string out the construction work over many years, it would be better for his city to suffer a short, sharp construction shock. Most of phase one of the tramway system was up and running by the middle of 2004, just four years after the work had started. In subsequent years, the network has continued to grow and there are now around 80km of track. An additional fourth line has been constructed, but most of this later work has been outside the centre of the city. When I arrived in the summer of 2003 it seemed that almost every main road (and a good number of the minor ones) was being dug up. The photographs that I took at the time reveal street after street of holes in the ground, fences, cranes, lorries and piles of construction materials. It was a genuinely impressive sight but beyond all the work I could see just how handsome the city was. One day, I thought, I will return.

Nearly twenty years later I was back. Arriving beside the River Garonne the previous evening it had been immediately obvious that the frenzy of work in the first few years of the 21st century had not been in vain. A wide esplanade which had previously been the fiefdom of the car had been transformed into gardens, fountains, walkways and, much to my delight, a long, wide cycleway. It escorted me beside the river and into the imposing expanse of the Place de la Bourse. When I was here in 2003 I was not even allowed to step foot in the square as it had been entirely fenced off and gaping holes had been dug deep into the ground. On this occasion, once I had negotiated the relatively narrow width of the road and tramway I was able to cycle freely, taking in the magnificence of the 18th-century architecture surrounding me. I circumnavigated the flamboyant fountain with its revealing Three Graces extolling mirth, elegance and beauty with not a hint of modesty. With a smile on my face, the virtues of the three young women seemed an apt metaphor for what I was experiencing.

I had spent the night in a high-rise budget hotel within a short walk of the city centre so bright and early on this Tuesday morning I set off for a stroll leaving Wanda in the hotel room. In my experience, the staff at Ibis hotels rarely raise objections to the suggestion that bicycles are stored in rooms and it was no different here in Bordeaux. She would remain there for the next 24 hours until the following morning when we would set off in the direction of the Canal de la Garonne after a second night in the hotel.

As per usual I had a few practical tasks on my mind, the most pressing of which was to get a haircut. I also needed my beard shaved off. It had reached the point where painful hacking with a cheap disposable razor would undoubtedly leave me with the appearance of someone who had just spent ten rounds in the ring with Tyson Fury. It was best to call in the professionals and I had noticed a barber shop en route to the hotel the previous evening that advertised both haircuts and beard removal for an all-in-one price. Unfortunately, when I arrived at their door at 9 am they were fully booked, but they did recommend a former colleague who now had his own shop nearby. I was in luck, or so I thought.

Jean-Baptiste was very friendly and we chatted as he snipped and shaved but I was somewhat taken aback when I was presented with a bill for €35, especially as I had only been sitting in the chair for a matter of ten minutes. It was a sharp reminder, if one was needed, that I was back in a big urban area and a very affluent one at that. Day after day of €10 campsites, baguettes, brie and €5 bottles of red might give the impression that France is a cheap country. Indeed it is if you restrict yourself to camping, bread, cheese and cheap wine. Veer outside this bubble of good value and you need to brace yourself to be fleeced just as comprehensively as you might be anywhere else on the planet.

Feeling somewhat deflated that within the first hour of the day I had managed to have my bank balance drained by such a considerable sum, I resolved to have a more frugal afternoon. Aside from investing in a new pair of sandals from the city centre Decathlon[41], most of my time was spent being a *flâneur* around town. I strolled aimlessly through the predominantly pedestrianised old streets, dodging trams, poking my head around random corners and staring far too long at inconsequential oddities. The colourful umbrellas and balloons strewn from building to building above my head. A bicycle stripped of its parts but still locked securely to a set of railings. The street names chiselled into the stone beside modern shiny blue plaques providing exactly the same information. The front end of a racing green Jaguar car that appeared to have smashed through the façade of the Parking Victor Hugo. (It was all in the name of modern art of course.) I even spent a few moments examining the *"bel appartements"* and *"hôtels particuliers"* offered for sale in the window of Propriétés Emile Garcin. Their prices were measured in the millions of euros. It was easy to see why my haircut had cost me 35. Perhaps it had been a bargain after all.

As the afternoon drew to a close I headed to the *hôtel de ville* or rather the terrace of Le Café Rohan that was squeezed into one corner of the square beside the town hall, overlooking the Cathédrale Saint-André. Where better to be inspired for an hour or so of podcast editing than your own patron saint's church? I also took the opportunity to take a closer look at the second of the three maps for the Canal des 2 Mers cycle route that I had picked up back in Royan. The maps were the best I had yet found with exactly the kind of detail your average cycle tourist may have wanted and I was, of course, that average cycle tourist. The scale was also perfect: the map for the Véloscénie from Paris to Mont-Saint-Michel had been comically simple and the maps for the Vélomaritime in Brittany ridiculously detailed. These were Goldilocks maps with a scale that was not too big but not too small. Just right.

The area covered by map two joined the great south-western cities of Bordeaux and Toulouse and much to my delight almost all of the route was on off-road *voie verte*. The route joined the Canal de la Garonne near a town called La Réole. This was 70km from Bordeaux so I suspected it would be my first overnight stop. It also had a town centre municipal campsite. That sealed the deal. The only section of on-road cycling (the map described it more poetically as *"voie partagée"* or "shared route") was a 20km section between a town called Sauveterre-de-Guyenne and La Réole. Thereafter the route followed the canal to Toulouse without once (as far as I could see) leaving the towpath. Between La Réole and Toulouse, it would be another

---

[41] If you remember, I had punched several holes in the bottom of the previous pair of sandals by using them to force tent pegs into the ground. I had also come very close to punching several holes in my feet.

200km of cycling so perhaps two or three overnight stops. It was now Tuesday so I could be in Toulouse by Saturday or Sunday at the latest. As plans went, that was pretty detailed by my standards and deserved a celebratory beer. Or two. I would worry about Toulouse to Sète at the weekend.

By the time I set off back to the Ibis Budget hotel, the sky was an ever-darkening shade of violet and the yellow tinge of the streetlamps was setting the stone buildings ablaze in a riot of warm colours. Again my mind cast back to 2003 when I had been standing in this very same square. At the time it was cordoned off to passers-by with construction lorries, rubble and equipment detracting somewhat from the view of the cathedral, town hall and café terraces. This evening, however, the place shone. Even some of the flagstones had been replaced by colourful lights giving a playful air to the scene. Then, as I made my way beside the Gothic buttresses at the eastern end of the church, a tram snaked quietly beside me, its interior lights picking out a slow blur of people as they headed home for the evening.

It is sometimes best not to return to a favourite town or city for fear of disappointment - I had experienced that with Venice - but it was certainly not the case with Bordeaux. Almost 20 years had passed between my two visits. I could only hope that it would not be so long before my third.

Day Thirty-Two: Bordeaux to La Réole (80km)
Wednesday 3rd August

There has not been a French winner of the Tour de France since 1985 when Bernard Hinault fought off the challenge of his teammate Greg Lemond to secure first place. The late 1970s and the first half of the 1980s witnessed multiple French victories, five of them for Hinault and another two each for Bernard Thévenet and Laurent Fignon. A previous period of French domination was the 1930s. Six of the ten editions of that decade's tours were won by Frenchmen, the last one being a certain Roger Lapébie in 1937. It was his only grand tour victory.

The race that year adopted a clockwise route from Paris to Paris via Lille, Metz, Geneva, Nice, Perpignan, Bordeaux, La Rochelle, Rennes and Caen on the north coast. Stretching out over 4,415km, it was somewhat shorter than the races of the 1920s but significantly longer than those of the modern-day. It was the first Tour de France to allow derailleur gears and fortune was on Lapébie's side when the favourite, Italian legend Gino Bartali, retired injured at the start of stage 12 in Marseille. (At least he had a cheap train fare home.) He was also aided by the Belgian team[42] who decided to quit en masse and in disgust after one of their members was given a time penalty, unjustifiably in their eyes. Only 46 of the 98 starters crossed the finishing line in Paris and with a winning time of 138 hours, 58 minutes and 31 seconds, Roger won with a margin of 7 minutes and 17 seconds over his nearest rival.

Why is all this relevant? Well, had Roger cared to glance east at the end of stage 16 of the race as he was approaching that day's finishing line in Bordeaux, he may have spotted the smoke from a steam train chugging its way beside the River Garonne. If he did, it was probably about to start climbing the hill to Créon and then trundle onwards to Sauveterre-de-Guyenne. As a Girondien himself, he would have been familiar with the countryside in these parts. He may even have taken the train. Who knows? I do hope he did as, following the closure of the line between Bordeaux and Sauveterre in 1979, the land and the stations were purchased by the local authorities who turned it into a rather good cycle path. They also decided to name it after him. It is now known as La Piste Roger Lapébie and it is not just good, it is magnificent.

---

[42] Between 1931 and 1961 teams were national rather than sponsored, as they were initially and as they are now.

If you cast your minds back to Dieppe and the start of the French section of the Avenue Verte, I made the following comments about the 40km cycle route to Forges-les-Eaux:

> "Never before in my years of being a cycle tourist had I encountered such a monumentally wonderful cycle route. Segregated? Tick. Quality surface? Tick. Bespoke signage? Tick. Maintained? Tick."

At the time I thought I had experienced the zenith of what a cycle path could possibly be. Yet here I was in south-western France marvelling at something even more fabulous. At 50km long it was also a bit longer than its northern cousin and it was immaculate. Kilometre after kilometre of pristine track that was maintained to a standard rare for main roads, even in France. The tunnels were just as they had been when the railway was in operation but lights had been installed to help cyclists see the way ahead. Every brick was still in place and as far as I could see, the tunnels were watertight. The junctions with roads were set out with give-way markings and lateral painted strips on the ground to encourage a slower speed. This was a cycle track masquerading as a road, just one from which cars, trucks and buses had been excluded. How strange. How novel. How marvellous!

In Créon, the former station had been taken over by the tourist office and a snack bar had opened up in a smaller building next door. Beyond the station, a long wooden hut had been erected on the former platform and named itself the Station Vélo de Créon. It provided most things that a cyclist might need including bike hire, simple repair and maintenance facilities, advice and even a "*vélo-école*" should you have forgotten the basic principles of riding a bike. There was a covered shed sheltering picnic tables on the opposite platform and a number of cyclists had chosen this spot to take a break from the pedalling to make the most of what was on offer. Alas, the chap in charge was a little stumped when I asked if he had one of those keys to tighten a Brooks saddle, but that was perhaps asking too much. In all other respects, it was utterly wonderful.

It did not finish there. Only 4km further along the line at the former train station at La Sauve, whetting the appetite for summers yet to come, there was a board explaining how €831,000 was being spent transforming the building and surrounding land into a "*gare touristique*". It would include accommodation, a bar, a restaurant, toilets, covered areas for picnicking and a secure bicycle storage garage. I had arrived a year too early to benefit but was nevertheless impressed.

To the east of La Sauve, I paused at a sign informing me that Sauveterre-de-Guyenne was another 25km away. I was reminded of a conversation that I had had earlier in the year with Declan Lyons for The Cycling Europe Podcast.[43] Declan had written the Cicerone cycling guidebooks for the Canal de la Garonne and the Canal du Midi, the two sections of the Canal des 2 Mers cycle route. He had made the following comments:

> "If you remember the former French prime minister Alain Juppé who became mayor of Bordeaux... He really put a huge effort into cycling and developed a lot of the cycleways in the area. He made a lot of them D-roads - departmental roads - which means that they have to be maintained by the local authority to that standard. The only difference between them and an ordinary departmental road is that there are no motorised vehicles allowed on them."

It was our friend Alain Juppé again, the man who was willing to risk political capital by causing chaos in his home city with an intensive period of construction for the tramway network. He was also willing to risk the opprobrium of the anti-cycling lobby (if it exists in France) by recategorising the cycling network as departmental roads. And it had worked rather brilliantly.

I glanced back at the post beside me. Above the distances and the signs for the cycle routes - including the EuroVelo 3 "Scandibérique" along this stretch of the path - was a small yellow sign. On it had been printed a number and three letters: D803. I was cycling along the *route départementale numéro 803*, otherwise known as La Piste Roger Lapébie. Genius!

The cycle path continued to wind its wonderful way east and then south in the direction of Sauveterre-de-Guyenne slicing a glorious path through cuttings and tunnels, woods and vineyards. It was all rather magical.

However, as the morning drew to a close, my mind began to wander and I started reflecting upon my chances of making it back to the Hook of Holland in time for my ferry home. After a few moments of thought something dawned upon me. If I were to say that my continental journey had started in the North Sea at midnight on Saturday 2nd of July and if it were to finish at midnight back out at sea on Saturday 3rd of September, the halfway point in terms of time would be today - August 3rd - at midday.

---

[43] It is episode 044 if you would like to listen to the full conversation.

4 weeks, 3 days and 12 hours down. 4 weeks, 3 days and 12 hours to go. It would be midday in… 8 minutes.

I quickly consulted an online map and noticed that I was approaching a village called Saint-Brice. It must surely have a church, I thought. I stepped up my speed and within a few minutes I was in the centre of the village in the shade of some trees, beside a small church with a tower. I waited. When midday arrived and much to my delight, the bell began to toll, twelve times. My cycle was halfway over, at least in terms of time. I spread my map of France over the ground and took a few moments to ponder the situation. *Had I reached the halfway point in terms of distance?* It was difficult to say. After the morning's efforts, I had probably now cycled about 2,100km. The next part of my journey - the ViaRhôna/EuroVelo 17 from Sète to Andermatt - was, according to the EuroVelo website, 1,000km long. The final part of my journey - the Rhine Cycle Route/EuroVelo 15 from Andermatt to Rotterdam - was another 1,500km. My current route was 800km from Royan to Sète but I could perhaps knock 200km off the total considering the distance travelled since Royan. That added up to 3,100km. But I had only used five of my ten planned trains and each could, theoretically, knock 100km (maximum) off the total which would bring it down to 2,600km. Five days so far had not involved much cycling. Today was cycling day 27. My average distance cycled on those days would be 79km by the time I arrived in La Réole. If I could reduce the number of days off in the next four and a half weeks and up the daily average, it might be possible. Perhaps. I was slightly scared by the prospect of defeat. I folded up the map and cracked on.

An early afternoon arrival in Sauveterre-de-Guyenne was bittersweet. It was good that I had made so much progress in the morning but the bastide town marked the end of the disused railway line which had been such joyous cycling territory. From here to La Réole I was back on the road. I drowned my sorrows not with a stiff drink but with a ham salad baguette and an ice cream from a snack bar in one of the arcades off the main square. I then went to sit on the steps of the nearby church where I watched a small lizard bask in the sun. It was a reminder that I was very much in the south of France. As were the terracotta roof tiles, abundance of lavender, hilltop villages… Just no sound of cicadas. That struck me as strange. Perhaps I was not so far south after all.

Had the afternoon not been preceded by the glorious morning on the Piste Roger Lapébie, I would have perhaps ranked it higher than I did. The country lanes were quiet, the views delightful and the undulating terrain not so taxing on the legs. The charming Moulin de Loubens gave me a reason to pause for ten minutes and take photographs. It was strangely familiar as

I had seen it several times on posters and in tourist brochures: an ancient vine-clad mill complete with a tower and arches over the water. The kind of building that no architect - past or present - would ever design that way but, mirrored in the green water below, was perfect. As the French would say, *malgré lui*: a reluctant attraction despite itself.

I had few expectations of La Réole. It represented the place where, the following morning, I would start following the Canal de la Garonne. I was, however, slightly taken aback by its lack of Frenchness. It was a bit run down and reminded me of somewhere in a forgotten corner of Italy. Its heyday was long since gone and it was clearly struggling to head in the direction of a new one. Before cycling down to the riverside campsite I popped into the small Proxi supermarket in the centre. It was a world away from the relative opulence of Bordeaux where I had started the day and the people around me gave every impression that this was not the happy corner of Gironde.

I descended the hill in the direction of the river with expectations lowered but then, as I turned the corner, was presented with an impressive suspension bridge. I could also see the campsite on the other side of the river. The bridge - designed and built by a certain Gustave Eiffel - was closed to motorised traffic. Nothing to do with Alain Juppé this time. It was simply because it too was suffering from a severe case of neglect and could no longer cope with the stresses associated with heavy vehicles.

Once I had pitched the tent on the elongated riverside campsite and the sun had begun its slow trudge towards the horizon, I settled down to eat my cheap Proxi meal and sip my cheap Proxi wine. From a distance, as the light dimmed and as my mind drifted off into an alcohol-induced fuzz, I could see La Réole on the opposite bank of the river. It was framed by the two metal uprights of the bridge. Its houses and its church tower were crammed along the riverbank, overgrown greenery softening the hard edges of the scene before me. Despite what I had experienced earlier, it struck me that faded glory might have its attractions after all. Perhaps there was a message there for us all.

With that, I crawled into the tent and let the wine do its business. Until, of course, I had to creep off to the toilet block at 2 am to empty my bladder. There was another message for us all.

Day Thirty-Three: La Réole to Agen (89km)
Thursday 4th August

As a single teacher in good health and without children, I was in the fortunate position of being able to embark upon long cycling journeys. Many others are forced to restrict their travels to fit in with the constraints of time, members of their family or physical ability. I was acutely aware of this - sometimes to the point of embarrassment - when I met other people of a similar age who also happened to be travelling by bicycle. On this first day of cycling along the Canal de la Garonne, I would have several encounters that put my own fortunate situation into sharp focus.

The first of these was not so much a first encounter as a first exchange of meaningful conversation. Since leaving Royan I had spotted two French cyclists in their 50s on numerous occasions. We had swapped cheery *bonjours* as I overtook them or as they overtook me and they had also stayed at the campsite on the northern bank of the Gironde between Royan and Bordeaux a few days earlier. In La Réole it was no surprise to find them at the *camping municipal* but it was not until the morning when we were packing away our tents that we got chatting.

"We started in Royan and today is our final day before we catch the train home from Agen," explained the taller of the two men, in French. "Perhaps next year we'll come back and continue along the cycle route from there, but we need to get back to work."

They had only had a week to complete their trip. The first week of my cycle had seen me travel along the coast from Rotterdam to Dieppe but looking back, I did not get into the swing of being a cycle tourist again until well after Dieppe. I had not even figured out which pannier for which bit of kit by that stage. I had completed relatively short cycling trips myself but had never been in a position of stopping before the end of a route with the intention of returning one day to complete it. It must, I reflected, be somewhat frustrating.

That said, the two chaps in front of me were in good spirits, enthusiastically looking forward to their final day of cycling before heading home. Perhaps it was the mindset that was more important: they had set themselves an objective and they had achieved it. My objective may have been somewhat grander in scale than theirs but I was kidding myself if I was expecting the sense of satisfaction to be ten times as great if or when I reached the finishing point. What *would* be significantly greater would be the sense of disappointment if I did *not* get to the end of the journey. Compared to the two French cyclists, the risks of doing so were much higher. It was a thought not to dwell upon, although it was something that I would return to reflect upon again later in the day.

What I should have been dwelling upon was my route. It was going to be a frustrating start to the day. I headed back over the impressive metal bridge in the direction of La Réole as the sun was creeping higher in the sky to my right, in the east... Which meant I was actually cycling north and in the wrong direction. No harm done. Indeed cycling over such a stunning structure on such a magnificent morning was a price worth paying. I turned around and started heading south, the sun now where it should be, on my left. But that was not the frustrating bit.

When I was cycling along the Nantes-Brest Canal in Brittany, it had become increasingly evident that when the canal was constructed, the engineers had made use of many pre-existing rivers to make their lives easier. Or rather, the lives of those who were doing the work easier. Looking at my map of the Canal des 2 Mers à Vélo, that did not seem to be the case with the Canal de la Garonne. I could see on my map that as far as Agen - today's destination - the canal was always a distinct entity to the south of the river. Thereafter and as far as Toulouse, its terminus, it had been constructed to the north of La Garonne. So on this first day of canal cycling here in the south-west of France, it should not have been too difficult to find the Canal de la Garonne. And it was not. Within 15 minutes of setting off - even taking into consideration my return journey over the river - I was on a small concrete bridge spanning the canal.

I consider myself to have a very good sense of direction. I instinctively knew that on the other side of the canal I needed to turn right and start cycling along the towpath in the direction of Agen and then Toulouse. A family on bikes - mum, dad and a young boy - arrived from the left and passed me on the bridge. "They clearly can't read a map or follow the signs," I thought to myself.

"*Bonjour*," beamed the fools.

"*Bonjour*," replied the smug Englishman.

There was a similar interaction with a nearby fisherman. His eyes followed me as I cycled past him before he also greeted me with a merry "*bonjour*". There was a hint of puzzlement in his regard.

A couple of kilometres after having turned right I noticed a village signposted to my left. As I had not passed through the centre of La Réole after leaving the campsite I had yet to find my breakfast so I decided to follow the sign and fill my stomach. My muscles remained cold and it was an arduous climb to Loupiac-de-la-Réole. *Had I made the wrong choice? Was a croissant and pain au chocolat worth all this effort?* I was torn between returning to the canal and continuing up the hill. Hunger won out and I kept pedalling.

Ten minutes after leaving the canal I arrived in the village. But I could not spot any of the *commerces* that had been promised on the signs. I quickly reached for Google Maps and found the Marché Minut', a tiny supermarket in what passed for the main square.

Breakfast purchased, I again consulted the online map to see if there was an alternative route back to the canal. As I zoomed out on my screen I could see the thick blue line of the River Garonne further north and the much thinner line of the Canal de la Garonne further south. I could see La Réole and the route that I had cycled. *That was strange.* Before deviating away from the canal I seemed to have been cycling west. I looked for the compass that would re-orientate the map so it was presenting itself as north-south, but there was no compass. The map was fixed north-south. That made no sense. I stared at the map for a few moments, flakes of croissant crumbling annoyingly onto the phone. At least they were not tears.

This smug Englishman with his excellent sense of direction had set off in the wrong direction along the canal. By the time I arrived back at the concrete bridge, I had managed to add an extra seven kilometres to the cycling day. I passed the fisherman for the second time. He nodded, a wry smile on his face.

It was not so much the extra distance that annoyed me (although the hill had been a pain). It was more my dented sense of directional infallibility. I could not ever remember making such a schoolboy error on any of my previous pan-European cycles. I had made lots of errors whilst cycling. I had frequently misjudged distances, not realised that the Peloponnese were some of the biggest mountains in Greece and nearly come to tears when the descent from the Col de Tende was almost impassable… But cycling west instead of east? I was blushing. I resolved never to mention the incident again to anyone, anywhere. I think I got away with it.

Fontet was the village where I should have turned left. It was also home to the impressively named Musée d'Artisanat, de Monuments en Allumettes et de Sciences Naturelles. It was the kind of place that I would have loved to spend some time exploring, especially the section dedicated to monuments constructed from matchsticks. It was housed in an old wooden shed and the faded poster outside showed the Palace of Versailles, in matchstick form, beside the yellowing image of Gérard, the matchstick maker. Alas I would have to wait until 2 pm and even then, give the man a call to book myself in. I had missed out on seeing the real Versailles by taking the train from Paris to Chartres. This would surely have been recompense, of sorts. With regrets and a serious hope that the museum had devoted more of its budget towards buying a good fire insurance policy than it had to extending its opening hours, I finally started cycling in the correct direction along the canal.

Accommodation was beginning to play on my mind. Agen did not appear to have a campsite so I looked on Warmshowers and fell upon the profile of Thierry and Marick, a retired couple with a love of foreign travel. They lived 50 metres from the cycleway and the town centre. I sent a quick message, apologising for the late request, and hoped for the best.

After my experiences along the Canal de Nantes à Brest, the Canal de la Garonne felt familiar. It made for easy, comfortable cycling: the towpath was well maintained and mature trees provided ample, almost continuous, shade from sun. It was also very straight. I could see on my map the River Garonne wriggling erratically along a seemingly endless number of meanders while the canal continued a sensible path heading south-east. The canal presented as a parent on a mission to get to the shops, the river as a young child who simply wanted to have a bit of fun running up and down the pavement despite being firmly attached to its mother.

It would make sense in the telling of the story of the Canal de la Garonne to start with that of the Canal du Midi, its southerly sibling. But I had chosen to cycle in an inconvenient direction around France confounding historical chronology, so please accept my apologies. I will come back to the Canal du Midi later but for the time being, all you need to remember is that it is much older than the Canal de la Garonne: the former opened in 1681, the latter in 1856.

Although it was envisaged as a logical Mediterranean-Atlantic-linking extension to the Canal du Midi as far back as the late 17th century, the incentive to start digging the Canal de la Garonne was the Industrial Revolution when more goods needed to be transported to the sea. The River Garonne was far too unpredictable with larger boats at risk of being grounded so construction of the 194km canal must have been considered a welcome arrival by the 19th-century industrialists of south-western France. As was, presumably, the railway line from Bordeaux to Sète which became fully operational just two years after the opening of the canal in 1858. As we have seen before, the railway was not great news for the waterways. A rescue, of sorts, arrived in the shape of the pleasure boats of the late 20th century, one of them carrying Rick Stein. His *French Odyssey* television series and accompanying book popularised the waterway in the English-speaking world. A celebrity chef from Cornwall cannot, however, have been upper most in the thoughts of the 19th-century navvies as they toiled in the mud.

My online contact David Naylor was also cycling around France with his wife, Christine. It was David who had recommended that I stay at the campsite in Domfront earlier in the trip. He had been in contact again after spotting my mid-trip tweet ("4 weeks, 3 days, 12 hours done... 4 weeks, 3 days, 12 hours remaining") from the previous day:

> "@CyclingEurope - Camping 7km from Agen today
> and heading towards Bordeaux tomorrow.
> If we see you we will shout."

As we were both travelling along the towpath of the Canal de la Garonne we would be unlucky if we were to miss each other. However, although I had told David to look out for an orange T-shirt, I had few clues as to what he and his wife might look like. There were a good number of couples cycling on the towpath. So it was with some relief (as well as some surprise as my mind had drifted off into the realms of inconsequential daydreaming that only towpath cycling can induce) that I heard my name being shouted by a man approaching me at speed: "Andrew!"

As noted at the start of this chapter, I am lucky to be a teacher who gets a long summer holiday to go off cycling. If you do not fancy the marking and are no fan of teenagers, there are other solutions. The first is, admittedly, a long-term strategy but works well for many: join the police force and retire after 30 years at a relatively young age and with a decent pension. That is exactly what David, a former police officer living on the south coast of England, had done.

"We started in Saint-Malo..." he explained.

"...And as of today we've done 3,000km," added his French-born wife.

She had not taken retirement from her job as a neo-natal nurse in the NHS but was on an extended career break. That was a second potential strategy to add to the list. If you are able to persuade your employer that the company or organisation that you work for will continue to function perfectly well if you do not come to work for three months - choose your words wisely - you too could be off on a long bike ride very soon.

Their experiences of cycling the canal were generally very positive but they were finding the route relatively busy:

"When we went through the Massif Central and the Cévennes we were lucky to see one cycle tourist a day," explained David before going on to detail the remainder of their route through France:

"After Bordeaux, we'll continue north but because of Brexit I'm restricted to 90 days so we are planning to return home on day 89."

My suggestion of overstaying the 90 days as a two-fingered salute to the Brexit bunch was dismissed by law-abiding David who pointed out that he did not want to mess up his chances of getting a long-term visa in the future. His French wife had no such issues of course. Had I been David I would have been filling in the forms for French citizenship faster than you could shout "*Vive La France!*".[44]

As they continued their cycling odyssey north-west in the direction of Bordeaux, I continued mine south-east in the direction of Agen. It was a wonderful place to be cycling. As with the Nantes-Brest Canal, each lock had an accompanying cottage and again, some of these cottages had been repurposed to cater for the needs of people travelling along the canal. One exceptional example was the cottage beside the Écluse de Berry. It was a simple construction with a jaunty asymmetrical roof which added a touch of character to an otherwise inconsequential building. With whitewashed walls, mint green shutters and multi-coloured bunting draped across its façade this was about as Instagrammable as lock keepers' cottages went, although I did resist the temptation myself. I was too busy chatting to the chap serving me a drink and a slice of cake. I asked him if he was also the *éclusier*, the lock keeper.

"No, the locks are automatic and have been for several years," he explained, in French, before going on to detail how the system worked.

"Above the canal, just before the lock, there's a cable across the water and a pole hanging from the cable. When the pole is pulled, the first door opens. Once inside the lock, there's a button to press in the cabin over there: the door closes, the water level is adjusted and the second door opens automatically."

There was none of that strenuous manual cranking open of locks as there is along my local canal in Yorkshire. None of those marital arguments as to whose turn it was to steer and whose turn it was to get off the boat and start working up a sweat. I had been seeing these cables and poles all morning and been somewhat bemused as to why they were there. I had thought they might be something to do with canoeing as the poles resembled those on a canoe slalom course but aside from that my theory had made little sense and it was nice to have solved the mystery.

I used the opportunity of my canal-side break to check on the status of my Warmshowers' request:

---

[44] Despite having worked throughout the COVID pandemic as a nurse in a British hospital, Christine explained the exasperating horror that she had had to endure in trying to obtain settled status in the UK. A shameful, shocking tale.

"Bonjour. OK pour ce soir après 18h. Bonne route."

Excellent. Just as I liked responses: to the point and positive. My accommodation was sorted.

I arrived in the centre of Agen about an hour before the agreed rendez-vous so I found a quiet bar in front of the town hall and indulged in a refreshing beer. I should, perhaps, have saved my money. When I arrived at Thierry and Marick's home on the southern side of the Garonne at 6 pm, I was showered with an embarrassment of hospitality. This included a comfortable room, a delicious evening meal and a seemingly endless supply of beer. I was able to wash my clothes, charge all my batteries and there was even a cute dog to keep me amused.

Yet all of that was inconsequential compared to Marick herself who was as charming a host as I could have wished for. What's more, I was the fifth cyclist she had welcomed into her home that week, and it was still only Thursday! Perhaps she liked the company when her husband was not at home. Although she was not a cyclist, her husband, Thierry, was. He was also a keen walker and had gone away for a few days on a hiking holiday with friends. Marick explained that, because of family caring responsibilities, it was impossible for them both to take a holiday at the same time.

Once again I had been reminded as to just how fortunate I was to be able to do what I was doing. With no caring responsibilities in my own family, I continued to benefit from a personal situation which was simply not available to many others. It was humbling to meet people like Marick, or the two chaps at the campsite in La Réole earlier in the day. They were all obliged to work around what life had thrown at them. People such as David, Christine and me were in a very fortunate position and it was always useful to be reminded of just how lucky we were to have the freedom to do what we were doing. Even if it did occasionally mean that I was not able to tell my east from my west…

Day Thirty-Four: Agen to Grisolles (94km)
Friday 5th August

Marick had been a superb host. Alas, her influence upon the mosquito population of Agen was limited and come the morning I had been assaulted by the little bastards to an extent that had me considering reporting them to the local *gendarmes*. Whilst sitting at Marick's kitchen table, simultaneously scratching at my skin and eating my breakfast, she was already preparing the evening meal for more Warmshowers visitors that evening but she took a few moments to advise me on my upcoming route. This included the recommendation that I visit the village of Auvillar, around 30km to the south-east of Agen. I would add it to the list of possible diversions for the day. David and Christine had also mentioned a strange canal-related contraption near Montech. I had not quite understood what it was but if I stumbled upon it, I would investigate.

Had Marick not come to my rescue and provided accommodation, there might have been an alternative option. However, I knew nothing of its existence prior to my arrival in Agen the previous afternoon. One of the great engineering feats of the Canal de la Garonne is Le Pont-Canal d'Agen. Extending over 580 metres and supported by 23 arches, it carries the canal above the River Garonne before they both continue their respective journeys south in the direction of Toulouse. As I cycled across the bridge en route to Marick's house on Thursday afternoon I had noticed a recently renovated building at its eastern end. Banners outside the building announced it as a "*café vélo*". I made a mental note to return the following morning and find out more which is why, at 8.30 am on Friday, I was standing outside its entrance.

Before me was another substantial slice of state investment in the cycling infrastructure of France, similar in scale to what I had seen along the Piste Roger Lapébie earlier in the week.[45] The building was only modest in size but in most other respects it proclaimed pretensions well beyond its physical footprint. Above my head, attached to the oversized pediment of the one-storey neo-classical construction was the coat of arms of Agen underneath which the capitalised words "*CHÂTEAU D'EAU*" had been carved. In its former life, this building had supplied the town with its water. Now it was supplying cyclists with food, maintenance and even accommodation courtesy of a small dormitory.

"*Morgan. Sprechen Sie Deutsch?*"

---

[45] According to a 2015 report in the *Dépêche du Midi* newspaper, over €1 million.

I turned to find a rotund man, naked from the waist up, awaiting my response.

"*Nein, Englisch,*" I replied. "*Ou français?*"

We settled for the latter. His name was Kurt, he was from Bern in Switzerland and he was not having a good week. He was on a long cycling trip around France, not dissimilar to my own, but his bike had serious mechanical issues. The derailleur and cassette on the rear wheel had become bent and he had struggled to find spares locally. He was waiting for them to be sent from Switzerland and had been holed up in the dormitory for two nights already. With the weekend fast approaching, he was worried that his delivery might not arrive before the start of the following week. Perhaps when he saw me arrive he had hoped that I could help him in some way but all I could do was offer sympathy. It is not an easy emotion to exchange via a shared second language and I am not sure if I was successful. When I glanced back to wave at him from the ramp leading up to the canal, he cut a forlorn (if substantial) figure but the encounter reminded me that so far I had been lucky. I had experienced no mechanicals whatsoever and I dearly hoped it would stay that way.

Perhaps Kurt needed some inspirational soundbites. Had he been cycling towards Toulouse that morning he would have found them. At regular intervals along the canal, carefully painted in serifed fonts onto the retaining walls of the canal, its locks, its bridges and even the towpath, were a series of thought-provoking quotations:

"Waterfall crashes, river swirls, stream whispers, canal soothes."
"Everything for the eyes seems so close and for the legs so far away."
"Do not acquire. Travel to impoverish. That's what you need."
"Old shoes can only take you where the path leads. Then you have to continue barefoot."[46]

Or, in the case of Kurt, without a functioning gear system. The quotations kept my mind occupied as I continued my cycle south in the direction of Auvillar, one of the most beautiful villages in France. This was not

---

[46] In the original French:
"*Cascade fracasse, fleuve tourbillonne, ruisseau murmure, canal apaise.*"
"*Tout pour les yeux semble si près et pour les jambes si loin.*"
"*Non non, pas acquérir. Voyager pour t'appauvrir. Voilà ce dont tu as besoin.*"
"*Les vieux souliers seuls peuvent parvenir où conduit le chemin. Après il faut continuer pieds nus.*"

Marick's opinion (although I am sure she would agree) but that of an outfit going by the name of Les Plus Beaux Villages de France.

The idea of creating the organisation came from a Reader's Digest publication of the same name in the early 1980s. It inspired the mayor of one of the featured villages to join forces with others appearing in the book "to promote and protect their remarkable heritage". 40 years later, they are still at it and the number of beautiful villages has tripled to nearly 180. There are, of course, boxes to tick if you would like to join the exclusive club including having listed buildings, harmonious architecture, quality public spaces and - my favourite - traffic-calming measures. Clip board in hand, I set off up the steep hill towards the centre of Auvillar.

I did not get very far very fast. After cycling back across the River Garonne I turned left along a quiet lane but it quickly defeated me. I was out of practice when it came to vertical challenges - especially unexpected ones - and, for the first time since leaving Rotterdam, I got off and pushed. I was not alone in the arduous trudge.

"*Bonjour,*" puffed a man in an accent that was certainly not French. It belonged to Ron, a youngish chap from New York.

"I'm here for the summer on a creative writing retreat," he explained.

Ron was hoping to find inspiration for his next murder-mystery novel before returning to his job as an English lecturer at a university on the East Coast of America in the autumn. We chatted about travelling and writing as I pushed and we both panted.

"Auvillar is a great place to find somewhere to sit and be inspired," were his parting words just before we went our separate ways.

Mine was through the arches of a tall clock tower that marked the entrance to the cobbled, pedestrianised village. That was one big tick already but I quickly cast aside my imaginary clipboard. It was immediately obvious that this was indeed one of France's most beautiful villages.

I slowly guided Wanda over the cobbles. It was approaching midday on another hot, sunny day and most of the shutters on the upper floors of the buildings beside me were closed to keep the cool air in and the hot air out. Their ground floors formed an arcade under which I was able to divert and benefit from the shade provided. For such a picture-perfect location, there were few people: just a handful of tourists and a few locals going about their business. After 100 metres or so, the narrow road fanned out into a small triangular "square" dominated by a perfectly circular market hall. It would be a stretch to call this a building: more a terracotta roof supported by a series of Romanesque columns. It had no walls but at their closest points the orange tiles were only metres from the buildings around the three-sided square. This was not just architecture, it was geometry. My inner mathematician was delighted.

I went to sit on the steps of the market hall and within seconds the silence had been pleasantly interrupted by the sound of an accordion shortly followed by the voice of a woman. I turned to see the musician and singer in the centre of the market hall. I was their audience of one.

For perhaps ten minutes I was happy to do nothing but glance around and watch the rarely changing scene before me. The bird perched above me on a balcony, tweeting. The man under the arcade, turning the pages of his book. The racing green Triumph, reflecting and contorting the shape of the cobbles in its shiny paintwork. I recalled the words of Ron: "Auvillar is a great place to find somewhere to sit and be inspired". It was indeed. So much of my days were spent actively forcing the scenery around me to change - that is the nature of travelling by bicycle - yet there was sometimes more to see when the scenery barely changed. The beauty was in the detail.

I finally dragged myself away from the Place de la Halle and wandered the short distance to another small square, this time with the more traditional four sides rather than just the three. Along one of them was the façade of the Église Saint-Pierre. Along another, behind a statue and some tall poplar trees, was a set of railings and beyond that the vastness of a flat plain. Behind me, unseen, the former province of Gascony, before me the former province of Quercy and immediately below me the River Garonne, efficiently dividing the two. However, from my elevated position, the thin line of the Canal de la Garonne - now several kilometres away - remained hidden beyond the trees, vineyards and fields.

It would be another half hour before I was back on the towpath, continuing my journey south and east. The wise words of writers and poets continued with a snippet from Goethe:

"Voyageur, je rafle ce que je peux" /
"Traveller, I'm grabbing what I can"

I did not quite understand this quote and it still bemuses me today. Were they words of warning from a pickpocket? Was that an issue in late 18th-century Germany? Very confusing.

Equally bemusing was the sight of two... Trains? Buses? From a distance, it was not easy to decide. Both had been painted in vibrant blocks of yellow, red, lavender and aquamarine (not a common combination in these parts) and the vehicles had been positioned on opposite sides of the canal which had now thinned significantly. In fact, was this still the canal? Although there was water at one end of the narrow canal, such was its incline that after about 20 metres it was simply bare concrete. As I cycled closer to the trains / buses I could see that each carriage was being supported by comically large wheels with pneumatic tyres. So it was a bus. But then again it was not. It was a ridiculously oversized toy train, on wheels. The kind of thing that Gulliver might have played with when he was relatively small.

I had found the Pente d'Eau de Montech, the Water Slope of Montech. Bear with me: this might take some explaining. It had confused me when it had been mentioned by David and Christine the previous day: it had confused me again today when I had set sight on it. Here goes...

We all know that canals climb hills via locks. It was none other than Leonardo de Vinci who invented the modern lock in 1497. It was called the Miter lock and it was ground-breaking as it was the first to make use of two gates that closed together at an angle. The pressure exerted upon the gates by the upstream water only served to close them tighter. However, when the level of the water in the lock equalled that outside the lock - and crucially the pressure of the water was the same on both sides of the gate - they would open easily. Genius!

Locks are fascinating things. To climb longer slopes, they can be positioned next to each other in a staircase. The longest in the UK is the Tardebigge staircase consisting of 30 locks but the most spectacular are those that climb rapidly through a succession of adjacent locks, for example at Caen Hill in Wiltshire. However, patience is required and according to the Canal and River Trust, it can take six hours to traverse all 29 of the locks in the Caen Hill system. (Far quicker on a bike.)

This, it seems, was the motivation for building the contraption near Montech. Here there were just five locks through which to travel and it took about an hour to pass through them. In the early 1970s when work was being planned to increase the size of the locks (to accommodate longer boats), it was decided to experiment and create a boat lift. Jean Aubert and his team of engineers came up with a system that would push 1,500 cubic metres of water (with a boat sitting on top of it) up a slope of 125 metres. In doing so the 5 locks could be avoided and 45 minutes would be saved. Opened in 1974, it was unique in the world, but when one of the engines failed in 2009 it closed and is now a museum piece. The story is told inside a barge that sits in what is now a dry dock beside the two train engines that remain fixed like conjoined twins to a yoke and a gate that once pushed the wedge of water up the hill.

"The Montech water slope is a rare technological curiosity that attracts an ever-increasing number of visitors," according to an information board.

I would describe it as wonderfully bonkers. A physical embodiment of an engineering culture that encourages innovation and experimentation. It is, perhaps, why there is a ridiculous 300-metre tower in the French capital that is now one of the world's most popular tourist attractions or why the country has a high-speed network of trains that is the envy of many others, especially the UK. I was reminded of the bike lift that I had discovered in Trondheim, Norway during my 2015 quest across the continent. Equally daft but the world is just a little bit better because of it. And you never know: it might have caught on...

There was a slightly surreal end to the day. I had located a campsite near a small town called Grisolles. It was never going to be on the list of the most beautiful places in France. Grisolles, it seemed, was the perfect name for Grisolles, so I did not hang around in the centre choosing instead to head directly to the campsite on the hill above the town.

Surrealism was not to be found in the town but in the reception of Camping Les Terraces Occitanes. Following a long wait for anyone to arrive, a man with few teeth turned up. He seemed somewhat confused by the arrival of a customer and, upon working out that I was not French, called for backup. A few minutes later his wife entered the darkened room and began to take details. This took time. A lot of time. Such was her unease when using the computer that I could only assume that she had never previously done so. Despite my name, she assumed I was Belgian - my accent perhaps? - but we eventually made it to the end of her questions and I was left to find my pitch. It was all a bit… Grisolles.

Day Thirty-Five: Grisolles to Toulouse (31km)
Saturday 6th August

I had been the first cyclist to arrive at the campsite near Grisolles the previous evening but over the next few hours almost all of the half dozen or so pitches that had been set aside for cyclists were filled. My comparative eagerness was repeated in the morning when I was the first to leave but not before an informative chat with a Frenchwoman called Marie. She was from a town about 20km from the south coast called Pézenas. It was a little off my planned route but it was a place that I had always wanted to visit.

Well, ever since the winter of 1985. Those were the days before the expression "interactive online learning" had ever been uttered by anyone, anywhere. At the time, one of the few ways to learn a foreign tongue was by tuning to BBC1 on a Sunday morning and watching one the corporation's language learning programmes. There was *Deutsch Direkt* if German was your thing, *España Viva* for the hispanophiles, and for lovers of all things French, *À Vous La France*. The presenters, Carole Rousseau and Patrick Simpson-Jones - who each spoke cut-glass English percolated through a French accent - guided viewers through the essentials of the language. At the end of each episode, after Carole and Patrick had stopped flirting with each other, we were transported to France itself to discover elements of life in Grenoble and, in the final few programmes of the series, Pézenas.

"I had no idea my town was so famous," declared Marie, in French. I played down the fact that this was a minority-interest programme to say the very least.

"If you do visit, you could stay at my house. I won't be there but I could arrange for someone to give you the key."

This was a remarkable offer. Marie was on holiday with her husband and two children and here she was offering me, a complete stranger, the use of her house. Carole and Patrick would be blushing at the thought that their efforts in fostering Anglo-French relations were still coming to fruition nearly 40 years later.[47]

Another place that I had always wanted to visit was Toulouse and it was my destination for today. With time an increasing concern, I was not keen to take another day off from cycling. It had only been four days since I had

---

[47] Both Patrick and Carole are still going strong after all these years. Patrick has retired to Florida and Carole is still hard at work recording material for secondary school language courses in the UK. I hear her voice regularly when teaching French!

done that in Bordeaux. However, the distance gods were looking down upon me favourably as I continued my cycle along the Canal de la Garonne. I was now only 30km north of Toulouse and if I could arrive in *la ville rose* before lunchtime, I could at least spend the remainder of the day exploring. To make the most of my limited time in Toulouse it made sense to stay close to the centre. So, before leaving Camping Les Terraces Occitanes, I abandoned tentative plans to find a campsite and booked myself a hotel only a stone's throw away from the city's main square.

Grisolles was still looking distinctly grisolles as I paused to buy breakfast from a *boulangerie* before rejoining the canal that slashed a straight blue line to the east of the town. Shortly after doing so, I stopped to read a noticeboard that told me what I had missed: the Theodore Calbet museum, the metal "Baltard-style" market hall[48] and the vaulted gate of the Église Saint-Martin. I could live with that. Of greater interest was the mention of a certain Jean Dargaties, or Jean Dargassies as he was known professionally. His profession? Cyclist.

But not just any cyclist. Dargassies was one of only 60 men to compete in the first edition of the Tour de France in 1903. Crucially, he was also one of the 21 who managed to complete the race. On a route that stretched out over 2,428km, he finished in a creditable 11th place. However, during stage 4 of the race that had started in Toulouse and would finish in Bordeaux, on a route that was remarkably similar to mine (albeit in the opposite direction) Dargassies was doing very well. Indeed after he sped through his home town of Grisolles at the head of the peloton, *L'Auto*, the newspaper of Henri Desgrange, the man who set up the Tour de France, reported it as follows:

"All Grisolles is on the road: it is in fact to see Dargassies pass, the regional champion who they've been following in *L'Auto* since the start of the Tour de France. Many local cyclists went to see him in Toulouse and Dargassies has now come to visit them. From four o'clock in the morning the national road that crosses Grisolles is black with people: on all sides can be heard exclamations, cries of impatience: all hands are preparing to applaud. But when Dargassies passed, it was an indescribable thing, everyone shouting their encouragement: it was like a long trail that began on the side of Toulouse and ended on the side of Montauban. Ah! These Grisollois, what enthusiasm!

[48] Named after Victor Baltard who was famous in the 19th century for designing ornate metal market halls including Les Halles in Paris. But clearly not the one in Grisolles.

Here is the order of the passages: Dargassies, Georget, Garin…" (L'Auto, 13th July 1903)

Garin was, of course, the eventual winner of the inaugural Tour de France and his name has gone down in the annals of cycling history. Dargassies has been largely forgotten.

119 years later, it was somewhat quieter beside the canal, but if I listened carefully there were perhaps the faint echoes of cheers ricocheting down through time. Or was it the leaves on the trees? Irrespective, Dargassies was - and still is - a local hero. He finished 4th in the 1904 Tour de France and in 1907, gained the accolade of becoming the first ever *domestique* cyclist when he escorted the moneyed Henri Pépin on a rather leisurely Tour de France. That was more my style.

After Grisolles there was little to distract me from the job of cycling to Toulouse: no more *"plus beaux villages de France"* or curious contraptions dreamt up by free-thinking French engineers. Just 30km of canal towpath to negotiate. It did not make for the most exciting of rides but it was easy going and shortly before 11 am I was approaching my destination.

The Canal de la Garonne finished abruptly - and somewhat noisily - at a bridge which, despite its age, now carried a wide slip road for the adjacent motorway that I had been shadowing for several kilometres. I was suddenly flung back into the *über*-urban world as I attempted to cross a three-lane road immediately followed by a four-lane road both of which had converged on this point in order to funnel their users onto the motorway.

Also converging upon this point, in decidedly more sedate fashion, were the three canals of Toulouse: de la Garonne, du Midi and de Brienne. The latter was a short channel linking the other two canals to the River Garonne. If I had arrived in a straight direction from 12 o'clock on the clock face, the Canal de Brienne set off in an equally straight direction towards 4 o'clock. Somewhere between 2 and 3 o'clock (just to be difficult) the Canal du Midi started meandering nonchalantly on a journey that would initially see it snake around the north and east of the city before slithering its way to the Mediterranean. I glanced down from a second bridge towards the narrow and overgrown starting point of the much older Canal du Midi. It was obvious that it would be a very different beast to cycle beside compared to the Canal de la Garonne or indeed the Canal de Nantes à Brest earlier in the trip. It was an ominous sign.

All that was for the following day. I had a big city to explore. I switched on Google Maps and asked for directions to the main square, the Place du Capitole. 15 minutes later I was there, feeling rather confused. The border may have been a further 100km to the south but somehow I had arrived not in a French city, but a Spanish one. Yes, the signs were in French, as were the voices. It was the French tricolour that had been hoisted above the façade of the magnificent town hall in front of me in the square. On a physical level, however, this was much more reminiscent of Pamplona or Madrid. It was a world away from Bordeaux which, in comparison, had been positively Parisian. But neither was it built from the blinding white limestone to be found in Nîmes or Montpellier. This was quite unique for France, but not so unique for Spain. And it certainly lived up to its reputation for being the pink city, *la ville rose*.

Although it was still not midday, I went to my hotel and asked if they could look after Wanda while I wandered. I was in luck. I had arrived well in advance of check-in time but the receptionist at the Hotel Royal Wilson was more than happy for me to deposit my panniers in the room. Perhaps, on reflection, he was more concerned with the fact that the building attached to his hotel was in the process of being demolished. All that remained were the ground floor windows of a restaurant and a hairdressers that now functioned as a safety barrier between passers-by and a big hole in the ground.

"It's all very compact and easily walkable" was the opinion of my Rough Guide. It was also very unplanned. Every street seemed to have adopted its own unique direction. Great for wandering. Wonderful for getting lost, which was my plan. Via a circuitous route I made my way back to the Place du Capitole with one question playing on my mind… *Why was everything so pink?*

It was actually more of a browny red. *The Red City? The Brown City?* Neither work so well as marketing epithets so let us stick with pink. It is all down to the iron oxide to be found in the clays of this corner of Languedoc. The Romans made bricks from it to build their town of Tolosa and these very same local bricks have been the building material of choice ever since.

My initial strolling did not take me far. After an hour or so I found a backstreet bar and indulged in a very early - 2 pm - beer. This proved to be fatal for my energy levels. Once again, accumulated fatigue as a result of consecutive days of cycling and repeated nights of sporadic sleep in the tent had caught up on me. It seemed appropriate that in very Spanish Toulouse I should require a siesta so I gave in to my body, made my way back to the hotel and indulged in a couple of hours slumber.

I re-emerged onto the streets in the late afternoon. With the temperature beginning to dip as the evening approached, this made for much less taxing wandering. As the light softened, the brown and red buildings began to reveal more of their shades of pink. None more so than the churches. It is strange to think that for even the most agnostic of travellers such as myself, buildings of prayer and contemplation are just as attractive - in a literal sense - as they are for the ardent believers. It goes beyond the undeniable beauty of the establishments. Perhaps it is because they offer a space to pause, think and reflect. A place to shut out the outside world and consider where one's life or journey has been, where it is now and where it will take us.

This was certainly the case with the Basilique Saint-Sernin on the northern edge of the historic centre. Its distant ornate brick tower could be seen from the Place du Capitole, leading the curious along the length of the Rue du Taur. The five octagonal tiers were topped with a sharp spire and the whole wedding-cake construction was perched precariously upon the centre of the cross of the basilica itself. Construction started in the 1070s and it is now the largest Romanesque church in France. It contains a serious number of pink bricks and it was all built to accommodate pilgrims en route to Santiago de Compostela. Just like me, they found - and continue to find - a place to pause, think and reflect on their journey so far. What's more, we all had our respective challenges: theirs to climb the Pyrenees mountains, mine to negotiate a way alongside the Canal du Midi.

I had long dreamt of cycling the length of the canal but as the day of departure approached I was increasingly apprehensive about the route. The more I read about it in my Cicerone guidebook, the more I looked at the detail on the maps and the more I thought back to my chat with Declan Lyons (the man who wrote the guidebook) earlier in the year, the more I worried. Cycling along the Canal du Midi would be a very different experience compared to the previous canals. It might just be easier to follow the pilgrims over the Pyrenees instead.

I inevitably found myself sitting on the terrace of another café sipping another beer. I opened up the third of my three maps covering the length of the Canal des 2 Mers à Vélo that I had picked up in Royan. This one showed me the route from Toulouse to Sète on the Mediterranean coast.

On a macro level the route formed a long arc that would see me head initially south-east from Toulouse but by the time I arrived in Sète my direction of travel would have rotated through 90° to see me travelling predominantly towards the north-east. Carcassonne, the famous fortified city, marked the approximate midway point between Toulouse and Sète but I would also pass through Béziers, further to the east. This was a place I had visited in 2013 as I made my way along the Mediterranean from Greece to Portugal. Indeed the entire section of my route from Béziers to Avignon would be repeating that journey. Was this another opportunity to take one of my five remaining trains? That was not an option I would consider until I set sight - again - on the flamingos of the Etang de Thau. Between a pink city deep inland and some pink birds on the coast it would be cycling and nothing but cycling.

When the 17th-century engineer Pierre-Paul Riquet started to plan his canal from Toulouse to the Mediterranean, he was very much a pioneer in the field: there were few shoulders upon which he could stand. The impetus for constructing a canal from the Mediterranean to Toulouse was, as noted previously, to avoid the route through the Strait of Gibraltar which was controlled by the pesky Spaniards. In 1666, Louis XIV - the Sun King - proclaimed in an edict that the canal should be constructed and the following year the digging started. It took 12,000 labourers - women as well as men - over 14 years to complete the work. But it was not just a case of digging a long hole in the ground. As with all canals it required a water supply and Riquet was persuaded to create just one sizeable reservoir - the Bassin de Saint-Ferréol - rather than a larger number of small ones. It required the construction of an 800-metre-long dam that was over 30 metres high. As the new lake was 20km from the canal's summit, a 25km channel also needed to be dug linking the two. The construction of the dam was the largest construction project in Europe at the time - the HS2 of its day - but that was not factoring in the Canal du Midi itself. To avoid inconvenient obstacles such as hills, the canal was designed to follow the contours of the land, but 65 locks were still needed to tame the gradient. Sadly, Riquet, who had provided a substantial chunk of the funding himself, died six months before the canal's completion. Yet his efforts were not in vain. In 1996 the Canal du Midi was attributed World Heritage status by UNESCO. Their citation described it as follows:

> "It is one of the most remarkable feats of civil engineering in modern times… The care that its creator, Pierre-Paul Riquet, took in the design and the way it blends with its surroundings turned a technical achievement into a work of art."

Riquet was not just an engineer: he was an artist, and I was about to set off along his very long gallery.

Day Thirty-Six: Toulouse to Alzonne (92km)
Sunday 7th August

I had wanted to start my day by returning to the Place du Capitole to fly the drone so as to capture the glory of the town hall - le Capitole - in the golden-hour light of the morning sunrise. Alas my plans were scuppered by the constant stream of revellers who, at 8 am, were making their semi-drunken way back home. One young guy seemed particularly keen to ride Wanda around the square but I managed to persuade him otherwise. I could only imagine that his enthusiasm for flying - and no doubt crashing - the drone would be even greater. He stayed off the bike and the drone stayed stowed away in my front-right pannier bag.

The Canal du Midi was only about 1km due east of the Place du Capitole. However, I felt compelled to join it at the start of its journey to Sète, the same point at which I had finished my cycle along the Canal de la Garonne the previous lunchtime. This meant retracing my steps to the meeting point of the two canals - 3km away - and then cycling the first 4km of the Canal du Midi that would bring me to the point 1km due east of the main square. The extra kilometres might have lengthened the cycling day by about half an hour but I was willing to make the sacrifice. I did want to cycle the whole of the Canal du Midi, not just the convenient bits.

My departure from the centre of Toulouse was further delayed as I was cycling along a path that was sandwiched between the canal and the eponymous Boulevard Pierre-Paul Riquet, the man responsible for the canal's construction. I noticed a large food market on the other side of the street. This being a Sunday in France, any opportunity to stock up on food supplies could not be ignored so I went to explore. It would take another 30 minutes to investigate the stalls of top-notch French produce and I came away laden with bread, salami, cherry tomatoes, goat's cheese and fruit. This included a peach that the woman in charge of the fruit stall insisted that I have for free. It made me wonder if the vagrant look that I had successfully managed to acquire on my previous long European trips was returning. If it meant offers of free food, so be it.

My plan for this first day along the canal was to cycle as far as a place called Alzonne. It had a campsite and when I had visited the website to check it out, it had the option of booking online in advance, so I paid the €13.60 and did just that. It was not often that I was able to set off in the knowledge that my accommodation for the evening was already sorted. Although it was something I would normally not worry about until the mid-afternoon, it was a weight off my mind. Added to the quiet, carefree (and predominantly car-free) Sunday morning atmosphere of the suburbs and a front-left pannier bag full of food, it was an especially zen start to the day.

Aside from its pink(ish) buildings, Toulouse was also famous for its students - over 100,000 of them - and for being the centre of the French aerospace industry. As I cycled through its southern suburbs that warm Sunday morning, it seemed that every aeronautical engineer who had not escaped the city for their annual summer holidays was outside, working hard at exercising. There were walkers (*"bonjour!"*), cyclists (*"bonjour!"*), joggers (*"bonjour!"*), rowers (*"bonjour!"*) and paddle boarders (*"bonjour!"*) every few metres. I had no evidence to prove that they were indeed aeronautical engineers but being so active so early on a Sunday morning suggested they all possessed the hard work ethic demanded by their profession. As they walked, cycled, jogged, rowed or paddled I could see their minds trying to pick over some thorny issue that they had encountered with Bernoulli's principle.[49] I could only hope they were not distracted from their trains of thought by my cheery salutations. If you have faith in the domino effect, the next great plane disaster might have its origins in those bright and breezy greetings. Condolences to all those affected.

The gentle 50-metre climb to the canal's summit at the village of Le Ségala stretched out over 50km. If it had not have been for the presence of the locks that provided a regular reminder otherwise, it would have been entirely possible to imagine I was cycling on the flat. Little effort was required and, contrary to expectations, the towpath was just as amenable to cycling as that of the Canal de la Garonne had been earlier in the week. A few annoying roots encased in the tarmac but aside from that, it was easy-going. I began to cast aside my concerns about the Canal du Midi being in any way challenging and concentrated instead on the important job of enjoying my Sunday-morning cycle. As the canal twisted and turned its way south, the trees gifted me protection from the harmful rays of the sun. The pretty lock keepers' cottages with their green-painted shutters and whitewashed walls were a gently fading reminder of the days when this was a busy trading thoroughfare. The only minor distraction was the noise of a more modern trading thoroughfare to my left: the Autoroute des Deux Mers and its fast-flowing stream of traffic.

Then, almost everything changed.

The clue had been staring me in the face since leaving Toulouse. The cycle route on my map was marked in green. As far as the summit of the

---

[49] When the internal pressure of a gas or a fluid goes down, the speed of the gas or liquid goes up. It helps explain why planes can fly but clearly it is not that simple.

canal it was a solid green line of *voie verte* (greenway). Thereafter it became a dotted green line and was described as *"chemin"* (path). The transition from the former to the latter took place within a couple of metres of me passing through a short tunnel under a railway line. Behind me was the cycling-friendly paved surface of the Haute Garonne *département*: ahead of me was the less-friendly unpaved surface of Aude, the *département* across which much of the remainder of the Canal du Midi passed. It would be my home for at least the next two days of cycling. The dotted green line on my map did not revert back to solid green until after Béziers, a city that was not even in the Aude *département*. I consulted the Cicerone guide to read what Declan Lyons had written about the upcoming section of the route. He did not pull any punches: "Gravel and hard clay - narrow and very difficult in places".

On the positive side, I was not cycling a high-end racing bike with wafer-thin tyres. Wanda's robust construction and wide Schwalbe Marathon Plus Tour tyres were more than a match for even the most unforgiving of surfaces. But it did make for an uncomfortable ride. Clutching at another positive, the day-trippers from Toulouse had reached their limit at the edge of Haute Garonne and had turned around to go back home. Traffic beside the canal was suddenly much reduced.

After a kilometre on the rough track, at the pretty Écluse de l'Océan, the cycle route crossed over a bridge to the western side of the canal. However, there were no signs to tell me that this was the case so I carried on regardless. Another 50 metres further along the canal, when the path petered out, I realised the error of my ways and quickly backtracked. Lack of signage would continue to be an issue for quite some time.

Having crossed over to the correct side of the water I now discovered that I usually had a choice of paths: one immediately beside the canal and one on the raised embankment, but it was very much Hobson's choice. I repeatedly crossed from one to the other at points where the two paths briefly met but invariably found myself wishing I had stayed put. It was, as Declan had noted, very hard going.

Added to these woes was the sad realisation that I was now witnessing, for the first time, the devastating effects of the fungus Ceratocystis Platani which, over recent decades, has spread amongst the plane trees that line the canal. The trees were not an original feature of the 17th-century canal but were added in the 1830s so as to strengthen the banks and provide shade. After nearly 200 years, they had met their match in the form of the fungus that is believed to have been brought over from North America in ammunition boxes used during the Second World War. The fungus has proved to be just as deadly as the bullets the boxes once contained and it is an ongoing battle to remove the diseased trees and replace them with fungus-resistant varieties.

A report in *La Dépêche du Midi*, the regional newspaper for the southwest of France, stated that by the end of 2022 30,100 of the canal's original 42,000 trees had been "felled and burned on the spot". Nearly 20,000 new trees have been planted but, inevitably, restoring the banks of the canal to their pre-fungus state will take many decades. I first encountered this programme of replanting to the west of the town of Castelnaudary. Everything was carefully explained on a large board erected by VNF, Voies Navigables de France, the authority responsible for French waterways. At this particular point, 95 new oak trees had been planted and I could see them lining the canal as it curved into the distance ahead of me. Only a few metres tall and with protective sheaths to prevent them from being nibbled by passing animals, it would be many years before they were able to offer any kind of shade to a passing cyclist.

Ironically, along the sections of the canal that had been replanted and in order to facilitate the restoration work, the tow path had been significantly upgraded so as to accommodate vehicles and machinery. The result was that I had a decent surface along which to cycle, but absolutely no shade. Of the two evils - rough track and lack of shade - I could have lived with the former if it meant that the beauty of the World Heritage Site had not been partially erased by an indiscriminate and lethal fungus. I consoled myself with the thought of returning to the Canal du Midi in 20, 30 or perhaps even 40 years' time to see the restoration work come to fruition. If, by then, I had not been felled myself.

Castelnaudary was the only town that I passed through between Toulouse and my destination of Alzonne. As I did so, a large canal basin opened up. More small lake, it must once have been a great hub of industrial activity when the Canal du Midi functioned as a key artery transporting wine and wheat from south to north. Now it had adopted a much more peaceful existence providing mooring facilities for the pleasure craft that chugged up and down the canal.

The main company hiring out these vehicles went by the name of Le Boat and the French teacher in me cringed every time I had to read the name. Water-born tourism had been modest (often non-existent) on the Canal de Nantes à Brest. There had been more of it on the Canal de la Garonne but it was only here, along the Canal du Midi, where it had become big business. Le Boat had a number of bases where budding ship captains could pick up or return their vessels. After my experiences with the towpath earlier in the day, I momentarily fantasised about hopping on board for a smoother, more comfortable journey to the Mediterranean. Alas only trains were part of my plan, not boats, but I was tempted.

I was now cycling through the hottest part of the day. The temperature in the shade was around 30°, the temperature in direct sunlight significantly higher and, for much of the time there continued to be minimal shielding because of the removal of the diseased trees. The locks however were delightful examples of Pierre-Paul Riquet's desire to create not just a functional channel of water but one with artistic credentials. Each was in the form of an oval, 30 metres long, 11 metres wide at the midpoint but only 6 metres wide at the gates. The gentle curves of the lock walls mirrored those of the hulls of boats and it was not difficult to imagine two barges being accommodated simultaneously should the need have arisen.

All the locks were identified by both numbers and names. It was between the distinctively named Écluse de Guerre - the Lock of War - and the Écluse de la Criminelle - the Lock of the (female) Criminal - where I paused at the much more poetic Écluse de la Peyruque. It was number 39 and in the adjacent former lock keeper's cottage a retired couple operated a small shop selling refreshments, local produce and home-made ceramics.

"I've never done the Canal du Midi, neither on a bike nor in a boat," explained Jean-Louis in French. He was in charge of serving customers while his wife toiled away on the ceramics in her studio inside the cottage.

"I was a teacher on the island of La Réunion before I retired. We came here for a quiet life 18 years ago."

"Has it changed much in 18 years?" I asked.

"When we arrived in 2005, all the lock keepers' cottages were inhabited by lock keepers. Except this one. The lock keeper lived with his family in the nearby town so we were able to move in. Now, most of the cottages are not lived in and the canal is not as well maintained."

I wondered what the attitude of the canal authority was towards cyclists, reflecting upon the quality of the route and lack of signage.

"Cyclists are tolerated. The focus of Voies Navigables de France is the canal. They don't worry about the towpath. There are two groups of tourists who travel along the canal. There are those who would like there to be traffic lights, pharmacies, supermarkets - I'm exaggerating of course! - and there are those who want it '*dans son jus*'[50]. There are cyclists who are happy and there are cyclists who are very, very unhappy."

I thought about his comments in the final few kilometres of the day. *Which camp was I in?* Perhaps there was a third group of cyclists who simply could not decide. My first day along the Canal du Midi had had its

---

[50] 'In its original condition'

frustrations but ultimately this was a canal and not a cycle path. It would be interesting to see if, by the time I arrived in Sète later in the week, my opinions had become more equivocal.

I found Camping l'Escale Occitane around 3km north of the canal on the far side of Alzonne. It was, perhaps, France's only airline-themed campsite. Rémy and Nadia had both worked in the airline industry before deciding to leave the jet set to run the campsite and restaurant. Air France memorabilia was strategically placed in the bar, including a row of seats from an Airbus. I could not spot the Airbus itself but would not have been at all surprised if it was on Rémy's list of future purchases. It would make an interesting addition to the range of accommodation options that the campsite offered. This included an area set aside for cyclists and I pitched the tent as the sky was just beginning to take on a pinkish hue generated by the slowly setting sun.

As I glanced towards the horizon I could see the hazy silhouettes of the foothills of the Pyrenees. They would always remain distant on this trip. However, as I neared the southernmost point of my Grand Tour of Europe and despite the idiosyncrasies of the Canal du Midi, it was a reminder that the greatest physical challenges of the journey were still ahead of me in the Alps. It was Sunday 7th August. I had now completed just over five weeks in the saddle and there remained only four weeks to complete my continental quest. *Had I bitten off far more than I was capable of chewing?* On which thought I went to order some airline-style food in the restaurant.

Day Thirty-Seven: Alzonne to Pouzols-Minervois (71km)
Monday 8th August

Whatever the Canal du Midi might throw at me today, I could at least take solace in two things. Firstly, I would be passing through the spectacular medieval town of Carcassonne. Secondly, I would finally start heading back to Rotterdam and the Hook of Holland as, shortly after Carcassonne, the direction of the canal changed very subtly from south to north. Thereafter, my route to the Netherlands, despite it taking in the eastern edge of Switzerland, appeared to be much more direct than it had been on the way south. I had estimated the total cycling distance of my Grand Tour to be around 4,500km, 5,500km including the ten train journeys. According to my calculations, I had cycled just over 2,400km and had taken five of my ten (maximum-100-km) trains. With fewer than four full weeks to accomplish my cycling quest, I persuaded myself that this was beginning to suggest that my ambitions were attainable. As long as, that is, I did not dig too deep into the statistics or the obstacles ahead of me. The minor issue of the Alps, for example.

After dinner in the campsite restaurant the previous evening I had spent a leisurely few minutes perusing Google Maps in a vain attempt to find a suitable campsite for the following day. With a full stomach, a couple of beers oozing through my veins and a nice sunset to admire, my lack of success had not concerned me. However, after strolling back to the tent I fell into conversation with a French cyclist of a similar age. He was also struggling to find campsites further along the canal but was somewhat more animated about the situation. As I went off to doze in my tent, he sat down to continue his investigations.

My French research assistant was the first person I encountered in the morning and he was keen to share with me the results of his efforts. His extensive notes mentioned a campsite at a place called Pouzols-Minervois so, feeling only slightly guilty about benefitting from his late-night toil, I took a photo of the details. Alas when I looked on my map, the town was a good number of kilometres away from the canal, many more than had been required to cycle to the campsite near Alzonne. Such a deviation would mean either missing out on a significant stretch of towpath or retracing my steps the following morning. Then again, if the towpath was anything like it had been on day one of cycling along the Canal du Midi, I might be eager to escape it towards the end of the day. It would be a decision to take in the afternoon. For the time being - as with my many other potential concerns - I would continue to ignore it.

Foreshadowing later events, instead of returning to the point where I had left the canal, I chose instead to head east from Alzonne in the direction of the towns of Sainte-Eulalie and then Villesèquelande. I followed five kilometres of quiet and immaculate country roads to rejoin the towpath to the east of Villesèquelande. The journey had me reminiscing fondly about the leisurely, unchallenging, comfortable, bump-free (I could go on…) paths that I had been cycling upon for much of my journey up until this point. With few concerns for the quality of the route below my wheels, I was again liberated to soak in all that surrounded me: the distant Pyrenees mountains, the hectares of exploding sunflowers and the fat black grapes hanging low from the vines. Everything was bathed sumptuously in the early morning golden light of the sun. I did not wish to be anywhere else apart from here, cycling, slowly edging my way towards the southernmost point of my epic journey. I had set off from Toulouse with the firm intention of cycling every metre of the Canal du Midi, "not just the convenient bits". It was only day two and I was already happily wavering from this hasty resolution.

I could at least look forward to my imminent arrival in Carcassonne which was now only 10km along the canal. Ignoring Declan's comments in his guidebook ("the towpath is not easy to cycle from here into Carcassonne"), after my dalliances with the rural road network, I did feel compelled to remain loyal to the canal and stuck it out, despite the somewhat unfriendly terrain. At the Écluse de Lalande, I paused briefly at a multi-coloured sign which had been erected to point out the directions to exotic destinations such as Hanoi, Sao Paulo and Trinidad. Despite their far-flung locations, surely those journeys could not be anywhere near as taxing as that required to get to Carcassonne only a few kilometres further east.

I left the canal on the western edge of the bastide town of Carcassonne and followed my nose across its grid pattern of streets in what I guessed was the correct direction. I knew what I was looking for but was not quite sure where it would be. I first caught a glimpse of it as I approached the Pont Vieux, a long, low bridge the ancient arches of which spanned the River Aude. And then there it was, above me and to the right: the elongated medieval splendour of the fortified town of Carcassonne.

It may have done a fine job masquerading as Nottingham Castle in *Robin Hood: Prince of Thieves*, but this was far removed from the English East Midlands. An imposing hilltop location, three kilometres of solid-stone fortifications and 52 turreted towers. A masterpiece of military defence born in the Middle Ages. Who needed to build a film set in Hollywood or Pinewood if the real thing had already been erected in south-west France? This is what France did very well. Almost too well… I was reminded of the

Château de Pierrefonds that I had stumbled upon in 2015 as I made my way from Paris to the Belgium border on the Spain to Norway cycle. Pristine history. Tailor-made for the movie moguls and TV executives. In the case of Pierrefonds, it had been those shouting "action" on the set of the BBC's *Merlin*. Both they and Kevin Costner had just one person to thank for making their set designers redundant: a certain 19th-century architect going by the name of Eugène Emmanuel Viollet-le-Duc.

The British and the French have very different attitudes when it comes to preservation and restoration. It is rare in the UK to visit a listed building or monument and find that it looks just as it did when the ribbon was cut in the 13th, 17th or whatever century. Admittedly, in those days, ribbons were probably not cut. Great wooden doors were no doubt flung open with great gusto and the local big wig (resembling Brian Blessed of course) would have roared in delight as their new palace, or church, or castle was declared open. The important business of excessive consumption, no-holes-barred orgies and general belligerence and debauchery could commence. I am, of course, pandering to historical stereotypes but hey! the Catholic does have a reputation. I digress.

The focus in Britain is towards conservation. Where restoration does take place it is usually purposefully designed to be obvious. The contrast between old (conserved) and new (restored) is often stark and that is what Historic England wants you to see and understand.

In France, the approach is somewhat different. Cast your mind back to my visit to the cathedral in Chartres. I wrote the following:

> "The stand-out attraction was a choir screen, 7-metres high and 100-metres long depicting the life of Christ in 40 sculpted scenes. Its detail was astonishing and recent renovation work had returned it to the day it had been chiselled in the early 16th century."

I dare say millions of Euros had been thrown at that choir screen. It was stunning. Pristine. Perfect. Not a blemish nor a pimple. Restoration in action, and no explanatory note to explain that perhaps what I was looking at was a modern take - replacement even? - on a very old work of art.

It is a contentious issue and not one confined to the 21st century. In the 19th century, Viollet-le-Duc was an exponent of recreating the past and he did this not just with Carcassonne and the Château de Pierrefonds but also with Notre Dame Cathedral in Paris.[51] He may not have been aware of it at the time, but his Carcassonne turrets were not typical of south-western France in the Middle Ages. He got it wrong, although they do now look the part.

On the other side of the channel, John Ruskin had a very different approach when it came to preserving the past, as summarised by David Spurr in his book, Architecture and Modern Literature:

> "Viollet-le-Duc devoted a successful career to restoring many of France's great architectural monuments of the Middle Ages and wrote extensively in defence of his practices. Ruskin, on the other hand, abhorred restoration of any kind, and defended the aesthetic value of ruins."

Plus ça change. Carcassonne is no ruin and the filmmakers are not complaining. Perhaps if Ruskin had known that a century later, the technicians, actors and movie producers would have to traipse to southern France to find an authentic Nottingham Castle, he might well have changed his mind.

Irrespective, I loved Carcassonne. It was in utter contrast to that other great architectural icon of France, the Mont-Saint-Michel. Whereas in Normandy the thousands of tourists had been squeezed into the confines of a small, fortified mound, in Carcassonne there was space. Lots of space. I did not have to lock Wanda at the entrance and hope she would be there when I returned. She could join me in exploring the network of cobbled streets, alleys and squares. If one lane looked too busy, there was always an alternative turning that led me along a quieter route at the end of which I would return to the throng.

As I was strolling around the old city of Carcassonne, the Canal du Midi had gone off on its own wander maintaining its position to the north of the River Aude. The mound upon which the walled city had been built seemed to have pushed the river - and its loyal neighbour the canal - as far north as it could. Upon leaving the fortifications via the Porte Narbonnaise on the eastern side of the medieval complex I intuitively continued cycling east in the hope of soon bumping into the canal again. Not appreciating the scale of the canal's northern detour, it would be another 10km before I was reacquainted with the towpath. This involved discovering some of

---

[51] It is interesting to note that the spire that collapsed during the fire at Notre Dame in 2019 was not the 13th-century original but that designed by Viollet-le-Duc and constructed in 1859.

Carcassonne's more modern attractions including a bustling out-of-town trading estate, the busy D6113 and the vast car park of a newly built hospital. At this point, I admitted defeat, turned on Google directions and was dispatched in the direction of Trèbes via a second instalment of the D6113. Robin Hood never had these issues, although perhaps Kevin Costner did. I later consulted the official website of the Canal des 2 Mers cycle route. I noted with more than a modicum of irony that the section between Carcassonne and Trèbes that I had managed to avoid was one of the few stretches of the towpath for which a mountain bike was *not* recommended.

For the next 20km (for which mountain bikes *were* recommended) I remained loyal to the canal again. It was here, just to the west of a village called Millegrand, where I arrived at the southernmost point of my Grand Tour. I was oblivious to this momentous moment when it happened, only working out later that I had indeed turned the corner at this particular point. Perhaps if I had realised at the time I might have jumped into the canal in celebration. I might even have tossed Wanda in beside me and shouted for rescue from one of the passing leisure craft. Perhaps they would have taken pity on me and allowed me to stay on board until Béziers. I had now come to the conclusion that by far the best way to cycle the Canal du Midi was to do so whilst sipping cocktails on board a boat.

I abandoned the canal for the final time that day at the small town of La Redorte after which I continued on a series of mercifully quiet D roads for the 15km as far as my destination of Pouzols-Minervois. Visiting Carcassonne had made the day memorable. In most other respects it had been a day to forget. The final nail in the coffin came in the form of Pouzols-Minervois itself. The campsite was easily found beside the main road. Most people staying there were hidden inside their small static caravans. There were few, if any, tents and I was allocated a patch of ground which presumably doubled up as a children's sandpit when not occupied by people such as me. My Hubba Hubba tent was freestanding. On a windless day such as today, it did not require any pegs. This was good fortune as the pit of sand was incapable of supporting anything hammered into it.

With the tent being held down by nothing more than the panniers sitting inside it, I cycled into the village itself. I was hoping to find a bar serving food or, failing that, at least a small *épicerie* where I could buy the simple necessities of life in France: bread, cheese and wine. Alas, the village was even quieter than the campsite and there was no evidence of a bar or a restaurant or any kind of shop. How did the people hiding behind the closed shutters in the small warren of streets survive without their daily dose of freshly made *baguette*? It may have been a Monday but I suspected that every day in Pouzols-Minervois was a Monday. I trudged back down the hill to the campsite where I knocked up yet another evening meal of spaghetti and pesto. What it lacked in variety it did at least make up for in calorific value. As I slurped the strings of pasta, I consoled myself with the knowledge that Tuesday might be my final day of cycling the Canal du Midi. Escape, I hoped, was in sight.

Day Thirty-Eight: Pouzols-Minervois to Montagnac, Via Sète (134km)
Tuesday 9th August

My cycling acquaintance from Alzonne who had found the campsite in Pouzols-Minervois never arrived himself. Or, if he did, had managed to do so without me noticing him. On such a small campsite it seemed unlikely, especially as he would probably have been allocated the other side of the sand pit. Come the morning, it remained unoccupied.

It would be an early start for me, one of the earliest of the trip. A symptom, perhaps, of my enthusiasm to move on to pastures new or at least to be cycling somewhere other than beside the Canal du Midi. Shortly after 7 am, I was standing at the gate of the campsite looking directly towards the rising sun. It was a moment of quiet contemplation. The previous two days had been hard work and, with Sète still 100km away, it seemed likely that today would be no different. My willingness - eagerness even - to give the towpath yet another opportunity to redeem itself was as annoying as it was bewildering. Before setting off from the UK, the Canal du Midi was firmly lodged in my mind as a highlight of the entire journey around Europe. Yet here I was just wishing for this section of the ride to be over and done with. I was annoyed with myself for having had such high expectations. I was annoyed with the authorities for not making any effort to accommodate cyclists. I was annoyed with the canal for having been built in an age when towpaths needed to be nothing more than rough paths for towing.

I had cycled 15km to get to the campsite from the canal the previous afternoon and it would be another 10km along the main road heading east before I could rejoin it near the town of Argeliers. I reasoned that at such an early hour, traffic would be light. It was almost non-existent. I was able to spend the first half hour of the cycling day pedalling in the direction of the rising sun along a very straight, high-quality road looking forward to the post-canal adventure. Montpellier, Avignon, the Rhône Valley, the Alps, the Furka Pass, the Rhine, the Bodensee, Basel and Strasbourg before a final week or so of cycling in the direction of Rotterdam and the Hook of Holland. My current mood may have been a little subdued, but I had every reason to believe it would not continue once the Canal du Midi was behind me.

It was the kind of day that was invented for stopping and staring. Upon arrival in Argeliers, I quickly found the main square and it had everything that Pouzols-Minervois did not, including a *boulangerie* where I bought breakfast. I ate it whilst sitting on a wall just outside the shop with a good view of the comings and goings in the square. The Place François Mitterrand contained most things that you might reasonably expect a small French town to offer: to my right a *charcuterie*, opposite me a post office, a small supermarket and a *tabac* and around the corner to my left a hairdressers. To my immediate left was a two-storey building with the words *liberté*, *égalité* and *fraternité* written in large stone capital letters on its pediment. The three colours of the French tricolour could just about be made out on a metal flag that had been planted upon the apex of the pediment. Such was the lack of upkeep of the building that I could not quite work out whether this was the current *hôtel de ville* or one from a previous, more prosperous, era. Indeed the whole square wreaked of neglect. It was nothing if not authentic and a perfect theatrical setting for the actors who were about to arrive. I was their non-paying audience of one.

Firstly a small group of men began to gather outside the *tabac*. They did not talk to each other. The youngest of them had carried a box of tools to where they were standing. I could not fathom why they were all standing in the same spot. There was no bus stop and when the shutters of the *tabac* opened they did not rush in to buy their packets of Gauloises Blondes. Neither did they move when the supermarket opened a few minutes later. Two women had now taken up residence at the table behind me, drinking coffee. They were just as silent as the men.

The calm was broken by a car that had no number plates. The driver was revving the car's engine in a way normally associated with a novice driver's first lesson. The vehicle stopped at an angle between the *tabac* and the supermarket, blocking the road. Out stepped an elderly woman. She took a moment to ponder her parking position before making her way, slowly, into the *tabac*. The men in the huddle and the women at the table watched her without commenting. A few moments later a police car arrived and stopped behind the old woman's car. Not able to pass, he flashed the blue lights mounted on the roof of his car. When nobody emerged from within, he gave a short blast from his siren. By this point, everyone - including me - was transfixed.

The policeman was now out of the vehicle, investigating. When he turned to the men, they shrugged their shoulders and gave no indication that the culprit was inside the *tabac*. After a few minutes, the woman left the *tabac* and made her way slowly back to her car. At this point, in an apoplectic fit of rage, completely out of kilter with the level of the crime committed, he shouted in the direction of the woman:

"You're not the only person in this village madame!"

The woman shuffled a little more quickly but did not respond. She got in her car, revved the engine excessively and drove out of the square in first gear. When the policeman cast his glances around the square, everyone looked away...

It was all very Manon des Sources. Tensions and seething resentment being played out in public in the searing heat of a rural village in southern France. It made for great entertainment. Alas, I did not have the time to wait around for Act One, Scene Two. I mounted Wanda, nodded in acknowledgement towards the group of men as I passed them and cycled out of the square in the direction of the canal on the lookout for a fishing cat.

The cat in question was not difficult to locate and I found it about 1km from the village square. Le Chat Qui Pêche was a restaurant beside a bridge over the canal that I had noticed earlier on the map. It was here where, by crossing the bridge, I could be reacquainted with the towpath. Come rain or shine it was my every intention to stick as close to the canal as possible for what I hoped would be my final day cycling along it. It would be diplomatic to describe the quality of the path so far as varied but it was with this hope in mind - that there would be good as well as bad - that I set off from the fishing cat restaurant.

Initially, the surface was excellent. The canal east of Argeliers had had most of its trees removed and, as I had previously witnessed, this corresponded to there being a decent track along which to cycle. What's more, I was soon to leave the *département* of Aude and start travelling through Hérault. This new *département* would be my home for at least the next couple of days and I was hopeful that the authorities in this littoral chunk of France had adopted a more enlightened approach to cycling than their colleagues further west.

The Ceratocystis Platani fungus may have wreaked havoc with the trees lining the Canal du Midi, but it had not had any noticeable effect on the landscape through which I was travelling. Indeed, with no trees to obscure the view, it could be argued that the fungus had finally done me a favour in allowing me to appreciate the magnificent spread of delights that had been laid out beside the canal. It was a constantly changing patchwork of vines, farmland and small villages punctuated with the occasional copse or line of trees that had not succumbed to the virus. In the far distance, behind a light blanket of haze were the faint outlines of the low foothills of the Pyrenees. I began, for the first time, to put the trials and tribulations of the previous few days into perspective.

Essentially, my problems were not with the canal itself but with my high expectations of what it might be like to cycle beside it. I had envisaged endless days of carefree cycling along an idyllic body of water through a *paysage* that ticked every box on the Peter Mayle list of French clichés. The canal itself and the landscape had delivered what I had ordered. It had simply not been so carefree because of the quality of the paths I was cycling upon. *Was that the fault of the canal authorities? Or the département of Aude?* Well, yes. But they were not the ones to have produced the glossy brochures or to have created the slick websites extolling the virtues of cycling along the canal. In fairness to them, they had been silent. The lack of cycling signage from the moment I had crossed into Aude had been the clue. Perhaps if at that point I had read a sign that said something along the lines of "cycling is tolerated but not encouraged - have a nice day!", by lowering my expectations, my experience would have been very different. Even an enthusiastic travelling cyclist such as me had to accept that sometimes, in some places, cycling was not the best way to travel from A to B or, in the case of the Canal du Midi, from Toulouse to Sète.

A few kilometres to the west of Béziers near the town of Colombiers, the canal began to draw my attention away from the sumptuous landscape through which it had been cut. Back in 1679, it had also been drawing the attention of our canal engineer, Monsieur Riquet, when he encountered a problem in the form of a hill. Hills are to canal engineers what environmental protestors are to London commuters, if somewhat more chronic. Until this point on his canal, Riquet had done a fine job in following the contours of the land. However, avoiding the Collines d'Ensérune would, in Pierre-Paul's mind, be a contour too far, so he started digging through the hill, despite the sandstone rock being susceptible to collapse. In far-off Paris, learning of this problem, Prime Minister Colbert ordered the work to be stopped immediately and experts were called in for advice. In a move that Michael Gove would have appreciated over 300 years later, Riquet had little time for these experts and ordered his men to keep digging in secret. In just eight days, the workers managed to cut a 170-metre tunnel through the hill and line it with concrete to prevent collapse. By the time Riquet and his diggers were celebrating their achievement, the formal order to halt the work had not even arrived from Paris. There is a lesson there for us all.

For a few minutes, I watched the small pleasure cruisers enter the arched hole in the side of the hill. I had no choice but to cross the contours and climb the hill, rejoining the northern bank of the canal on the other side of Colombiers.

It would now be fewer than 10km before I was in Béziers but it was still only lunchtime. I was aware of a campsite in the town but was calling a halt to the cycling day after barely 50km really an option? As I descended beside the staircase of nine locks to the west of Béziers, I pondered my options. I had contacted a Warmshowers host in the coastal town of Agde - about

25km east of Béziers - but had heard nothing back. That was not looking hopeful. Continuing as far as Sète remained an option. If I did, it would require me to cycle another 50km, but after Béziers, my map was giving me every indication that it would be easy going as far as the cycling conditions were concerned. Yet there was no campsite in Sète and I dared not even look at the prices of the hotels in this honeypot destination beside the Mediterranean. Once again, I ignored my problems and continued cycling.

Between Béziers and the coast, as I had hoped, the Canal du Midi had been seized upon by the Hérault département as a key way of promoting cycle tourism. Large information boards extolled its virtues:

"Cycling is an original way[52] to discover the canal's interesting architectural features. Slowly and silently you can admire the fauna and flora of the canal salt meadows and farmland."

Well, thank you very much. I will. And I did.

Approaching Agde, the route was on road and my ability to appreciate the flora and fauna was somewhat limited by the preponderance of mega-campsites that were as inappropriate for accommodating a lone cyclist on a budget as would be the luxury Hôtel George V in Paris. After rejoining it momentarily, I left the Canal du Midi for the final time a few kilometres to the west of Agde. No tears were shed.

I had now discounted the Warmshowers option in Agde and was en route to Sète, still ignorant as to where I might be sleeping that evening. The glorious cycleway that I followed, the Mediterranean Sea and its beaches to my right, the Étang de Thau and its pink flamingos to my left, was sufficient to soothe my troubled mind. By 5 pm I was in the centre of Sète and had dismounted from the bike. My journey along the Canal des 2 Mers cycle route from Royan on the Atlantic coast to here in Sète on the shores of the Mediterranean was complete. *But was my day of cycling?*

I had agreed with friends Basil and Liz to meet them the following morning in the town of Pézenas. This was about 20km inland from Sète, probably nearer 30 on a bike as sitting between the two was the Étang de Thau and its flamingos. It was now a week since my last non-cycling day so I was due a day off and that was what I planned to do in Pézenas with Basil and Liz. There was no train linking the two towns. *Should I stay in Sète overnight and cycle to Pézenas in the morning?* That would mean finding somewhere to stay on the coast and, confirming what I had

---

[52] Are you sure?

suspected, a quick look online revealed that budget options in Sète did not appear to exist. The alternative was to continue cycling in the direction of Pézenas and hope that some other accommodation option would present itself before darkness fell.

I remembered Marie, the woman with whom I had chatted back at the campsite in Grisolles. "Stay in my house!" she had implored when discovering my desire to visit her hometown. I had her phone number on a piece of paper in front of me but she had explained that she would still be on holiday when I was due to cycle along the Mediterranean coast. That was not a problem according to Marie as a friend of hers could let me into the house. However kind and convenient her offer might have been, I did not feel at all comfortable engaging in what seemed like legal short-term squatting.

I then remembered the HomeCamper option that I had used in Brittany. When I looked on their website there were several options in the Pézenas area including the opportunity to stay on the grounds of a vineyard near the town of Montagnac, just 5km north-east of Pézenas. Google directions told me it would be a further 34km to cycle and take me a couple more hours. It was now nearly 6 pm but it would be light for several more hours.

I sent a request to the vineyard and within a couple of minutes I received a response:

"Bonne nouvelle Andrew, votre demande a été acceptée."

With that I set off cycling into the evening, destination Domaine De La Conseillère.

Le Grand Tour

PART SEVEN:

The ViaRhôna / EuroVelo 17

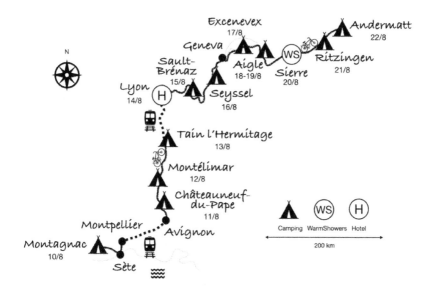

Day Forty: Montagnac to Châteauneuf-du-Pape (77km + Train + 24km) Thursday 11th August

Fear not! Pages have not been ripped from your book. Day thirty-nine did of course exist. It was, however, the ultimate day off from cycling and travelling. It merits a mention as it was spent catching up with friends Basil and Liz in the town of Pézenas, the town made famous - to me at least - by the BBC's *À Vous La France* television language course of the 1980s.

Basil had been a teaching colleague from my days living and working in Reading, Berkshire. We toiled away in a local secondary school trying to instil into the children our love of all things French and Italian. Admittedly our efforts had limited impact. If those children - now adults in their mid-30s - happen to throw a friendly *"merci"* or *"ciao"* in the direction of a local serving them pints of beer when on holiday, our valiant efforts were not completely in vain. He was instrumental in my decision to cycle to southern Italy in the summer of 2010 as he had purchased a property in Puglia and both he and Liz featured in the final chapters of my first book, *Crossing Europe*. Several years later they decided to move to south-west France and our meeting in Pézenas was the first for quite some time. We spent the day catching up, strolling, drinking and eating before I bid them farewell and returned for a second night in the tent at the Domaine De La Conseillère.

The cycle up to the winery had been surprisingly enjoyable considering that I had not left Sète until almost 6 pm. Having just cycled 100km to arrive where I was, the prospect of having to cycle at least another 30km to my accommodation did not fill me with joy. Yet the suburban cycling facilities of Sète were excellent and they guided me out of town in segregated safety and security beside the fast-flowing traffic heading along the north-eastern shores of the Étang de Thau. After Mèze, Google sent me in a straight line through the dwindling remnants of suburbia and then along the route of a disused railway line to Montagnac. Since setting off from the Hook of Holland, it was, by far, my greatest escape from the named routes that I had been following. I was delighted to discover that cycling investment was not only being ploughed into the headline-stealing big boys of the French national cycle network. The run-of-the-mill routes were also receiving their fair share: money was being spent for the benefit of all cyclists, not just the tourists with their panniers.

After breakfast in Montagnac, day forty started with me retracing my route back to Sète. With the canals behind me, today would see me embark upon the penultimate stage of the Grand Tour, all 1,000km of the EuroVelo 17 that would take me to Andermatt, high in the Swiss Alps. 800 of these kilometres would be in France along the route known locally as the ViaRhôna. With two possible starting points on the Mediterranean, I would be setting off from Sète.[53] My first interim destination was Montpellier where I planned to catch the sixth of my ten trains, in this case as far as Avignon. This was another portion of the Grand Tour that I had previously cycled, in 2013 as I made my way along the Mediterranean. Taking a train was a logical, pre-envisaged part of this trip. Once in Avignon, I would start to cycle along the ViaRhôna in the hope of finding a campsite somewhere to the north of the former papal city.

While perusing my map as I sipped my morning coffee in Montagnac, it struck me that a shortcut that avoided Sète might be possible. As I made my way back towards the coast, I toyed with the idea of following the D613, a direct road from Mèze to the centre of Montpellier. However, the 300 metres of the D613 that I was forced to use as I arrived in Mèze had me swiftly changing my mind and I continued in the direction of Sète along the segregated routes that I had cycled upon two days earlier. In any case, I liked my iconic starting and finishing points. I knew that at the Alpine end of the EuroVelo 17, I would be welcomed by the sight of the isolated town of Andermatt at the far end of a gorgeous Swiss valley. There may not have been any magnificent mountains to frame an iconic departure point by the Mediterranean but surely Sète must have made an effort to celebrate the spot, no?

Upon arrival in Sète, I consulted OpenStreetMap in an attempt to identify the exact starting point of the ViaRhôna / EuroVelo 17. *The lighthouse at the end of the harbour wall? The square opposite the elegant town hall? Or perhaps one of the bridges spanning Sète's famous town-splitting canal?* Alas not. It appeared to be a roundabout, the Rond-Point Jacques Mareschal. Situated beside the sea at the end of the harbour wall, I had cycled over this roundabout upon arrival in Sète two days earlier. Nothing about it had struck me as iconic.[54] In addition, it would require me to cycle an extra few hundred metres and then turn back to retrace my route. So,

---

[53] The alternative starting / finishing point of the ViaRhôna is at the southern end of the Rhône near the town of Port-Saint-Louis-du-Rhône.

[54] It turns out that Jacques Mareschal was an 18th-century mapmaker and engineer. He was responsible for the construction of the Saint Louis tower in Port-Saint-Louis-du-Rhône no less. Perhaps in choosing his roundabout in Sète, the cycle route planners of the 21st century had indeed found an iconic spot to start their route by giving a nod to the town at the very end of the Rhône (see previous footnote). That said, I do prefer my iconic starting points to be visual and not to be discovered via Google several months later.

when I noticed a sign for the ViaRhôna pointing east over the Pont Virla, that was sufficiently iconic for me. I set off from there instead.

By the time I started cycling the ViaRhôna, it was past 10.30 am and I had already travelled over 35km. I had identified a train that left Montpellier station at 2 pm: with only another 40km to cycle, this seemed entirely doable, and so it turned out to be. Much of the route along the coast was on segregated bike paths and, as I cycled along a long spit of land to the east of Frontignan, I was able to gaze leisurely across the expanse of the Étang d'Ingril to my left and the even greater expanse of the Mediterranean Sea to my right. Beyond a low crash barrier, traffic on the road beside me was extremely light. With a flawless sky above me, barely a whiff of wind and the distant pink dots of more flamingos on the salt lagoon, it was both a good day and a good place to be cycling. The contrast with my love-hate relationship with the Canal du Midi was stark. It had been the part of my route around Europe to which I had looked forward the most yet on many levels it had both frustrated and disappointed. Here I was at the start of my next route and I was already being blown away by everything that I was experiencing. Everything, that is, apart from the wind itself.

During the planning stages of the trip, I discovered the existence of the ViaRhôna with great delight. Not particularly because of its own merits but simply because it would signpost my way from the south-west of France to the Alps, from the Canal du Midi to the start of the Rhine Cycle Route. My expectations of the ViaRhôna were low and I had given little thought to it in advance. This low bar was only further lowered by my lack of success in getting hold of the Cicerone guidebook for the route. It had seemingly gone out of print, a consequence, I assumed, of a lack of interest in the route.[55] I was fully prepared for ten days or so of mundane cycling through a no-doubt pleasant but far-from-spectacular part of France and Switzerland.

At Plage Frontignan, the cycle route headed back onto the mainland and for the next hour or so I continued to enjoy the delights of this first section of the ViaRhôna. Every turn was well signposted and every effort had been made to keep me away from anything that might kill me. Through pine forest, on quiet lanes beside the railway and then, as I skirted around the town of Villeneuve-lès-Maguelone, a return to a dedicated cycle path beside the road.

Shortly after Villeneuve, I needed to turn left and head in the direction of Montpellier to catch my train. It was slightly disappointing to have to abandon the ViaRhôna at such an early stage of our relationship, especially

---

[55] Those wishing to follow the ViaRhôna will be delighted to discover that in early 2023, a new second edition was published by Cicerone.

as I knew that it would soon be crossing the mystical flatlands of the Camargue delta in the direction of historic Arles. My 2013 cycle across this part of France had not seen me follow the exact route that I was about to abandon. On that occasion, upon arrival in Avignon from the east I had initially followed the route of the Rhône but then deviated away from it to visit the famous Roman aqueduct - the Pont du Gard - further north. I had not crossed the marshland of the Camargue at all. I had not experienced seeing its grazing wild horses or breathing in the salty odours of its lakes. Its famously magical landscape would remain unexplored.

Yet for seemingly unjustifiable reasons, I was committed to my train journey from Montpellier to Avignon. Perhaps it was simply the countdown clock that continued to tick in my head to the moment when my ferry back to England would depart on September 3rd. I had barely three weeks remaining to achieve my goal of returning to the Hook of Holland. It did seem to be an increasingly unrealistic target. At the roundabout where I was required to cycle north to Montpellier, I paused at the signs for the Méditerranée à Vélo and ViaRhôna routes, the EuroVelos 8 and 17 respectively. They pointed right but I turned left.

There remained only 10km to the centre of Montpellier and most of this was on a cycle path beside the River Lez. Some top-notch graffiti that had entered the realm of street art kept me amused for a few moments under the concrete and metal span of a motorway bridge. As did a residential tower block that had balconies exploding out in all directions from its numerous floors. It was more pin cushion than tower block and was a nod to the vibrancy of this young southern city, a third of whose million-strong population consisted of students. What an enviable place to study!

I was now getting used to taking the train. It was another modern TER that transported me and Wanda in the direction of Avignon. I was delighted to note from my electronic ticket that the distance by train between Montpellier and Avignon came in at 99km. Since taking my first train from Calais to Le Touquet, it had been a concern that I might inadvertently break my self-imposed rule that none of the ten rides should cover a distance of more than 100km. I had bent the rule (to myself, secretly) when travelling from La Rochelle to Royan as I suspected that the two trains that I needed to take might add up to more than 100km. The as-the-crow-flies distance, however, was still only 60km. I considered this to be a clarification of the rule rather than a change of the rule. The train journey from Montpellier to Avignon was considerably more direct so to have proof that it only came to 99km was a moment of relief, delight even. The justification for taking my ten trains was built upon the premise that by doing so I could knock 1,000km from the total distance of 5,500km. This would hopefully make the entire Grand Tour a more cycleable 4,500km. By seriously undercutting the 100km on most of the journeys so far, I had squandered some of those 1,000km. It would inevitably make life more difficult for me in the final few weeks of the trip. Perhaps another (ahem...) clarification of the rule might be needed as I headed north.

When not fretting about train distances, I spent my time on the TER trying to locate a campsite somewhere conveniently north of Avignon and discovered a place near Châteauneuf-du-Pape with the enticing name of Camping L'Art de Vivre. *The art of living campsite?* I was up for a bit of that. It would mean cycling another 20km or so in the late afternoon but after my previous evening dash from Sète to Montagnac, that would be a walk in the park, or rather, a nice cycle by the Rhône. What's more, the campsite bigged up its credentials as a haven for ViaRhôna cyclists. It looked perfect so I booked a pitch from the train.

Having visited Avignon on a couple of previous occasions, I was happy to limit my time in the city but I did want to pass by the tourist office to pick up a map for the ViaRhôna. Map secured, I headed to the bridge across the Rhône because, well, that is what everyone is supposed to do in Avignon. The bridge now serves no function other than to have tourists dance upon it whilst singing *"Sur le pont d'Avignon, on y danse, on y danse..."*. Being a smug know-it-all, I chose instead to cross multiple lanes of heavy traffic in order to stand with the bike under the bridge. It is now thought that the good folk of medieval Avignon never stood on the bridge to dance but beneath its arches. After my tribulations with the traffic, I muttered *"Sous le pont d'Avignon..."* but was not in the mood for dancing. A feeling of sanctimonious historical superiority has minimal impact when there is no one to witness it and when you have just come close to being run over by several coaches full of pensioners.

I had thought that by making my way to the river I would easily find the ViaRhôna cycle route. I should have studied the route more carefully as, after mumbling my smug song, I realised that I would need to leave the city via its eastern Porte Thiers. More death-defying feats would be required to cross back over the roads that had been squeezed in between the river and the city walls. It was with muted enthusiasm that I eventually set off cycling beside the Canal de Vaucluse in the direction of Châteauneuf-du-Pape.

My bad mood soon evaporated as I continued to follow the exceptionally well-signed route. It effortlessly wound its way through the suburbs of Avignon and not once was I required to double back and correct myself. In the first hour of cycling, I must surely have encountered more signs than I had in three days along the Canal du Midi, and not one rough path to boot.

I was beginning to wonder if there was perhaps more to this ViaRhôna thing than I had initially thought.

Further joy was gifted on a plate when I started to follow a section of the route that ran adjacent to the railway line heading north. Beyond the flat fields to my right I could see the distinctive outline of a long hill. Curiously, it appeared to have snow on its ridge. *A hill? With snow? In August?* I paused to take a photograph but when I zoomed in to crop the image I was delighted to realise that this was no nearby hill. It was a distant mountain. And that was not snow. It was the unmistakable profile of Mont Ventoux with its treeless upper slopes of white stone. It was another reminder of my 2013 cycle when I had moved away from the EuroVelo 8 to climb the peak with a French acquaintance. Nearly a decade later, to be able to see it so clearly from a distance of 40km reminded me of the feat that I had accomplished. It had been over 1,600 metres of continuous ascent and I had not paused once to take a rest. I was younger and I was undoubtedly fitter but it had been a challenge that had pushed me to my limits. It was a non-too-subtle reminder that the greatest physical challenge of this particular trip in 2022 was yet to come. At the very end of the EuroVelo 17 was the climb to the Furka Pass at over 2,400 metres.

Mont Ventoux would be an almost constant, if distant, companion for the remainder of the day, but approaching Châteauneuf-du-Pape things became a little confusing. Beside a turning that would, if followed, see me cross a secondary meander of the Rhône[56] there was a sign for the ViaRhôna pointing straight ahead with the added words *"itinéraire provisoire"*. According to the official online route, I should turn left and cross the bridge. The ViaRhôna website explained the situation as follows:

> "On certain stretches, we propose provisional routes for very experienced cyclists, allowing them to tackle an unofficial unbroken route. These sections may follow un-signposted roads, roads on which the surface may be uneven, or even very busy roads, awaiting the completion of all ViaRhôna's sections."

It read like a description of the Canal du Midi.

---

[56] Take a look at a detailed map of the Rhône and you will appreciate this comment. It frequently splits into two distinct rivers only to coalesce again several kilometres further along its path. Some of these splits have been canalised. It can make for confusing route finding.

Somewhat confused, I followed the *itinéraire provisoire*, not because I fancied living fast for a few kilometres but because my campsite was in that direction. My mind was soon soothed by the appearance of the hilltop town of Châteauneuf-du-Pape. Before me, the narrow road wound its way towards the base of the hill, vines to my left and vines to my right. The most distinctive building was the *château neuf* (new castle) itself, its high walls dominating the town and the rooftops down upon which it gazed. It had been built for Pope John XXII in the 14th century and he was the only pope ever to stay there. A shadow of its former self - it had survived being plundered for its stone, being flogged by the revolutionaries of the 18th century and even the Nazis who tried to blow it up - it still cut an imposing silhouette at the top of the town. I would return in the morning to explore but as it was now nearing 6 pm, I needed to find the campsite and, continuing to follow the *itinéraire provisoire*, I did so beside the secondary meander of the Rhône.

For a campsite with such good facilities, Camping L'Art de Vivre was strangely quiet but as a place to rest and recuperate without the screams of children, it was perfect. A few other cyclists were in residence - I had seen very few on the route itself - and I treated myself to a beer and evening meal at the campsite restaurant. The menu offered "*assiette de cyclo*" which consisted of lentils, melon, cheese and a slab of pork smeared in pesto. I suspected that the somewhat generic *assiette de cyclo* gave the chef licence to stick in the dish anything in his fridge that was nearing its use-by date knowing full well that ravenous cyclists would probably eat anything after a hard day in the saddle. It was an eclectic mix that hit the spot. I was not complaining.

Day Forty-One: Châteauneuf-du-Pape to Montélimar (93km)
Friday 12th August

"It's because of the climatic conditions," explained the owner when I asked him why his excellent campsite was so quiet. "With the heat people prefer air-conditioned mobile homes and they're afraid of staying in tents."
The heatwave was continuing and there was no sign that it might end anytime soon. I could not remember a day since leaving Dieppe which I would not describe as anything other than very hot.
I asked him if he had lots of cyclists staying.
"You see that wooden hut? I bought it for cyclists to use. But then I had a problem with the mayor. The ViaRhôna was diverted over there," he said, pointing towards the far side of his campsite. "Before, it passed right in front of the campsite."
There was perhaps more to this *itinéraire provisoire* malarky than I had previously thought.
"Politics! There was €650,000 European funding up for grabs for the route and the mayor - who is also the president of the *conseil départemental*[57] - wanted his share, so the route was changed."
The murky politics of the EuroVelo network. Lest he tell me more than I needed to know and for fear of waking up in the tent beside a horse's head, I left it there. (It would, on reflection, need to be a pony, and a small one at that.)
I ventured up the hill into the centre of Châteauneuf-du-Pape. It was predictably somewhat wine-themed but I managed to find a *boulangerie* that did not insist on me washing down my *croissant* with a glass of the local red. Further up the hill, it was astonishing just how little of the *château neuf* was still standing. From afar, it had looked like a substantial building but up close, just two sides of the building remained. The stone pilferers, revolutionaries and Nazis had been far better at their jobs than I had initially given them credit.
Having deviated away from the route - both of them - to get my breakfast, I now had to trundle back down the hill in the direction of the river to rejoin the ViaRhôna. The signage at the *halte fluviale* - a newly built landing pier for passing boats - suggested that I had now cycled beyond the contentious area where official and *itinéraire provisoire* versions of the ViaRhôna fought it out for supremacy and, of course, chunks of European funding.

---

[57] The county council

I would be destined to remain loyal to the route for the remainder of the day and my loyalty was handsomely rewarded with one of the best days of cycling I had experienced since setting foot on the continent at the start of July.

Indeed from a purely cycling perspective, the ten kilometres after rejoining the path beside the Rhône were simply magnificent. It was very easy to see where those €650,000 had been invested. I was not fussed about which mayor had control of the funds: whoever it was, they had put them to good use. It was not so much cycling, more gliding on the ground. The smooth segregated path had been carefully built in such a way as to descend gently to the level of the adjacent road when it was necessary to cross to the other side and then gently regain height at the opposite kerb. It was almost as if someone had ironed away the bumps. It is rare - even after millions have been poured into inner city cycling schemes - for kerbs to be crossed without at least a jolt of the bike. Here things were different. I could not help but conclude that the designer, the architect, the builders and the maintenance team were all cyclists themselves and they were making every effort not to create more work for the orthopaedic ward at the local hospital 30 years down the line. By mid-morning, my bones were singing sweet melodies to the glory of the ViaRhôna.

Along many stretches of the Canal du Midi, my eyes had been all-too-frequently glued to the rough track before me to avoid being flung into the water by an errant tree root. On the silky surface of this part of the ViaRhôna, my glances were free to be cast elsewhere and so they were. The landscape had taken on an altogether different aspect. Until this point of the trip, the hills had been undoubtedly pretty and the mountains - on the rare occasions that I had seen them - had been impressive but distant. I had always been at least 50km from the Pyrenees and even on the previous afternoon as I was approaching Châteauneuf-du-Pape, Mont Ventoux had been tens of kilometres away. But here, for the first time since leaving Rotterdam, as I started to make my way north along the valley of the Rhône, things were changing.

To the north of the town of Mornas, the nearby river - still to my left - had squeezed the traffic infrastructure together and pushed it against a rocky outcrop. As I was shunted closer and closer to the motorway, the main road and the railway line, the natural barrier to my right was increasingly dominant. Rising perhaps 200 metres into the sky, the sheer cliff would have made for a formidable climbing challenge. The reason why, presumably, the counts of Toulouse had chosen to build a mighty fortress at its head. The fortress was looking rather good for its age. I wondered if our old friend the ever-enthusiastic renovator Monsieur Viollet-le-Duc had

had it on his list of projects.[58] Irrespective, the ensemble of cliff face and ancient castle provided the Grand Tour with something that it had been so far lacking: topographical drama.

I had been expecting this to happen at some point but was surprised that it had happened so soon after leaving Avignon. Yet it was easy to forget just how far the influence of the Alps extended into this part of Europe and how much of this south-eastern quadrant of France was mountainous. Until now, my Grand Tour had literally gone out of its way to avoid serious topography. With the exception of a few hills in Brittany, I had been tracing a flat profile through the Netherlands, Belgium and along France's northern and western coastlines. Even beside the canals of south-western France, the Pyrenees and the Massif Central had kept a respectable distance from my chosen path. It was only here, in the valley of the Rhône, as I began to be funnelled further north along the course of the river that the mountains were beginning to seriously encroach. From this point until I escaped the narrow confines of the Rhine Valley in Germany, mountains would be an almost ever-present feature of the landscape. I welcomed that with open arms. My legs, on the other hand, might soon be disagreeing.

Although the ViaRhôna had taken its name from the river, it did not appear to be slavishly following its course. Indeed for the 30km after Mornas, I was kept well away from the Rhône as the cycle path continued along a series of narrow country lanes. It was pleasant if uneventful cycling and for the two hours that it lasted, with every twist and turn clearly signposted and with barely any excuses to pause, I entered a period of calm, carefree travel. My mind could drift and, with little effort required to keep moving, my body could relax. It was, perhaps, the nearest you could get to meditation on a bicycle.

I was reacquainted with the Rhône at Bourg-Saint-Andéol, a town which occupied an elongated position on the western bank of the river. It was a multi-roofed Romanesque church that initially drew my attention as I crossed the modern bridge over the water. Then, as I began to make my way along the tree-lined promenade next to the buildings, I noticed a bicycle wheel, of sorts.

It was, in fact, a bicycle pump housed inside a round container with spokes painted on its sides. Remembering that it had been quite some time since I had made any effort to re-inflate Wanda's tyres, I stopped cycling and parked up. There followed a Crystal Maze moment of looking and

---

[58] He did not. The renovation work on the Mornas Fortress took place in the late 1970s and 80s and was at the behest of a local group called the Friends of Mornas. Having died in 1879, Viollet-le-Duc was not one of them.

trying to work out how the contraption functioned but once I had worked out the mechanics, I picked up the rubber tube, clamped it to the valve of my front inner tube and started pumping. This involved pushing a metal bar with my foot but the ergonomics seemed somehow wrong. *Was it me? Or was it the design of the pump?* Little if any air seemed to be moving through the tube. I reattached the valve several times but whenever I pumped nothing happened. The pressure gauge on top of the machine showed no sign of life. Standing back to reflect upon my failed efforts I noticed a sign: "*en panne*". It was broken. At least I was not at fault. It was an inconsequential moment but one that I would reflect upon later with a certain amount of regret.

North of Bourg-Saint-Andéol a sign announced that I was about to start following a segregated *voie verte*. I would stay on this greenway for much of the remainder of the day and it was in its first kilometre that I noticed another cyclist. She had paused beside the path and I tossed her a merry "*bonjour*". A few minutes later she had caught up with me and we exchanged a few words in French. She was in her 30s and had adopted a very bohemian look that was distinct from all the other cycle tourists that I had so far encountered. With her flowery cotton trousers and shirt and her white sunhat she was dressed more appropriately for a leisurely morning reading a newspaper in the garden, but her distinctive look was not holding her back. Far from it. She explained that she was cycling as far as Lyon and she was putting in some serious daily distances, most of which were significantly greater than 100km. Perhaps I should ditch my Lycra shorts immediately.

She was amiable company and over the next hour or so we chatted about our respective journeys although her insistence upon speaking in English was a touch exasperating, at times comical.

"What do you do for a job?" she enquired.

"I'm a French teacher."

"Why do not you do the route of the tower of France?"

"The Tour de France?"

"Yes, the tower of France…"

Eventually, I held back my gentle corrections and let her continue. Her unorthodox use of the English language was just as commendable as her unorthodox cycling attire. And who was I to comment? It worked fine for her and I understood every word she uttered.

Following a few more river crossings, I found myself back on the eastern bank of the Rhône in the final few kilometres of the day as I approached Montélimar. I had found a campsite just to the north of the town but my guidebook reminded me that this was the home of French nougat, the sickly sweet almond-laced confectionary that has done wonders for the profits of the dental industry down the centuries. After a long day in the saddle, I reasoned that despite the risks to my teeth, chewing my way through a prime slab of *nougat de Montélimar* would be a fine way to end the day.

So, instead of heading directly to the campsite, I deviated into the centre of Montélimar in search of nougat. Alas, my late-afternoon arrival appeared to have coincided with most of the shops being closed, so instead of an end-of-day munch of nougat, I had to resort to an end-of-day beer instead. The sacrifice of the long-distance cyclist. I took it bravely for my one-man and one-bicycle team. The Rough Guide had described the town as "attractive". That did seem to stretch the adjective a little far. Perhaps "not unattractive" might have been more appropriate. Beer consumed I cycled off to the campsite via a local Intermarché where I *did* manage to purchase some nougat for just €1.50. A fraction, no doubt, of the price I might have had to pay in one of the town-centre boutiques.

"Not unattractive" may have been appropriate for the town but the meaning was being stretched when it came to describing Camping L'Île Blanc. I was welcomed by an ugly entrance which, with its corrugated roof and penitentiary-style main gate transported me to a lawless small town in South America. The only thing to suggest that this was not a far-flung prison outpost was the sign and several poorly painted cartoon images of the inmates having fun on a lake. Distant screams could be heard. I assumed from children on water but they could have passed for something altogether different. First impressions are important and at Camping L'Île Blanc they were not great.

Following signs for the reception, I walked through a series of dark corridors and into what passed as a bar but was stopped in my tracks by three vicious-looking barking dogs. However, I could now see the children on the lake and, in fairness, they did seem to be enjoying themselves. I was further put at ease by the receptionist who was an amiable young guy wearing a corporate-style Camping L'Île Blanc t-shirt. But an idyllic country campsite in the Dordogne this was not. I was instructed to find myself a spot in an area where the lakeside positions had all been taken by large campervans, at least some of which looked roadworthy. I pitched my tent, heated some pasta and wrote up my notes whilst watching the not-inconsiderable life of the campsite go by.

In what must rank as the saddest sights of the entire trip, my attention was drawn towards a father and his young son. They had pitched their tent not far from my own and the man was drinking cans of strong beer. His son, who was perhaps seven- or eight-years old was desperate to play but all his increasingly drunken father could do was chastise him. There appeared to be no mother or brother or sister or friend for the boy to spend his time with. Just his father, who had little time and a dwindling amount of energy to devote to his offspring. The boy, silenced by the comments of his father sat cross-legged on the ground, a safe distance from his father. He occasionally jabbed at the ground with his wooden sword whilst the unshaven man stared at the screen of his phone, smoking.

It had been a good day on the bike, perhaps one of the best, and my love for the ViaRhôna was only growing as I continued my journey north. Yet the scene playing out before me on this drab, unkempt campsite had suddenly plunged my mood. I was reminded of some of the children that I taught back home in Britain: the ones who cannot communicate effectively, have little imagination and barely any zest for life. The ones who will probably never set off on a bike to cycle thousands of miles around the continent. I looked again at the boy just a few metres from where I was sitting. He could one day be one of them. As I lay in the tent I could not get his plight out of my mind. It had been an unwelcome and melancholic end to the day. Holidays were meant to be escapes. This boy was trapped: not by the prison-like campsite but by the callous attitude of his father and his unjust sentence could be a long one.

Day Forty-Two: Montélimar to Tain L'Hermitage (96km) Saturday 13th August

The evening of the 12th may have ended darkly, but the morning of the 13th was bright. Very bright. I was keen to get off the campsite and found myself back outside the gates at 7 am. The sun had only just crept over the horizon and its soft low-angle light had me and the bike casting long shadows across the grass as I cycled the short distance back to the Rhône. At this point in its journey south, the river had split into two distinct bodies of water. To the west, it cut its entirely natural course and formed the dividing line between the *départements* of Ardèche and Drôme. To the east was the somewhat less natural Canal de Dérivation de Montélimar. Opened in 1957 it formed part of a grand scheme by the Compagnie Nationale du Rhône to regulate the flow of the river south of Lyon. In doing so, boat traffic could be both increased and speeded up, hydroelectric stations built and irrigation of neighbouring farmland improved.

On a personal level, it meant that I had not one but two bridges to cross before I could continue to follow the ViaRhôna along the west bank of the river north of Rochemaure. The first of these bridges - the one spanning the canal - was, as bridges go, nothing special. Its greatest asset was the view that it afforded across the wide expanse of the canal below me and the nearby tree-smothered hills of the Ardèche. Although still a carpet of green, such were the continuing drought conditions that the forests were increasingly embracing shades of brown and yellow.

In the far distance, beyond a curve in the river, were the tall cooling towers of a power station, clouds of vapour rising vertically above the conical walls of concrete. There was no wind of which to speak. The unblemished surface of the canal mirrored perfectly the hills, the towers and the clouds of vapour and as I joined the canal-side tarmac path below the bridge I was rewarded with not one but two suns: one real and one reflected. The only perceptible movement was that of Wanda and me. It was a beautiful way to start the day, but the best was yet to come.

Turning away from the canal to cycle in the direction of the river I could see ahead of me an ornate tower. As I approached I noted that it was, in fact, the bridge over the Rhône that I had been expecting but with trees obscuring my view of the river there was little else to see. I continued to cycle in the direction of the tower and was delighted to discover that this was a footbridge, albeit a very grand footbridge. The tower had recently been renovated and, rather incongruously, great blocks of concrete had been installed beside the path to secure long metal cables that shot off through the archway of the tower to supporting posts beyond.

Ignoring the no cycling signs (it was, after all, still only 7.30 on a Saturday morning) I continued and passed through the arch of the tower before pausing to take in the astonishing scene before me. Two more towers - identical to the first - could be seen and a walkway was suspended from the cables that linked all three towers together. It was a rather clever reimagining of a very old bridge. And very Instagrammable, so I delayed my crossing by a few moments to take some pictures.

There was also an element of adventure about the construction. Had this been an Indiana Jones movie, Harrison Ford would now be running away from hordes of arrow-wielding locals and he would, inevitably, have ended up dangling from severed portions of the bridge as they hung perilously above the Rhône. Admittedly, some kind of oxy-acetylene cutting equipment may have been required by the arrow-wielding locals and Indiana would not have had far to fall into the river but let's not quibble: this was exciting stuff! I set off and clattered across the metal grids forming the walkway. It was great fun.

The story of the bridge, or rather bridges, was a chequered one. The first was opened in 1842 and consisted of not three but five towers from which a wooden deck was suspended. Alas, this bridge - along with two of its supporting pillars - was swept away by the Great Floods of 1856 but it was rebuilt with the three remaining towers.

Fast forward to 1937 when a heavy fuel truck whose driver had ignored the weight limit signs managed to punch a hole in the deck of the bridge sufficiently large to see him and his lorry plunge into the Rhône. It foreshadowed a somewhat troubled period for the bridge.

In 1940, retreating French forces destroyed part of the deck but it was repaired two years later. Now under German control, it was bombed by the Allies on August 19th 1944 before the resistance got their hands on it the following day and blew up the central tower. It was repaired and reopened in 1946 and the next couple of decades in the life of the bridge were mercifully uneventful. Until 1968 when another overladen truck went through the deck. This resulted in all motorised traffic being banned from the bridge and it became pedestrians and cyclists only. But we are not quite finished.

In 1982 the bridge was seriously damaged by two arson attacks at which point the *département* of the Ardèche had had enough and proposed knocking down the troublesome structure. The locals were having none of that and they battled to keep it standing, taking ownership a couple of years later. But what would they do with a bridge that was no longer a functioning bridge? It took ten years for the answer to materialise and it arrived in the form of a proposal to include it on the route of, you guessed, the ViaRhôna! The bridge in its current incarnation was opened in 2013. Only one question remained: if it was saved by the creation of a long-distance cycle route, why had cycling across it been banned?

When I arrived in the medieval village of Rochemaure, it was not yet 8 am and I had only cycled 6km but I had the distinct feeling that I might have already experienced the highlight of the day. In one way I had but in another, the 340-metre-long "*passerelle himalayenne*" at Rochemaure had just been part of one of the main highlights of travelling beside the Rhône: its bridges. The previous day had seen me cross at least six and today, including the two that I had already passed over I would be destined to cross another ten. The Rhône and its adjoining stretches of canal were bridge heaven if that was your thing. Bridge hell if it was not. I was in luck: I loved them. They came in all shapes and sizes. Some were functional, some almost ornamental. Some were suspended, others not. Some for everyone, others just for pedestrians and cyclists. Most were at the very least aesthetically pleasing: some were works of art but admittedly there were a handful of real shockers. And there were even some whose primary purpose was not to function as a bridge. These were the hydroelectric barrages that had become a regular feature of the river.[59]

After breakfast from a *boulangerie-café* at the foot of the hill in Rochemaure, I continued cycling north and a short-term plan began to be constructed in my mind. Rob Watkins, a well-travelled cyclist who had provided some content for an episode of The Cycling Europe Podcast earlier in the year had contacted me. He had noticed that I was approaching the town of Tain l'Hermitage and he recommended I stay overnight at the riverside municipal campsite. That was about 80km from Rochemaure so ideally located. Furthermore, I had noticed that there was a train station in Tain l'Hermitage. For the first time since leaving the Hook of Holland nearly six weeks earlier, inclement weather was being forecast, especially for the following morning of Sunday 14th when heavy storms were expected. Tain l'Hermitage was about 75km south of Lyon so it might be an opportune moment for me to use the seventh of my maximum-100-km trains. Earlier in the trip it had been pointed out to me that the infrastructure of the ViaRhôna was not quite so developed in the area immediately south of Lyon so this sealed the deal. If I could arrive in Lyon by lunchtime on

---

[59] According to the CNR (Compagnie Nationale du Rhône) there are 49 hydro power plants on the river south of Lyon and combined with its 59 wind farms and 59 solar farms the company is the largest producer of renewable energy in France.

Sunday, the weather may have improved sufficiently for me to continue cycling in search of a campsite further along the Rhône to the east of the city. I checked the train times and there was one at 9.40 in the morning. Perfect. This was a plan that was not simply beginning to be built: it had put all its bricks neatly in order, cemented them together and found a subcontractor to sort out the roof. I just needed to make sure I was in Tain l'Hermitage by the end of the day.

The distant cooling towers were now somewhat less distant. Their position beside the river, sucking up the cooling waters of the Rhône, imposed a slight detour away from the riverbank. After a few shimmies to the left and a few shimmies to the right, normality was restored and I continued to follow an off-road path heading north. Having failed on Friday to pump up my tyres at the broken contraption in Bourg-Saint-Andéol (I suspected that I had, if anything, deflated them slightly before seeing the "out-of-order" sign) I was on the lookout for a bike shop. Once located, I hoped to revert to the tried and tested method of asking to borrow a pump. I found one in Le Pouzin and set about chatting to the owner as I pumped. We bonded over a mutual love.

"Tain L'Hermitage is an area for good wine," he announced upon learning that it was my destination. He was remaining loyal to the local tipple. "I don't like Bordeaux."

When I informed him that the wines of the Rhône Valley had been my red wine of choice when living in France in the 1990s he elevated me to the status of his long-lost son. I held back from pointing out that my preference was more financial than anything oenological.

The man was also a fan of the ViaRhôna - unsurprising as it passed in front of his bike shop door - but was keen to emphasise the diversity of those deciding to cycle along it.

"The ViaRhôna is increasingly popular with all kinds of cyclists, even women," he explained, a little clumsily, but I sensed he was not being overtly sexist. He just wanted to highlight that the received stereotype of the MAMIL was increasingly outdated, certainly from what he could see through his shop window.

Usage statistics of the EuroVelo network do not break down the figures by gender but the European Cyclists' Federation - the organisation responsible for managing and developing the network - do point out that 40% of visitors to the EuroVelo.com website are female. As for his anecdotal comment about the ViaRhôna / EuroVelo 17 being "increasingly popular" - presumably based upon evidence that included more people like me asking to borrow his pump - he was right. Of all the EuroVelo routes, the EuroVelo 17 saw the greatest increase in usage in 2022, a whopping

35%. This followed a leap of 18% in 2021 compared to the pre-pandemic levels of 2019, again putting it at the top of the list.

In absolute terms, the number of people cycling the route, either partially or in its entirety, is a more elusive statistic. A 2023 report for the Auvergne-Rhône-Alpes regional government[60] estimated a figure of 2.6 million in 2022. The majority - 81% - were *"excursionnistes"* (cyclists staying in their own homes overnight), 12% were *"touristes"* (cyclists staying away from home for at least one night) and 7% were *"itinérants"*. According to the methodology, I was one of the latter and was distinguished from a plain old *"touriste"* by the fact that I was on a touring bike, carrying pannier bags over the back wheel and had a map holder attached to the handlebars. The 102-page report is a fascinating insight into who I am and what I do. Of those 7% *"itinérants"*, about two-thirds are French and a third from other countries. Irrespective of our nationality, we cycle 72km per day (7km more than the *"touristes"*!) and, on average, we spend €25 per day on food and €20 on accommodation. After 41 days of being on the continent (of which 35 had been cycling days), my average daily distance cycled was 81km and my average spend on accommodation €21.85. The methodology seemed to have validity.

Three more bridges - an ugly girder construction at Le Pouzin, a simple modern corridor of steel for bikes and pedestrians overlooking the confluence of the Drôme and the Rhône and then an elegant 19th-century cable suspension beauty - assisted me in cycling to La Voulte-sur-Rhône. Here I paused to spend some of my daily allowance of €25 on lunch before continuing my tour of Rhône river crossings further north.

Approaching the centre of Valence, the ViaRhôna moved away from the banks of the river to accommodate the needs of the Autoroute du Soleil which had temporarily taken up prime position by the water. Having never previously visited the city, I did not mind the diversion. It was, at least, a change of scenery but I did not pause my journey and the delights of Valence would remain unexplored in preparation for a future visit. I trundled on through the inner suburbs until regaining my rightful place beside the river once the motorway had ended its flirtation with the Rhône. It was here that things got rather exciting.

I had heard the low hum of a propellor-driven plane on a few occasions during the early afternoon but thought little of it. It was not, after all, an uncommon sound. I had also noticed some distant plumes of smoke to the west. It was here where the parched mountains of the Ardèche were located.

---

[60] *ViaRhôna: Evaluation de la fréquentation et des retombées économiques*, Indigo for La Région Auvergne-Rhône-Alpes, July 2023

Forest fires were not, alas, uncommon in this drought-ridden summer that France - and much of the rest of Europe - was experiencing. The forecast of rain in the coming days must have been welcome news to many. It certainly was to me. The novelty of a cool, damp atmosphere for a day or two would come as blessed relief after the extended period of heat and tinderbox dryness. The connection between the hum and the smoke became apparent north of Valence as I approached a long, straight canalised section of the river where a significant number of people had assembled. They were all looking at the sky.

As I started to cycle past them, the distant hum slowly became louder and its pitch gradually increased. It was an approaching plane. I paused and turned around to see three brightly coloured red and yellow aircraft not only approaching but also descending. These were not just any brightly coloured planes: they were Canadair fire-fighting planes and I was about to witness them filling their bellies with water from the Rhône. The people beside me had their cameras poised and I dismounted from Wanda to watch the spectacle unfold.

It was somewhat disconcerting to see a large plane about to crash into the water even when I knew that it was going to do no such thing. The first of the three aircraft approached the water and immediately a low spray of white water was thrown up from the point of contact as the tanks of the aircraft started to fill. The plane bounced slightly but its speed did not discernibly slow. It was an astonishing sight. After perhaps ten seconds of capturing water, the pitch of the engine began to rise and the Canadair moved off into the sky on a mission to deposit its load over the fires of the Ardèche. Within a matter of a couple of minutes, all three aircraft had filled up and had disappeared over the crest of the hill to the west. Spontaneous applause broke out amongst the audience and I joined in enthusiastically. A sad thing to have to witness but, for the moment it happened, an aeronautical engineering spectacle to behold and remember.

By late afternoon I was approaching my destination of Tain l'Hermitage and my final bridge of the day. I could see the campsite that I was aiming for stretching out along the opposite bank of the river and after 96km of cycling, I arrived at its gate. The sky remained cloudless. It was difficult to imagine that storms were indeed on their way. Perhaps the forecasts were wrong. Perhaps there would be no respite from the heat and the sun after all. It seemed almost cruel to have been promised something but see no evidence whatsoever that it would be delivered.

Day Forty-Three: Tain L'Hermitage To Lyon (Train)
Sunday 14th August

The low rumble of distant thunder started in the early hours of Sunday morning. I was, of course, in the tent. It was proving to be yet another night of on-off sleep. It is said that we only remember the dreams we have immediately before waking. The fact that I could often remember multiple dreams suggested that I was waking on multiple occasions before eventually nodding off for a few more minutes of slumber. However, the noises outside the tent gave me reason to listen, and hope.

The pattern of short periods of sleep followed by short periods of being awake had been broken and I was now alert to further suggestions that a storm was indeed approaching. The rumbles became louder. There were flashes of light and cracks of thunder. Then started the glorious sound of rain on the skin of the tent. After six weeks of almost continuous drought - just a short shower as I was approaching Saint-Malo on the northern coast - it was happening. The heavens were finally releasing their long-overdue payload. Yet my delight was more profound than the circumstances might dictate.

Why was the white noise of rain on a tent so pleasing? Even during extended periods of wet weather when I have prayed relentlessly for blue skies, I have always felt a deeply enjoyable sense of comfort when droplets of rain hit the tent. *Was it an inner sense of joy provoked by the knowledge that I was being protected from something that could feasibly be detrimental to my well-being? Did it remind me of my time in the womb, encased within a small defensive pocket, natural fluids gently washing past me in all directions? Was it that my chronic sense of fear of attack from animals or fellow humans abated in the knowledge that anything or anyone wishing me ill will had probably been dissuaded by the rain? Or could it be that the chillingly misconstrued noises of the night - the crack of a twig, a fluttering of leaves - had been all but drowned out by the steady crashing of droplets on the man-made fibre of my Hubba Hubba?*

Probably a combination of them all. The sheer novelty of what I could hear was the icing on the cake. Proper, good old rain. Wonderful. That night I spent many, many minutes listening to the noise. Seemingly wide awake, I abandoned any effort to fall asleep but eventually I did. When I awoke, I could only remember one dream and I reasoned that I must have slept well. If, as the longer-term forecast was predicting, rain continued to fall as my journey progressed along the upper stretches of the Rhône and into

Switzerland, I might well benefit from several nights of comparatively good quality sleep.

Within a matter of days, I would be ruing my thoughts. For the moment, however, I remained ignorant of rain-induced problems to come. Packing my four panniers whilst still in the tent was an art that I had mastered when cycling across Europe during the summer of 2010. That year the continent witnessed its wettest August on record and I had chosen to spend much of it in a tent that was significantly smaller than the one I was currently using. However, in the area set aside for those travelling with just a tent at the campsite in Tain l'Hermitage a small marquee had been erected under which a picnic table had been placed. It was here where I could brew my morning coffee. As I waited for the pot to boil I chatted to a young German cyclist who was heading south along the ViaRhôna. We both agreed that the turn in the weather was welcome although I did think that if further storms were to develop, it was me who had more to worry about as I headed into the foothills of the Alps.

It was an aspect of cycling that I could dismiss for the next few hours as I was booked onto the 9.40 train to Lyon, a journey which I estimated to be around 90km, comfortably within my 100km limit. Rain was continuing to fall heavily as I cycled the short distance from the campsite to the well-maintained Gare de Tain l'Hermitage-Tournon. The optimistic pale orange of the station's exterior walls was in contrast with the sullen grey of the sky and upon arrival I wheeled Wanda along the platform to make use of a shelter where I could wait and begin to drip dry.

Over the next half hour or so, I was joined by several other cycle tourists who had made the same decision as me to cut their losses and sit out the storm whilst on board a train. After having been out all night in the rain and having just sliced her way along the gathering pools of water along the wet main road of Tain l'Hermitage, Wanda was spotless. Cleaner than she had probably been at any point since leaving my house back in Yorkshire. As with all bikes, she functioned much better in the rain. Admittedly a sweeping statement but one that I am willing to argue. Every working part of her anatomy was now lubricated by a fine - if temporary - glazing of water. Above all, her carbon belt - which would often squeak in dry, dusty conditions - was silent. All that could be heard was the gentle purr of the Rohloff hub. Another reason to embrace the wet conditions. As I sat, I admired her beauty. She was a good-looking beast of the road, especially when wet.

As 9.40 approached, we had become a small gathering of six bicycles and six riders. That would not be an issue as the TERs were almost always modern trains with step-free access into their carriages, each of which contained a large area set aside for bicycles. Alas when the train appeared in the distance, my heart sank as I realised that this was not one of the modern TERs. This was more like the train that I had caught from Paris to Chartres. However, whereas at Montparnasse station in the capital I had the luxury of time on my side as the train stood patiently in the station waiting for its allocated time of departure, here in Tain l'Hermitage, clambering aboard would be altogether more stressful. There was no risk of the train driver setting off as I was in the middle of hoisting Wanda up the flight of three deep steps. However, with six bicycles to hoist, the train guard might feasibly blow his whistle if he thought the process had become too elongated or if he felt that his train could not take any more bikes. The prospect of several of the cyclists being left behind on the platform was a real possibility. As the slowing carriages flashed past I noticed a bicycle sign on the front door of the first so, in an attempt to minimise the risk of being left behind, I set off jogging in that direction, determined to be first in the queue.

Several manic minutes later we had all managed to board. To say the train was busy with bicycles would be somewhat of an understatement. Most of the unoccupied floor space in the carriage was accommodating a bike of some description, many carrying panniers or bikepacking bags. Having set off from Marseille earlier in the day, it was apparent that the train was gathering up rain-sodden cyclists at each stop. I could only guess as to how many more might join us before we arrived at our destination further north. Many did.

With an hour ahead of me before we arrived in Lyon, I set about some medium-term route planning. After unfolding my map, I began to study the path of the ViaRhôna to the east of Lyon. It was the first time that I had given it serious consideration. The route wiggled to a far greater extent than it had done between Avignon and Tain l'Hermitage as the river itself cut a more arduous path between the hills. Using a list of distances found on the back of the map, I added up the number of kilometres that I still needed to cycle to arrive at the eastern extremity of Lac Léman at Saint-Gingolph. It came to 323km or 4 days of cycling approximately 80km per day. At least three more days would be required to get to the source of the Rhône and the nearby end of the EuroVelo 17 in Andermatt. This latter section promised to provide the most physically taxing cycling of my Grand Tour as I would be required to climb over the Furka Pass. That said, if I were able to reach Andermatt after three days in Switzerland, that would amount to just one week of cycling from Lyon. With under three weeks before my return ferry was due to set off from Rotterdam, it would leave me with nearly two weeks to cycle the length of the Rhine. Things were indeed looking up as I had initially envisaged that I would need at least 10 days to do just that. 14 days seemed positively ostentatious. But then again, I had not taken into account any rest days. *I could not possibly cycle for 21 consecutive days, could I?*

I glanced out at the storm which was continuing to drench the valley of the Rhône. I then glanced at the bike, still dripping water after our journey to the station. Finally I glanced at the wet tent Wanda was carrying. Mmm… Might it be an idea to book into a hotel in Lyon? Indulge in a bit of rest and relaxation in preparation for what could be 20 days of consecutive cycling if I made it no further than Lyon today? I whipped out my phone and found a cheap hotel on Booking.com. Within a matter of seconds the Hôtel du Helder had become my home for the evening.

With accommodation sorted, I spent a few minutes catching up on the news. A headline on the BBC News website caught my eye:

"Climate activists fill golf holes with
cement after water ban exemption"

The article went on to explain that golf courses in France would be allowed to continue watering their greens despite many French villages being on the verge of running out of water. Extinction Rebellion had, rather ingeniously, taken to filling the holes with cement to highlight the issue and it had worked. "A golf course without a green is like an ice rink without ice," bleated Gérard Rougier of the French Golf Federation. The report concluded by reminding readers what most of them were probably already aware of, especially those of us who happened to be in France:

"Some parts of the River Loire have virtually dried up.
Across two-thirds of France, a state of crisis has been
declared, with rainfall down by some 85%."

Again, I glanced out of the window. It would take many, many days of rain to solve the problem. The golfers of France might just have to get used to playing their game on parched grass. There was little sympathy in this carriage of the 9.40 to Lyon Part-Dieu.

The Hôtel du Helder was close to the river. It had faded elegance written all over it. Perhaps if the surrounding area had not become a mecca for fast food outlets, mini-markets and run down cafés it might still be living the high life on the social circuit of Lyon. Admittedly if it had, it would have priced itself out of my budget. I secured Wanda to a radiator in what must surely have been one of Lyon's most desirable pre-war bars (much of the decor and furniture appeared to date from the 1930s). I then headed off to visit one of the most desirable places for a 21st-century touring cyclist to hang out: the nearby laundrette.

In desperate need of a couple new t-shirts, it had been my plan to do a little retail therapy whilst in France's third city but despite its size, Lyon seemed to hang firmly onto the concept of Sunday being special. Perhaps it did not help that the following day - August 15th - was a national bank holiday, the festival of the Assumption of Mary. Most people seemed to have escaped the city for the long weekend and almost all of the shops were closed, including those in the Westfield shopping centre next to Lyon Part-Dieu station. Walking there and back took time and energy. My afternoon of not cycling was turning into yet another where rest had been shunted off the agenda. Somewhat wearily I sauntered back towards the river to ponder life on the road. The drizzle had now stopped and blue patches of sky were returning. I wondered whether I had made a good decision in staying in Lyon. *Might it have been better to continue cycling?* It was a question not worth answering as the deed had been done. I was staying in Lyon for the night and that was that. As the light dimmed over the city I headed back to the Hôtel du Helder and settled down for a night in front of the box. After the news came the weather: the unsettled conditions would continue for the next few days. Through the window I could hear a distant collective cry of delight from the golfers of France. All they needed to do now was get rid of all that concrete.

Day Forty-Four: Lyon to Sault-Brénaz (81km)
Monday 15th August

With the Hôtel du Helder being just a stone's throw away from the left bank of the Rhône, it was only a matter of minutes before the triumvirate of cyclist, bicycle and river were reunited. After a few moments of quiet contemplation, Wanda and I turned right and started travelling north. The Rhône continued its journey south towards the Mediterranean and, with gravity on its side, it had an easier task ahead of it than we did. We were setting off from an elevation of 175 metres in Lyon. The Furka Pass - still some 500km to the east - was at 2,436 metres. The final day of cycling to the pass would require us to climb around 1,000 metres from the valley floor. The remaining 1,200 vertical metres would be spread out over at least the next six days, so it was an entirely manageable feat to take on. It was, however, the first extended section of my Grand Tour that would see day after day after day of ascent. I knew from experience that this kind of slow-burn climbing could be energy-sapping stuff. The crucial thing was that I knew what was coming. I had been preparing for this section of the trip for months: not by pumping iron in the gym or by cycling multiple times up Stainland Road (although I *had* done that thanks to my daily commutes home from work) but by thinking and anticipating. My physical preparedness was not guaranteed but I knew my mental strength was good. Bring on the Alps!

Today was the feast day of the Assumption of Mary. I could not quite work out what Mary's assumption might have been, but this being a Monday, Andrew's assumption was that none of the shops would be open, especially as it was also a French bank holiday. I had made sure that my breakfast at the hotel in Lyon had stretched the definition of all-you-can-eat to the point of it being all-you-can-eat-and-quite-a-few-things-that-you-cannot. I secreted a couple of bread rolls and a handful of Babybel in the pockets of my raincoat. I exited the building in profile lest the receptionist spot any suspicious bulges in my attire. These, along with a small box of peanuts that I had been nibbling for several days might have to see me through until I could cook something at a campsite later in the day.

That said, beside the river and through the expansive parks to the east of the city, it could have been any day of the week as there were no shops to be either open or closed. It felt like a lazy Sunday morning with few people around: just a handful of joggers, one or two fellow cyclists and, as I crossed the Rhône on the edge of Villeurbanne, the burnt out shell of a Citroën. I was, after all, leaving a large French city at the end of a weekend in August.

For many, a spot of *fin-de-semaine* summer rioting was a right of Gallic passage and they had done a remarkably good job in destroying this shapely C3. I had never previously appreciated just how innovative the model's curving windscreen-cum-sunroof was. Along with all the other windows it had been completely removed. Impressive work!

The river cut a complicated path through the parks with at least three contenders vying to be the bona-fide Rhône. The Old Rhône was in with a good shout until in melted into the Lac des Eaux Bleues (and a number of other lakes) before briefly re-emerging further east and then disappearing altogether. To the north was the Canal de Miribel and to the south the Canal de Jonage which eventually joined to reform the Rhône proper. I had been following the Canal de Jonage, more or less, and near the point where it stopped being a canal and started being a river again, the cycle path turned right. *Or did it?* I was not convinced and here ensued a little head scratching.

In areas where signage was lacking - not just along the ViaRhôna but elsewhere during my Grand Tour - I had often been following the trace of the route available online via OpenStreetMap. Signs, OpenStreetMap and my paper maps usually provided all of the answers and they rarely contradicted each other. But here they did. OpenStreetMap was telling me to continue to follow the river. However, some of the *itinéraire provisoire* signs – reminding me of those I had followed near Châteauneuf-du-Pape a few days earlier - were wanting to send me up a very steep bank to my right. *Really?* Furthermore, at this point on my paper map the words *"opérationnel à partir de juillet 2022"* had been printed. *Could I believe that?* It was only August 2022 and my map could feasibly have been printed years ago. *Was this another murky tale of a local mayor wanting to get their hands on the European cycle infrastructure subsidies?*

After a few moments of thought, I dismounted and pushed Wanda up the vertiginous path for a minute or two before spotting more *itinéraire provisoire* signs and continuing to cycle. There followed 45 minutes of left-right-left-right angle-poise cycling through the suburbs of a series of small towns until the point where, as I suspected, I found it. Another big sign telling me how the *département* - Isère - was investing money to improve the quality of my life. In this case, €1.1million for a kilometre or so of newly paved track across fields and through woods. It was all very nice but I could not help but wonder if the deviation away from the river and all the faffing around through the nearby housing estates had been worth all the fuss. Several kilometres later I was, mercifully, back in my comfort zone beside the river.

Shortly before midday, I noticed two cyclists in the distance. As they approached I could see one of them waving in my direction. It quickly became apparent that they were somewhat outside their own comfort zone. There were barely any pleasantries. The female in the couple cut straight to the chase.

"Excuse me, *monsieur*. Have you found an *épicerie* that's open?" she asked, in French and in desperation.

"I'm sorry," I replied "but I have the same problem. I've not seen anything open since Lyon."

The woman turned to her male companion and started sobbing, dismounted from her bike and beat her fists on the ground.

"I can't go on," she cried. "Is this it? Death from starvation on the route of the ViaRhôna?"

Her words were slightly muffled and it could be that she had simply dropped something on the floor but irrespective, I shuffled slightly so as not to reveal the Babybels protruding from my pocket.

"We've not been able to buy any food since setting off this morning," explained the male cyclist a little wearily.

It did not bode well for my onward journey but I wished them "*bon courage*" and they reciprocated. Lest I be mugged by other desperate cyclists on the look out for sustenance on this bank holiday Monday in France, I decided to pause in the pretty village of Hières-sur-Amby to sit beside the church and eat lunch. As the bells of the clocktower chimed twelve, I munched my way through the bread and processed cheese and nibbled my nuts as a dessert. I was not going to be sharing my tasty *cacahuètes* with anyone!

On the train the previous morning I had identified several candidate campsites to use over the coming days. The one at Sault-Brénaz was only a further 25km along the Rhône by which point I would probably have cycled some 80km so I set it as my destination for the day. As the crow flew, it was perhaps only 10km from Hières-sur-Amby but I was now cycling towards the north-east and just to the south of a town called Lagnieu, the river abruptly changed direction by 90° to head south-east. This, combined with the wiggly nature of the cycle path, would add at least another 15km to the direct distance. Taking the shorter route was not really an option, or rather, was an option that would require me to climb another steep (and much longer) hill to my right. Indeed at some points the hill was actually a sheer rock face leading to a tree-smothered balcony: perhaps the cycling option to the top did not even exist. From the cycle path beside the river it was difficult to spot any roads or paths heading in that direction and anyway, I was happy continuing to pootle my way along the relatively flat path of the ViaRhôna.

Crossing the river at the Pont de Lagnieu, it was apparent that the recent storms and heavy rain had increased the level of the water significantly. It flowed beneath me with powerful determination. The river was also beginning to change colour: it was noticeably more turquoise than it had been back in Lyon and it was a gradual change that would become increasingly obvious the further into the Alps I cycled.

According to NASA's Earth Observatory, it is all to do with glacial flour:

> "The glaciers function like bulldozers, grinding away and pulverising rocks along valley floors and walls. The process produces a fine-grained powder of silt and clay - glacial flour - that is picked up by meltwater streams. Since the particles are so fine, they are slow to sink to the bottom, remaining suspended in the water column instead. When sunlight hits the water, these particles absorb the shortest wavelengths: the purples and indigos. Meanwhile, the water absorbs the longer wavelength reds, oranges, and yellows. That leaves mainly blues and greens to get scattered back to our eyes."[61]

And there was I thinking NASA was all about missions to the moon and inventing Teflon.[62]

Of greater importance was what I found on the northern side of the Rhône: a sign for a Lidl supermarket. I paused to check on my phone how far away it was. Half a kilometre, if that. It was worth the slight detour, especially as Google was suggesting that it was open. The algorithm in California might not be *au fait* with the idiosyncrasies of French public holidays but I was willing to take the risk. My gamble paid off.

I could not quite believe that the shop was not overrun with desperate French people seeking sustenance on this Monday bank holiday. Somewhat counter-intuitively, it seemed to be simply another day at Lidl with only a handful of customers pushing their trolleys across the car park. I just needed to negotiate the entrance to the store with the bike.

It consisted of two automatic doors and an airlock (that I assumed was no such thing). I wheeled Wanda through the first door and it closed behind

---

[61] earthobservatory.nasa.gov: 'How Glaciers Turn Lakes Turquoise'

[62] NASA did get to the moon but it turns out that they did not invent Teflon. That said, according to research in 2022 by the EU, 25% of Europeans do not believe they got to the moon either but I digress...

us. There was sufficient space in the "airlock" for Wanda to be secured without disturbing anyone entering behind us so I left her there and proceeded, on my own, though the second automatic door which duly closed behind me. They may never have invented Teflon but, bearing in mind its complexity, NASA must surely have been instrumental in designing the entrance to this Lidl store in rural France.

Alas, I had not thought this through. The second door opened immediately onto the first aisle of the shop. The only exit was via the narrow checkouts. I picked up a few items that would see me through the next 24 hours, paid for them and went back outside into the car park before returning to the airlock to retrieve Wanda. The first door then closed automatically behind me. Ah… We were trapped.

The few people who had been in the car park had now disappeared. I could not be seen by any of the Lidl employees and I doubted they would have approved if I had tried to wheel the bike through their shop and force Wanda's width through the space next to the checkout. Bags-for-life, chewing gum and mobile phone top-up cards would be strewn far and wide. Perhaps if NASA *had* been involved it might well be an airlock after all. I waited and waited, periodically checking my breathing.

Finally, about ten minutes later, an elderly lady got out of her car and started walking towards the shop. It was torture. She walked slowly. At one point she paused. *Do not turn back, not now: I'm getting low on oxygen.* As she approached the door it slid open. She looked up, a little startled to see a cyclist gasping for breath but we exchanged *bonjours* and I escaped. Neil Armstrong never had these issues.

All that remained was to cycle the final few kilometres of the day to the campsite which was located on an island to the south of Sault-Brénaz. It was somewhat busier than the Lidl. The enterprising owners of the campsite had cut a meandering narrow channel across the island through which the fast-flowing waters of the Rhône were able to flow. The result was a very popular wild-water canoe and kayaking course, the Espace Eau-Vive. After such a quiet, sedate day on the bike it was very much a shock to the system to be confronted with people and noise, but welcome nevertheless. There was ample space for camping at a suitable distance away from the hullabaloo and after a beer in the bar, I set about making camp for the night.

It would be the usual fare of spaghetti and pesto (with the added delight of Lidl Parmesan cheese) but what was not so usual was the cool evening. The sunset came and went at around 9 pm and thereafter the temperature dropped rapidly. After so many nights spent simmering in the tent, as I headed further and further into the mountains, things were gradually changing and it was not just the colour of the water.

Day Forty-Five: Sault-Brénaz to Seyssel (112km)
Tuesday 16th August

Not a drop of rain had fallen but such had been the relative coolness of the night, come the morning, the exterior skin of the tent was sopping wet. Previously, in the almost certain expectation that come the evening I would be erecting it in warm sunlight, I might have wrapped up the tent regardless. Here in the Alps, I was somewhat more sceptical about how the weather might pan out, especially after the storms of recent days. With the sun creeping over the summit of the hill to the east, I removed the fly sheet, spread it over the ground and waited for it to dry in the direct sunlight that had only just arrived.

In the meantime, my neighbours - a young Swiss couple - were cooking up breakfast and we got chatting. They were cycling in the opposite direction along the ViaRhôna and recommended a campsite where they had stayed in a town called Seyssel. Referring to my onward journey over the border into Switzerland, they broke the least surprising news of my Grand Tour so far.

"Switzerland is very expensive," revealed the man, laughing nervously.

"But going by bike is one way to discover it in a good price range," added the woman, keen to defend the honour of her home country, "because the campsites are only €30 to €40 for a cyclist".

I tried not to make it too obvious that I was now fighting the urge to spit out my morning coffee. It seemed it was not only the temperature which was beginning to fluctuate: so was the cost of living. I had paid just €9 for my night at the campsite in Sault-Brénaz and my many nights of camping in France had rarely cost me more than €15. Many had been under €10 so "€30 to €40" was, from my perspective, eye-watering.

Seyssel was a little further than I had anticipated cycling but my new Swiss friends had emphasised just how flat the route would be. With the added recommendation of a decent campsite close to the centre of the town, it was worth making the effort. I had been maintaining my average cycling distance at a smidgen over 80km. So, making hay whilst the sun was shining - and the terrain quite flat - was no bad thing, especially bearing in mind the more strenuous challenges of the mountains in the coming days. These would surely dent my average quite considerably.

It was a wonderfully peaceful morning beside the Rhône and, as I started to make my way south following the idiosyncratic path of the river, I tried to soak in everything around me. The green hills to the east, the cloudless expanse of sky above me, the sporadic clumps of tall poplar trees beside the water and the gentle flow of the river itself, its surface reflecting all the fineries that the valley had to offer. It was an overload of beauty.

The rusting and overgrown tracks of a long-abandoned railway line to my right were somewhat curious, perhaps even a little out of place. *Had they once transported the genteel folk of Lyon from their smoggy industrial age slums in the city to this pristine stretch of the Rhône to applaud the serenity of the natural landscape and breathe in its pollution-free and naturally perfumed air?*

Probably yes, but also… cement. Yes, cement.

Unbeknownst to me I was entering an area of very well-hidden quarries and an industrial processing plant operated by the Vicat company, one of France's leading manufacturers of the lucrative legal white stuff.

The story of Louis Vicat, the man who gave the company its name, is a humbling one. Born in 1786 in central France, Louis trained as an engineer of roads and bridges but it would be on a mission to build a new bridge over the Dordogne near Souillac where he would make his name. It was proving difficult to build the bridge due to unsuitable mortars so Louis set about researching how to improve the mix. He came up with a solution that, using the correct proportions of clay and limestone, allowed the mixture to set underwater. Instead of filing a patent, he published his findings for anyone to use and in doing so transformed the world of construction. It was his son who set up the Vicat company and Louis was showered with awards and accolades for his great work and generosity. He died in 1861 but when the Eiffel Tower was opened in 1889 he was one of the 72 celebrated scholars and engineers whose names were chosen to adorn the first tier of the building.[63]

As I cycled, there were an increasing number of reminders that this pretty corner of France had once been - and to a certain extent continued to be - a hotbed of industrial endeavour. It being an area rich in both clay and limestone, it was ideally suited for the Vicat company to set up a cement factory in the early 20th century but the company was not alone. The manufacturer Baron-Vialle had constructed buses here in the inter-war years and in the second half of the century, several aluminium foundries were opened. A handful of quarries remained, as did Vicat in their large processing plant beside the Rhône.

---

[63] The list of 72 names is a roll call of the great and good of the French scientific world during the country's first 100 years as a republic. As long as, that is, their surname was not too long. With limited space available for each name, he set a maximum of 12 letters per name. No problem for Vicat, but an issue for the celebrated 19th-century French naturalist Étienne Geoffroy-Saint-Hilaire. He's not up there. One other issue: it seems that you had to be a man. None of the 72 names is that of a woman.

The rusting railway lines that I had noticed shortly after leaving the campsite were once part of the Est Lyonnais line, the path of which I now realised that I had been following for much of the time since leaving Lyon. Yet the ViaRhôna was not the first to exploit the line after its closure. For much of the route between the Vicat factory in Montalieu and the quarry at Mépieu, I was cycling beside a long but low concrete tunnel. Inside this tunnel was once a 6.5km conveyor belt built upon the route of the railway line to transport the limestone from the quarry to the cement factory. It seems that in this corner of France, it was not the cycle planners who were first to see the recycled utility of having someone build a long, flat track for their trains only to abandon it when it became uneconomical to exploit.

By the time I arrived in the town of Morestel, the ViaRhôna had again deviated from its namesake, in this case by some 7km. However, following a sharp left turn and lurch to the north-east, we rejoined the river beside the bridge at Groslée. For the remainder of the day, we never ventured more than a few hundred metres at most from the water and it was a welcome return to the life of an enthusiastic bridge-spotter and crosser. In my evening write-up of events for August 16th, I would later comment that what was about to unfold was one of the best - if not the best - days of cycling so far.

Perhaps what nudged it to that position in the pantheon of cycling days was the sheer novelty of the scenery that was increasingly engulfing me. My route to this point had rarely been anything below pretty, often beautiful and occasionally bucolic, but the topology was now adding an extra dimension - literally - to what I was seeing. Mountains were no longer distant objects strung low on the horizon: they had become unavoidable - and welcome - features of the landscape. The river itself had done the hard work over the millions of years of its existence, cutting a wide path into what was presumably once a terrain just as featureless as the contemporary flat plains of the west of France. The resulting drama of the land was now the river's crowning glory, all its epoch-spanning efforts coming to fruition as I, a humble and fleetingly insignificant cyclist, looked up from the handlebars of my bike to admire the view.

The greatest visual delight of the day, however, remained somewhat hidden until 60km into the cycling day when the path of the ViaRhôna turned nearly 180° on itself and headed north in the direction of the small town of Belley. Some 30km ahead of me was the not inconsiderable hulk of Le Grand Colombier, a distinctive lump of rock hidden to a greater extent under a tablecloth of forest and home to a climb that had occasionally featured on the route of the Tour de France. It was my waymarker for the afternoon as my destination, Seyssel, was located at its northern extremity. The signs of the cycle path were now somewhat redundant: with such a sizeable finishing post, if I were to get lost I would only have myself to blame.

I crossed the river yet again near the town of La Balme via a modern suspended footbridge. It was near here that those who had been trying to tame the river over the centuries had, at some point, decided to construct another of the river's *canals de dérivation*. It was a canal that did a remarkably good job of masquerading as a river and stretched over nearly 20km as far as Chanaz whilst the Rhône itself meandered along a much narrower course first to the east and then to the north. Indeed such was the extent of the fluctuating width of the canal that at points it took its deceit to an altogether new level and gave every indication of being a lake before admitting its trickery and officially calling itself the Lac du Lit au Roi.

I was keen to maintain my energy levels on what I fully expected to be one of the longest rides of my continental odyssey. So, when I spotted a café overlooking the lake, I decided to pause my journey and sit down for a proper lunch served to me at one of the tables on its shaded terrace. It was around 2 pm and there were already a few bicycles parked up beside the building. I walked inside but it was not obvious from anything I could see what was on offer. Not being able to spot a menu, I asked what I thought was a perfectly logical question:

"*Qu'est-ce que vous avez pour le déjeuner madame?*"

The two women behind the counter looked anxiously at each other without speaking. In unison, they each turned to stare at a young lad in the kitchen. He stared back for a few seconds. No words were exchanged. In a seemingly choreographed manoeuvre, all three of them then turned back to look at me. I smiled, nervously. *Was it such a strange question to ask in a, err... café? Had I got my days wrong? Was it still Monday and had they just turned up to do a bit of cleaning?* The few customers on the terrace would suggest otherwise.

Eventually one of the women suggested that the chef could perhaps rustle up a plate of cold meat and cheese. This had me instantly salivating and I eagerly awaited his response.

"*Oui, je pense que c'est possible...*" he responded, hesitantly.

I could understand that I might have arrived towards the end of their lunch period, but their exaggerated reactions were utterly out of kilter with the problems that seemed to have been thrown up by that scenario. Was there a local by-law preventing the sale of food to anyone after 1.30 pm? Or to cyclists?

The meat and cheese were delicious but more bizarre events were about to unfold. In a country where it would not have surprised me in the least if the street beggars accepted payment by debit card, this café did not. I only had a few coins in my pocket and not enough of them to pay the modest €7 bill.

The payment was eventually made by international bank transfer. I was not the only customer stunned at being asked to open up our banking apps and punch the required 28-digit IBAN into our phones. The two other cashless customers were just as bemused as me.

The payment palaver had delayed my departure so it was not until past three when I set off again. The views of Le Grand Colombier were increasingly stunning. They reached their zenith just outside Chanaz where the oyster-shell profile of the mountain was reflected almost without blemish in the turquoise water of the Rhône that had just reappeared following its jaunt to the east. It was, perhaps, the biggest wow! moment of the trip so far.

Viewed from the northern bank of its canal, Chanaz might also have provoked a few quiet wows. By far the busiest place I had stumbled upon all day, it was a town that certainly drew in the crowds. The short but steeply arched footbridge that spanned the canal artistically framed the pretty three-storey houses that lined the opposite bank. As I trundled on, a modest passenger boat full of tourists chuffed its way under the bridge. It was as charming as it was unexpected. A few cyclists had made the effort to push their bikes up and over the bridge but with four panniers and a tent I was not tempted to follow them. However, a comment on social media later in the day spoke glowingly of Chanaz and I regretted not pausing and making more of an effort to cross the canal to discover the delights it had to offer.

In the final 20km of the cycling day, I was surprised as to just how much energy I still had in my legs. Even when the small Cat Eye odometer that was clamped to my handlebars ticked over into three figures, I felt just as alive as I had done when setting off from the campsite. On the previous day, cycling from the centre of Lyon had, at times, been a physical struggle. That was after a non-cycling day on Sunday. Yet here I was on Tuesday feeling none the worse for wear having cycled more than 100km. *How did that work? Was it the enormous pile of pasta that I had eaten at Camping Espace Eau Vive the previous evening? Was it the succulent range of meats and cheeses consumed in the early afternoon?* Probably both but it left me wondering why anyone would want to waste their money on energy snacks and drinks when all you needed to do was pack in the staples of pasta, meat and cheese. Just not so convenient to pop in your pocket.

Seyssel took up an imposing position beside the Rhône. The riverside church dominated the town's profile at a pinch point where the two banks of the river were linked by a solid suspension bridge dating from the mid-19th century. It being relatively late in the day I cycled straight through the town in search of the campsite and found it a few minutes to the north of the centre. With my evening meal (more pasta…) purchased from the conveniently located Carrefour supermarket outside the entrance, I pitched the tent and headed off to the campsite bar to celebrate the success of the day. The view looking south along the river towards the church and the bridge seemed to shout "Haute Savoie". Yet my eyes were distracted by something closer to home. *Was it a car? Was it a bicycle? Was it a tricycle?* A man called Stéphane, who had pitched his own small tent quite close to the bar, provided the answers.

"It's a vélomobile," he revealed. "It has three wheels: two on the front and one at the back and it's completely enclosed in fibreglass. It can travel up to 80km per hour and weighs around 25 kg, 40 with my luggage."

It was a three-wheeled recumbent bicycle dressed as a fighter jet. I pointed to his t-shirt which referred to an *"association"* of vélomobile riders.

"There are quite a lot of us but most of them live in flat parts of France." I guessed the fighter jet was not so great on the hills.

"Do you have a normal touring bike?" I asked.

"What is a normal bike?" he replied, making a good point in the process.

"Does it have a name?"

"Sputnik! Because in French this is what we call the medicine that you put in your bottom."

I could see the resemblance. Cycling could sometimes be a pain in the arse, literally. But this took things to a whole new level.

Day Forty-Six: Seyssel to Excenevex (97km)
Wednesday 17th August

If yesterday had been the yin, today would ultimately be the yang. Tuesday had been a glorious day of cycling. Everything I might have dreamt about in the months and years leading up to this long cycle around France. Wednesday was not too shabby: it would see me cross my first international border for nearly six weeks and have me cycling along the shore of Lac Léman. But there would be a sharp sting in the tail of the day and the clues were there from the very start. Standing on the old bridge across the Rhône in the centre of Seyssel, munching my crumbling *croissant* and sipping my takeaway coffee, the storm clouds were beginning to gather and they were heading in the same direction as me.

In other news, shortly after leaving Seyssel something happened for the first time on my Grand Tour: I was confronted with a big hill. I had encountered hills in Brittany but none of them were of this magnitude. Around 300 metres of ascent to a modest (by Alpine standards) 550 meters and I loved every second. Correction: I loved every second when I arrived at the summit (it was nothing more than a junction of roads and paths close to a hamlet called Traînant). My lungs were finally being tested over an extended period - 1 hour 23 minutes to be precise - and I was rewarded with a wonderful view of Le Crêt du Feu-Arcine.

Fear not, I had never heard of it either but that was what I was looking down upon. As far as I could understand, it was the geographical feature on the other side of the valley, not dissimilar to Le Grand Colombier that I had passed beneath on the previous day. The view of Le Crêt (it translates as an escarpment) du Feu-Arcine was annotated in excessive detail on a large information board at the viewpoint. I started reading but it required a degree in geology to interpret. Ideally a French degree in geology. I soon gave up and stuck to staring at the mercifully unannotated real thing.

I was joined by someone that I recognised from the campsite. Not Stéphane (he had passed me on the hill at an astonishing speed in his three-wheeled contraption) but a woman who was cycling using a more traditional (dare I say normal?) bicycle. We chatted in French for a few minutes until it dawned upon us that we shared the same first language.

"I'm from Vancouver but I live in Lyon teaching English," she explained. She was en route to visit her cousin in Zurich and she had found the climb quite tough.

"I was cycling 150km a week commuting to work but COVID fucked everything up. All my teaching is now online. I need a new job!" she declared.

We were joined by a French woman who had also been camping overnight in Seyssel. She was cycling with her son and daughter and they had set off from Lyon also along the ViaRhôna. Over the next hour as we approached the Swiss border, just as we had done on the ascent, we all crossed each other on multiple occasions exchanging cheery motivational salutations. It may have been fleeting but there was a common bond of mutual encouragement within our small stretched-out peloton. After so many days - weeks even - of encountering so few cyclists who were travelling in the same direction as me it was here, at the summit of this climb, where I was able to engage in some quality en-route group banter. But it made perfect sense: summits were great places to meet fellow cyclists as most cyclists stopped when they arrived at one. On my flat route around France, I had not previously climbed to any summits worthy of the name and had missed out on the opportunities for idle mutual back-slapping chit-chat. Another reason to love the hills!

After deviating slightly from the route of the ViaRhôna to stock up on cheap food from a French supermarket (I was not 100% certain that I would be back in France by the end of the day) I crossed the border into Switzerland. This happened in the middle of a dense forest to the south-west of Geneva. The track on the French side had been paved but this ended abruptly at the stone border post that simply had "F" chiselled on one side and "S" on the other. Two and a half hours later after diligently following the signage through the increasingly urban landscape to the west of Geneva, I arrived at the shores of Lac Léman.

I paused briefly to look out over the water in the direction of the city's iconic jet of water but did not hang around lest I be tempted to spend some money and immediately regret doing so. Although not yet raining, the sky had clouded over to such an extent that there was no blue to be seen. It seemed almost inevitable that at some point the rain would start falling as the afternoon morphed into the evening. I just needed to make sure that when it did I had found myself a campsite, erected the tent and was sitting inside it in the dry. *But where would that campsite be?* It was already 3 pm and I had yet to search for a campsite let alone pick one and set it as my destination for the day. It was playing on my mind, but so was getting out of Switzerland and back into France to avoid having to pay "€30 to €40" for a pitch here in one of Europe's most achingly affluent countries. I decided to prioritise escaping Switzerland and set off along the southern shore of the lake.

Everything, especially the houses and their swimming pools and tennis courts, oozed wealth. I wondered what the locals might think of a cyclist such as me passing in front of their living room windows with his tent and four panniers. I could only imagine it would be a mixture of bemusement and pity. But then again asking the filthy rich why anyone would travel long distances by bicycle and repeatedly camp overnight is a bit like asking a giraffe why he never goes to the cinema. It is a concept that has simply never entered most of their minds. If you happen to be filthy rich (or a giraffe), give it a go. You might find it quite enjoyable. (Giraffes: mind your head on the door and sit in the back row so as not to annoy the other cinemagoers.)

After about 5km my route headed inland, away from the shore of Lac Léman. As did the road. It was at this point where the filthy rich became the filthy stinking rich. No longer did they have to entertain the idea of the likes of me passing in front of their living room window as their living rooms looked out directly upon the lake. The only things blocking their views were their private piers and yachts moored at the end of their manicured gardens.

The French border was just beyond the small Swiss town of Hermance. There was a campsite on the Swiss side of the border. The reasons as to why I chose not to pull on the brakes at this point of my journey have been lost in the mists of time. I even made a short detour to pass by the reception of the site. I can only imagine that I genuinely believed that just over the border in France there would be a campsite that would charge me a quarter of the price. I did not even bother checking the price of the Swiss site. I simply cycled on and at that moment my fate was sealed.

Now having returned to relatively cheap France, I identified a campsite about 10km from the border, Camping Le Nant des Mules. By 5.30 pm I was standing outside its entrance looking at the sign hanging over the welcome board. It confirmed the distressing information in no less than five languages:

Complet
Komplett
Volgeboekt
Completo
No Vacancy

The apology came in just four (*désolé / dispiace / apenado /* sorry - perhaps the Dutch and the Germans do not apologise...). I cycled past the reception but there was nobody around. I could, I thought, knock on a door and ask the owners if they could squeeze in just one small tent. But I did not. Why? This time I did have a reason. A few kilometres further along the road was the town of Excenevex and it was home to a cluster of campsites on the shore of the lake. I set off again. *Was that a drop of rain?* My mind was immediately distracted away from my accommodation issues and the weather when a large fly flew into my mouth at high speed and gave every impression of wanting to set up camp at the top of my windpipe. I pulled on the brakes and forced myself to cough in an exaggerated fashion whilst plunging my fingers into my mouth in an attempt to extract the unwanted visitor. It worked, or so I thought. The lifeless torso of the beast now lay motionless on the tarmac of the road. *Was that another drop of rain?*

At least the road was now taking me downhill. Upon arrival in the suburbs of Excenevex, I quickly spotted some signs for campsites and followed them. Yes, it was now raining very lightly. Nothing too serious. I arrived at a roundabout. There was a campsite to my left and a campsite to my right. The one on the right looked more my style. It was a one-star affair. Perfect. Basic, nice and cheap. Crucially, there was no "*complet*" sign outside. Finally, I had found my home for the night.

"*Bonjour*. Do you have space for a small tent?" I asked, rhetorically (of course they did!)

"I'm very sorry, *monsieur*, but we are only a campsite for caravans and motorhomes," explained the woman behind the reception desk, very politely.

"In that case why the hell do you call yourself a campsite?! There are laws against that!" I did not retort.

"I think it's about to start raining," she added.

"It already is," I confirmed.

"Sorry."

"Fuck off!" I did not shout.

"Why not try the campsite over the road?"

A few minutes later I was repeating the conversation at the four-star Camping La Pinède.

"*Bonjour*. Do you have space for a small tent?" I asked wearily and even more rhetorically than before. The vast campsite was strewn with tents, camper vans and caravans of all descriptions.

"Yes, of course," smiled the young woman dealing with me. Dressed in a smart-but-casual blue uniform complete with pin badges informing me she spoke French, English and Spanish, she was a slave to the corporate monster that was Camping La Pinède. "It's beginning to rain quite hard, isn't it?"

"Yes."

"That will be €35 sir."

A large clap of thunder broke the shocked silence. I winced.

"€35?"

"Yes."

I winced again.

I had no choice but to pay up. Outside the storm had not just arrived: it had arrived and asked all its mates around for a party. Rivers of water were flowing in places that they had no right to flow. More corporate slaves were now rushing into the building for shelter. Others had mops in their hands and were beginning to try and persuade the water to stay outside the reception area. The ever-increasing pool of water by the entrance was evidence that they were not succeeding.

My allocated pitch was a couple of minutes' walk from the main reception but so torrential was the rain that it seemed churlish even to consider venturing out and attempting to pitch the tent. But there was no sign that the rain was going to ease off and, after about 30 minutes in the dry reception building, I plucked up the courage, mounted Wanda and headed off to emplacement 462.

A nearby wash block provided shelter for Wanda and all my chattels but I needed to get the tent erected. In a moment of madness worthy of a philandering politician I took the tent off the bike, ran over to the pitch and started erecting.

I remembered buying the MSR Hubba Hubba tent a couple of years earlier and reading the instructions. There *was* an alternative method of erecting it that meant the outer shell could be put up before the inner, but I was buggered if I could remember how that was done, so I did not. It was not a wise move. By the time I had managed to put the poles together and secure them to the fishnet inner, there was already a considerable amount of water washing around inside the tent. There was, however, no going back. I continued to battle, in the wind and the rain, and stretched the flysheet over the frame. Finally, it was watertight. Never again will I sneer at a relieved amateur builder on *Grand Designs* who is ecstatic to have fitted the windows and tiled the roof.

I returned to the wash block to wait with Wanda. What a man needs in these situations is Pringles, chocolate and wine. In a masterstroke of planning, these were the three items that I had purchased from the campsite shop. They provided solace as I watched the rain continue to fall. The rumbles of thunder were a distraction from my internal sobbing. Some time passed.

I had inadvertently managed to pitch the tent on a slight incline. I noticed this having completed the erection process and remarking that the small swimming pool inside the tent had a deep end and shallow end. Running / Pushing / Shouting / Ducking / Petting / Bombing / Smoking were, however, the least of my worries. I just needed to empty the pool of its water. Noticing that the wash block was stocked with, rather ironically, at least €35 worth of paper towels, it struck me that they might be my saviour.

Piles of paper towels in hand, I returned to pitch 462…

I may have emptied the wash block of every single paper towel but it worked. By 8 pm I had managed to dry the tent sufficiently to move in.

As I lay in my moist Hubba Hubba eating the final hyperbolic paraboloids of Pringles and sucking the final remnants of wine from the bottle, I cast my mind back to earlier in the day as I had been cycling beside the shores of Lac Léman:

> "I wondered what the locals might think of a cyclist such as me passing in front of their living room windows with his tent and four panniers. I could only imagine it would be a mixture of bemusement and pity."

I was beginning to appreciate their thinking.

Day Forty-Seven: Excenevex To Aigle (67km)
Thursday 18th August

It rained much of the night but, such is the design miracle of the modern tent, the inside continued to dry. At around 6 am I dared peak outside and there were glimmers of hope. The rain had abated in the preceding hour and now stopped. The sun had yet to rise but the clouds above me were no longer pregnant with precipitation. There were even a few patches of gloomy blue. I coughed. My throat was sore. I remembered the incident with the fly. I suspected that some of it was still lodged in there.

By 7 am I was up and pondering the scene around me. The designers of quick-drying tents have yet to turn their skills to wet clothes which have been sitting in a pile all night so I draped my cycling gear over poor Wanda. She had spent her night in the elements. At least she was now spotlessly clean. And at least we had survived the ordeal. Close by I could see a mangled pile of tent poles, guy ropes and man-made fabric. One family's holiday had come to an abrupt end at some point during the previous 12 hours.

By 8 am I had packed everything away and had pulled on my wet shorts and a sweaty, stained t-shirt that had been relegated to the washing bag a couple of days earlier. But needs must. It was at least dry. Well, dryish. Carrying the damp odour of a vagrant I set off back towards the reception area and the adjacent exit. There were few people out of their tents, mobile homes or campervans to see - or indeed smell - me. The minions of the Camping La Pinède corporation were equally thin on the ground. Just a refuse collector chugging from bin to bin in his converted golf cart and the cleaner of the nearby wash block. She was refilling the paper towel dispensers and had a puzzled look on her face. I whispered a quiet "*bonjour*" as I cycled slowly by. She eyed me suspiciously and did not respond...

The route of the ViaRhôna kindly passed the gates of Camping La Pinède so it was not a challenging start to the cycling day. Initially, a segregated cycle path guided me away from the shore of Lac Léman before a deserted country lane took over the reins and sent me in the direction of nearby Sciez. Above me, the sky was perhaps 50% grey cloud. Or, rather, 50% blue. Ever the eternal optimist my heart clung to the latter statistic but my head had already worked out that the former was a steadily increasing number. The bank of clouds to the south-west was travelling in the same direction as me and it seemed unlikely that the day would be completely dry.

I was keen not to repeat the evening scramble for accommodation of the previous day so, as I ate breakfast in the café area of a roadside *boulangerie*, I attempted to hatch a plan. My second foray into Switzerland was now only 40km away at the point where the ViaRhôna finished on the French side of the border-straddling town of Saint-Gingolph. I could no longer consider campsites in France an option and would need to bite the financial bullet of finding accommodation in Switzerland. One way of blunting this outlay to the point of it disappearing altogether was to secure a night with a Warmshowers host. I located two possible members in the area where the Rhône re-established its course heading south at the eastern end of Lac Léman and dispatched a couple of messages. If nothing came of those requests I would explore the camping options.

Another concern was power. I could usually survive up to a maximum of three days once my iPhone and 20,000 mAH[64] battery pack had been fully charged. I had done this back at the campsite in Seyssel by creeping into an unoccupied glamping tent and pilfering some overnight electricity. (I will come quietly if the gendarmes start asking questions.) That was only 36 hours ago so I should not yet be suffering from charge anxiety but when I attempted to plug my battery pack into my phone in the tent at Camping La Pinède, nothing happened. Either my phone or the battery pack had been affected by the water thrown down from the sky during the storm.

I dearly hoped the issue was with the battery pack but feared it might be my phone. If this turned out to be the case it would pose serious questions regarding my ability to keep travelling. Although the world would no doubt survive without my regular tweets, Instagram photos, Facebook posts and blog updates, my ability to go online and find accommodation or work out the route when I could not find a sign beside the road would be severely curtailed. *How would I record audio for the podcasts that I was continuing to publish as I cycled? How would I record the videos that I intended to use for a post-trip film? And how would I manage to board the ferry home from Rotterdam when my tickets were stored on the phone?* Oh to live in the 1950s when phones were still ignorantly stupid and wired into a box by the front door. The modern-day mobile phone has become the portable electronic Behemoth of the 21st century.

At least my phone was still working, for the time being. The level of charge was around 35% (a level that back home in the UK would have me in a cold sweat) and all I could do was wait. Wait until the battery dried

---

[64] mAH - milliampere-hour: a measurement of how much energy charge a battery can hold. A single Duracell AA battery typically holds a charge of around 3,000 mAH.

(and hopefully started working again) or until I could plug in the phone to mains electricity to see if that was where the problem was to be found.

This stretch of shoreline on the southern side of Lac Léman was dominated by the spa towns of Thonon-les-Bains and Évian-les-Bains. Perhaps they could soothe my woes by simply cycling past their therapeutic institutions. This would have been tricky in Thonon as the cycle route kept well clear of the town centre adopting a route close to the water. However, I did pause in the town's port area. Its dozen or so piers were home to several hundred modest yachts. (Nothing remotely as vulgar as those I had seen in Switzerland.) More exciting to this landlubber, however, was the tourist office kiosk and the availability of some benches in a small park sandwiched between the lakeside road and the quayside.

I started to explain my battery/phone predicament to the tourism woman in the large wooden hut but she was a bit bored by the tale I was recounting and interrupted me:

"Would you like to charge your phone here?" she offered, keen for me to shut up so that she could move on to serving someone who at least had the intention of spending some money in Thonon.

"It's charging!" she declared from under the counter where the socket was located. Somewhat relieved, I went to sit on one of the park benches to wait for 30% to become at least 80%. The problem was with the battery pack, not the phone.

It was actually quite nice sitting on the bench for 45 minutes watching the world go by without the distraction of the phone. The old folk chatting politics. The young couples walking hand-in-hand along the promenade. The families buying ice-creams from the parlour on wheels. The kids screaming in excitement as they played in the fenced-off pirate-themed playground. And me, still drying out… Perhaps, I thought, it might one day be interesting to set off on an epic cycling journey with only an old-style Nokia brick or burner phone (or no phone), a film camera, a notebook and a pen. Just like they did in those Cyclists' Touring Club films from the 50s and 60s. They were always smiling, having fun. A fit and healthy bunch who were living through the final decades of a world without access to instant information, push notifications and breaking news. No weather forecasts refreshed by the swiping down of a finger. No online dating by swiping left.

Prime Minister Harold Macmillan told Britain in 1957 that "most of our people have never had it so good".

Perhaps he had a point.[65]
With its town centre sitting firmly beside the water, it was more difficult to avoid Évian-les-Bains. Its main attraction - the large Casino complex - was semi-hidden behind boards erected to keep out anyone apart from those involved in its restoration. Beyond its future regained charms, large *Belle-Époque* mansion blocks jostled for position amongst the more modern apartment complexes. Chief amongst the older buildings was the turn-of-the-century splendour of the Palais Lumière. Behind its ornate façade, a small army once administered "up to 1,200 treatments a day: baths, showers, massages and electrical treatments..." I hope they were more careful mixing water and electricity than I had been. The consequences for them would surely have been somewhat more serious.

My attention, however, was focused further ahead. 15km ahead to be precise. That would be the end of my journey along the ViaRhôna at the border with Switzerland. Most of these 15km were on the busy lakeside road. There was no cycle lane beyond Évian and it did not make for the most pleasant of cycling conditions. Until that is, I arrived in a small village called Locum. It was here where, for the final 3.5km, the cycle route moved off the road and onto a delightful twisting and undulating cycle path. It ran parallel(ish) to a disused single-track railway line that itself shadowed the route of the busy road below and the shore of the lake. Perhaps the authorities hope to reopen the line one day as it remains intact, complete with its original rails, rusting gently away ever since the last train passed this way in 1988. This was one abandoned railway that had not yet been handed over to the greenway cycle planners.

By the time I descended the few metres back to the shore as I approached the centre of Saint-Gingolph - I was not sure of the pronunciation - I had cycled around 50km and it was just after 2 pm. The official end of the ViaRhôna was next to the lake and very close to the border. It was marked by a wooden bus-stop-like structure under which an electronic display had been installed. It set out, interactively, the route "*au fil du Rhône... du Léman à la Méditerranée*". I recognised many of the locations that flashed up in front of me on the screen. It had taken me eight days to travel from the Mediterranean to Lac Léman. I had cycled around 600 of its 800 kilometres with the remainder being travelled on the two trains, from

---

[65] He did not: Post-war austerity / Widespread racial discrimination / Food rationing / Smog and pollution / UK's diminishing world status / Bomb sites / The Cold War / Sporting humiliation (England 3, Hungary 6) / 80% of men smoked (and half of them were killed by the habit) / Sexual expression frowned upon and often illegal. (10 not-so-great things about the 1950s, BBC website, 2007)

Montpellier and then from Tain l'Hermitage. It was a moment of satisfaction but not one I could dwell upon for long. Although I had reached the end of the French-administered ViaRhôna, I had not yet completed the route of the EuroVelo 17. That finished in Andermatt, some 200km further along the valley of the Rhône and beyond the Furka pass. And then there was the small matter of the Rhine. I had just 16 days remaining to travel some 1,700km and I had only three of my ten train journeys remaining. It would be close run thing.

Of more pressing concern was tonight's accommodation. One of the two Warmshowers hosts had replied to my request, but it was not with good news. They were themselves away on a long cycle. There was no news from the other person. I sat under the roof of the wannabe bus shelter and searched for a campsite somewhere along the Rhône valley in Switzerland no more than 30km from the French border. I found one quite quickly, in Aigle. I had never heard of the place before. *Why would I? It was just another small town along the way to Rotterdam.* I gave Camping de la Piscine a call and booked myself a pitch for the night for a relatively cheap (by rumoured Swiss standards) €23.

Leading off from the bus stop was an angled metal walkway that protruded slightly over the lake. Bunting consisting of alternating French and Swiss flags was attached to the railings. They fluttered vigorously in the breeze. At the Swiss end of the walkway was a pile of rubble and a makeshift tarmac path leading back to the road. This was an international frontier where the French had clearly made much more of an effort than their cousins in the Confederation of Helvetica.

Switzerland was blessed with a network of top-notch active-travel infrastructure. It went by the name of SwitzerlandMobility and I had first encountered it whilst cycling from southern England to southern Italy in 2010. On that particular occasion, I had crossed the country from Basel to Chiasso via the Gotthard Pass and followed the signs for Swiss cycle route number 3, the North-South Route. 12 years later I was back and preparing to follow cycle route number 1 no less, the Rhône Route which would take me to Andermatt. My expectations were high and it was only a matter of moments before I spotted my first distinctive light blue sign for, as it is called in French-speaking Valais, La Route du Rhône.

I found it geographically curious that a river that flowed from its source in the mountains to a lake as large as Lac Léman (70km long, 15km wide and over 300 metres deep in places) could still be considered the same river when it exited that lake at its other end. But it did. This was, from the perspective of geographers, the very same river that I had been following since Avignon, and who was I to question their judgement? But I still thought it strange.

I rejoined the path of the Rhône after a further 5km back on the busy road along the shore of the lake. When I did, the contrast with the road was stark. The river snaked across the wide patchwork of fields that made up much of the four-kilometre-wide flat plain of the valley and the cycle route followed it loyally on a high quality path of its own. With high mountains to my left and to my right, I could not help but think how fortunate I had been to follow the river in the direction from sea to source. I had not made a conscious decision to do so, it just happened that way. I had of course made a decision to cycle anticlockwise around France but in no way was the direction I would cycle the Rhône a factor in that decision. But this was the spectacular end of the route, heading into the Alps. I could only imagine that arriving at the roundabout in Sète might be somewhat of a disappointment. That said, any celebratory swim in the Mediterranean would surely be more pleasant than a glacial swim in the Alps. If the opportunity arose, I would restrict myself to a short paddle.

It was only mid-afternoon when I was approaching Aigle but, with my weather app predicting more rain from about 4 pm, I might have arrived just in time. For those of you who did their French homework at school it will come as no surprise that Camping de la Piscine was located next to the town's swimming pool. And, indeed, the town's crazy golf course but Camping du Minigolf has less of a ring to it I feel. Good choice. The site was everything I needed after my uncomfortably damp night at Camping La Pinède. The tent was erected before any rain fell and it set about the job of drying out in anticipation of me moving back in.

As I waited I took up residence at one of the trestle tables that had been set up in a small marquee that was for the exclusive use of cycle-campers. I used the opportunity to sort through my things, do some washing and, after a trip to a nearby supermarket, rustle up an evening meal. Just as I had feared, the food prices were high to the point of me considering whether the checkout woman might accept kidney donation as a valid method of payment. Kidneys still in situ, I resurrected a technique honed to perfection whilst cycling through pricey Norway in 2015: find the cheapest food in the supermarket and eat it every night during your stay. Just as they had been in Norway all those years previously, a packet of spaghetti and (admittedly fake) pesto seemed to be priced within range of my budget. On a calorific level, they were at least very cycling-friendly.

No rain had fallen by 5 pm and by 6 pm - the time at which the BBC weather app told me that there was a 99% certainty of it raining in Aigle -

it had yet to do so. Even by 9 pm, despite the cloud, it was still dry. Perhaps here in Switzerland, unlike in Spain, the rain really did not fall on the plain.

Day Forty-Eight: Aigle
Friday 19th August

It turned out I was wrong. The rain most certainly fell on the plain of the Rhône valley in Switzerland, especially during the night of the 18th to the 19th of August. It was late evening and I was gently simmering in my sleeping bag when the comforting (see previous comments…) pitter-patter of rain on the outer skin of the tent began. It was destined to continue uninterrupted until the middle of Friday afternoon.

When I emerged from the tent in the morning and scurried over to the marquee to brew my morning coffee, the decision to go nowhere was easy. It might have only been five days since my last day off the bike - the Sunday in Lyon - but this would be a proper day off. No cultural enrichment. No shopping. No traipsing around ticking off the attractions listed in the Rough Guide. I doubted if out-of-the-way Aigle even got a mention. There was bugger all to do here and the prospect of lounging around and sipping more coffee was not just appealing, it was actually exciting. *When had I last had a proper rest?* I could not remember. After nearly seven weeks of travelling, today was definitely going to be that day of rest I was craving.

I was sharing the marquee with a Spanish family. Mother, father and their two teenage daughters. They were also cycling and camping but were clearly made of hardier stuff than me. I chatted to the father and we compared notes about our respective journeys but then they set off, under their raincoats, in the direction of France. With everyone else at Camping de la Piscine holed up inside their campervans, even fraternising with fellow campers was now added to the growing list of things that I could not do in Aigle. I was beginning to enjoy this.

It seemed sensible to use the time that I had been afforded to do a little forward planning. The next point on my mid-term cycling horizon was the town of Andermatt. It was here where the EuroVelo 17 finished and where the EuroVelo 15 - the Rhine Cycle Route - started. To get there, I needed to continue to follow the valley of the Rhône passing through Martigny (where the river took a dogleg 90° turn to the left and started heading north-east), Sion, Visp and Goms. A few kilometres after Goms, at Obergoms, the climb to the Furka pass would start. Once over the pass I could hopefully freewheel all the way down to Andermatt via Realp and Hospental. Google suggested a distance of about 190km to Andermatt. Bearing in mind the climb on the final day, perhaps a 70-70-50 split across three days might be the best way to approach this, the most physically challenging section of my Grand Tour.

A town called Sierre was approximately 70km further along the valley from Aigle. This would make an appropriate place to pause overnight. *There were a handful of campsites beyond Sierre, but were there any Warmshowers hosts?* Yes, two, near the centre. One was "more a runner than a cyclist" according to his profile and he lived on the top floor of an apartment building. That might be an issue with the bike. The other looked more promising: Jean-Daniel and Célien, father and son. Detached house, small garden. *"Le vélo est mon mode de transport au Quotidien, mon exutoire, mon sport."*[66] They sounded perfect potential hosts so I dispatched a request to stay on Saturday night.

As for the second night en route to Andermatt, another 70km along the valley would take me to Goms, or thereabouts. I found at campsite called Camping Brigga, a kilometre or so to the south of Goms and gave them a call.

"Allo. Parlez-vous français? Or English?"

"Nein. Einen Moment," replied the woman. I heard her call someone to the phone.

"Hallo," said a man.

"Allo. Parlez-vous français? Or English?" I repeated.

"Nein."

Dragging the few words of German that I knew from the dark corners of my mind, I tried to bridge the linguistic impasse.

"Ein nacht? Sams...? Ein... tent?"

I was confident that the word for a tent in German was not tent. I was more confident that Saturday was *sams*-something but as to how it finished, I could not quite remember.

The man replied with a phrase that utterly escaped my rudimentary level of German. Then the line went dead.

Mmm... Had I just reserved a pitch for Sunday night or not?

Within the hour there was more concrete news from Jean-Daniel in Sierre.

"Yes, you can stay tomorrow but it will be a bit different because we are having a party to celebrate my father's 87th birthday. If you are happy to do so, you can eat with us. It will be raclette, a local speciality."

Happy? I was delighted! I replied immediately to accept the invitation.

As for the third night, hopefully in Andermatt, I knew exactly where I would be staying. Gotthard Camping was as basic a campsite as you could find. I had stayed there in 2010 as I cycled along the EuroVelo 5 to southern

---

[66] "Cycling is my daily mode of transport, my outlet, my sport."

Italy. It was essentially a field next to the cable car station close to the centre of town and the facilities were those provided for the comforts of skiers in winter. From what I could see online, it was still open for business. Again, I attempted to call. This time there was no answer but I was less concerned: the large field could happily accommodate all-comers. I was confident that another small tent would not be a problem.

This flurry of planning, interspersed between long periods of staring at the rain through the plastic window of the marquee, consulting social media, reading junk emails and intensive, high quality procrastination, filled up my morning. Come early afternoon I was feeling rested but, admittedly, a tad bored. Donning my rain jacket, I went for a wander around the campsite and then gave the modern wash block a thorough inspection. When I noticed that the reception had reopened, I sauntered over to book myself in for a second night. Time passed, slowly...

By 2 pm, the rain was beginning to ease. As I needed to get some cash from a dispenser, I decided to cycle the short distance into the centre of Aigle. It was a branch of UBS that obliged. *Could there be a country that had more colourful banknotes than Switzerland?* I doubted it. Also colourful was the bunting strewn across the rue du Bourg. Yellow, green, red polka dot... The penny did not drop.

I wandered around the corner, into the Place du marché and noticed some writing had been stencilled onto the ground in bright yellow ink:

À VOS VÉLOS?
PRÊTS?
DÉCOUVREZ LA ROUTE DU TOUR!

...beside which was the stylised logo of the Tour de France.

A glance online revealed that stage 9 of this year's tour had started in Aigle on July 10th. On the day that I had been setting off from Dieppe along the Avenue Verte, the professionals had been setting off on their own 193km ride. (Mine had been a more leisurely 57.) Indeed not only had the stage started in Aigle, following a long loop to the north of the town, it had returned to Aigle before climbing the mountains on the western side of the Rhône valley to finish at Châtel in France. I wondered what nice-but-nondescript Aigle had done to merit this accolade of featuring not just once but twice on the same stage of the Tour de France. *How strange.*

Perhaps there was more to Aigle than I had first given it credit. Turning around I noticed I was standing close to the tourist office so, leaving Wanda parked outside, I went inside to see what else I could learn about the town. The woman on duty smiled and said *"bonjour"* but she was busy dealing with a man from Norway. *Was he renegotiating the terms of the bilateral pasta and (fake) pesto bulk-purchasing agreement for the benefit of cheapskate touring cyclists?* No, but he was here on equally serious business. The tourist office doubled as a retailer of the local wines and the man seemed intent on buying most of the available stock. This took some considerable time. However, once he had agreed on a price and arranged for the wine to be delivered in a shipping container to Oslo (or so it seemed), the woman could return to her day job of advising tourists as to what they could do on a wet afternoon in Aigle. I was that tourist and to kick off our conversation I mentioned the Tour de France markings outside in the square.

"Have you visited the world headquarters of cycling?" she enquired.

What was she talking about? We were not in Paris or London or even Geneva.

"The world headquarters of cycling?" I queried.

"The headquarters of the UCI. It's here in Aigle."

"Really?"

The UCI - the Union Cycliste Internationale - is the organisation that governs competitive cycling on a global level. It was set up in 1900 in Paris by the national cycling federations of Belgium, France, Italy, Switzerland and the United States. Not Britain. The Belgians, French, Italians, Swiss and Americans were not very happy that the British, by virtue of being made up of England, Scotland, Ireland and Wales, had an unfair advantage when it came to international competitions as they could enter four teams. They decided to break away from the British-based International Cycling Association (founded by none other than Mr Henry Sturmey of Sturmey-Archer fame) to create the UCI, and their ruse worked. The British were only admitted as members when they agreed to amalgamate their four national teams into one. They did so in 1903 and the International Cycling Association was no more. The UCI moved its headquarters to Switzerland in the 1990s and to Aigle in 2004 where it took up residence in the World Cycling Centre.

"It's not very far. Just next to the river," explained the woman in the tourist office, "and it's open until 5 pm if you want to visit."

My self-enforced "boring" day in Aigle was about to get significantly more interesting. Somewhat inadvertently, my Grand Tour of Europe had stumbled upon the world headquarters of... cycling!

The World Cycling Centre was located in a modern building made of concrete, metal and glass a few kilometres from the centre of Aigle on the eastern bank of the Rhône. Approaching alongside the river from the south, the first hint that the building might contain something cycling-themed was the bumpy tracks of at least two BMX circuits. Beyond them was the building itself embossed with the logo and letters of the UCI.

Leaving a rather slimline Wanda (I was not used to seeing her without four panniers and a tent) chained to a deserted bike rack (*did nobody cycle to work at the headquarters of world cycling?*) I went off to explore.

The modern construction ahead of me could have passed for another high-tech Swiss pharmaceutical laboratory but as I ambled over a wooden footbridge towards the entrance there were clues that this was something a little more sporty. The Olympic rings above the entrance, an oversized yellow jersey of the Tour de France emblazoned across several panes of glass and the almost-windowless curve of the arena-like building to my right.

Once inside, the first thing to catch my eye was a series of bicycles suspended at a jaunty angle from a bare concrete wall. They told the story of the evolution of the bicycle from Baron Karl Von Drais' running machine to a high-spec Scott racing bicycle of modern times in seven steps. They were essentially all the same: two wheels, a frame and a seat. A simple device which, for reasons unknown, only entered into the human consciousness some 200 years ago.[67] We will return to Baron Von Drais later in the story.

Beyond the bikes was a café but my attention was drawn by the Tour de France exhibition on the opposite side of the entrance hall. Tall yellow boards told the history - in text and images - of the annual French institution that had passed through Aigle earlier in the summer. Merckx, Hinault, Indurin... (No mention here of Armstrong as there had been at the Musée du Vélo in Normandy.) An enormous photograph of the Arc de Triomphe in Paris, sun setting and racers blurred by their speed. Such was the height of the boards that nothing could be seen of what lay beyond. Aside from in one corner where there was a door-sized gap. A steep wooden bank could be glimpsed in the distance. I climbed the step through the gap and there it was: the most astonishing sight of my visit to Aigle. The exterior shape of the building had been the clue. Before me was a full-scale, fully functioning velodrome.

Velodromes do not come cheap. The one built for the London 2012 Olympic Games cost over £100 million and even more modest affairs such as the velodrome in Derby in the English Midlands run to tens of millions. The velodrome at the UCI World Cycling Centre was built in an attempt to

---

[67] Some believe that Leonardo Da Vinci's sketched a bicycle in 1493. It is a nice idea but the acclaimed cycle historian Dr. Hans-Erhard Lessing proved in 1997 that he did not. The drawings were faked.

remove that significant barrier to entry into track cycling. It is made available to countries for whom constructing a velodrome would simply not be a viable option either because of a lack of money or because of the relatively low level of potential participation in the sport.

On the day that I visited, just one athlete was in training. In the distance, slowly pedalling on a static bike, on his phone… It was, after all, nearly the end of the working week.

Someone who certainly had not been static on his bicycle was the man with the familiar face back at Camping de la Piscine. We exchanged knowing glances although neither of us seemed to know why they were indeed knowing.

"Have we met before?" I asked, in French.

There was a pause as we both thought.

"Agen. The café under the bridge," replied the man. Of course!

"Kurt? From Bern?"

He confirmed that he was. It was no wonder I did not recognise him immediately as the last time we had met he was naked from the waist up. Here in Aigle, he had decided to cover up his rotund upper body. Perhaps it was the rain. He explained how he had finally managed to solve his mechanical woes with the derailleur and had continued his cycle - on a much more direct route than my own - across France. Tomorrow he was hoping to be back home in Bern. I explained to him my plans for the coming days and how I was aiming to be in Andermatt after three days following a climb to the Furka Pass.

"Three days? Andermatt?" he replied, scepticism oozing from each word.

Might I need a plan B?

Day Forty-Nine: Aigle to Sierre (81km)
Saturday 20th August

When I woke, the KFM - Kung Fu Masters - Crew were on my mind. I am all for keeping local youths off the street and busy doing culturally enriching activities such as breakdancing. However, if they insist on doing it near me, I wish they would keep the volume down and preferably not perform it in their Portakabin opposite the entrance to Camping de la Piscine in Aigle. But they did and it had provided a loud and somewhat annoying soundtrack to my Friday evening at the campsite. Internally I was questioning whether my cycling plans were over-ambitious. Externally I was being berated by hip-hop. It was not a great motivational combination and come the morning I was in a grumpy mood.

Lest I provide him with the opportunity to pick apart any other aspect of my onward route to Rotterdam, I kept my distance from Kurt and simply waved in his direction as I scuttled down the road in the direction of Aigle town centre. There I sought solace in a *croissant*, a strong black coffee and some hardcore mathematics.

Perusing my map I noted that, on a geometrical level, today was destined to be a pleasing one. 25km (or thereabouts) in a straight line to Martigny, a 90° left turn and another 40km (or thereabouts) in a straight line to Sierre. I was cycling two sides of a right-angled triangle, the opposite and adjacent, and as all students of Pythagoras should know:

$$a^2 + b^2 = c^2$$
$$25^2 + 40^2 = c^2$$
$$c^2 = 2{,}225$$
$$c = 47\text{km (or thereabouts)}$$

The point-to-point distance between Aigle and Sierre, over the mountains. (I have checked and Pythagoras was not wrong.) After so many years of cycling I found it so wonderfully satisfying that, on a macro level, I was finally going to be travelling in such a geometrically precise way. I remained uncertain as to why the Rhône had decided to take such a precise 90° turn to the right as it flowed from its source high in the mountains. My head assumed the answer was to be found in the composition of the rocks through which it was cutting. My heart told me that even rivers enjoy the intrinsic delight of mathematical beauty.

After having located a local bike shop where I could pump up Wanda's tyres, I set off back in the direction of the Rhône to pick up the signs for

Swiss National Route 1 and the EuroVelo 17. On a micro level of course, the route was anything but straight, oscillating as it did around the sides of my triangle. That said, after crossing the river near Aigle, the entirety of the morning was spent on the western side of Rhône as I made my way to Martingny. The bridge-crossing antics of the French ViaRhôna were not, it seemed, being continued to any great extent here on the Swiss side of the border.

In a country as mountainous as Switzerland the valley floors were inevitably going to be busy places. The narrowing strip of flat land - its width soon measured just a kilometre - needed to accommodate all those things that in a more vertically challenged country would be strewn across a far greater area. In addition to the river, there was a motorway, a main road, a railway, and an electricity power line as well as the cycle path itself which, for most of the time, remained loyal to the bank of the river. Much of the land between these elongated strands of communication was taken up by small towns, housing estates and industry. The remaining gaps were filled with a fragmented stained-glass patchwork of farmers' fields, each cut to a precise shape to fit snugly onto the plain. Barely a patch of land went unused until, that is, the steep-sided mountains rose abruptly from the valley floor at angles approaching - occasionally surpassing - 45°. It was here where wilderness thrived in a deep shag pile of green forest.

Situated to the south of the abrupt change in direction of the river, and slightly above it, the town of Martigny was announced first by its 13th-century tower, La Bâtiaz. From its position on the hill, its medieval occupants must have enjoyed commanding - and militarily strategic - views to the north and to the east. With the tower now being in the hands of restaurateurs rather than feuding knights those views were for the benefit of fine diners. But not for me. My own fine dining would be courtesy of a panini purchased in a fast-food outlet in the centre of town.

Amongst the well-heeled and well-dressed residents of smart Martigny, I felt a little out of place so I did not loiter lest I get questioned on suspicion of vagrancy. I did, however, pause to gaze longingly at the achingly arresting cuboid edifice on the rue du Simplon. Consisting of four storeys of high-spec polished black metal and mirrored floor-to-ceiling glass, it was a stunning example of modern Swiss architecture. Yet what made it truly exceptional was its function in life. *A Swiss bank? A museum of modern art? A research institute of world renown?* None of these. It was a humble secondary school housed in a building that was anything but humble. I thought of my own place of work - a comprehensive school in West Yorkshire - with its hotchpotch of buildings old and older, holes in the ceilings, doors that do not close, malfunctioning windows and tattered blinds. A purist might argue that a school is not its buildings but its pupils and its teachers. Given the choice, I knew where those purists would prefer to send their children to be educated every morning. I was standing in front of it.

The Rhône valley north-east of Martigny was a distinctly different beast following the dogleg turn. The plain was at least three times as wide, the Alpine slopes not quite so steep and the transition from valley floor to mountainside somewhat less abrupt. The towns and villages now melted rather than crashed into the mountains and the slopes themselves were no longer covered from tip to toe in trees. Facing south, the hills to my left were ripe territory for the cultivation of vines and many of their lower reaches were home to a seemingly countless number of vineyards. Having never in my life knowingly purchased a bottle of Swiss wine, this came as something of a surprise.

According to the tongue-twisting Interprofession de la Vigne et du Vin Suisse (IVVS), vines have been grown in the country for around 2,000 years. Swiss vineyards cover 14,696 hectares, with more than 2,500 winemakers in six regions of which Valais - the valley of the Rhône - is the largest. The conditions are favourable: dry and sunny and a *"foehn"* wind that keeps temperatures higher than would normally be expected at such high altitudes. The wines are both red and white with the pinot noir, chasselas and gamay varieties making up more than half of the crop grown by the 390 producers in the area. After our earlier discussion regarding right-angled triangles and then Martigny's perfectly cuboid comp, I feel as though we have now entered into the statistical section of today's maths lesson. I will pause here but there may be a test later.

Aside from all the numbers, the vines were very pretty to look at as I cycled along the valley bottom. Most were some distance from the cycle route beside the river but on occasions, I was able to get up close and personal with some fat bunches of black grapes. They looked delicious and indeed (if you promise to not breathe a word to the IVVS), they tasted delicious as well. It would only be a matter of weeks before they were harvested and en route to the tables of the... well, Swiss. Switzerland Tourism (presumably in an attempt to get you into the country) reveal that "only about 1% [of Swiss wine] is exported [as] the Swiss prefer to keep their wine to drink themselves". A fact which begins to explain why I had never knowingly drunk any Swiss wine elsewhere. The chances are I had not. It also explains why, when you think of Switzerland, you think of chocolate, watches and stolen Nazi gold, not bottles of wine.

In contrast to the slopes, most of the agriculture on the valley floor was fruit: apples, pears, strawberries, tomatoes and many others that I could not quite recognise. Combined with the ever-more-stunning scenery as I edged closer and closer to the highest mountains, the cycle was turning out to be a real treat for not just the visual senses but also for the olfactory ones. With an ever-so-slight tail wind to boot, what was not to like?

Yet something was not quite right. Here I was travelling closer and closer to the source of the Rhône, but I had the distinct impression that I was actually cycling slightly downhill. Which I was not. I knew this as when I periodically examined my GPS altitude profile, there was no question of me doing anything other than climbing. I had started the day at just under 400 metres in Aigle and had consistently cycled uphill all day. My arrival in Sierre would see me reach 550 metres. But that was not what my brain was telling me. And it was not just the effect of the slight breeze. It was more fundamental than that.

I had been here before. Well, not here, but in northern Spain in 2019. On that occasion, I had been cycling into the Picos de Europa mountains from sea level. I knew my destination - Potes - was at around 300 metres and I became increasingly concerned as the day progressed that I was not climbing. Fearing a sudden sharp climb to compensate for the lack of change of altitude I checked the route profile. It revealed that I had been climbing all day. Then I arrived in Potes. It was utterly bemusing. In Spain I had been cycling along a narrow gorge. *Might that have tricked my mind?*

It turns out that the illusion of cycling uphill but feeling as though you are not cycling uphill is indeed a thing. It is referred to as a false flat and for lean, mean cycling machines who wear bright Lycra, weigh perhaps half of what I weigh and ride around on their über-lightweight Pinarellos, it can be a real problem. They are competing - either against another cyclist or simply against their own PB - pushing their bodies to the limit and, when they see a flat bit of road ahead of them, they seize the opportunity to put ever more energy into their riding. Yet they find themselves out of breath and their speed not accelerating to the level they are expecting. They end up utterly exhausted and just as bemused as I had been in Spain and how I was here in Switzerland.

It is, in fact, an optical illusion brought about in mountainous areas where the encroaching hills play tricks on the mind and send signals to the brain that you are cycling on the flat. Or even slightly downhill. For the high-performing cyclists of the professional tours, the sensation must be an exasperating one. Yet for me, trundling along at low speed on a path that appeared to be going ever-so-slightly downhill, I was fooled, and happy to be fooled. The persuasive forces of the mountains were convincing my brain that we were cycling in one particular direction and, as I was not pushing myself to the limit - far from it - it was those forces that won out. I was not feeling in the least bit tired. It was just another section of very gradual downhill riding. But a section of downhill riding that was anything but. If this continued, climbing to the Furka Pass might be easier than I had imagined.

I arrived early in Sierre which was a much more modern town than Martigny. As I had a little time on my hands before I met up with my Warmshowers host Jean-Daniel, I went for a beer in one of the bars beside the main pedestrianised area of the town centre. The cost of doing so was, inevitably, extortionate so I was not tempted to go for a second choosing instead to sit beside a nearby fountain and snooze. Shortly before our arranged meeting time of 6 pm, I cycled the couple of kilometres to Jean-Daniel's house where I received a very warm welcome.

It was immediately obvious that Jean-Daniel, a nurse at the local hospital, was a socially gregarious chap, as was his bearded son Célien. The ground floor of their house was home to several bicycles. Wanda was parked amongst them and we all climbed to the first floor to be introduced to other family members who had already arrived to celebrate Jean-Daniel's father's birthday. I quickly made my excuses and went to shower and change into what might remotely pass as evening wear (but was anything but) before descending back to the first floor where the party was just beginning.

Jean-Daniel's family - brothers and sisters and their respective husbands, wives, partners… - were numerous and I did not rate my chances of remembering many of their names as the evening progressed. They asked me about my journey to date and gave advice on what was to come. I felt a little uneasy being the temporary centre of attention as this was a birthday party not for me but for André, the 87-year-old father of my host. Thankfully, when he arrived, the focus turned to him. More hands were shaken and after aperitifs we all sat down to eat. Then came a succession of raclette-themed courses. Every variation of freshly melted cheese was delicious and for a cyclist who was preparing to embark upon the toughest section of his big cycle around Europe, much welcome.

Throughout the meal (as well as before and after), wine was served. Swiss wine. Multiple bottles were opened, discussed and emptied and, as we all sang *"bon anniversaire"* to André, I began to wonder if, in 2022, the the number of bottles of Swiss wine available for export might be somewhat reduced. That 1% which was destined to be sent around the world must surely now be measured in only fractions of a percentage. A suitably mathematical end to a very mathematical day.

Day Fifty: Sierre to Ritzingen (74km)
Sunday 21st August

Since leaving Lyon on day 44, there had been five days of cycling. The ascents and descents on each of those days could be summarised as follows:

Lyon to Sault-Brénaz:
  ascent - 118m / descent - 81m / net ascent - 37m
Sault-Brénaz to Seyssel:
  ascent - 180m / descent - 105m / net ascent - 75m
Seyssel to Excenevex:
  ascent - 694m / descent - 548m / net ascent - 101m
Excenevex to Aigle:
  ascent - 215m / descent - 171m / net ascent - 44m
Aigle to Sierre:
  ascent - 168m / descent - 35m / net ascent - 133m

Although the cycle from Seyssel to Excenevex included a not inconsiderable 300-metre hill near the Swiss border, by Alpine standards, I had yet to test myself. What's more, since arriving in Switzerland, I had being doing most of my cycling at below 500 metres. All this was about to change. The net ascent on day 50 would jump to 800 metres and still more on day 51 as I made my way to the Furka Pass. The seriously strenuous work was still ahead of me.

Both Jean-Daniel and his son Célien were keen cyclists and knew the local cycling conditions well. Over breakfast they offered more advice about my onward journey without any Kurtesque hints that I might have bitten off more than I could chew.

"When you arrive in Mörel do not follow route 1, stay on the road," suggested Jean-Daniel. "It's a very rough path and adds a significant amount of climbing. You can rejoin the route in Niederwald."

It was this kind of local knowledge that made Warmshowers such a great concept. Well that, the delicious raclette and copious quantities of Swiss wine.

I returned to the centre of Sierre and, mindful of the calories that I would be burning during the day, indulged in a second breakfast at a high street *boulangerie*. At least that was my excuse. I had become very accustomed to my French breakfasts ever since crossing the border into France near Dunkirk. Most days had started with a *croissant* and *pain au chocolat* or *pain au raisin*. Occasionally all three. Today was a three-patisserie day. I was also mindful that this might be my last opportunity to indulge in a traditional French breakfast until I was again within reach of France along the Rhine north of Basel. The Swiss canton of Valais through which I had been cycling for most of my time since crossing the border at Saint-Gingolph was bilingual. French as far as Sierre. Thereafter, German. I was about to move outside of not just my breakfast comfort zone but my linguistic one as well.

The first 10km east of Sierre was also outside my cycling comfort zone. As far as the town of Susten, Swiss Route 1 followed the main road. This might not have been so bad had construction of the A9 motorway not terminated just to the south of Sierre. Somewhat abruptly, all the traffic from four lanes of motorway was funnelled onto a single-carriageway main road. It was at precisely this point where cycling route 1 also joined the party. All that separated me from a string of fast-moving cars was a line painted on the ground. The yellow bicycles that sporadically adorned my thin band of tarmac were at least reassurance that I was meant to be cycling here even if I did not necessarily want to. It was not the most pleasant of experiences but it was a Sunday morning. Had I been cycling here on any other day of the week, I would also have had to endure the thunderous noise of close-passing lorries. As in many civilised countries across mainland Europe, the freedom to drive an HGV is severely curtailed in Switzerland on the Sabbath. Another case of God moving in mysterious ways. Or, if he happened to own a truck, at home with his feet up quaffing communion wine.

More tribulations were to come, but an altogether different nature. Route 1 moved away from the busy road shortly after Susten, crossed the Rhône and continued its journey east on a quiet lane beside the river. Order had finally been restored to my cycle touring world. *Or had it?*

I had noticed a sign at the point where the cycle route branched away from the lane along a good quality riverside path. It read "*Umleitung*". I might have been inclined to take more notice of it (and work out what it meant) had it not been moved away from the path itself and laid flat on the ground. It was yellow so I assumed it to be a deviation sign of some description but clearly one that was no longer in use. I continued along the path by the river. 500 metres later a high metal fence stopped me in my tracks. I could continue no further.

To my left was a vast village of tents, white gazebos and the occasional long row of blue portable toilets. Mingling in between them were attendees of the Open Air Gampel music festival. For more than 35 years the young people of Switzerland had been descending upon this village every August for a weekend of sex, (probably) drugs and rock 'n' roll. And, in 2022, unwittingly and without benefitting from any of the things in the aforementioned list, so had I.

The fence in front of me extended as far as the eye could see across the plain of the valley, completely encircling the event. It reminded me of stumbling upon the rock festival on the dam back in the Netherlands at the start of the trip. Just as I had done before, I trudged back along the path to the point where I should have taken more notice of the sign.

I rejoined the lane where the path had started and set about cycling along it again. Another 500 metres or so later I was back at the fence, a few metres north of where we had first encountered each other. A security guard stared at me from her side of the fence. I was tempted to enter into an argument about the nonsensical placement of the deviation sign. At the point where it was, the only alternative route was the lane. However, the manner in which she was drawing smoke from her cigarette suggested she might not see the merits of my nuanced point of order.

Instead, in what must surely be recorded as one of the dumbest decisions of my entire Grand Tour, I decided to make my point by leaving the confines of the lane and pushing Wanda around the perimeter of the festival to where I could join another road. This might not have been so bad had the festival not being taking place in a farmer's field. For another 500 metres I toiled over mounds, across ditches and through mud with every moment of exertion and exasperation being witnessed by a small but growing crowd of bronzed, semi-naked festival goers on the other side of the fence.

The final ditch - the one that I needed to cross to access the road that I had finally found - was, of course, the widest, deepest and wettest. My attempts to cross it were watched with equal amounts of amusement and bemusement by the crowd. Once back on tarmac I remonstrated with another security guard who was at the wheel of a passing pick-up truck using a choice selection of Chaucerian profanity. He looked at me, derision written large over his face. My humiliation was complete. Following an angular deviation around the perimeter of the festival, I rejoined the path by the river some 3km later.

What remained of the morning was much less eventful. The path again moved away from the river on several occasions but this time everything was planned and signposted. Close to Visp I passed through a short tunnel under the railway line and, after coming back up to the surface spent a few minutes trainspotting. Swiss trains had been gliding past me for days. Their effortless movement under suspended power cables and along pristine tracks was testament to a network that famously works. The Swiss train system had not just been built: it had been built, maintained and modernised. Probably several times over. The train tracks looked as good as they did on the day they had been laid.

Of particular note were the Glacier Express trains with their bright red and white livery and their panoramic windows allowing uninterrupted views of the mountains. On a route from Zermatt in the west to St. Moritz in the east, it was here in Visp where the trains joined the Rhône valley. Over the next few days, they would become a regular feature of the landscape as they climbed to the Furka Tunnel and the Oberalp Pass before descending beside the Rhine. Alas it seemed that these beauties on wheel sets would only be part of my own journey across Switzerland from afar and not from within.

By the time I arrived in Brig after around 45km of cycling, only a modest amount of climbing - perhaps 150 metres - had taken place. Things were, however, about to change. Jean-Daniel's advice to stay on the road from Mörel was uppermost in my mind. As I cycled through Brig I was a little anxious about what was to come and my nerves were not calmed by an information-laden sign that I stumbled upon near the centre of the town.

1 / Rhône Cycle Route
Ernen 18km
Via Mörel
16km on a busy main road climbing 500 metres over 18km
Recommendation: Take the train

This was the road that Jean-Daniel was suggesting I use yet the people in charge of the Swiss cycle network were suggesting I take the train! The only thing they seemed to agree upon was not following the official cycle route after Mörel.

I had time to consider my options as between Brig and Mörel - still 7km away - there was no option (other than opting to take the train, and I was not going to do that). My choice was between sticking to the busy road or following the rough, steep cycle route that Jean-Daniel had warned me against. *Was it better to live my final moments falling off a steep precipice or being run over by a truck?* Then again it was still Sunday so there were no trucks. Perhaps being run over by a Swiss businessman out for a high-octane drive in the mountains in his Ferrari was more likely.

Leaving Brig there was a good example of the Swiss railways not having just been built but rebuilt. In this case replaced. For a couple of kilometres I was able to stay well clear of the main road by following a short-lived disused railway track but as the incline started to increase I had no choice but to rejoin the road. Traffic was mercifully light so after passing through

Mörel I ignored the cycling signs sending me across to the opposite side of the valley and stayed where I was, on the road. The narrowing landscape had now become no more than two steep-sided hills, their bases colliding at a point where the river flowed. The road and the railway fought for space, occasionally crossing each other courtesy of increasingly spectacular feats of civil engineering. After 55km of cycling I reached my first mountain-climbing switchback road. There was no mistaking the moment. The Alps were finally showing me their teeth.

Looking towards the south and east I could begin to understand why Jean-Michel had recommended I stay on the road. Although from such a distance I could not comment on the state of the path, I could just about work out the direction of the official cycling route, the EuroVelo 17. It had all but disappeared along a side valley following the River Binna, a tributary of the Rhône, at the end of which my map showed me that the route would double back towards the main valley of the Rhône. It certainly looked adventurous stuff. *But with four panniers and a tent on a heavy touring bike?* I was not sure. Yet I was slightly envious, annoyed even that I might be missing out so, at a point shortly after Lax where I could clearly see a road that would take me across to the other side of the valley, I made my move. It required a short sharp descent towards the river and then more strenuous climbing but, after a further 3km I arrived in the mountain village of Ernen where I was able to rejoin the official route of the EuroVelo 17.

Ernen was, without doubt, a very pretty mountain settlement. Approaching from the south it painted an almost picture-perfect scene: a cluster of wooden chalets and barns with a lime-washed church complete with sharply pointed spire at its centre. The backdrop was hardcore Alps that included the Finsteraarhorn which, at 4,274 metres lay claim to being the most prominent of Switzerland.[68] However, the centre of the village was ruined somewhat by the construction of staging required for an outdoor theatre festival. Scaffolding, lights, banners and the like all conspired to make me wish I had arrived on a different day. Nevertheless, Ernen did contain something of interest: my first cycling sign for Andermatt, now just 47km away on the other side of the Furka Pass.

The final 10km of the day saw a return to more modest - but no less spectacular - climbing. Along quiet roads and mountain tracks the route linked village to village beside lush late-summer meadows. On the northern side of the valley the red and white trains continued to glide up and down

---

[68] The prominence of a mountain is measured from its peak to the lowest contour line that completely encircles it. Basically, and in lay man's terms, how much it sticks out from other peaks in the area.

on their spotless tracks. No leaves on the line here in Switzerland. The businessmen in their Ferraris roared up and down the road. On my side of the valley there was just me, a few other cyclists and the cows ringing their bells. This was peak Switzerland. All that was missing was a chocolate-eating cuckoo telling me the time.

It had been a spectacular day of cycling, not without its challenges, but certainly one of the most memorable since setting off from Rotterdam some fifty days earlier. In the final few kilometres, the route joined the path of the river in the valley bottom and I arrived at Camping Brigga close to Ritzingen. It was at this point when I remembered the phone call that I had made from Aigle: I had been cut off as soon as it had become apparent that we did not share a common language. The *physical* challenges of the day may have been overcome but the *linguistic* challenges had yet to begin.

Day Fifty-One: Ritzingen to Andermatt (54km)
Monday 22nd August

Eleven days earlier I had set off from Sète with the intention of following the River Rhône from sea to source. That source - the Rhône Glacier - was now just 20km away from the campsite near Ritzingen. Camping Brigga was set on a hill in a peaceful location and frequented mainly by people who had a caravan permanently stationed on the site. Many had grown considerably in size (the caravans that is, not their owners) with the addition of awnings, tents and some even had their own garden, of sorts, cordoned off by a low picket fence. However, on this particular Monday morning in August, there were campers around to see me noseying around the site waiting for time to pass.

I had a problem. Nothing linguistic. I had paid my €25 (the warning from the Swiss couple back in France of having to pay at least €35 had not, so far, come to fruition) and had been given free rein to pitch the tent wherever I chose. It had required very little interaction between me and the ageing couple who ran the place. The issues that I did have were to do with electrical power. Following the Lac Léman storm, I had managed to buy a replacement powerbank at a supermarket in Aigle, but Jean-Daniel's sockets at his house in Sierre had been completely incompatible with my adaptors. As a result it was now 48 hours since I had been able to charge everything to max.

I might normally have squeezed a third day from the phone and the battery by being *über* frugal with their use but today was not just any day. It was the day when I would face my greatest physical challenge of the trip, the day when the views would be their most spectacular, the day when I would climb to the highest point I had ever cycled in my life. A day, no less, which would go down in the annals of cycling history... Well, perhaps not, but it would at least be memorable. *If I was not able to photograph it, video it, blog it, podcast it and GPS track it, who would ever believe that I had done it?* I may have been up and out of the tent at 7 am but, after a long wait at the reception chalet to stock up on electrical charge, it would not be until past 9.30 am that I finally set off.

The first 15km would be a flat ride as far as Obergoms. Route 1 / The Rhône Route / EuroVelo 17 / Rhône Cycle Route (all four names had their place on the small blue signs that I had been following since arriving in Switzerland) actually passed through the middle of Camping Brigga. I would have struggled to erect the tent any closer to it than I did. For most of the cycle to Obergoms the route stayed on the southern side of the river and the Rhône was rarely not in sight. That said, it was no longer the imposing river that it would become further downstream. Had I chosen to clamber over the rocks that separated me and Wanda from the water, I could have easily pushed her across. After the muddy experiences in the festival field on the previous day, it might not have been a bad idea.

Cycling in the cool air of the morning was a joy. Through forests, meadows and pretty Alpine villages I cycled. What surrounded me was in constant flux. A remote airport here, a complex of nuclear bunkers there. What never changed was the wall of rock at the end of the valley. It was difficult to imagine that a route existed over these mountains, but it did, and at some point later in the day I would be a very slow moving dot in those mountains. It was quite a thought.

By the time I arrived in Obergoms I had ascended just over 50 metres. This was taking the calm before the storm to a whole new level. I had barely broken sweat. A consequence of not just the forgiving terrain but also the temperature which remained comfortably low. I paused the cycling to ponder my onward journey but my contemplations did not get far as I was distracted by one of the pretty red and white trains. However, this particular train - which consisted of just one carriage - was not on the railway tracks. It had been positioned beside the road on a patch of grass and was open at one end for passers-by to enter.

Inside was a small exhibition about a proposed tunnel - the Grimseltunnel - the construction of which was scheduled to start in 2027. It would run for over 20km under the Grimsel Pass from Obergoms to Innertkirchen. All very exciting. For me, however, of greater significance was the train itself. This carriage was identical to the Glacier Express trains that I had been watching from afar for days, complete with ceiling windows to take in the majestic views of the mountains. *Oh to be a traveller on such a train!* One day, I thought, I would return to Switzerland to experience such a thrilling ride.

Anticipating the long climb that was about to start, I went to a nearby shop to stock up on high-calorie snacks (including the largest bar of Toblerone that they had on the shelves). When I came out of the shop I found a youth hanging around my bike. Mercifully she was only about four-years old and her Belgian parents were keeping her in check.

"What is that?" she asked, in Dutch, pointing at the green bag on the back of the bike. Her father translated as we spoke.

"It's a tent. It's where I sleep every night," I explained. She looked somewhat puzzled.

"What is that?" she asked, pointing at one of the panniers.

"It's where I put all my clothes," I explained.

"What is that?" she asked, pointing at the shiny brass Japanese Crane Bell Suzu attached to the handlebars.

"It's my bell," I explained. This was rapidly turning into an Alpine version of Sesame Street.

She was also on a bike and, for a four-year-old, it was an impressive machine. It came complete with a bell (we compared dings), a lookalike Brooks saddle, fat tyres and... a carbon belt. It was identical to Wanda's belt in every way apart from its length.

"They are very popular on children's bikes in the Low Countries," explained her father.

"My daughter wants to know where you are going on your bike," he added.

Pointing up the mountain I explained that I was about to climb the big hill in the direction of the Furka Pass.

"It's about 1,000 metres up there."

She did not look impressed, turned to her parents and started to plead with them.

"Can we please get rid of this English bloke and go play on the swings?" she said, perhaps. No translation was offered so I could only imagine the worst.

Her reaction had put me in my place. Whatever her words, she clearly wanted to move on and do something more interesting. We said our goodbyes, I took a deep breath and headed for the Furkastrasse.

I was setting off on a climb of just over 1,000 metres. It would be 17km to the pass but the road designers had done me a considerable favour in managing to iron out the steepness to a steady yet chronic incline of 6%. The gradient never let up but it had been tamed through the construction of carefully placed switchback roads and it was not long after leaving Obergoms that the first of the corners kicked in. At this stage just a handful linked together by roads that would have me turning almost 180° and see me cycling back in the direction of Camping Brigga. What I was sacrificing in direction, however, I was making up for in ascent and in the knowledge that I was inextricably edging vertically towards the pass itself.

The Glacier Express trains never make it anywhere near the Furka Pass. Not now. At Obergoms they plunge into the 15 kilometres of the Furka Base Tunnel, reappearing on the other side of the mountain at Realp some 10km west of Andermatt. However, a small tourist train - the Dampfbahn Furka-Bergstrecke - does maintain the railway link to the Furka Summit Tunnel, just 300 metres below the pass. Not having the ability to wind itself along mountain roads, its route was somewhat more direct than my own. It followed a narrow-gauge rack-and-pinion line that, at times, saw it climb at a rate of nearly 12%. This was most evident on the couple of occasions that I cycled under its bridges and witnessed their almost comical inclines.

What could not be witnessed is what happened to the train shortly before it arrived in Gletsch. As I was slowly toiling up another set of switchback roads, the valley had become so steep that even the rack-and-pinion system could not cope. Instead, the train entered a long tunnel in the mountain, looped back on itself and remerged from the rock just 100 metres from where it had disappeared. When it did so it was travelling at 90° to its original direction. Crucially, it had gained sufficient height to see it pull into Gletsch on time. Quite a trick! Alas on this day - August 22nd 2022 - I spotted no steam trains puffing their way up the mountain, through looping tunnels or across any of the steep bridges.

Had I been at the Furka Pass on August 22nd 1868, there would have been excitement of an altogether different kind. It came in the form of a short woman from England dressed head to toe in black.

The Furka Pass has been used as a gateway between east to west for centuries. The Romans used it to transport their goods and for moving their soldiers. Yet it was not until the 1860s that a paved road was opened and over the last century and a half it has earned its spurs as one of the most iconic of Swiss mountain destinations. One of the first to venture this way was that short woman in black: Queen Victoria.

In 1868 she was at a low ebb. Prince Albert had died in 1861 and she was growing tired of the bickering Gladstone and Disraeli. She needed a break and headed off for the Alps - the place so beloved of Albert - incognito. Well, kind of. Accompanied by her daughter, Princess Louise, she travelled initially to France on the royal yacht before taking Napoleon III's train to Paris and onwards to Lucerne where she checked in at the local Premier Inn as the Countess of Kent. Apologies: it was the elegant Pension Wallace but she did sign in under her assumed identity. She was also accompanied by her (ahem…) friend John Brown as well as a couple of her favourite ponies (as you do…).

On one of her forays away from Lucerne, she ventured to the Furka Pass to take a peek at the Rhône Glacier. Along with her not inconsiderable entourage, she took over a local inn for three days, much to the disgust of those who had booked in advance. Having travelled up the mountain from the east, she arrived at the pass on August 22nd 1868, exactly 154 years to the day before I was due to accomplish the same feat, albeit from the other direction.

Initially, she must have wondered why she had bothered, as she noted in her diary:

"Very shortly after Realp we began the tremendous ascent of the Furca... we reached the desolate little Inn... Unfortunately, the mist began to come down, & as we got higher & higher it became very cold & damp... It is, in fact, a miserable little 'Schenke', very small rooms poorly & badly furnished, but clean, & not uncomfortable, if there were only fireplaces as one would find in every small Highland Inn... It blew dreadfully & rained & was very cheerless."

The chief attraction for visiting the pass was to marvel at the mighty Rhône Glacier that was sitting in the valley to the west. Victoria made the short trip to see it from above on the first day of her visit. On the second day, she got in her carriage and was taken to Gletsch to see it from below. She had a cracking view:

"We again gazed with wonder & astonishment at the splendid glaciers... Went up to the Hotel du Rhone Glacier, where a good many people seemed to be stopping. Here, we had to get out... & Alpenstock in hand, walked about ½ a mile along a path, crossing a little stream over rough stones, till we came to the glacier itself where it was level. With the help of Brown & Hoffmann, I walked a little way on it & back. It cracked a little, but the thickness of the ice is quite enormous. It looks brown & rather dirty."

When I arrived in Gletsch at around midday on August 22nd 2022, things had changed considerably, notably the glacier which was nowhere to be seen. The fortunes of the glacier were mirrored in the fortunes of the mountain settlement itself. A small number of large hotels - including the Grand Hôtel Glacier du Rhône where Victoria had alighted her carriage - dominated. But they were no longer the 19th-century busy summer retreats welcoming Europe's well-heeled grand tourists. Now just a collection of oversized, neglected and predominantly closed-down hostelries, they marked the point at which you choose to either turn left and climb over the Grimselpass or continue up the valley to the Furka.

I paused in a small car park at the far end of the village adjacent to a small Anglican church. It was from here that Victoria must have set off on her wander towards the foot of the glacier. If I had been inclined to do the same it would have taken a considerable amount of time and required me to clamber up a rocky slope a couple of kilometres away. Even then I would have been craning my neck before glimpsing any of the ice. According to a

2022 report in *The Guardian* "If greenhouse gas emissions continue to rise, the Alps glaciers are expected to lose more than 80% of their current mass by 2100". Anyone returning in another 150 years may well find no Rhône Glacier at all.

Gletsch had been a touch depressing but it did at least afford a splendid view of my onward journey. As I looked along the valley to the east I could see a monumental wall of predominantly bare rock. Onto its face was etched a zig-zag line, first left then right. Eight times the line changed abruptly its direction. This would be my route for the next couple of hours.

I do love a long, slow climb on the bike, as long as I know it is coming. This one I had been contemplating for months. Mental preparation is key. Physical preparation is useful but not, I would argue, essential. After Gletsch I would be cycling up a 6% gradient for 10km. It would take me two and a half hours. Professional cyclists have completed the same ride in under 30 minutes but I was not in such a rush, far from it. I wanted to make the most of the experience and would certainly not be pushing myself. My ride time (minus all the stops) would be 80 minutes so at around 7.5km per hour, not too shabby, but certainly not award-winning.

It seemed that most of the trucks that had been passing me between Obergoms and Gletsch had decided to take that left turn and head north over the Grimselpass to deliver their goods to the needy folk of Interlaken. This left the road to me, a few cars and my fellow cyclists, of which there was a good number. Some were the speedy folk in Lycra who were presumably aiming to break their PB. Some were on eBikes and they passed me effortlessly and without breaking a sweat. Those carrying luggage were almost all doing so bikepacking style with their minimal kit stowed neatly away in bags under their saddles and attached to their handlebars. They also passed by frequently but were not so fixated on their time and on occasions I would overtake them as they paused to take in the view. Then there was me with four panniers and a tent. In my sub-category of cycling, on that day and at that time, I was the undisputed king of the mountain.

The road to the Furka pass is only open for around five months every year but in late August 2022, there was not a hint of inclement weather. Although the air was cool and the wind had been gradually gaining strength throughout the day, the sky remained predominantly cloudless and the views that it afforded were, from the perspective of a cyclist with limited experience in the high mountains, unprecedented. After several kilometres of contouring beside the railway line east of Gletsch - its tracks crossed the road before shooting off into the Furka Summit Tunnel - I hit the wall of rock and the final series of switchbacks kicked in. Eight corners in total, each flipping my direction (great for an even tan!) and finally an opportunity to gaze at the view back down the valley. I could trace my route since Gletsch and far below me on the valley floor was the Rhône, meandering its way across the plain as a freshly born offspring of the still unseen glacier.

Shortly before pausing opposite the iconic Hôtel Belvédere, I was passed by one of the bikepackers. He was travelling at perhaps double my speed and wearing a white shirt complete with multicoloured cycling-world-champion bands. We exchanged greetings in French (I was still in my linguistic zone mentally even if I was out of it physically) and I was slightly envious of his speed, his drive, his age... Perhaps he really was a world champion.

The hotel itself had been built in the loop of corner number six. Alas, its windows were boarded up and, just like the hotels I had seen in Gletsch, its glory days had long since tumbled down the steep sides of the valley. Queen Victoria's visit to the Furka Pass launched an era of mass tourism which lasted until the outbreak of war in 1914. Thereafter, the fortunes of the few Belle Époque hotels that are still physically standing have diminished considerably. Even the visit of Sean Connery / James Bond to the Furka Pass in 1964's Goldfinger did not arrest the decline. The Hôtel Belvédère can be seen in the film, as can the Rhône Glacier. Those were the days when the view from the hotel included the glacier: now it requires a 700-metre trudge down a rough path to get to a cave that has been dug out of the ice. The hotel closed in 2015 and rusting metal sheets over the windows render the panoramic restaurant redundant.

In a parking area opposite the hotel, there was a café which also served as the access gate to the glacier path. I decided not to venture along it. I sensed I would be disappointed by what I found and it would remain unexplored.

It was in the car park where I got chatting to the world champion bikepacker.

"I'm studying at a *grande école* in Paris and I'm on my way to complete a four-month internship in Milan," he explained. "But I'm not a world champion, it's just fashion." I put my signature book away.

"Don't buy a sandwich here. The guy inside is charging seven Swiss francs," he warned. I wandered across to have a look at £6.50 worth of sandwich. Two slices of white bread with a slither of processed cheese. I was not in the least bit tempted, despite my developing hunger after the climb. I would wait until the pass itself.

The backpacker's English was impeccable. His studies at an extremely selective and elite *grande école* put him at the top of the French educational pyramid and his motivation to cycle to Milan rather than jump on a train or drive suggested he had a glittering future ahead of him.

"Perhaps in 20 years when you are the French president I can come and pitch my tent on the lawns of the Élysée Palace," I suggested after offering my admiration for his academic as well as physical achievements. He laughed and we both rejoined the route albeit one of us at a somewhat steadier pace than the other.

The final three kilometres to the pass appeared to be steeper, but they were not. *Was it my fatigue? Was it the northern wind beginning to have more of an influence as I neared the ridge of the mountain? Or was I being paced subliminally by Monsieur le Président du Futur?* Perhaps a combination of all three.

Shortly after 2.30 pm, I glanced down at the Rhône for the final time. I had been following its course for 12 days. At the planning stage, it had been a conveniently functional way of getting from the Mediterranean to the start of the Rhine in the Alps. Expectations had been low, so low that I had given it little thought before setting off. It would be a case of knuckling down and getting from A to B. From Sète to the Furka Pass. How wrong could I have been? Despite the challenges of the inclement weather, cycling beside the Rhône had been an adventure in itself and the route could proudly hold its head high amongst any of the more widely known routes that I had been following. Thoroughly enjoyable cycling. Thoroughly enjoyable travelling.

As the Rhône disappeared from view, the road flattened out and within a few hundred metres I arrived at the pass. There was not a great deal there. Just another car park, a mobile sausage van and a small blue sign:

Furkapass
2436 m. ū. M.

The fourth-highest pass in Switzerland. I had never cycled to such a height before. There was only one way to celebrate. I reached inside my front-left pannier bag and pulled out the Toblerone. Washed down with a *bratwurst mit brot* from the sausage stall it seemed a fitting way to complete an epic river-inspired journey in German-speaking Switzerland.

Monsieur le Président du Futur joined me and we discussed French foreign policy before again setting off. He planned to cycle over the Gotthard Pass (and sort out the Middle East crisis) before the end of the day. That was the route I had followed back in 2010 but my journey today would be all downhill to Andermatt, the official end of the EuroVelo 17 and the official start of the EuroVelo 15.

It was only a few hundred metres after setting off that I passed the patch of ground where Victoria's "miserable little Schenke" had once stood. It ended its life as a target for the Swiss military and when they could fire at it no more it was turned into yet another car park. She would have liked that (although probably not enough to raise a smile).

In terms of distance, the descent into the valley was almost as long as the climb had been but a little steeper and considerably quicker. However, I could not quite release the brakes and freewheel downhill. The wind was now much more of an issue than it had been on the way up and, although the route had its fair share of switchbacks seeing me temporarily change direction, for most of the time I was cycling directly into it. This might not have been so problematic had I not been cycling on the right-hand side - the valley side - of the road. There was no wall or fence to stop me from falling down the hill, just a concrete bollard every few metres. Nothing much had changed since Sean Connery had driven his Aston Martin down this side of the pass in the early 1960s. At least I was not being followed by a woman taking potshots in my direction. I was never planning to adopt an aerodynamic position on the bike and slice through the air at top speed as they do in the mountainous stages of the Tour de France. But neither had I thought that my descent would be so hesitant.

Eventually, I built up enough confidence to go a little faster and could begin to enjoy the view unfolding in front of me. As the final ladder of switchback roads kicked in just to the west of Realp, I had finally sped up from a slow trundle to a modest gallop. Channelling my inner secret agent on a bicycle (in our environmentally conscious times it might happen, one day…), I started to lean into the corners, just a little. "The name's Sykes, Andrew P. Sykes."

The authorities might not have erected a sign to mark my descent, but in a small lay-by close to one of the sharp turns the real (albeit fictional) secret agent had been honoured with a green sign at the top of a pole:

JAMES BOND STR.

Underneath the sign was a picture of Sean Connery standing beside his DB5 looking worryingly back up the hill for the crazy woman with the rifle. The black-and-white view in the photograph was almost identical to the one I could see myself. At the end of the long valley was Andermatt and before it the village of Hospental.

The gradient in the final section of my route was slight but, with the wind continuing to blow, the cycling was perhaps the most challenging it had been since the start of the day. I pulled on my jacket, not because of its ability to keep out the rain but because it also claimed to be windproof. It helped, a little and at just after 4 pm I was approaching my destination and the end of the EuroVelo 17, Andermatt.

Queen Victoria described it as a "small, dirty village" and after my first visit to the town in 2010, I said something along similar lines. This is what I wrote in Crossing Europe:

> "Initially, I wondered if I had indeed found the town with the picturesque campsite that I had admired so much on the tourist office leaflet in Altdorf. All I could see were large car parks and what appeared to be empty industrial land... It had all the charm of your typical out-of-season ski resort: far too much concrete which was clearly designed to support pretty snow in the winter months but which in summer just looked plain ugly."

Ouch! A lot has to do with the weather. It had not been great for Victoria in 1868 and in 2010 I was cycling through what remains as Europe's wettest-ever August. In 2022 things were looking up. The sky continued to be unblemished with cloud and the wind had abated. With the road to the Oberalp Pass - which I would be climbing the following morning - in the background and surrounded by high mountains, Andermatt looked quite... pretty. That was an improvement on 2010 and certainly 1868.

The campsite - Gotthard Camping - where I had stayed 12 years earlier looked identical to how I remembered it, with the addition of a spruced-up reception cabin in the car park. A functional place on the edge of town and close to a cable car station, it was perfect for my needs. I paid my CHF 19 and set up camp before wandering into town in search of food.

It was Monday 22nd August. I had 12 days remaining before the ferry from Rotterdam set sail. Just one cycle route - the Rhine Cycle Route / EuroVelo 15 - and 1,450km stood between me and that signpost at the Hook of Holland where it had all started just over seven weeks previously.

It was not the moment to reflect upon the fact that it had taken me 12 days to travel the 1,000km of the Rhône Cycle Route, EuroVelo 17. At least from here to the finishing line it would all be downhill, no?

PART EIGHT:

The Rhine Cycle Route / EuroVelo 15

Day Fifty-Two: Andermatt to Valendas (Train + 62km)
Tuesday 23rd August

Earlier in the summer as I was wilting under the heatwave that was punishing most of northern Europe, I received an email from Switzerland.

Dear Andrew,
I am an avid cycle tourer and a great admirer of your books. I re-read them now and again to either motivate myself for touring or for bridging long winter periods without cycling. I am also following your blog and thus your current tour virtually. I have noticed that you will eventually cycle through Switzerland. If you like we could cycle a day's route together. Lunch and dinner would be on me.
Best regards,
Claud Butler

At the time the Alps were very much at the back of mind. *And Claud Butler? Really?* I had been having a few issues with prank calls to my mobile phone. *Was this a prank email?* The original Claud Butler had set up a successful chain of bicycle shops in the inter-war years in Britain and although his company had gone bust many years ago, the brand endures to this day. *Could the man himself have sold up before the business went down the pan and exiled himself to a life of luxury in the Alps?*

No. A quick search online revealed that he had died in 1978 and if he had lived on he would have reached the ripe old age of 119 by 2022. And anyway, it would have been a very subtle prank. Far too subtle for the pupils back at school who had managed to get hold of my mobile phone number. I took Claud Butler at his word, emailed him back and promised to get in touch once I had arrived in Switzerland. A few days earlier we had arranged to meet next to the lighthouse at the Oberalp Pass at midday on Tuesday 23rd August. Today.

According to the Swiss Federal Office of Topography (in a country of so many hills it is entirely understandable that such an institution exists), the source of the Rhine is a little to the north of Lake Toma. With the Oberalp Pass being the nearest paved road to the source, it would seem to be the ideal place for the Rhine Cycle Route to begin. But it does not. It starts down the hill in Andermatt at the same place where the Rhône Cycle Route officially finishes, 25km from what is left of the Rhône Glacier.

As I packed up the tent at Gotthard Camping, I had some decisions to make. A helicopter hovered above the campsite picking up metal girders from an adjacent field and flying them off into the mountains to be deposited elsewhere. Every few minutes it would return to repeat the operation. I fell into conversation - when it was possible - with my neighbours, Rich and Becca from Ilkley, the posh corner of my home county of West Yorkshire. They were also travelling by bike and had set off from Nantes earlier in the summer. Their route would eventually take them to Rome but up to this point, it had been almost identical to my own.

"16km of unrelenting hill. Two hours of leg-burning pain. Exactly what I thought it would be," noted Rich reflecting on his experience of climbing to the Furka Pass.

"At least the nice hill outside Geneva got us prepared for the Alps," added Becca before being drowned out by the rotors of the returning helicopter.

Their comments got me thinking. None of us had anything to prove. We had all earned our cycling spurs in the days since leaving Lyon as the foothills became hills and then mountains. We could all be rightly proud of what we had achieved.

I was trying to build an argument to support a decision that I had been toying with for a few days. I could cycle to the Oberalp Pass. Alternatively, I could take the train. It was on the route of the Glacier Express, as was Andermatt. Instead of gazing at the pretty red and white trains from afar, I had the opportunity to be inside one. Not just a static carriage promoting a new railway tunnel: one that climbed a steep hill with me gazing out through the windows. It was all very tempting.

The counterargument was, however, strong. Until this point, I had used seven of my ten maximum-100-km trains. With only 12 days remaining, up to 300 kilometres worth of train journeys would be useful, essential even. It was only 10km to the Oberalp Pass. I would be squandering 90 kilometres of train journey. I had been maintaining a daily average cycling distance of just over 80km for some time now. By opting to take this train I was in effect adding an extra day of cycling to my tour. However, it was the Glacier Express...

After finishing my packing and fully cognisant of doing something that might, in the long term, return to haunt me, I cycled into town, found the train station and bought myself a one-way ticket for the 11.29 train to the Oberalp Pass. In the short term, who cared? I was delighted by my indulgence.

The 20-minute journey was an astonishing display of civil engineering genius, the train winding its way up the hill switching back on itself in incomprehensibly tight loops on its metre-gauge tracks.[69] Unfortunately, this particular train did not have the panoramic windows of its more modern cousins but that was only a minor complaint. The views looking back along the valley towards the Furka Pass were glorious. As we steadily climbed the hill, Andermatt edged slowly away from its prominent place in the foreground to be just another pretty mountain village in the distance. All that was needed to complete this epic Alpine scene was Julie Andrews twirling in a frock and blasting out "The hills are alive with the sound of music…".

OK. That was Austria but let's not quibble. This was spine-tingling travel at its best and, admittedly, easiest. I loved every second.

As we began to approach the pass, the track levelled off somewhat and then skirted around the edge of a lake before pulling into the station. Hauling Wanda off the train was no mean feat as the level of the carriage was some way above the level of the platform. There were no steps to the door of the bike compartment but after offering to help a couple of pensioners with their bikes, they reciprocated in assisting me and everything - and everyone - was returned safely to terra firma.

The pass itself was only a short ride up the hill from the station but nothing that required me to break into a sweat. There was much more here than there had been at the Furka Pass: what looked like a small military base, a *gasthaus*, a couple of restaurants… and that lighthouse. I had not given it a second thought before but the incongruity of the modest red and white structure now dawned upon me.

"Why do they need a lighthouse here? They probably don't get a lot of ships," Andreas Pfister of the building department at the local council was quoted as saying when he spoke to the Swiss Broadcasting Corporation in 2010 shortly after the lighthouse was erected. He graciously offered an answer to his rhetorical questions.

"This lighthouse is supposed to send a message, so people will stop and wonder," he added.

And if they happened to be wondering why a lighthouse, the answer was that it is a small-scale replica of the one that stands at the Hook of Holland at the other extremity of the Rhine. I would look out for it if or when I arrived there. The initial plan was to bring a Dutch barge to the top of the mountain as well but with no barge to be seen, I assumed the idea had been quietly shelved. Perhaps those melting glaciers and rising sea levels might one day make Andreas' task a little easier.

---

[69] For reasons of comparison, standard-gauge tracks measure 1.435 metres and the railway to the top of Yr Wyddfa (Mount Snowden) is 0.8 metres.

When I spotted Claud (he was the only other cyclist at the pass) he had his earphones in and was listening intently to something on his phone.

"Hi. I'm listening to your latest podcast," he revealed.

This was quite an achievement as I had only finished editing it whilst waiting for the train in Andermatt.

"I know so much about you," he declared. If he had listened to all of the seven episodes of The Cycling Europe Podcast that I had recorded, edited and published since setting off from Rotterdam at the start of July, he had a fair point.

"And I know so little about you, apart from you having a famous cycling name," I replied. He laughed in recognition. Perhaps I was not the first person to have pointed it out.

"How was the climb?" he asked.

"Very easy," I blushed. "I took the train."

"Are you hungry?"

"I'm a cyclist. I'm always hungry."

Reinforcing what he had already said in his email earlier in the summer, he made it very clear that he would be paying.

"Switzerland is a very expensive country," he explained, "unless you earn a Swiss salary."

It was another very good point and I was not prepared to argue.

Claud was about my age and very easy-going. He lived with his wife and son Cedric (also a keen cyclist but without a name to match) in a town halfway between Bern and Zurich and he worked in financial regulation for the government but we spoke no more of it. I was much more interested in finding out about my onward journey through Switzerland and, over a delicious lunch on the terrace of one of the Oberalp Pass restaurants, Claud happily spilled the beans.

"The best bit of the route is here at the start. Lots of quaint little villages with old houses. After that, it can be a bit industrial until Lake Constance. The river's been canalised as you pass along the border with Liechtenstein and Austria. It's flat but you have mountains on either side."

I noted that the official route of the EuroVelo 15 stayed on the southern side of Lake Constance but Claud had another suggestion.

"Even though I'm Swiss I'd have to recommend the German side. Nicer villages, nicer cycle paths. If you change your mind, you can always cross on a boat from north to south."

"Is there an option to take a boat from one end of the lake to the other?" I asked.

"Yes, you can take a boat in Bregenz in Austria to Konstanz. It takes about four hours."

Would it break the rules of my trip to take such a boat? I was not sure. I had a rule about trains but had never got around to drafting any regulations about boats.

Although Claud was not from this part of the country, he knew the area well. One of the nicest aspects of the day was not just being able to freewheel down the road into the valley but to do so in the knowledge that someone else was taking responsibility for the route finding. For the first 20km, we stuck to the main road sweeping around its wide bends, freewheeling effortlessly through small towns and villages and shadowing - occasionally at very close quarters - the railway line and the frequently passing Glacier Express trains.

At Disentis, with the valley having widened slightly, the route moved away from the main road, crossed a bridge over the fledging Rhine and began to contour on the southern side of the river along deserted country lanes and farmers' tracks. Past whitewashed churches and darkly stained timber houses, through meadows and beside ancient barns. This was the stuff of chocolate boxes.

I was very conscious of having spent a lot of time pressing my brakes into action over the previous 24 hours. Since leaving Yorkshire I had not taken the opportunity to ask anyone to look at the bike in any way so I was keen to pause at a bike shop for someone to examine Wanda's disc brake pads. The one great disadvantage of disc brakes is your average cyclist's inability to see how worn down they are. I was that average cyclist and I needed the eye of someone who was an expert in the field. Or should that be Alpine meadow?

We passed through a couple of towns but without any luck. Then, as we arrived in the main square of Ilanz - the town where Claud would take the train back home and from where I would continue to my campsite - we found what we had been searching for: a bike shop that was open.

Claud did the talking with a man who must surely have ranked as one of Switzerland's most elderly bike shop owners. Indeed I did wonder whether Claud Butler the middle-aged Swiss civil servant from Zurich was actually in conversation with his British namesake who had faked his death in 1978, emigrated in secret to Switzerland and was still in action at the age of 119. On reflection, it seemed unlikely. Whoever he was he was very dismissive of my brakes.

"I explained your concerns but he says there is plenty of brake pad left," explained Claud, the younger. Claud the elder interjected with a question to which the response from Claud the younger was "Rotterdam".

At this point Claud the elder laughed and with a dismissive sweep of the arm uttered a withering sentence.

"He says it's flat all the way to Rotterdam and you won't need your brakes," explained Claud, the younger.

The old man had a point.

After drinks and more food in a nearby bar, I thanked Claud for having guided me on my first day along the Rhine. After so many days of cycling alone, working things out for myself, quietly rejoicing when I made a wise decision and having no one to blame but myself when I made a poor one, it was nice to have sub-contracted out most of the thinking. Claud had been good company.

Yet the life of a solitary cyclist on a quest to catch his ferry must return to its natural position. I said my goodbyes and plodded on up the hill for 10 kilometres in the direction of Camping Carrera, alone.

Some campsites are just how you imagine. Some campsites you look forward to but they disappoint. There are, however, some campsites for which expectations are low - perhaps even non-existent - but which delight. I had come across Camping Carrera earlier in the day via a quick search online. It appeared to be very close to the cycle route and that was good enough for me. It had been a busy day and I had not had an opportunity to revisit my initial choice.

Thank goodness for that as what I found was wonderful. Tucked away at the top of a small gorge leading down to the Rhine, it was set back from the road by a few hundred metres. Surrounded by forest and frequented mainly by people travelling independently in tents, some with bikes, some in small motorhomes, there were no caravans and certainly no picket fences.

A very good end to a very good day travelling by bike. (And one rather extravagant train...)

Day Fifty-Three: Valendas to Buchs (83km)
Wednesday 24th August

10,000 years ago (or thereabouts) there was a deep rumble in the mountains overlooking the Rhine Valley at the point where you can now visit the town of Flims. Not great news if you happened to be a hunter-gatherer in these parts as you were about to be hit by a landslide of blockbuster proportions. In addition to wiping you and all your berries off the face of the earth, it completely damned the river at Ilanz. However, all was not lost. Over time, the Rhine fought back and it again established its presence in the valley. It did so by carving a deep 14-kilometre-long gorge through the landslide which, all these years later, is rather spectacular. Those berries - and their gatherer - were not squashed in vain.

Camping Carrera was close to the western end of the gorge but the only way to continue to follow the river at this point was on foot, on a boat or on the train. None of these were an option for me so I continued east for several kilometres along the cycle route, the gorge remaining hidden beyond very attractive meadows, trees and villages. To help complete the bingo card of cycling in the Swiss countryside there was also one spectacularly pretty white-washed church. Sitting prominently in a freshly mown field of grass, tree-smothered mountains in the distance and its pointy spire poking up into the sky, it was a postcard-in-waiting. But it was not a gorge. I kept cycling.

A big hint that things were becoming more dramatic came shortly after the church when I found myself suddenly sweeping back and forth along a series of switchback roads. *Was I finally plunging deep into the gorge?* Not quite yet. This was merely a tributary gorge leading to the real thing but as *hors d'oeuvres* went, it was mouth-watering. 70 metres above the Rabiusa River were two bridges: one modern, constructed from concrete and one much older, constructed from metal. Leaving the more modern bridge to the few cars that happened to be out so early this Wednesday morning, I had the old bridge to myself.

It had been a while since I had put the drone through its paces, fearful that I might anger large Alpine birds which might take a dislike to a UFO on their patch, as the seagulls had done back in Brittany. But it was early in the day - just past 9 - and surely any predatory bird worthy of the name would be too busy warming themselves in the fledgling rays of sun that were beginning to cascade across the landscape. I launched the drone and watched the images on the screen of my phone as it edged its way through the narrow valley. Slartibartfast could not have done a better job. The overlapping profiles of the 45° hills on either side of the Rabiusa took turns coming into and then out of shot as the river meandered back and forth far below. Amazing footage from my eye in the sky. It was without any doubt a stunning gorge. But it was still not the gorge I was looking for. Again, I kept cycling.

The route I was following now clung to the side of the valley that I had just been filming. There was, at times, little or no protection to my left to prevent anything - or anyone - from falling over the edge. However, in contrast to the descent from the Furka Pass, my position on the right-hand side of the road was to my advantage and I was kept safe as I climbed higher and higher. There was a short tunnel hewn from an outcrop of rock and immediately after the tunnel, the view of the valley was obscured by tall trees. Then, as the road approached its pinnacle, a substantial crash barrier appeared on my left, a vertical rock face below it and a tantalising glimpse of the Rhine Gorge in the distance. Suddenly everything disappeared as I entered a series of three more tunnels. It was all very frustrating!

After the third tunnel, I slowed to a crawl but sensing that I was still approaching the Rhine from the south, I did not stop cycling. It would have been dangerous to do so as the road had now thinned considerably and drivers would, quite understandably, have their attention distracted by the view. As did I. Keen to get to the other side of the road to stop and stare, I eventually found what I had been looking for: a viewing platform. Its location was well chosen, at the crest of the hill and at the point closest to the river far below.

The platform reminded me of the ones that I had found in Norway several years earlier, strategically placed along the coastal road and cleverly designed to raise the viewer off the ground so as to reduce the visual impact of anything nearby. This platform in Switzerland took the form of a winding ramp that had been wrapped rather elegantly around a chunk of rock beside the road. As the path wound back on itself I turned to see the Rhine Gorge in all its glory.

It was here where the Rhine had cut deepest through the landslide. Behind me, the hill stretched upwards by at least 100 metres. Below me, the land fell away steeply for another 150. At the bottom of the gorge, the turquoise river slithered first one way and then the other around bends that it had created over thousands of years. Such was the depth of the valley that the sunlight had yet to complete its journey down the south-facing flank of rock opposite where I stood but there was no mistaking the majesty of what I was witnessing. And then, the glacé cherry on the cake. Along the wide curve of a track that mirrored the geometry of the river, the red snake of the Glacier Express train appeared from nowhere before disappearing into a tunnel a few moments later. Magical.

I really did need to crack on. That ferry was still leaving at 8 pm on Saturday 3rd September and I had to be on it. The good news was that according to Mike Wells, the writer of the Cicerone guide to cycling the Rhine Cycle Route, the viewing rock that I had just been standing on marked the point after which there would be no more climbing. That did not mean that every single metre of the route from here to the Hook of Holland would be downhill or on the flat but I could be confident in thinking that there would be no more energy-sapping uphill slogs.

The long, straight road running into the centre of the small town of Bonaduz was a joyous freewheel back towards civilisation. I needed this as, again, I was on the lookout for a bike shop. Not to check my brakes this time but to check the tyre pressure. I had last done so in Aigle only a few days earlier but the bike was already feeling decidedly bouncy again.

The Bieler Sport shop in Bonaduz was more bicycle clinic than bicycle shop. I walked into the plush emporium of high-end sports gear and asked an assistant if I could borrow a pump. Before I got past the word "borrow" the man in front of me held up his hand and ushered me silently outside. Half expecting him to tell me (a scruffy, sweating, unshaven cyclist) to sling my hook using language that I probably would not understand, he escorted me to the side of the building and down a short ramp before waving at a colleague for help. He then promptly - and equally silently - disappeared. The Mr Ben of Switzerland.

"Could I possibly borrow a pump for my tyres?" I asked, in English, euphemistically. Experience had taught me that this question, if understood, would usually be interpreted as "Could you pump up my tyres for me?". In this case, it was. Without speaking, the mechanic, a youngish chap dressed in a spotless white t-shirt took hold of Wanda's handlebars and pushed her over the spotless floor. He sat on a spotless stool and reached for the spotless hose of compressed air. This bike mechanic had elevated his workshop working environment to that of an operating theatre. Impressive!

More air went into the front than the back. My ongoing suspicion that I had a very slow puncture on the front wheel seemed to be confirmed but with only just over a week of cycling to go, I was reluctant to start changing the inner tube. Not in itself a monumentally difficult task but with the front wheel hub containing a dynamo, there was an extra level of complexity involving wires. A lame excuse but simply a reflection of my lack of confidence when it came to the technical side of cycling. The price would have to be paid in several more visits to bike shops over the coming few days.

I crossed to the northern bank of the Rhine shortly after leaving Bonaduz. Although until this point I have been referring to the river as the Rhine it was, in fact, the Vorderrhein. It only became the Rhine after it coalesced with the Hinterrhein close to the bridge I had just crossed. All that might be useful if you ever appear on a TV quiz show. That aside, it will also mean that I do not get pedantic emails from disgruntled hydrologists. (Although I suspect it will not stop them telling me that rivers converge, not coalesce.)

The town of Chur was to the Rhine what the town of Martigny had been to the Rhône. In Martigny, the direction of the Rhône had changed - somewhat abruptly - from predominantly to the south to predominantly to the east. In Chur, the direction of the Rhine changed from predominantly to the east to predominantly to the north. The capital of the canton of Grisons, it claimed to be the oldest city in the country. According to the Historical Dictionary of Switzerland, flint objects have been found there dating back over 10,000 years, around the same time as the great landslide blocking the course of the Rhine. Sorry, the Vorderrhein. Some of those hunter-gatherers survived and prospered, albeit a few kilometres further along the valley, and their descendants had done a remarkable job in creating a very attractive city.

The old part of Chur - the Altstadt - was made up of a collection of narrow streets lined by pastel-coloured four- and five-storey buildings with small squares filling the gaps in between and the sound of water trickling down ornamental fountains rarely distant. The whole area had been pedestrianised. Then again, perhaps it had always been that way. Minus the accoutrements of the 21st century, it was not difficult to imagine how the city might have looked hundreds of years ago. A time when the rich nobles clomped past on their stallions, ordinary Alpine folk wandered the streets in their finery and street urchins scrambled around on the cobbles in search of discarded coins.

North of Chur the cycle route passed beside a succession of industrial plants staying close to the river but also the *autobahn*. This was just how Claud had described. Then, on the edge of the town of Landquart, the signs for National Route 2 - the Rhine route - suddenly instructed me to turn along a path that ran beside another tributary of the Rhine. However, after around 3km of following the tributary, I was beginning to wonder if I had misread the signs. I was cycling due east when I could see on my map that the Rhine itself was heading north-west along one of its canalised sections. *Should I turn around and cut my losses?* The distance that I had cycled would inevitably have to be made up for at some point with a return towards the river. *Had I made a serious navigational error?*

As I was beginning to contemplate stopping and retracing my path, a wooden bridge came into view. It straddled the Landquart (the tributary adopting the same name as the town) and, much to my delight (mixed with a certain dollop of perplexity) there was another sign for National Route 2 pointing over the bridge. I duly crossed the river, at least certain that I was continuing to follow the Rhine Cycle Route albeit not the Rhine itself. As pedestrian-cycle bridges go, it was an impressive one with the wide wooden platform beneath Wanda's tyres supported by the graceful yet sturdy arc of two heavy-duty girders made from laminated planks of wood. A wonderful combination of form and function.

Confident that I was still on track, I was still struggling to find definitive answers as to why I had been forced to deviate by such a distance away from the Rhine. Over the course of the next hour, all would become clear. Now travelling in the same direction as the river, albeit from a distance of at least a couple of kilometres, I eventually started to climb a little, especially between the villages of Malans and Greisinger. They were both exceptionally pretty places with their old buildings painted white or in similar pale shades to those that I had admired back in Chur. The imposing *gasthaus* in the centre of Malans was straight from a film romanticising the lives of the good folk of rural Switzerland in centuries gone by. This idyll of all things quintessentially Swiss was further embellished as the path ascended towards Greisinger passing as it did through vast vineyards, the long lines of vines funnelling my gaze to the bottom of the wide valley. It was there where the Rhine continued its own journey north beside the sporadic pockets of industry, now hidden amongst large clumps of trees. After Greisinger the route slowly descended back in the direction of the river passing to the north of Maienfeld through more meadows and vineyards. The excessive beauty of the scene was set amongst a backdrop of high mountains in all directions. Beautiful!

It came as little surprise to discover that this area was known as Heidiland, taking its name from the 19th-century novel Heidi. The book's author, Johanna Spryi, had spent her childhood summers in the region. Since the book's publication in 1880, the good folk of Maienfeld - the town where the entirely fictitious Heidi had been born to her ill-fated parents - have been laughing all the way to the Swiss bank. The book, it seems, has been instrumental in defining a bucolic vision of Switzerland in the minds of many people around the world. This is especially the case with the Japanese, who have been particularly inspired by an animated version of the tale. They now visit the area en masse. Yet Heidiland did not disappoint. It was undeniably ravishing and notwithstanding its entirely spurious Heidihaus and Heididorf, I was delighted to have been shunted away from the uninspiring, canalised and at times industrial Rhine to see it.

On the subject of which, I crossed to the western bank of the river at around 2.30 pm at a point where it was indeed relatively uninspiring, definitely canalised but mercifully industry-free. The Rhine has long since marked the international border between several countries. It forms the frontier between Switzerland and Austria, Switzerland and Germany and then further north between France and Germany. One of the river's lesser-known international borders is that which exists between Switzerland and its diminutive yet ludicrously wealthy neighbour Liechtenstein. Shortly after crossing the Rhine at the northern extremity of Heidiland, I could see it looming up in the distance.

And loom it does as most of the country's 160 square kilometres are very mountainous. The wealth-generating activities of its 40,000 citizens (and the thousands more who flock over the border to work there) take place on the eastern bank of the Rhine in a narrow strip of flat land some 25km long but just a few kilometres wide. According to the CIA Factbook, it is one of only two double-landlocked countries in the world in that the countries that surround it - Switzerland and Austria - are themselves landlocked.[70] And make money it does. The World Bank rank it at number two in the list of GDP per capita with $184,083, second only to Monaco with an eye-watering $234,317. (Switzerland is 7th on the list with $92,102 and the UK - brace yourself - 31st with a modest $45,850.)

With it being such a tiny place, it would have been remiss of me not to step foot in the country. However, it did require a detour back over the river via the Alte Rheinbrücke, a windowless wooden pedestrian tunnel of a bridge that took me to a roundabout in Liechtenstein. Contrary to expectations, the roads were not paved with marble and the cats' eyes did not sparkle with precious jewels. The greatest surprise about Liechtenstein was its ordinariness. I spent a happy half hour slowly cycling along the main street of Vaduz, the capital, trying to spot something - anything - that was distinctly Liechtensteinian but I failed miserably. It was smart, well maintained, clean, quiet, functional… Aside from the castle on the hill and the Regierungsgebäude des Fürstentums Liechtenstein (Government Building of the Principality of Liechtenstein) which had a modicum of splendour about its façade in the large main square, there was little to turn the head. Perhaps that is the secret to becoming obscenely rich. Take note.

Back over the wooden bridge in poverty-stricken Switzerland, I continued along the bank of the Rhine for a few more kilometres as far as Buchs. It was here that I had located a tiny town-centre campsite, Camping Werdenberg. Again, most of the campers were long-term summer residents with the awnings and picket fences that went with their style of camping.

---

[70] Should it crop up as a question on that quiz show, the other is Uzbekistan, surrounded by Kazakhstan, Kyrgyzstan, Tajikistan, Afghanistan and Turkmenistan.

However, there was a patch of grass in the centre where (dare I say) normal campers could erect their tent for the night. It was the camping equivalent of being a goldfish in a bowl, every movement scrutinised by several sets of eyes looking on from the other side of the circular road around the site. Oh to have been a naturist! That would have ruffled some feathers. As it was, I remained clothed, erected the tent, boiled up some pasta and fell asleep in the tent.

Day Fifty-Four: Buchs to Konstanz (64km + ferry)
Thursday 25th August

The online reviews for Camping Werdenberg in Buchs had warned me about the bells. They were hanging high in the slender pink clocktower next to the campsite, poised for action. However, as an early riser, I was not too perturbed when my fellow campers and I were subjected to the first peal of the day at 6 am. The bells were certainly loud and slightly off-key but at least they did not rouse me from my slumber. That had happened some hours earlier after a longer-than-usual period of sleep that had left me feeling somewhat groggy. Unfortunately, instead of turning over at 3 am and closing my eyes, I reached for my phone and started to browse online. No further sleep took place.

A few hours later I recorded the following comments for the podcast about my nocturnal scrolling:

> "I was looking at the map and it suddenly dawned upon me [that] I'm actually going to find it really difficult to get to Rotterdam in 10 days… Even with two train journeys of a maximum of 100km - probably one from Basel to Strasbourg and another further north - I'm going to struggle. In his Cicerone guide, Mike Wells recommends at least two weeks to get from source to sea. I'm not at the source but I've not gone that far… I don't really know what's going to happen over the next week and a bit."

I was worried but I continued to record my thoughts. My plan for later in the day was to start cycling along the northern shore of the Bodensee (Lake Constance). This would mean leaving Switzerland and entering Germany. At least it would be much cheaper on that other side of the border. To access the German shoreline of the Bodensee I would need to cycle into Austria and pass through Bregenz, the country's only city along its 20-km share of waterfront. I had arranged to meet an old friend from Germany for lunch in Bregenz but that was not my only planned encounter of the day. At 8 am I had also arranged to meet a British cyclist called Ken Wynn back in Liechtenstein.

Today would be the most international day of my trip by far as it would see me travel through four countries: Switzerland, Liechtenstein, Austria and Germany. But that was nothing compared to what Ken was attempting: 12 countries in 12 days for charity, from his adopted home in Amsterdam to Barcelona. Liechtenstein was country number six. Reflecting upon the predicament of my narrowing window of opportunity to get back to the Hook of Holland and catch my ferry home, Ken might be the perfect person to help inspire me.

"My average needs to be about 175km per day," he explained shortly after we sat down for coffee and *croissant* outside a café in the town of Schaan.

"My average is currently just 81km," I admitted. Ken smiled sympathetically.

"Once you hit the Netherlands it will be completely flat so you'll pick up time there," he pointed out. It was worth the reminder although his supportive words did not calm my growing sense of unease.

Today promised to be the most challenging day of Ken's cycle as he planned to cross the Alps and travel as far as the northern tip of Lake Como in Italy. 180km and 2,500 metres of climbing. My plan to ride slowly north towards the shore of the Bodensee and indulge in a leisurely (and no doubt liquid) lunch with an old friend seemed positively ostentatious. And feeble. *Was there any wonder I was at severe risk of missing that ferry home?*

I wished Ken well and as he sped off south I trundled back over the Rhine to rejoin the cycle route and continue my journey north still wondering how the hell I was going to make up time and distance. I passed the bell tower in Buchs just as it was striking nine, the morning detour to meet Ken having added an extra 8km to the journey. For the first 15km of the cycling day proper, I was kept well away from the Rhine for reasons known only to the cycle planners of Switzerland. Perhaps, just as they had done on the previous day as I cycled through Heidiland, those in charge wanted to show me Switzerland at its best and who was I to complain? The route guided me through vast open fields along the wide plain of the Rhine with spectacular views of the surrounding hills, mountains and craggy balconies high above. Yet these were the last hurrahs of the Alps. Within a matter of hours I would have escaped the alluring grip of Europe's most celebrated mountain range and swapped it for the more gentle but no-less-appealing pastoral landscape of southern Germany.

Once I had rejoined the left bank of the Rhine the cycling became a little more… run-of-the-mill. Boring would be too-harsh-a word but I could perhaps understand why the Rhine Cycle Route planning committee had chosen not to have their cycle path follow the river so slavishly earlier in the day. I passed into Austria with minimal formality - just a small blue sign announcing the arrival of the Republik Österreich - and no change whatsoever in cycling conditions. The well maintained riverside tarmac path continued to point me effortlessly in the direction of the approaching lake.

For much of its journey north the Rhine Cycle Route, EuroVelo 15, offered the cyclist a choice of either cycling along the left bank or the right bank of the river. This was particularly the case where the Rhine formed the border between France and Germany. In the days to come it would, on occasions, prove to be a somewhat confusing arrangement but it presumably kept the rival cycling bureaucrats of France and Germany happy. Indeed this dual-route arrangement also extended into Switzerland from Basel as far as Konstanz on the Bodensee: one route in Switzerland, one in Germany. However, to cycle the length of the Bodensee there was no choice. If you wanted to be loyal to the official route of the EuroVelo 15, you had to adopt the southern shore of the Bodensee through Switzerland.

However, a couple of days earlier, Claud Butler had been equivocal in his recommendation to follow the German side of the lake to the north and that was my plan. What's more, my meeting with old friend Claus in Bregenz was only a few kilometres from the Austro-German border. Everything pointed at me continuing along the northern shore and abandoning the official route.

The city of Bregenz was announced not on land but in the sky with a blue and white airship circling in the sky. Ferdinand von Zeppelin had flown his first airships over the Bodensee from nearby Friedrichshafen. It seemed that his influence was still lingering, and the floating ovoid gave me something to aim for as I followed the local cycling signs towards the centre of Bregenz. A few days earlier I would have been hard pressed to place Bregenz on a map of Europe let alone one of Austria or even the Bodensee. However, Claus had suggested it as a place to meet and from what I could see, he had chosen well. It was a smart lakeside resort with a wide tree-lined walkway beside the water and was clearly popular with the tourists who had come here to take a leisurely stroll whilst gazing across the lake.

Claus, a fellow teacher from Stuttgart, was on holiday with his wife and two children in nearby Bavaria. Leaving the family in Germany he had driven down into Austria to meet me. Having not seen him for over a decade, I was a little unsure if I would recognise him immediately but after an exchange of WhatsApp messages, we were soon approaching each other along the promenade. I was in luck. He looked exactly as he had done in Strasbourg in 2010.

If that sounds familiar, it is probably because you have read my first book, Crossing Europe, in which I recounted the story of my cycle from southern England to Puglia in southern Italy. I arranged to meet up with Claus for a drink when I arrived on the Rhine after ten days of cycling. He was having a tough time of things back in 2010 having just split up from his then partner so it was good to see that he had managed to turn his life around in the intervening years. Life for Claus now appeared to be good.

After a short detour to visit Bregenz's opera amphitheatre that had been constructed half on land, half on water and which had featured in the James Bond film Quantum of Solace (that man gets everywhere!) we chatted over beer and food in a restaurant overlooking the lake. The waiter took a severe dislike to me parking Wanda in a spot where I could keep an eye on her (*"Keine Fahrräder!"* he repeated sternly) but I was persuaded by Claus not to argue ("don't mess with the Austrians when it comes to rules and regulations" he warned) and I reluctantly agreed to lock her to a nearby designated bike rack.

The perceived hostility of the waiter was in stark contrast to the serene views across the lake. Elegant white ferries of the BSB line passed before us either setting off or finishing their journeys along the Bodensee. And it got me thinking...

"How far do the ferries go?" I asked Claus.

"At least as far as Konstanz, but they're not direct. They stop in every town along the shore," he explained.

"How long does it take to get to Konstanz?"

"Quite a few hours. In school in Germany we are taught that the Bodensee is so long that you can't see from one end to the other because of the curvature of the Earth," he added.

I reached for my phone and found the BSB website. There was a ferry leaving Bregenz at 3.30 pm and, via a change of boat in Meersburg, I could potentially be in Konstanz by 7.30 pm. The direct distance between Bregenz and Konstanz was around 50km but if I opted to cycle along the northern shore it would inevitably be much longer, at least a day of cycling. After several beers with Claus, although it was still only early afternoon, the prospects of cycling much further were slim. If I chose to stay on the bike, my cycle around the lake would only start the following morning. However, I had stumbled upon a way in which to eliminate tomorrow's cycle from the schedule altogether.

I did not feel entirely comfortable taking a ferry on such a long journey. *That would be breaking the rules, no?* Some might even accuse me of cheating. Then again, what rule would I be breaking? The only rule in the book was the one about trains: a maximum of ten train journeys for a maximum of 100km each. This was a ferry, not a train. And anyway, it would not be my first ferry. I had taken quite a long one way back on day one to cross Rotterdam harbour to avoid retracing my steps beside the estuary west of the city. There had also been the ferry that had taken me across the Gironde near Bordeaux. Admittedly neither of those two ferries was anything like 50km from departure point to destination. Yet they were ferries. If I had broken any rule about such things, I had done so many weeks previously. But there was no rule about ferries in the first place!

"Just buy the goddam ticket," pleaded Claus after having put up with my verbal anguish for far too long. He was right. Ultimately if taking a boat to Konstanz shaved a full day of cycling off what remained of my journey I should do it.

Bearing in mind she had been plying her trade on the Bodensee since 1937, the *MS Schwaben* was in fine fettle and, during the afternoon and early evening, I cruised around the curvature of the Earth in art-deco style. Aside from the distance covered, it was also what I needed physically: an enforced period of doing nothing but watch the world go by.

That evening I booked into an Ibis Budget hotel on the outskirts of Konstanz with a renewed sense of hope that I was capable of completing my journey on time albeit tinged with a modicum of sadness. I picked up my microphone again and recorded more thoughts for the podcast:

> "There's a little bit of me that regrets doing what I've just done because looking from the boat this afternoon, this is a beautiful part of the world. I wish I had the time to cycle along the coast of the Bodensee... but it was a sensible decision. I've got to get back to Rotterdam for a week on Saturday."

And ultimately, you cannot break a rule if there is no rule to break.

Day Fifty-Five: Konstanz to Kembs (59km + train + 19km)
Friday 26th August

After the Netherlands, Belgium, France, Switzerland, Liechtenstein and Austria, I was now in the seventh and final country of my Grand Tour of Europe. When I woke in the hotel on the morning of August 26th I did so for the first time in Germany. It was a sign that the end was nigh, kind of. I was unsure as to how many times I would need to pass over the border from Germany into Switzerland or France (and back) in the coming few days. Indeed, when I examined the map carefully, I could envisage doing so on multiple occasions today thanks to the rather idiosyncratic nature of the border in this corner of Switzerland. It did not slavishly follow the Rhine (as it did for the entire border between France and Germany further north). Far from it. There were small pockets of Swiss territory north of the Rhine (although no pockets of German territory south of the Rhine). There was even a tiny exclave of Germany - Büsingen am Hochrhein - just to the east of Schaffhausen that I would probably need to cycle through. Passport at the ready I set off from the hotel to retrace my route back into the centre of Konstanz before starting my onward journey for proper. Via a trip to the laundrette.

I have long spoken about the joys of using continental laundrettes and how they compare very favourably with their British counterparts. Come to think of it, not just favourably. They are in a different league altogether. The laundrette I located close to the hotel was a classic of the European genre. At one end of the establishment were the washing machines and driers. They all worked and were linked electronically to a pay-by-card console on the wall. At the other end were a couple of large Chesterfield sofas that would not have looked out of place in the foyer of a four-star hotel. The same could be said for the oversized designer clock that had been integrated into the wall above the sofas. There was a rustic wooden coffee table that was home to a few magazines that had been published in recent weeks rather than at some point in the 1990s. Pot plants that were still living introduced an element of the natural world into this otherwise clinical environment and a coffee machine offered me a range of fine beverages. Everything was spotlessly clean.

My error was to wheel Wanda inside this temple to clean laundry. I placed my clothes in one of the washing machines, paid, pushed the start button and took a seat on one of the Chesterfields. Another customer joined me and we exchanged *morgens*. The bike was leaning on her stand in the area between machines and sofas.

Then the owner arrived.

He was clearly not happy but it was not immediately obvious as to why. He was speaking German and although directing his comments to both his customers, only one could understand his words. However, his gestures suggested it was the bicycle that was the issue. Ahh... I held my hands up, apologised for not understanding and went to wheel Wanda outside. The man was now speaking broken English to me whilst continuing to justify his argument (I assumed) to the other customer in German. I stayed mute although did break my silence with a few *entschuldigungs*[71]. But the owner was not ready to calm down and continued to ask lots of rhetorical questions (his tone of voice was the clue) in German that I neither understood nor had the ability to respond to. I stood outside hoping that he would not take his protests to the next level by retrieving my clothes from the machine and throwing them at me in the street. Eventually, he got back into his black Mercedes and, with a screech of tyres, headed off down the road. I went back inside the laundrette and examined the floor. There was the faintest mark of a tyre tread on the tiles. When the washing machine cycle finished I gave my clothes a cursory spin in the dryer and escaped the scene of the crime. At least I would soon be back in Switzerland. Although I was sure that the formalities of extradition would be minimal, I would hopefully be long gone by the time the paperwork had been completed.

Although my primary concern was to arrive back in Rotterdam to catch the ferry on September 3rd, I now had the added risk of extradition to consider. I formulated a plan. As noted earlier, west of Konstanz there were two versions of the Rhine Cycle Route / EuroVelo 15 that I could follow, one to the north of the river, one to the south. However, as far as Stein am Rhein (in Switzerland), I would be cycling along the southern shore of the Bodensee Untersee, the lower lake (as opposed to the Bodensee Obersee or Upper Lake that I had crossed by ferry). This, I thought, would compensate in part for the disappointment of having missed out on cycling around the lake the previous afternoon.

After Stein am Rhein there was only one version of the Rhine Cycle Route as far as Schaffhausen. It followed the northern bank of the river and it was along this section of cycling that I would be passing over the multiple international borders between Switzerland and Germany. In Schaffhausen I would take a train to Basel, but not before I had cycled a little further west to the famous Rheinfall, a series of spectacular waterfalls stretching across the river that prevent any boats from travelling further upstream. It would add a few kilometres to the cycling day but it was a must-see destination.

---

[71] "Sorry"

The direct distance to Basel on the train was around 75km so comfortably below my 100km limit. However, it was not so far below 100km to make the choice of journey profligate, as the previous train journey from Andermatt to the Oberalp Pass had arguably been. Come to think of it, there was no argument to be had: it had been a waste of most of the 100km but at least I got my chance to travel on one of the pretty red Alpine trains. It had been worth every kilometre sacrificed.

Once in Basel, I had hoped to make use of the campsite in which I had stayed back in 2010 just over the border in France at a place called Huningue. Much to my disappointment it had not re-opened for the 2022 season citing COVID, "lack of security due to the presence of people from the travelling community" and nearby building work. That was a shame but there were other camping options further north along the river. I would use one of those.

So that was the plan. It all seemed a little complicated - convoluted even - but if it worked out I would travel the equivalent of over 150 cycling kilometres. The decision to take the ferry had gifted me a day of cycling and hopefully, today's train ride would do the same, leaving me with under 1,000km to cycle in eight days. If chosen very carefully, my one remaining train journey might knock another 100km from the distance. *900km in eight days? An average of just over 110km per day?* I had achieved that back in 2013 when cycling along the Mediterranean coast from Greece to Portugal. *Nine years later?* It would be tough but it was no longer in the realms of the fanciful. It was with a renewed sense of optimism that I pedalled out of Konstanz crossing my first international border back into Switzerland at just before 10 am. As I did, I glanced over my shoulder. *Was that a black Mercedes?*

It was another warm, sunny morning - those Alpine storms in the vicinity of Lac Léman now seemed very distant - and I was soon hugging the shoreline of the lake on an off-road path that followed an almost identical route to the railway line. The white Thurbo trains had doors painted green, yellow and blue and, as they quietly passed beside me at speed, each of the colours blurred across my vision. At one point there was barely any space between me and the carriages of the trains (not even a cursory fence) and it made for a fun, exhilarating race albeit one that I was always destined to lose very badly.

The views across the narrowing expanse of the Bodensee were sublime. The BSB ferries that ventured beyond Konstanz were few and far between, for much of the time leaving the water very much to the swans and the yachters in their wooden boats. The cycle path guided me gently over the slightly undulating landscape, but it rarely demanded much of an effort from the cyclist who more often than not used his momentum from the short downhills to conquer the equally short uphills. Then I would pass through a smart, well-preserved town of half-timbered buildings - the Germanic influence was less than subtle - before pausing at a pier to stare across the water towards the towns and villages from where the influence originated: Germany itself. This really was cycling heaven and I could not quite stop kicking myself at having taken the ferry the previous afternoon. This, I assumed, is what I could have won if I had not been so keen to jump on the *MS Schwaben*. However much my head argued that it had made a good decision, my heart was just as vehement in its disagreement. I would leave them to their petty argument while I continued to soak up the beauty of everything that surrounded me.

Located at the point where the Rhine re-established itself as a river after its journey across the Bodensee, the town of Stein am Rhein took things to an altogether different level. The Cicerone guide had bigged it up as "one of the best preserved medieval towns in Switzerland" but having already cycled through several well-preserved towns I did not think it would be much different. How wrong could I have been?

Crossing a modern bridge from the south, Stein am Rhein certainly had credentials. Centuries-old three- and four-storey buildings lined the bank of the river and the sharply pointed spire of a church tower protruded high above the red-tiled roofs that surrounded it. Then, as I arrived on the northern side of the Rhine, I was squeezed along a narrow street shared with cars at the end of which they had no choice but to turn right. On my bike, I could turn left into a pedestrianised square. After a few moments, I squeezed on the brakes and uttered just one word.

"Wow!"

There had been a few wow moments on the Grand Tour. The château beside the Avenue Verte at Mesnières-en-Bray. The price of the campsite in Domfront: just €4. (The price of the campsite on the shores of Lac Léman: an extortionate €35.) The morning mist lingering over the fields near Saint-Gilles-Croix-de-Vie. Auvillar on the Garonne. The Place du Capitole in Toulouse. The suspension bridge over the Rhône at Rochemaure. Le Grand Colombier. The Furka Pass. And more recently the magnificent Rhine Gorge. But there had been nothing quite so wow! as the main square in Stein am Rhein.

It was actually a square that rapidly morphed into a narrow main street at its furthest point. I had entered at the broader end to one side of the 16th-century *Rathaus*, the town hall, but what made the Rathausplatz so memorable was not its size nor its shape: it was the buildings and their façades. Curiously the *Rathaus* itself was relatively toned down compared to the two long lines of buildings that snaked away into the distance. Each medieval construction was unique but in perfect harmony with all of its neighbours. Most had four storeys but some had five and a handful just three. Yet the architect of each building had seemingly prescribed a different measurement for the height of a storey. None of the windows followed the same line from building to building. And the pitch of each tiled roof was again at the whim of the architect. Many contained dormer windows and some even supported full-blown gable ends. The result was pleasingly chaotic in a very organised kind of way.

However, what elevated the square from very beautiful to astonishing was the decoration. Many of the buildings were half-timbered but what was not was plastered and it was onto this plaster that a series of astonishingly detailed frescos had been painted. The themes were many and varied: science, the arts, agriculture, military prowess… all mixed in with brightly painted *trompe l'oeil* trickery. A wow! sight to beat most others.

I pushed Wanda slowly along the street, craning my neck to examine the colourful frescos whilst trying to avoid crashing into my fellow tourists, of which there were many. It was interesting to note just how many of them were cyclists. Was it a sign of things to come? Although the Rhine Cycle Route to this point had had its fair share of cyclists, it had never been busy. However, I suspected that from this point that might change as people chose to start their cycling journeys at some of the more iconic Rhine locations. Stein am Rhein was one of those, as was the Rheinfall and that was next on my itinerary.

Time, however, was an issue. I was leaving Stein am Rhein shortly after 1 pm and the train I needed to catch to Basel left Schaffhausen at 3 pm.[72] It was about 20km to Schaffhausen but I was keen to visit the Rheinfall which was a few kilometres further along the river. It was time to crack on with a bit of hardcore cycle touring. Alas, the route was not quite as flat as I might have hoped for but it was at least almost all off-road on a path with a good surface. It did, at times, feel as though I was on a roller coaster hurtling up and down the hills, through the woods and the farmers' fields and across international borders. (I must surely have shaken off the laundrette man in his Mercedes by now.) Even my pause to admire the old, covered bridge and pretty waterfront buildings at Diessenhofen was perfunctory: just the

---

[72] Although later trains were available, this was a regional Deutsche Bahn train that I could take for just €9. During the summer of 2022, the German government was heavily subsidising train travel and the €9-tickets had proved very popular. They were, however, only valid on regional trains and not on Swiss trains. Most trains from Schaffhausen to Basel were Swiss trains and most of the German trains were not regional ones. Life would get complicated - and potentially expensive - if I missed the 3 pm train.

time needed to take a photo. Then I was off again on my quest to make all the timings work.

It was already well past 2 pm when I cycled through Schaffhausen. I was now battling with the urban environment: left-right-left-right cycle paths, junctions, crossings, roadworks, people... but I ploughed on beside the river past a large hydroelectric plant and under several lofty bridges. The path narrowed somewhat and then I was obliged to dismount as a no cycling sign stopped me in my tracks. It was impossible to see much further ahead as the river had now entered a sharp meander in its path. Not that I could see much of the river as it was hidden behind a bank of trees. Hoping that the ban on cycling was due to the narrowness of the path rather than a long flight of steps, I continued. I could now hear the waterfalls but still had no sight of them.

Then, finally, the trees started to thin out and the path joined a steep road. At the bottom of the road, I found what I had been searching for: the Rheinfall.

In recent days I had had exchanges - online and in person - with various people who had been a little disparaging about the waterfalls. My first impression was more positive. The majesty of these falls was not their height - just 23 metres - but their width and the volume of water that passed over them. Stretching across 150 metres, at their summer peak 600,000 litres of water per second cascade across the rocky outcrops. The greatest recorded flow was in 1965 when it reached an astonishing 1,250,000 litres per second. An Olympic-sized swimming pool contains (rather conveniently) 2,500,000 litres of water. So if you happened to be there back in the mid-60s that was an Olympic-sized pool of water every two seconds.

After the very dry summer of 2022 I suspected that the peak flow of 600,000 was probably way off the mark for the day I visited. Not great news if you had come with your Olympic-sized pool in the hope of getting it filled: you might have had to hang around for six or seven seconds. I had not packed my pool so I just stared at the scene before me. Much of the rock was visible but the flow was still sufficient for great clouds of spray to be thrown up into the air. The raincoats of the people on the tourist boats edging as close as they could to the foot of the waterfall would still be of use.

It was 2.30 pm when I pushed Wanda back up the steep hill but instead of retracing my route along the path I switched on Google Maps and followed directions. 25 minutes later I was standing on the platform at Schaffhausen station waiting to board the train. My timings had worked with just a few minutes to spare but my day was far from over.

It was 4.30 pm when I pushed Wanda off the train at Basel. I had fond memories of the city from the 2010 cycle. After a night at the campsite in Huningue I had pedalled over the Rhine and along quaint cobbled streets, savouring every moment of being in what I perceived to be a very attractive Swiss city.

12 years later I wondered if I had arrived in the same place. There was no functioning lift from the platform down to the subway tunnel so I was obliged to haul the heavily-laden bike down a long flight of stairs. When I emerged from the station and consulted my phone there was no mobile coverage. I switched off the phone in the hope that it would find a signal upon being restarted. It did not. I had no paper map to consult. I stood and stared at the busy thoroughfare in front of me. The signs that I could see gave no clues and a street map was an unfathomable maze of roads. *What had happened to the quaint cobbled streets of 2010?*

The small compass attached to Wanda's handlebars did at least suggest a way forward. I knew that France was - very approximately - towards the north west of Basel so I turned right as that would mean me cycling - very approximately - towards the north west. About 10 minutes later, still without any mobile signal, I paused at a road junction. To my left were several concrete motorway flyovers. To my right a busy road heading in the direction of... who knows?

I was, for the first time on my Grand Tour, lost. Not in the middle of a forest or on a remote mountain path but in Switzerland's third largest city. I turned right for the simple reason that I would be heading north but there were no visual hints that I was making a good choice. Five minutes later I crossed back into Germany. I had envisaged cycling from Basel straight into France. This was not part of the plan but I continued cycling north. Eventually I noticed a sign for the EuroVelo 15 and turned left. This took me to a hydroelectric barrage across the Rhine and back into France.

It was 5.30 pm when I cycled Wanda through the gates of Camping du Canal near Kembs. It had been an exasperating end to one of the most memorable days of cycling. I pitched the tent, headed back to the campsite restaurant and sunk my teeth into a hamburger and a large pile of chips.

Day Fifty-Six: Kembs to Kehl (120km)
Saturday 27th August

There were many things to like about day 56 of this jaunt around Europe. Bearing in mind my need to be back at my starting point in exactly one week, the fact that I managed to cycle 120km in a very straight line north must rank as number one. (Remember that I was now aiming to cycle on average 110km per day.) I was also cycling very gradually downhill for the entire day. I was in France and firmly back in my linguistic comfort zone. And although quite humid due to the cloud cover, it was not raining and the temperature was hitting the sweet spot for cycling: not too hot but certainly not cold.

But it was deathly dull.

Perhaps the day was suffering from not being its predecessor which, despite a frustrating end, had been a highlight of the Grand Tour so far. And perhaps it was also because it was a section of my loop around Europe that I had never intended to cycle in the first place. When planning the trip, having decided to allow myself to take the ten trains, I thought it would make eminent sense to use a few of these to avoid travelling along routes that I had previously cycled. That had been the case from La Rochelle to Royan, a route that I had cycled (albeit in the opposite direction) in 2015. Similarly from Montpellier to Avignon, a route that I had cycled as part of the Mediterranean trip in 2013. Going one step further back in time, I had cycled from Strasbourg to Basel in 2010 en route to southern Italy. But whereas the journeys to Royan and Avignon were completed when I still had a good number of train journeys left at my disposal, that was not the case when setting off from Kembs. Only one of my trains remained and I needed to keep it in reserve for the final few days of the entire Grand Tour when I suspected I would be sprinting like an Olympian to the finishing line. It was doubly frustrating as the distance from Mulhouse - the nearest train station to the campsite in Kembs - to Strasbourg was almost exactly 100km so it would have been a very efficient train to take. But I simply could not risk it so consigned myself to the long slog north on the bike.

It would be a tale of two cycles: on generally well maintained segregated paths across farmers' fields and beside quiet roads until Marckolsheim, and then along the towpath of the Canal du Rhône au Rhin to Strasbourg. For most of the day I was a slave to the signs of the EuroVelo 15. Nothing went wrong. I never got lost. But I was bored to tears. Indeed it was one of those days when you begin to wonder, often fancifully, just how far you might be able to cycle before the end of the day.

I could only remember this strategy coming to fruition on one previous occasion, in Spain during the 2013 cycle. I had arrived at a campsite a few kilometres to the north of Tarragona on the Costa Dorada just south of Barcelona. My situation at the time was not dissimilar to what I was facing in 2022 in that I was running out of time to get to my destination of Cape St. Vincent in Portugal. I set off early from Tarragona, the weather was perfect - hot but not a whisper of wind - and the coastal road predominantly flat and straight. I kept cycling and cycling, constantly re-evaluating how far I could travel in one day. It eventually dawned upon me that I might be able to make it as far as Valencia and, after over 11 hours of cycling and an astonishing 278km, that is exactly what happened. My efforts put the entire trip back on track and after another ten days of cycling I arrived at my destination in time to catch a plane home to the UK and be back in the classroom for the start of the new academic year.

That said, I was not expecting to cycle another 278km along the Rhine in 2022. To put the Spanish ride into some kind of context, if I had repeated the feat, I would have finished somewhere close to Mannheim. Yet I did begin to wonder whether I might make it as far as France's most easterly town, Lauterbourg. It had a nice looking *camping municipal* and was very close to the point at which the Rhine became entirely German. It would mean cycling 160km before the end of the day. With that thought in mind, I cracked on.

Nondescript Kembs did not have much in the way of facilities when it came to supplying a hungry cyclist with his breakfast although it did have a hairdresser and a bicycle shop. Perhaps the latter benefitted from the small town being a meeting point for three of the EuroVelo routes. Route 15 was the reason why I was there but route 5 passed nearby on its way to Brindisi, as did route 6 on its way to Constanta on the Black Sea. This was all explained very clearly on an information board next to the entrance of the campsite. It was interesting to note that the routes for EuroVelo 5 and EuroVelo 15 between Strasbourg and Basel were very different. Whereas the 15 stuck close to the Rhine, the EuroVelo 5 followed a path several kilometres to the west passing through Colmar and Mulhouse. When I had cycled the EuroVelo 5 in 2010, it was often no more than a line on a very big map of Europe. I was frequently left guessing as to where I should be cycling. I usually followed regional or national routes that were signposted such as the EuroVelo 15 or, as it was at the time before its elevation to the status of a EuroVelo, the plain old Rhine Cycle Route.

Surely Kembs, at such a pivotal point on the EuroVelo network would have a boulangerie with tables groaning under the weight of croissants, pains au chocolat and pains au raison all ready to be devoured by ravenous cyclists. But it did not. You could trim your hair and pump up your tyres but you were stuffed (in the non-food sense) if you hoped to buy breakfast there.

A few kilometres north, the much more enterprising people of the wonderfully named Niffer did have a shop where I could buy breakfast. It was a community-run café-cum-very-mini supermarket and reminded me of the shop in the village of Ambridge (of Archers fame). I was served by the French Susan Carter who was keen for me to buy as much of her fresh stock as I possibly could as the shop would be closing for the holidays later in the day. What's more the coffee was free, much to the disgust of a grumpy Gallic Jim Lloyd who was toiling away in the corner of the room rearranging less-perishable stock. With its well-maintained streets and brightly coloured houses, Niffer was everything that Kembs was not and I was delighted to have stumbled upon it.

Alas there was not much else to stumble upon over the next few hours. The Rhine Cycle Route passed through a series of *heims*: Ottmarsheim, Rumersheim, Kunheim... and at Artzenheim I joined the canal for a few kilometres as far as my lunch stop in Marckolsheim. Here I was subjected to a cacophonous ten-minute peeling of the church bells at midday. It was almost as if the local priest was having a tantrum about reduced attendance on Sunday mornings and had inflicted upon his heathen flock this noise (there was little musical merit in the chimes) as some form of punishment.

What Marckolsheim lacked in tranquillity it more than made up for in its sandwiches. For a mere €3 I was able to munch away for many minutes on an enormous *demi-baguette* stuffed with cheese, ham and salad. The whole construction dripped volumes of mayonnaise. It was no wonder that the queue outside the *patisserie* had been so long. Perhaps the local priest should take note and whip out his fishes and loaves rather than berate his parishioners from the bell tower.

My Marckolsheim pit stop came after I had cycled some 60km. As I nibbled away on the sandwich I reflected upon the prospects of me cycling all the way to Lauterbourg. It would be another 60km to Strasbourg and then another 40km after that. Did I have the energy to cycle 100km before the end of the day?

Once the chimes had finished (there were a few frustrating false stops), I put in a call to Camping de Strasbourg, a large site in the southern suburbs of the city.

"*Camping de Strasbourg. Bonjour.*"

"Hi. Do you have any…"

"We are full. Goodbye."

Then the phone went dead.

At least they had not wasted much of my time.

Now a little unsure as to where I would end up staying overnight, I rejoined the canal and continued cycling north.

As with the other major canals that I had followed earlier in the summer, the Canal du Rhône au Rhin had lofty ambitions when building started in the late 18th century. The Nantes-Brest Canal had been built to avoid risky trips around the coast of north-western France which at the time was under the watchful eyes of the British. The combined effect of the Canal de la Garonne and the Canal du Midi had been to link the Atlantic to the Mediterranean and avoid having to traipse around the Iberian Peninsula where the Spaniards might steal your cargo (or at least tax it). However, the ambitions of the engineers of the Rhône-Rhine Canal were somewhat more audacious. As the name implies, the purpose of constructing the canal was to link the two rivers but in doing so they would also connect the North Sea to the Mediterranean.

As we have already seen, navigating the Rhine much further than Basel is somewhat problematic thanks to the Rheinfall. However, the canal was built to connect with the Rhine much further north at Strasbourg (albeit with a linking canal to Huningue and the port of Basel). From there, along a series of phenomenally straight sections of canal via Marckolsheim and Neuf-Brisach, it continued to Mulhouse before heading west, not in the direction of the Rhône but the Saône which in turn linked with the Rhône at Lyon. If you have a little time on your hands, find the canal on an online map or Google Earth and try to follow its path between the Rhine at Strasbourg and the Rhône at Lyon. It is a fascinating armchair adventure. It involves navigating a fragmented chain of sections of canal, sections of river and sections of canalised river where the pesky Saône has decided to take, quite frankly, juvenile meanders. No thought whatsoever for the poor buggers who had to try and sail their barges along the route!

There were plans to upgrade the link in the second half of the 20th century. Presumably, this would have seen the larger barges that can be found in the lower stretches of the Rhine and the Rhône take their cargos from Rotterdam to Marseille. The plan was, however, abandoned in the late 1990s.

None of this fascinating canal chat made the route from Marckolsheim to Strasbourg that Saturday afternoon anything other than relentlessly boring. The tedium of a cycle where the view from the saddle barely changed for 60km cannot be underestimated. By the time I was finally approaching Strasbourg I had abandoned any tentative plans to stretch the day to 160km even if, north of Strasbourg, it was reasonable to assume that there might have been more variety. I had had my fill of cycling for one day thank you very much.

The accommodation situation had not, however, been sorted. *Should I cave in and book another night in a cheap hotel?* I pulled out my phone and somewhat half-heartedly searched online for an alternative campsite. No, nothing in France, but... there was something in the town opposite Strasbourg on the other side of the Rhine in Germany: Campingplatz Kehl. I was a little reluctant as this was my final opportunity of the trip to stay in France. The following morning I would leave France for the last time and the final week of the Grand Tour would be spent either in Germany or the Netherlands. But needs must. I switched on Google directions and within 30 minutes I had booked in, erected the tent and was on my way to the shower block to freshen up. My choice of campsite had been a good one.

Situated on the right bank of the Rhine, the campsite was set amongst a thinned-out wood of mature trees not far from an open-air swimming pool. The screams of children were the giveaway. Either that or some horrendous crimes were being committed within earshot. There were a few sports pitches nearby as well as a running track and a small lake. In the back of my mind had been the thought that the German side of the Rhine would be an endless sprawl of industrial plants. I had no idea why I might think that but I did. So to find this green oasis dedicated to all things healthy and outdoors was as delightful as it was surprising.

There was even a substantial area of the campsite set aside for those travelling without a caravan or large motorhome. During the late afternoon and evening, I fell into conversation with a number of my fellow cyclists, all against the backdrop of a very audible rock concert. It provided a nasty sting in the tail/tale of the day and was taking place on the French side of the river in a park beside the Rhine. It was a sound that was destined to continue until 2 am thanks to the combined efforts of Mad Rey, Driss Bennis aka OCB, Anna Haleta, GREG and Ostalgie. I could have happily throttled the lot.

Day Fifty-Seven: Kehl to Philippsburg (123km)
Sunday 28th August

Eating breakfast that Sunday morning at the campsite in Kehl, I was reminded of the arrangements at Camping Gouarec in Brittany where Geoff Husband and his team had laid on a breakfast for the cyclists staying at the site. In Kehl, it was a much more impromptu affair and involved the small group of people I had met the previous afternoon. There was a family of cyclists from France consisting of mum, dad and their two primary-school-aged sons, a retired German cyclist called Frank from Braunschweig, and American Dave from the mountains near Seattle. All of us were undertaking European cycles that stretched into months rather than just weeks.

With the support of their school, the French parents had taken the young boys out of education earlier in the year. After ten weeks of cycling, retired Volkswagen engineer Frank was now on his way home as he had promised his wife he would be back by mid-September. Dave - of similar age to me - was being loyal to the stereotype of a laid-back west-coast American and was making the whole thing up as he went along. We all agreed that we would happily slaughter every single one of the musicians at the festival if the opportunity should arise.

Dave was a person of particular interest. His attitude to preparing for his trip was very different to my own.

"I just figured that when I arrived in Europe for the first time I would buy the cheapest new bike that I could but which was of sufficient quality to handle the load. This one cost €120 and it's now been on four tours. It means I don't have to box it up or pay for the shipping. I've been lucky to meet people who have stored the bike for me when I go back home."

He explained that he had managed to sell two previous bikes whilst busking playing his trumpet but at the end of his current trip he was planning on giving away this bike to Ukrainian refugees via a collection centre he had heard about.

"As for everything else - the panniers, the kit… - it probably cost about $100 in total and often bought second-hand. The tent is 20 years old and cost me something like $50."

Unsurprisingly, Dave was also an advocate of wild camping.

"I guess if I'm paying nothing for accommodation I can shell out the money on a good lunch instead."

He made some good points and, to a certain extent, shamed me. Some of my investments in kit prior to setting off had run into the hundreds of pounds, the bike itself into the thousands. In my defence, if there are no mugs like me around to buy everything new, there will never be any of the second-hand stuff available for the likes of Dave to buy. As for wild camping, it was a concept that I had still to embrace in any meaningful way despite having cycled some 20,000km around the continent over the years. I doubt I ever will.

One thing that I was able to embrace was following signs, in this case for the EuroVelo 15 / Rhine Cycle Route / Véloroute Rhin / Rheinradweg. Again, this being a frontier zone, everything was multilingual. You could choose your language and you could also choose your route, either in France or in Germany. Keen to make the most of my final opportunity of cycling in France, I chose to do just that, returning over the bridge to Strasbourg to pick up from where I had left off the previous afternoon.

It was not long before I had escaped the suburbs of the city and was again cycling through a mixture of open countryside, dense forest and farmers' fields with the occasional Alsatian town thrown in for good measure. After yesterday's rather tedious long cycle along the never-changing landscape of the canal bank, it was much welcome. *But was I welcome?* Close to the swanky Hôtel Château de Pourtalès, nearly all of the bicycle signs and markings on the segregated path had been defaced or struck out with large red crosses. At one point the words *"Interdit aux Vélo"* (forbidden to bike) had been spray painted on the path. There was no question of me not being on the route of the EuroVelo 15 but the changes were neither convincingly official nor convincingly unofficial for me to make a definitive decision one way or the other. Only the grammatical error in the spray-painted phrase (*vélo*, not *vélos*, which would be implied by the use of *aux*) gave any hint that this might be the work of a disgruntled local rather than that of the Strasbourg city council. I kept an eye out for angry residents shaking fists but none were spotted. I would not have missed the opportunity to correct their grammar.

Yet again the day was developing into a hot one and I was not alone in appreciating the canopy of trees in the forest north of Strasbourg. It being a Sunday morning, the area was busy not only with cyclists but also joggers and walkers, especially those with dogs. As for the Rhine, I was oblivious as to where it might be. Such was the path of the Rhine Cycle Route, aside from crossing the river to get to the campsite in Kehl, the last time I had seen the Rhine was way back near Basel. And so it was to continue until early afternoon and after almost 60km of cycling when I paused for lunch at a mobile snack bar which had been positioned on the bank of the Rhine near Seltz.

Perhaps if I had chosen the alternative route in Germany, I may have seen more of the river. As it was I had decided to stay in France and follow the signs for the EuroVelo 15. In the Cicerone guidebook, Mike Wells referred to taking a ferry across the Rhine at Drusenheim. I could not work out why. Comparing the various versions of the route that I had at my disposal - the guidebook, online at OpenStreetMap and the signs that I could see on the ground - I could only conclude that there were at times not two versions of the Rhine Cycle Route, but three. It was all very confusing but as long as my handlebar-mounted compass was telling me that I was heading north far more frequently than I was heading east, south or west, I was happy to continue cycling.

It would be another 15km before I crossed the border into Germany for the final time near Lauterbourg. This was the town to which I had initially planned to cycle the previous afternoon, estimating it to be about 40km north of Strasbourg. If I had chosen to continue my journey into the evening and not stayed at the campsite in Kehl, I would have ended up cycling nearly 200km on an odyssey approaching Tarragona-Valencian proportions. I was happy to have made the decision that I did. Nearly ten years after the epic Spanish cycle, I was sceptical that my ageing body was quite up for that kind of challenge.

These were not the only distances on my mind. A few kilometres after my lunch stop I paused briefly in the village of Munchhausen. On a post below a weather vane, a large number of colourful signs had been attached, each pointing in a different named direction and listing as-the-crow-flies distances. They included Strasbourg - 47km, Toulouse - 783km (it had taken me 1,624), Tahiti - 16,000km (seemingly rounded but, after checking, apparently not) and Rotterdam - 423km. This was the first time I had seen a sign referencing the distance to the finishing point of my Grand Tour. However I was not a crow and according to the Cicerone guidebook there were still another 812km to cycle from Strasbourg to the Hook of Holland along the Rhine Cycle Route. That said it was a sign - literally - that the end of the long trek was approaching.

More confusing were the kilometre markers positioned on the banks of the Rhine itself. The first I noticed was close to Lauterbourg. The number 350 had been painted on a large slab of upright concrete. The individual digits of the number were at least a metre tall. On the opposite bank of the river in Germany, there was a similar large slab of concrete also with the number 350. Having only fleetingly cycled beside the river since Switzerland, I could not remember seeing any similar signs earlier in the week. *What did this number refer to?* My initial assumption was that it was the number of kilometres to Rotterdam. On quick reflection, that was impossible if the direct distance from nearby Munchhausen had been 423km. *In the other direction to the source?* Equally impossible bearing in mind how far I had so far cycled (including the boat and the train, well over 500km). *So what did the 350 refer to?*

It turned out that the number did indeed refer to kilometres but the starting point for measurement was neither the source nor the mouth of the Rhine. It was the Alte Rheinbrücke - the Old Rhine Bridge - in Konstanz. If I had cared to look for it at the time, I would have seen the 0 kilometre sign as I cycled beside the bridge on my way from the Bodensee ferry to my hotel three days earlier. Since that sign, the numbers had been ticking over gradually and had reached 350 close to the point where I would leave France for the last time. It seemed strange that these navigational signs - which were the size that they were in order that they could be read from boats passing up and down the river - started in Konstanz. It was, after all, impossible to navigate the river beyond the Rheinfall close to Schaffhausen. Some of the mystery remained.

During the final week of the cycle, the kilometre signs would become a regular feature of the journey slowly counting up to the finishing line. An online search told me that the sign closest to the Hook of Holland carried the number 1,031. 681 signs and 681km of Rhine remained. I passed over the border into Germany at shortly before 3 pm somewhere near the concrete block carrying the number 352.

By this point in proceedings, I had located a suitable campsite for the evening, in a town to the east of the Rhine called Philippsburg. The route north of the Franco-German border seemed more exposed. There were fewer trees to protect me from the wind. My weather app told me it was only a "gentle breeze" blowing at around 15km per hour from the north. However, because I was cycling from the south at around 15km per hour, the combined effect of the wind resistance was doubled. It was energy-sapping stuff and my water supplies were as exhausted as I was. Approaching a modern bridge that would take me across the river near Karlsruhe, I pleaded with a woman who happened to be doing a bit of gardening in front of her house to fill up my bottles. She kindly did so, twice, as I quickly emptied one of the bottles whilst standing in front of her. My energy levels were momentarily restored.

I continued to struggle into the late afternoon. *Was the accumulated fatigue of cycling almost every day for over eight weeks finally catching up with me?* I had not benefitted from a full day of rest since Aigle in Switzerland. Today was my ninth consecutive day on the bike, a period during which I had climbed to the Furka Pass and which was culminating in me ramping up the number of daily kilometres in order to arrive at my destination on time. The previous day had seen me cycle 120km and when I arrived at the campsite in Philippsburg I had recorded another 123. *It was great for my chances of succeeding in my epic quest but was I risking complete burnout?*

It could not be denied that there was another factor at play which was more mental than physical. It was something that I had experienced before on previous trips and I was very conscious of it happening again in the final few days of this particular journey. My mind knew the end was in sight. The euphoria of completing my task was only a matter of days away and half of the signals from my brain were in celebratory mood. They were telling my body it could begin to ease off and relax. The other half of the signals were having none of that. They were shouting at my body to keep going and push even harder. The biggest battle in the remaining six days of the Grand Tour would not be against the terrain nor the wind but against the contradictory noises in my head.

Day Fifty-Eight: Phlippsburg to Gernsheim (110km)
Monday 29th August

The day that cycling came home. Kind of.

In the early summer of 2019, I was heading for the continent. Not on a bicycle, but on a plane. I flew to Basel and from there, a coach took me to Strasbourg and a river cruise ship on the Rhine. I had been asked to deliver some talks about cycling across the continent to the holidaymakers on board the *MS Brabant*. They were not my natural audience and the cycling exploits of many - perhaps most - of the people on the boat were long distant. However, that had not stopped the cruise company from making available a small number of eBikes for their clients to make use of, and a few did, perhaps inspired by my tales of trans-continental adventure.

When not indulging in the prodigious amounts of food and drink on offer on the boat, there was plenty of tourism to be done. The *Brabant* made regular stops at towns and cities along the Rhine: Speyer, Mannheim, Mainz, Koblenz, Bonn, Cologne... and in each place we had the opportunity of disembarking and exploring independently. The eat-as-much-as-you-can-because-you-burn-off-the-calories-whilst-exercising philosophy of the long-distance cyclist (which is perfectly valid) was not going to work on a river cruise. So, fearing that I might return home somewhat heavier than when I set off, I attempted to make the most of the visits and indulged in some hardcore walking tourism. As a result I became quite familiar with the places I explored.

Three years later, on a cycling mission to get to Rotterdam before the end of the week, this strenuous effort from 2019 was about to pay dividends. As I had previously explored many of the places I was about to pass through, I could focus on the cycling rather than the tourism. That was the theory and, as I set off back towards the banks of the Rhine from the campsite in Philippsburg, I was looking forward to another long day in the saddle. Admittedly my legs were somewhat less enthusiastic but they would just have to grin and bear it.

I had been suffering (within reason...) without a physical paper map for some time. Switzerland had embraced the Internet as a primary source of detailed cycle mapping like few other countries. Their excellent SwitzerlandMobility app for the Swiss "non-motorised traffic network" was a model for others to emulate. The easy-to-use interface had given me access to all the twists and turns of the Swiss cycle routes, both on- and off-road. Should I have chosen to abandon the bike, it also provided me with detailed hiking, roller-skating, canoeing, skiing and even sledging routes.

Everything was colour-coded: hiking was green, mountain biking yellow etc... I had followed the blue signs for cycling. Very often at points where several of these active travel networks crossed, extraordinary multicoloured signposts could be found pointing adventurers in a myriad of appropriate directions. On occasions, it was not an exaggeration to call these signposts works of art. However, the downside to all the excellent online support was scant offline support in the form of free paper maps from local tourist offices. I was missing the security blanket of such things and when I arrived in Speyer, I went on a mission to find one.

Speyer was the kind of compact city any self-respecting human being might want to live in. The cars had been all but banished from the main street, the historic bits preserved immaculately and the modern bits melted into the urban landscape seamlessly. I slowly cycled over the flat cobbles and past all the café terraces that were beginning to fill with morning coffee drinkers. I wondered if I should stop my journey and seek permanent asylum.

Back in the real world (albeit online...) Google told me there was a bookshop close by and once located it supplied me with exactly what I was looking for. A German version of the French IGN 924 cycle map of France: the Kompass Radfernwege Deutschland. It showed me where the major cycle routes were but, crucially, also the train lines. Very useful as I had yet to decide when and where to take that final 100-km maximum train. The map was not sufficiently detailed to use as a step-by-step guide, but good enough to give me a clear overview of where I was, where I was going and where I might end up at the end of the day. Next stop Mannheim.

It is no secret that the Rhine is a hotbed of the industrial might of the German republic so it should not have come as a surprise to find myself getting up close and personal with plenty of it as I continued my journey north. But it did. Perhaps seeing the Rhine from the comfort of a cruise boat three years earlier had given me a false impression of this section of the river. Or perhaps after many weeks of seeing only sporadic pockets of industry, when it did start to appear en masse it made much more of an indelible impression.

As I approached Mannheim the right bank of the Rhine was littered with oil storage tanks, factories and chemical plants. Then, at the point where I was required to take a short ferry across the river just to the north of Rheinau, there was a monumental coal-fired power station. The coal itself was piled high on adjacent patches of land, cranes busy hoisting more of the filthy black stuff from an exceptionally long barge on the river. The numerous buildings that made up the power plant were trying their best to be symmetrical but the detail was letting them down. The chimney on the left was white, the one on the right dark grey. The building on the right was slightly taller than the one on the left.

It was, however, magnificent. I use the word advisable but it was. A living monument to the Western world's desire to boil water whenever you fancy a cuppa or watch rubbish TV in the afternoon. Admittedly it was also keeping babies alive in incubators and was no doubt helping to manufacture many of Wanda's numerous German-made bicycle components. Waiting on the opposite bank for the push-me-pull-me ferry to glide across the water to pick up not just me but a lengthening queue of cars, I stood and admired the ugly beauty of the edifice. An admirably horrific blot on the Rhine landscape. A physical embodiment of the oxymoron.

It would be another 20 minutes before I had managed to circumnavigate the power plant after which the normal greenery of the Rhineland returned. The industry would also return later in the day but not before I had managed to stumble upon something that I had been looking forward to seeing for quite some time. Three years in fact.

Baron Karl von Drais, the man most often accredited with the invention of the bicycle, took the first ride on his "two-wheel running machine" from Mannheim in 1817. 202 years later in 2019, I arrived in Mannheim on the cruise boat determined to explore the connection between the man and the city. Alas, I failed miserably. With only a short window of opportunity to do my research - I had to be back on the boat after only three hours - it did not help that the tourist office had closed its doors for lunch, but I persevered. Alas the only connection I could find that linked anything in the centre of Mannheim to the good Baron himself was the logo that adorned the city's hire bicycles. It could, possibly, have been interpreted as a Draisienne bike. Aside from that, nothing. *Nichts!*

Had the city forgotten one of its most celebrated residents? Perhaps I would have more luck 205 years after von Drais' first ride. On this occasion, by the time I had arrived at the Barockschloss Mannheim, a sprawling 18th-century palace that was now part of the city's university, I already had. It was from this precise point on June 12th 1817 that von Drais had set off riding his machine. He had no pedals to turn: he was propelled only by his feet on the ground and by any pockets of gravity he could make use of. He cycled south for around 9km to a coaching inn - the Altes Relaishaus - in Rheinau, only a short distance from the power station that I had been admiring earlier in the morning. He then turned around and went back home along a path that was not too dissimilar to my own.

To mark the 200th anniversary of his ride in 2017, the Mannheim authorities had erected an information board near the castle and commissioned several photographs of local cyclists. These had been sliced vertically with each slither being displayed on a slender square pillar at an angle. There were two slices from two different images on two adjacent sides of each pillar. (Still following?) The effect was that as you passed by, one image of a cyclist slowly morphed into a contrasting image of a different cyclist. Very clever. (If you have any idea what I am trying to explain.)

As I was walking backwards and forwards to sample the effect I fell into conversation with a man who was pushing an elderly relative in a wheelchair. He did initially think that I had a problem due to my movement up and down the cycle path but I quickly reassured him that everything was OK.

"Are the people of Mannheim very proud of Drais and his invention?" I asked.

"Yes, they are. But it's not just Drais. It's also Benz. He invented the automobile here as well!"

How ironic that the city which gave birth to arguably the most efficient method of transportation ever invented should later in the same century also give birth to the machine that has, without any argument, caused the greatest damage to our world. Perhaps one day the bicycle will reign supreme again as it did for a brief flicker of time between the inspirational thoughts of the two Karls of Mannheim. We can but hope.

I cycled straight through the centre of Mannheim's grid pattern centre emerging at a bridge over the River Neckar where I turned left. A few kilometres later I rejoined the bank of the Rhine at the point where the two rivers met. There was more industrial might on show north of Mannheim but this time it was not quite so pretty. At least it was all on the opposite side of the river. I kept following the signs and looked forward to escaping to more verdant sections of the valley further north. The next city was Mainz but that was out of reach for today. I had identified a handful of potential campsites by the river and all that I had to do was catch a short ferry across another tributary of the Rhine and it would be plain sailing for the remainder of the day.

I arrived at the ferry ramp a few kilometres north of the centre of Mannheim in good spirits following my discovery that the city had not consigned Baron von Drais to the refuse skip of history quite yet. The small platform ferry was tied up at the bottom of the concrete ramp but there were no people preparing to operate it. Checking the route online, this was indeed part of the EuroVelo 15. It was 1.50 pm. *Perhaps they were at lunch.* I hung around for a few minutes. *The personnel would no doubt be back at 2 pm to restart the short crossings for the afternoon.*

My eyes fell upon a sign that I tried to fathom, more to keep my mind occupied than anything else.

Fährzeiten:
Altrheinfähre
Friesenheimer Insel - Sandhofen
01. April - 30. September
von 10:00 - 20:00 Uhr
Montag: Ruhetag

I could guess the meanings of much of what it said. Ferry. 1st April to 30th September. 10 am to 8 pm. That was good for me. *Montag?* That was Monday. Today was Monday. *Ruhetag?* No idea. I typed it into Google Translate. "Rest day". Bugger.

There was a bridge about a kilometre to the east of the ferry ramp but there was no path to follow by the water. I had no choice but to retrace my steps past all the industry north of Mannheim. It was not looking any better than it had done 15 minutes earlier. The detour added around 5km of cycling but then I was left searching for the cycle route. Once again I relied upon the handlebar compass and continued cycling north in the hope that at some point I would see a sign for the Rheinradweg. I would, but only after another 5km of hapless searching for signs. At least I had cycled through the centre of a small town and been able to indulge in a small feast of a sandwich and a cake. *Was I really that hungry or was it comfort food?*

The final 40km of the day were comparatively straightforward but not devoid of challenge. The wind continued to be a force to be reckoned with, especially when the cycle path adopted a position on the elevated flood bank of the river. At least it was chronic. The slabs of concrete that formed much of the surface were somewhat more testing. The cycling equivalent of Chinese water torture. Unlike continuous tarmac or gravel, the slabs of concrete had been laid in sections of around 5 metres. The gaps between the slabs resulted in a short, sharp jolt of the bike. It was indeed tortuous and if they are looking to update their methods, the Chinese really should pay a visit to the Rhine.

Escape came in the form of Camping Rheinblick near Gernsheim, a curious establishment that had been all but abandoned by its clientele of weekend caravaners. They had presumably all returned home after spending a few days by the Rhine. Their caravans remained but none were occupied. I happened to arrive at the same time as a young French couple. We were not so much checked in as processed by the disgruntled chap who was in charge. More cyclists arrived and we spent an amiable evening comparing notes as we cooked food under the roof of an open-air shed set aside for our use.

Shortly before heading back to the tent I recorded my thoughts for the podcast and there was an important update regarding the train situation.

"I'm continuing to make good progress. Today was 110km although it would have been just 100km if it had not been for the non-functioning ferry. Am I on course for getting to Rotterdam by the 3rd? I'm not sure. I'd like to think another two days of cycling would get me to Cologne. At Cologne, I'm going to take the train for 100km and that will leave me with three days of cycling - Thursday, Friday, Saturday - to get to Rotterdam. It's still pretty touch-and-go as to whether I'll do it. But I'll keep trying."

Day Fifty-Nine: Gernsheim to Braubach (135km)
Tuesday 30th August

The three days of cycling since Basel had not been a highlight of the trip. Of the 50 days spent cycling, all three would have easily taken up places in the bottom ten of the rankings. The Rhine as far as Schaffhausen had been wonderful: far more interesting and diverse than I might have imagined. Between Basel and Mainz, the Rhine meandered across a wide plain rarely narrower than 30 kilometres wide. Its principal attraction was never going to be the geography of the land that surrounded it.

Mercifully, things were about to change, courtesy of the Rheinisches Schiefergebirge or Rhine Massif, an upland area through which the river had cut a deep channel creating the Mittelrhein or Middle Rhine. This is the section of the Rhine Valley made famous by the postcards: a narrow steep-sided valley often smothered in vines and home to numerous hillside castles. Indeed such is the cultural importance of the area, since 2002 the section from Bingen to Koblenz has been listed as a World Heritage Site:

> "The 65km stretch of the Middle Rhine Valley, with its castles, historic towns and vineyards, graphically illustrates the long history of human involvement with a dramatic and varied natural landscape. It is intimately associated with history and legend and for centuries has exercised a powerful influence on writers, artists and composers."[73]

It certainly had a powerful positive influence on this particular writer who would later in the day rate the cycle from Gernsheim to Braubach as one of the most rewarding of his entire continental journey. But let us not get ahead of ourselves. Back to the almost deserted campsite beside the Rhine.

There was something autumnal about the early morning. Not altogether surprising: the start of September was now fewer than 48 hours away. The air was cooler, the sunshine slightly hazier as it rose gradually through a thin veil of wispy clouds and the wind was blowing earlier than it had done on previous days. On higher stretches of the Rhine, I usually had to wait until the afternoon for the gusts to build up sufficient strength to be noticeable, but not today. Before setting off I wrapped up. It was the first time I could remember doing so. On previous mornings I had occasionally

---

[73] whc.unesco.org

donned my jacket as a pre-emptive measure against the rain if I suspected it might fall, but I had no recollection of worrying about the cold.

I would not enter the Rhine Gorge until later in the day. Bingen was still some 70km further along the river. After heading north in the direction of Mainz and Wiesbaden, the river took a turn to the west as it flowed along the southern flank of the Rhine Massif for around 30km. Only at Bingen did it see fit to throw a left hook and punch a channel into the rock to regain its northwards flow.

As a result, the geography would only get interesting again once I had passed between Mainz on the left bank and Wiesbaden on the right bank. The EuroVelo 15 was maintaining its dual-path approach: one on each bank of the river and, as I had camped on the right bank overnight, I saw no reason to move over to the left. In any case, outside of the big urban areas, options for doing so were limited. Had the ViaRhôna also adopted such a dual-path approach, it would rarely have been an issue transferring from one side of the Rhône to the other such was the frequency of the bridges. Here in Germany on the Rhine, it was altogether different. Bridges were often few and far between, although river ferries were an increasingly common sight. However, unless you just happened to be lucky, taking one of the ferries did usually result in an enforced halt to proceedings. For a man on a mission to beat a fast-approaching deadline, that could be frustrating.

I paused briefly for breakfast at a bakery in Stockstadt am Rhein, a small town which was no longer on the Rhine thanks to canalisation work. I was delighted to discover that the cycle route now seemed to be devoid of the horrible concrete slabs that had blighted much of the previous afternoon. As the path followed the course of the severely emaciated meander of the old Rhine, it did so along wooded paths, quiet roads and at one point over some comically bone-shaking cobbles… but no slabs of concrete. I was not quite ready for that torture again.

The land enclosed within the former Rhine meander had been designated as a nature reserve back in the 1950s and it was very much a taste of things to come throughout the morning. Although the reserve was soon behind me, my cycle took me through the open countryside beside the river on a thoroughly invigorating ride. For much of the time, the route positioned itself on top of the long flood protection barriers and with such an elevated position I was afforded far-reaching views over the river to my left and great swathes of Rhineland to my right. It did appear that this was the secret to enjoying a journey through a flat, featureless landscape. Perhaps it should be a long-term project for the cycle route north of Basel. Rise above it, literally.

Neither Mainz - on the opposite side of the river - nor Wiesbaden - on my side of the river - seemed to have been blighted by the industrial sprawl that had welcomed me to Mannheim. My direction of travel was adjusting from predominantly northward to predominantly westward along the long gentle bend of the Rhine between the two cities. I had now hit the southern flank of the Rhine Massif. The view to my right contrasted sharply with what I could see to my left. Looking south it was no different to what I had been witnessing for days. To the north, however, there was now a gently rising hill, much of it covered in vines or dense woodland. There was a sprinkling of small farming settlements and the occasional tower of a church. Nothing anywhere near as dramatic as what I had discovered in Heidiland the previous week but most definitely a nod in the direction of what was to come once I entered the confines of the Middle Rhine after Bingen.

About 10km before Bingen, the Rhine Cycle Routes joined. Or, rather, the one that I was following on the right bank of the river stopped and I was obliged to cross the river. Fortunately, there was a ferry to take me to the left bank and the wait was not long: just ten minutes for a ten-minute crossing on another push-me-pull-me boat.

Within the hour I was approaching Bingen and getting lost. The signs for the cycle route appeared to have dried up. They were not alone. Just as on the previous day, I had struggled to find anywhere to replenish my stocks of water. I was lost and I was very thirsty. I must have given every impression of being in a state of distress as I heard a female voice. She sounded concerned.

"*Geht es dir gut?*" the woman asked.

"*Entschuldigung. Ich spreche kein Deutsch,*" I replied using one of the few expressions I did know. I have long thought the use of such phrases might confuse so I tried to say it without a hint of a German accent. The woman was not confused.

"Sorry. Are you OK?"

"Yes, I'm just a bit lost and thirsty," I explained.

Much to my delight, I seemed to have stumbled upon the Mother Teresa of the Middle Rhine as she quickly took me under her wing to rescue me from my plight. We were standing in front of a modern one-storey wooden-clad building. Its appearance suggested its function was something environmental and indeed it was. The local branch of NABU, the Nature and Biodiversity Conservation Union. She was a volunteer and was in the middle of doing some work in the garden.

"We are here to protect wildlife between Mainz and Bingen," she explained. "This is our new building. It opened in February and is next to a nature reserve just over there," she added, pointing in the direction of the Rhine.

"Does your mission extend to helping humans who have no water?"

She smiled and went off to find a tap before returning and sending me off in the correct direction.

It was one of those brief encounters which made me glad to be alive and be living in a world where, despite screaming headlines to the contrary, people generally rubbed along with each other just fine.

My error had been in missing a sign that would have taken me around the perimeter of the nature reserve that the woman helped protect. Ironically now I knew it was a nature reserve I might have appreciated it even more but it would remain unexplored by me as I headed off on a much more direct route towards Bingen.

After cycling beside a long modern housing development that had been constructed on the bank of the river at Bingen and which was blocking me from seeing so much as a drop of water in the river, I was suddenly presented with a memorable view. It was at this point that the Rhine had thrown its left hook, punched through the massif and continued its journey north. The river itself took an abrupt turn but the steep-sided hill on the opposite bank prevented me from seeing much beyond the corner. A point of strategic military importance, the ruins of the 13th-century Ehrensfels Castle took up a prominent position looking down upon the river and marked the southernmost point of the World Heritage Site. As I cycled around the corner I passed the sign for Rhine kilometre 531. There remained precisely 500km of the river to cycle.

It was 3 pm and I had travelled just over 80km. I had identified a campsite at Braubach called Green Camping am Rhein. It was perhaps 50km further along the river but according to the recorded message that I had listened to - twice - when I had attempted to call the site, the reception closed at 6 pm. Three hours to cycle 50km. That seemed eminently doable. I set off.

Lots of things were working in my favour, not least the valley itself. I had suddenly moved from an open plain into a narrow gorge. It was the equivalent of sticking go-faster stripes on your Ford Capri and attaching a spoiler on the boot. It had no physical effect whatsoever but somehow it was an environment that encouraged fast movement in one direction. Trains were whizzing past my left shoulder on my side of the river and there were more on the opposite bank doing the same thing. Although the path was segregated for almost all of the 50km, there was a constant rush of cars pacing my speed. I had no chance of beating the trains or the cars but the barges and cruise ships on the river? I gave it my best shot but then again they did have the current on their side. When it came to speed it was only my fellow cyclists who were at risk of being caught, aside from the eBikers of course. With its twists and turns, the gorge was never visible for more than a few hundred metres ahead of me so there was no risk of getting disheartened by a seemingly unattainable feature on the horizon as objectives were reached after only a few minutes. Added to all this I had no route finding to worry about. Unless I fancied climbing the hill (and I did not), there were only two options to choose from: straight ahead or turn around. There were pretty castles to admire - some ruined, some resembling five-star hotels - and vineyards galore. The sun was shining (those extra layers of the morning had long since been shed) and to top everything, the wind had changed direction. Even the cyclist's nemesis was willing me on.

Cycle touring has never been - and never will be - about travelling great distances in as short a time as possible. I will leave that to the ultra-endurance athletes. In 2015 it took me 96 days of cycling to pedal from Europe's most southerly point at Tarifa in Spain to its most northerly point at Nordkapp in Norway. The world record for that journey stands at 16 days and 21 minutes.[74] But on occasions, there is joy in pushing yourself, in striving to get somewhere by a certain time in order to do a certain thing. For me, it was securing my accommodation for the night. It might have been a curry house or a pub calling final orders. Irrespective, it did add an element of fun and from time to time, I had no problem with entering a race with no competitors.

By the time I was approaching Boppard, I had cycled over 120km. It was just before 5.30 pm. The Rhine was about to enter its biggest meander yet in the gorge. I could not see around the corner into the centre of Boppard but I had noticed from OpenStreetMap that it was at this point where the EuroVelo 15 re-adopted its dual-path approach. One route followed the left bank (where I was cycling) and one followed the right bank (where the campsite was located some 15km around the bend).

I never questioned that there might not be a bridge but, upon arrival in Boppard, I was somewhat alarmed to discover that, err... there was no bridge. Retrospective logic started to berate me. *There had not been a bridge over the Rhine since Wiesbaden. Why would I assume that there would be one in Boppard?* There was, however, a ferry. I dearly hoped it was still running (and that Tuesday was not the crew's rest day). The next bridge was not until Koblenz, a further 20km along the river.

---

[74] Albeit in the opposite direction: "The fastest cycle across Europe (North Cape to Tarifa) - individual is 16 days 20 hr 59 min and was achieved by Ian Walker from 21 June to 8 July 2019." (GuinnessWorldRecords.com) You can listen to Ian talking about his record in episode 027 of The Cycling Europe Podcast.

Fortunately, the ferry was waiting beside the quay on my side of the river. There were cars on board and within a matter of minutes, I had joined them. But the ferry seemed in no hurry to move off. I waited. Finally, 15 minutes after boarding we did indeed set sail. I disembarked on the right bank of the Rhine at 5.40 pm. I had 20 minutes to cycle 10km.

My average speed in the morning had been around 18km/hr. Since entering the gorge this had notched up to around 22km/hr. During the final 10km, I was pushing 25km/hr. Did I make the campsite for 6 pm?

No.

Panting, I climbed the flight of steps to the elevated reception area at Green Camping am Rhein. It was 6.10 pm. A couple of people were sitting on the sofas outside smoking and drinking a beer. I tried the door of the reception. It was open.

"I thought you closed at 6 pm?" I asked.

"Sometimes we do," replied the young woman. She gave no impression that she was keen to clock off for the evening.

It had been the longest cycling day yet. 135km. Somewhat relieved, I went to erect the tent. Although I was not aware of it at the time, it would be my 42nd and final erection of the trip. Who said that cycle touring did not have sex appeal?

Day Sixty: Braubach to Cologne (121km)
Wednesday 31st August

I had been offered a pitch in the "wild camping" area of Green Camping am Rhein and had gladly accepted. As previous mentioned, my wild camping credentials had never been good so perhaps this was a way of nudging myself in the direction of embracing a less formal way of camping. It turned out that "wild camping" was simply a euphemism for exploiting a section of the campsite that the owners did not feel obliged to maintain. More scruffy than wild. Keen to bag a pitch by the river I had ended up erecting the tent between a motorhome and a large slab of concrete that was probably an integral part of the local sewage system. I tried not to overthink the situation and escaped to a nearby restaurant for a large pizza.

My night of sleep in the tent had been sporadic, to say the least. With trains continuing to operate on both sides of the Rhine and large barges and cruise ships chugging up and down the river itself, it was rarely quiet. The more naturally soporific sound of rain on the tent only went so far in masking the less pleasant sounds of the Rhine transport network. When I emerged from the tent in the morning, I comforted myself in the knowledge that I would be spending the next night in a quiet bedroom and on a comfortable bed.

During the 2015 96-day cycle across the continent when I narrowly missed out on having my own entry in the Guinness Book of Records (by a mere 79 days…), I passed through Cologne. I had cycled into the city from the west and over the next two days, I would follow the Rhine north as far as Duisburg before branching away from the river in the direction of Münster, Bremen and eventually Hamburg. That experience would impact upon the current cycle in two ways. Firstly, I had every incentive to start my final train journey in Cologne to avoid repeating the cycle to Duisburg. Secondly, I had met up with a friend, Janina, in Cologne in 2015 but she was not able to spend much time with me as she had bought tickets for an Oli Murs concert that evening. Seven years later, Oli had clearly seen my plans and had done the decent thing of avoiding being anywhere near Cologne on the evening of August 31st. Janina could not use the same excuse. Indeed she had noticed that I would be passing through her home city again and had invited me to stay with her family. A quiet bedroom and comfortable bed awaited if, that is, I could cycle as far as Cologne by the end of the day.

Since leaving Basel, my plan to increase significantly the number of kilometres cycled each day was working. In the previous four days, I had averaged 122km per day and pushed my daily average for the entire trip from 81 to 84km. Shortly before arriving at the campsite in Braubach, I had cycled past Rhine kilometre sign 579. Another 452km remained before the river emptied out into the sea at the Hook of Holland. As the cycle route deviated to some extent from the river, this might mean cycling another 500km before I arrived at my destination. According to the Cicerone guidebook, I would need to cycle 470km from Koblenz to the Hook of Holland. As I was setting off from about 15km south of Koblenz this seemed to confirm that 500km was a reasonable estimate of what remained. If my train journey from Cologne the following morning could be as close as possible to 100km, this would reduce the cycling down to around 400km and I had four days in which to accomplish the feat. At the very minimum, I still needed to cycle 100km each day for the rest of the trip so I could not sit back and relax just yet.

It was still raining when I left the campsite and made my way under the railway line to access the centre of Braubach and, crucially, my breakfast. However, after an hour or so I had arrived in Koblenz and although I was still cycling under grey skies, it had at least dried up. I could have continued to cycle on the right bank of the river but chose to cross the bridge in Koblenz to pick up the path on the left bank. I remained there for the rest of the day.

By crossing the bridge I would cycle through the middle of the city. Koblenz had been one of the stops during my 2019 river cruise so I had no plans to linger. Nevertheless, it was an important point on the Rhine as it was here where (as the tourist office phrased it) "Father Rhine meets Mother Mosel" after the latter's 700-km journey though France and Luxembourg. The Deutsches Eck (German Corner) marked the point where the two rivers met. Throughout the 20th century, the Deutsches Eck has been a focus for German unification and then reunification. Kaiser Wilhelm I was not only the first Wilhelm to rule Germany, he was the first kaiser to do so following the founding of the German Empire in 1871. After his death in 1888, his grandson Wilhelm II (who became the Kaiser only 99 days after his grandfather had died following the short-lived reign of his father Frederick III) commissioned a 14-metre-high statue of his namesake on a horse and placed it on a 30-metre-high plinth at the Deutsches Eck. It is still standing today. Or so you would think. In 1945 the statue was all but destroyed by American artillery and the plinth remained empty until 1993 when, following the reunification of Germany and somewhat controversially, a replacement statue of Wilhelm I was installed.

Quite what he would have made of the preparations for an open-air rock concert beneath his stirrups and his horse on August 31st 2022 is not known. The upshot for me was that my access to the corner was blocked and I was not able to stand and appreciate the full glory of His Imperial Majesty and his horse. Just their rear ends.

To continue my journey along the Rhine I needed to cross a bridge over the Mosel. During my 2019 cruise, the boat had ventured along the Mosel as far as Bernkastel-Kues before turning around and heading back towards the Rhine at Koblenz. Looking down from the bridge in 2022 it was difficult to understand how many boats could have possibly made the journey such was the level of the water. The partially dried up riverbed was a reflection of the continuing widespread drought that I had been experiencing all summer. A report published by the Global Drought Observatory in mid-August 2022 stated that the Rhine was suffering from "very rare to extremely rare low flow levels" not seen for 500 years. As a consequence "the River Rhine discharge has been shrinking, causing multi-sectorial impacts... on water distribution systems, dike stability and commercial navigation". Although conditions did appear to be easing a little with the recent rain showers, I suspected it would be a good few months before things returned to anything like normal. If ever there was a year to be riding a bicycle beside the Rhine rather than living it up on a river cruise, 2022 seemed to be it.

Koblenz marked the northern end of the World Heritage Site so, as I continued north, it came as no surprise that the Rhine Valley slowly began to slide back down the scale of the spectacular. The topography of the flat plain was thankfully never reinstated to its full pre-Mainz state but I was again left bereft of geographical drama. That said, it was not a bad ride to the next major point on the map, Bonn. Some of the surfaces were uncomfortable but not as tortuous as the great slabs of concrete had been earlier in the week. Many of the paths were made up of interlocking bricks which could be quite bumpy at times. There was even a permanent warning sign alerting me to the fact that the path was in a poor state of repair. I did wonder if the time and money would have been better allocated to relaying the bricks rather than apologising for them.

Close to Remagen there was a six-kilometre deviation inland replacing a one-kilometre section of the cycle path beside the river. A wooden bridge had been washed away by flooding (which seemed ironic bearing in mind the level of the water back in Koblenz) and had yet to be replaced.[75] It did, however, allow me to spend a few minutes conversing with perhaps Germany's most delightfully boring man. He was also cycling and he

---

[75] If you are reading this as a form of travel guide (more fool you!) you will be delighted to discover that a replacement bridge has now been lifted into place.

explained the tedium of his life in great detail but there was something about the man that made me feel immediate warmth towards him. I thoroughly enjoyed our chat. Perhaps he also had a book in him and perhaps I sympathised with his desire to recount in excessive detail the daily trials and tribulations of a 21st-century cyclist.

One of the joys of cycling anywhere is that you are presented with a cross-section of the place through which you are travelling. I remember discovering this obvious but little-appreciated fact when I had the opportunity of cycling the length of Italy in 2010. I had previously visited the country on several occasions having flown to Milan and Rome and having travelled by train to Puglia in the south. However, during that first trans-continental cycle I was required to experience all the bits in between. The dirty suburbs of Milan and Rome, the flat Po Valley, the not-insignificant Apennine mountains and the great tracts of sun-beaten farmland of Campania. It was not just a case of travelling through these areas: I was experiencing them in a way that would have been impossible not just by plane but even by train or in a car. Thanks to my slow speed and lack of separation, I was afforded the time and space to see, smell, feel and - crucially - begin to understand what the country was all about. Looking back on that experience, Italy now means something to me that is perhaps very different - and arguably more accurate - than what it means to many others. I have similar recollections of travelling through Greece, Spain, France, Norway… in fact all of the countries across which I have had the pleasure to travel by bicycle.

But back to the Rhine. My journey from Koblenz to Bonn was one of those occasions when I was able to pull away the veil and see the river for what it really was. There were no picturesque towns or castles or vineyards or spectacular views. Just ordinary places full of ordinary people like me, you and my new boring German friend. Run-down places, abandoned hotels, vacant plots of land. It was the margarine that made the rest of the sandwich stick together and be so delicious. You would never choose to stick your finger into a tub of Flora and feast upon its delights, but when would you ever consider not putting it on your bread? And if you are lucky, the margarine sometimes turns out to be butter and worth appreciating on its own merits. That, my friends, is the joy of long-distance travel by bicycle.

Affluent Bonn, the former capital of the Federal Republic of Germany came and went. It may well have been more butter than margarine but I had neither the time nor the inclination to explore. A few kilometres later, after consulting my map carefully, I branched away from the cycle route in order to find Janina's home in the suburbs of Cologne. Deprived of the guidance of the signs for the EuroVelo 15 I set my destination as Hürth - 6km south-west of the city centre - and followed Google's instructions instead.

When she had messaged me earlier in the day she had suggested I aim to arrive at 6 pm as that was when they were planning to eat. It was eerily reminiscent of the previous day when I had been racing to ensure I was not locked out of the campsite. There was no risk of me being locked out of Janina's house but neither did I want to miss out on a good family meal. I doubted if her two young children would have appreciated having to wait.

The evening was a good one. Not only was it wonderful to catch up with Janina and her husband Henning - both teachers in local secondary schools - but also meet their children for the first time. They were quite bemused by a bloke turning up at their house on a bicycle and not speaking a word of their language (the children that is, not their parents). What four- or two-year-olds would not be? The bedroom (the living room…) was indeed quiet and the bed (the sofa…) was indeed comfortable. Crucially, with local knowledge on hand, I was able to reserve my final train journey of the trip. In the morning I would cycle into the centre of Cologne and take a train for Xanten, 90km to the north and only 30km from the Dutch border. Just 72 hours of the Grand Tour remained.

Day Sixty-One: Cologne to Arnhem (16km + Train + 70km) Thursday 1st September

"Today has been a real joy. Everything came together in a celestial meeting of cycle touring, travelling, people, places, weather... I loved it. Even the trains joined the party after an initial reluctance to play ball at Cologne station this morning. With only 48 hours of this continental odyssey remaining, I could not wish to have spent a more enjoyable day in the saddle. Even that pesky wind came to the party and blew me along the banks of the Rhine willing me to get to Rotterdam on time. Fabulous."

Praise indeed. That was how I started my evening write-up of the events of day 61. It was a day that would see me make significant progress towards meeting the 8 pm deadline of the ferry slipping away from the dock at the port of Rotterdam on Saturday evening. As the crow flew, Arnhem was roughly 140km from Cologne and the ferry terminal roughly 140km from Arnhem. But it was never going to be quite so simply as the flight plan of that now-knackered crow.

The Germans do breakfast well. Meat and cheese are rarely on the morning menu in British homes (unless you are one of the dwindling few who start the day with a full English). Not so in Germany and not so in Janina's house where everyone tucked into a hearty meal of salami and cheese. Not a bowl of low-fat, high-fibre cereal in sight. With a full stomach the cycling day did, however, start with an admonishment from Leona, Janina's four-year-old daughter. Although it required translation, she was insistent that I put on my cycling helmet and I obliged, for a few minutes at least. (She clearly has a future in the German health and safety industry.) As they all prepared to head off to their respective schools or childcare facilities I said my goodbyes and cycled off in the direction of the centre of Cologne and its vast main railway station.

Oh to be a cycling commuter in Germany! Almost every metre of the 16-kilometre ride from Janina's house to the square beside the station was on high-quality segregated cycle path. The rising sun under-lit the mackerel sky above me. I was a meerkat on a bicycle, slowly warming in the first hour of the day in preparation for another arduous day of adventure. And what a location in which to be warmed. Meteorological autumn had now arrived and this was evidenced in the foliage of the trees and bushes that lined my route, tinged as they were with pretty orange decay, a beauty only accentuated by the golden rays flooding across the farmers' fields and onto my path.

It would require a British train company to puncture my bubble of Teutonic transcendental travel.

A heavy touring bicycle laden with four panniers and a tent is not always compatible with a busy mainline station. Most of the previous nine train journeys I had taken since leaving Rotterdam in early July had been from and to much quieter stations. On most occasions I had been one of a small number of people boarding or alighting from the train and usually the only cyclist. I had managed to avoid busy commuter trains and the stations had usually offered step-free access to the platform either via a lift or a ramp. Basel had been the only exception. Köln Hauptbahnhof (to give it its full German title) was in a league of its own. A vast monument to the logistical infrastructure of the Federal Republic, its footprint was several times that of its neighbour, the mighty Cologne Cathedral. What it lacked in height compared to the Kölner Dom just a few metres away, it made up for in length with its 11 parallel platforms dispatching hundreds of thousands of travellers across Nordrhein-Westfalen and beyond on a daily basis. It seemed that most of them had decided to congregate on platform 4B at 8.30 on the morning of September 1st.

Xanten, my destination, was a terminus station on the rural RB 31 line from Duisburg. That, I suspected, would be reminiscent of the previous train journeys that I had made. Getting to Duisburg was proving more problematic. The trains were being run by National Express, the British coach company. It is difficult to fathom why any bureaucrat in the German department for transport might have thought it a good idea to hand out a contract to a British company when it came to transport, but they had. Perhaps they had suffered from a minor stroke whilst overdoing it on the salami and cheese that morning before work. The train I had my eye on was cancelled. No problems: I would catch the next one. Alas by the time it arrived, the number of people standing on the platform had more than doubled. They included a good number who were also travelling with a bicycle. I stood aside and let the throng cram into the National-Express-liveried coaches. And so it continued...

Over the next 90 minutes, National Express trains that were not cancelled arrived, filled to the brim with commuters and departed, without me. Had it ever been a good idea to take a train from one of Germany's busiest stations?

Then something strange happened. The crowds suddenly evaporated, a train arrived and I wheeled Wanda on board with barely another person - or bicycle - in the carriage. It was almost as if my exasperation was being monitored by CCTV and the managers of Cologne station had taken pity on me, closed the gates to platform 4B and provided me with my own personal train to Duisburg. Perhaps they had. How kind.

There were more issues to come after I changed trains. In France, bicycles needed to be booked onto the TER trains but there was no charge. Here in Germany there was a charge but for the train to Xanten I had not bought a ticket for the bike.

"I'm sorry but you'll have to get off the train at the next station and buy one from the ticket office," explained the train conductor in impeccable English. Perhaps it was a well-worn phrase in his lexicon.

Time was an issue. Most of the morning had been wiped out by the delay in Cologne and the train I was now on was not due to arrive at its destination until midday. The frequency of the trains to Xanten was only one per hour and I had already had a lengthy wait in Duisburg. My heart sank at the prospect of yet more delays. The long cycle to Arnhem had yet to begin.

I had been using the phone apps for the SNCF, SBB (in Switzerland) and Deutsche Bahn very successfully throughout the trip. English was not just an option, it was the language in which the apps had been automatically downloaded so there were no translation issues. However, I had failed to find the option for booking a bike on a train in Germany via the app. I managed to get away with it when travelling on the Deutsche Bahn train from Schaffhausen to Basel as my ticket had not been checked. En route to Xanten, I was now in a frantic race with time to find the option and buy a ticket for Wanda whilst still on the train.

It was a cliff-hanger moment. The arrival at the next station had been announced, the train was beginning to slow… and the conductor was walking back in my direction. 60 minutes were at stake. I had about a minute remaining - if that - to buy a bike ticket online.

As the train pulled out of the station I held up the screen of my phone in triumph. The conductor nodded.

"*Gut.*"

I had, somehow, managed to find the bike option and buy the ticket. 60 minutes had been saved.

In theory, that was it for the trains. I had used the last of my self-imposed allocation of ten journeys. To take another train before I arrived back home in the UK would be a failure, but it could not be discounted as a possible necessity.

Until the previous evening I had never heard of Xanten yet it was a town famous across Germany for its Roman ruins. When we think of the Romans we think of York, Hadrian's Wall, the Mediterranean fringe and, of course, Rome. The lower stretches of the Rhine are not at the forefront of our thoughts but logic would dictate that the Romans had indeed made their way along the river once they had managed to cross the Alps. The Roman settlement of Colonia Claudia Ara Agrippinensium would eventually come to be known as simply Cologne. Indeed in 2021 UNESCO designated 400km of the lower Rhine valley north of the Rhenish Massif as another World Heritage Site. This one went by the name of "Frontiers of the Roman Empire - The Lower German Limes". It is a title that perhaps needs some work.

It appeared that most of the Roman ruins of Xanten were contained within a square plot of land north-west of the town centre. I cycled beside a high wall behind which the archaeological jewels were located but chose not to explore further. I could only hope that any restoration work that I could not see was of greater quality than the wall that I could. Built in the style of a Roman fort complete with ramparts and gatehouse towers, it was a little too unblemished to be convincingly Roman even if it was an accurate representation of what might have been built 2,000 years ago. We expect our Roman ruins to be at least a little tumbledown. Alas, it was all a bit too *Carry On Cleo* for its own good.

I had managed to pick up the route of the EuroVelo 15 in the centre of Xanten. The dual path approach - one on either side of the Rhine - would continue as far as the Dutch border before reverting to a single path for the remainder of my journey to the Hook of Holland. However, as far as the border I would stay on the left bank which was increasingly to the south of the river as the Rhine turned its final corner to head west in the direction of the North Sea.

Having cycled for a few kilometres beside a couple of lakes under the shade of trees, there remained 40km of cycling to get me to the Netherlands. It was mainly on either slightly elevated and exposed paths on the ridge of flood protection banks or beside more shady country roads where the trees again offered an escape from the heat of the sun. Such was the topography, such were the buildings and such were the cycling facilities, if I had not known that I was still cycling in Germany, I would have assumed that I had already crossed the border. It was now that I was feeling the full force of the assisting wind as it pushed me along the banks of the river. I paused sporadically to take a photo, read a sign or simply admire the view. It was a cycle-touring utopia and my mood was as high as it had been throughout my long Grand Tour of Europe. The only blot on the landscape was that at some point in the next two or three days, it would all be over. *Would they really miss me if I did not turn up at school on Monday?* The thought of continuing north along the coast of the Netherlands fleetingly passed through my mind before the harsh realities of having to pay bills threw a bucket load of water onto the kindling of my dreams.

The final landmark in Germany was a bright red suspension bridge that slung its platform low across the Rhine. It had still been the case that there were very few bridges spanning the river compared to the number that I had seen whilst cycling the length of the Rhône. The Germans excelled in many areas but perhaps building bridges was simply not their thing. At least with their final effort on the Rhine, they had done a fine job. The bridge at Emmerich seemed to fit into its landscape perfectly and only served to improve the view from the saddle.

Staying south of the river I would never cross the distinctive red bridge and within a matter of minutes, I was approaching my final border crossing on continental soil. On day three of the cycle I had cycled across the border from the Netherlands into Belgium over a cattle grid. It seemed fitting that as I cycled back into the Netherlands on day 61 I was doing so - again - over a cattle grid. *Too many Friesian cows?*[76] The first of my seven countries had returned to guide me home and I would be doing so along the Rijnfietsroute, the Dutch section of the EuroVelo 15 that I had first encountered, for a few short kilometres, on day one of the cycle.

Within minutes of crossing the border, the signs for the Rhine Cycle Route pointed me in the direction of a ramp leading down to the water. At this point of its journey, the river was increasingly wide as it slowed to pass over the flatlands of the Netherlands and a 300-metre swim to the northern bank did not seem to be an option. Fortunately for me and the dozen or so other people queuing on the ramp, a small ferry was approaching at speed. The flow of the water may only have been slight but the wind was proving more of a challenge for the little blue and white boat. As it approached the bank it did so at an increasingly unnatural angle. The skipper had done this job a thousand times before as the ferry and the ramp kissed gently with centimetre precision and the wide metal gangplank was lowered into position with a less-than-romantic clank. A stream of pedestrians and cyclists disembarked and the gathering crowd replaced them. Within 5 minutes we were disembarking and I was en route to Arnhem.

My plan had always been to stay in Arnhem overnight, preferably at a local campsite not too far from the centre but there was not good news when I called ahead. It was full. The reason why would become apparent later in

---

[76] Since you ask... According to the Dutch Centraal Bureau voor de Statistiek, there are 3.8 million heads of cattle in the Netherlands of which around a half are dairy cattle. Far outnumbered by pigs. There are around 11 million of them. Perhaps all the 'cattle' grids had been installed to keep the errant pigs in check.

the day. After so many nights either in the tent or in free accommodation courtesy of Warmshowers (as well as at Janina's in Cologne), my budget could probably stretch to another night in a hotel. I did not resist the temptation of whipping out my phone and booking into the city centre luxury of the Holiday Inn. It would see my daily average spend on accommodation nudge upwards from €21.70 to €23.01 but at this late stage of proceedings, it was a price worth paying.

Due to its flat terrain, the rivers of the Netherlands are complicated and I do not claim to have all the answers. However, from what I could work out, shortly after the ferry, the river split in two with the wider Waal eventually meeting the sea to the south of Rotterdam. The more dainty Rhine continued as the Nederrijn until it became the Lek at Wijk bij Duurstede. Just to the east of Rotterdam the Lek in turn became the Nieuwe Maas which to the west of the city became the Nieuwe Waterweg. It was next to this latter river where I had stood beside the wonky sign at the Hook of Holland on July 3rd and where the Rhine Cycle Route officially started/ended. As to where the River Rhine went, I had no idea.

Cycling beside the Rhine in the Netherlands was remarkably similar to cycling beside the Rhine in Germany earlier in the day. However, I was now back in *knooppunten* territory and I reactivated the app I had been using in the first few days of the cycle. At *knooppunt* 63 I could continue to follow the EuroVelo 15, but this involved another short ferry across the river. Instead, I put myself at the mercy of the *knooppunten* network and, more specifically, *knooppunten* 61, 89, 82 (via a bridge over the River IJssel - I told you they were complicated!) before getting lost for a few minutes... then, well, I was never lost of course. This was a city in the Netherlands. Every street had a segregated cycle path and there were enough cycling signs to have your average London cabby driver frothing at the mouth. I had arrived and, after 70km of cycling, was standing beneath the famous bridge which, before it was destroyed in 1944, was *A Bridge Too Far*. Replaced shortly after the end of the war in 1948, it was renamed the John Frostbrug in 1977 in honour of Major-General John Dutton Frost who led the small group of soldiers attempting to defend it from advancing German forces. In the film, he was played by Anthony Hopkins.

Every year on the first Saturday in September, the Airbourne March takes place in remembrance of the Battle of Arnhem in 1944. I had already noticed a large number of distinctive dark red banners hanging from posts and flagpoles outside people's houses. When I arrived at the reception desk of the Holiday Inn, there was a long queue of veterans who had just arrived from Britain. Although not many veterans would have been camping, the event attracted thousands of people of all ages to Arnhem and I suspected it was the reason why the campsite had been full.

I waited patiently in line but it took time as the group of pensioners were checked in. They were in their 70s and 80s so they would not have taken part in the events of 1944 but listening to them talk it was an event that they had attended many times over the years, presumably because of family or army connections. They were sharing rooms but one man seemed particularly concerned:

"Could we have an extra key card for the room as some of us might be out late on the beers," he explained to the smiling young woman behind the desk. Age, it seemed, was not wearying these old soldiers and certainly not stopping them from hitting the late-night bars of Arnhem.

Had I been waiting behind a large group of twenty-somethings on a stag weekend, by the time I arrived to collect my own key card, I may have been somewhat disgruntled. In the circumstances that was not an option and I admired the pensioners for keeping alive a spirit of adventure in their advancing years.

My evening ended outside the Iveau Wijnbar along the pedestrianised street from the hotel. I asked the waitress to recommend a beer and she delivered an 8.5% Dikke Prins Sterk Blond, three times. I opened up the Cicerone Guidebook on my phone to work out the distance that remained to be cycled. Nearly 170km. *Was I celebrating my success somewhat prematurely?*

Day Sixty-Two: Arnhem to Rotterdam (161km)
Friday 2nd September

"It's the biggest annual march in the world," explained Raymond, a policeman and member of a re-enactment group. They were helping to add an element of authenticity to the events that were scheduled to take place on the 3rd. He was standing with a small group of fellow volunteers to the rear of the Airborne Museum at Hartenstein, a few kilometres from the centre of Arnhem. The men were dressed in military uniforms of the 1940s including the maroon berets of the British Parachute Regiment. The group included a small number of women who were wearing civilian clothes of the period. Beside them were a few American army jeeps.

"35,000 people will be walking. It's not just military. It's for everyone."

"Are you expecting many visitors from Britain?" I asked, wondering if the pensioners I had encountered at the hotel the previous evening were the only ones.

"Yes, but not as many as in the past. Because of Brexit, it's very expensive just to come over for the march. Many people came with vintage vehicles on a trailer but now they have to pay extra because they are counted as exports on the way out and imports on the way back."

The irony did not escape me. The European Union, or EEC as it then was, was set up in the years following the Second World War in the hope that it would encourage the fractious nations of the continent to work together rather than fight each other. It had done a remarkable job in achieving that aim to such an extent that it is now inconceivable that Germany would ever invade any of its neighbours again. It helped cement the peace and freedom that the paratroopers who were dropped into Arnhem were fighting for. Britain, alas, had turned its back on those post-war European structures and the whole continent was now a little bit less secure as a result. The continent needed the EU but its founding motives had all too often been drowned out by the ridiculous fallacy of bent bananas and the like. The nonsense of having to export and import your own vehicle to attend a rally aimed at commemorating peace was evidence of those structures fraying at the edges. Let us hope it stops there. My onward route would see me pass several monuments to the fallen. They included a cemetery at Grebbeberg containing the bodies of hundreds of young men - mostly in their late teens and twenties - who had been killed in the vain attempt to repel the German invasion of 1940. The costs of war are high.

The western suburbs of Arnhem were about as leafy as they come. Almost every house was immaculate and most were displaying the same banners commemorating the Airborne events that I had seen on the other side of town the previous afternoon. The streets were litter-free and bustling with people: the roads were pothole-free and respect appeared to be the mantra of the drivers. There were no man-made bumps in the road, no artificially tight chicanes or lurking speed cameras. I could only imagine that it was the norm. The drivers seemed to be driving with an innate sense of wanting to look out for those around them. Perhaps it was in the national psyche that having lost the peace but then regained it at such a heavy cost, the Dutch had collectively - but subconsciously - agreed to maintain the civility of their country at the highest of standards. It was probably also the case that the vast majority of the drivers were also regular cyclists.

Then again, was I being naïve? Perhaps it was just in this pristine corner of the Netherlands where social nirvana flourished. During the first few days of the trip I had cycled along the sparsely populated coastal fringe, but it was far removed from the urban reality of ordinary Dutch folk. It had been an insight into the country but in no way had it been typical or genuinely representative. Yet here I was on probably the penultimate day of my cycle travelling from close to the eastern border with Germany to within a few tens of kilometres of the North Sea. It would be interesting to reflect upon my positive morning impressions when I arrived in Rotterdam later in the day. *Did everyone benefit from a high-quality environment in which to live their lives? Surely even the Netherlands had its fair share of deprivation, no?*

Beyond the western suburbs of Arnhem was an area of dense woodland. That in itself was not surprising. What was surprising was just how hilly it was. After so many days of cycling on the flat, it was a delightful novelty to find myself freewheeling down paths in the forests and trying to use my momentum to carry me part of the way up the next hill. It did not last for long but whilst it did, was good fun. Then, suddenly, I was flung back into suburbia. It was perhaps not quite as well-heeled as its counterpart near Arnhem, but nonetheless pleasant and eminently liveable. The changing environment was being flung in my direction at an alarming rate and I was loving it.

If I stuck to the official route of the EuroVelo 15 my route would initially follow the Nederrijn before taking a sharp left turn via Wijk bij Duurstede across country in the direction of the River Waal. At Gorinchem I would need to take a ferry across the Waal and continue my route on the south side of the river before crossing back to the northern bank on a second ferry to the east of Dordrecht. Finally, I would need to cycle gradually north-west in the direction of Rotterdam via the outskirts of Dordrecht and encounters with the Lek and the Nieuwe Maas. For a country famed for being so cycling-friendly, it appeared to be rather complicated. And it was.

So much of my Grand Tour had involved following disused railway lines, canals, and since leaving the Mediterranean, rivers. I had tried my best to follow the prescribed route but had rarely been concerned if I appeared to have lost it as long as there was evidence of the railway line, canal or river being somewhere in the vicinity. When a cycle path ended, it usually meant that I had to follow a sign to turn left or right and more often than not, I found one.

Here in the Netherlands, it was very different. Due to the rather complicated nature of the river system, I could no longer guarantee that the EuroVelo 15 would follow the river that I could see beside me. What's more, cycle paths rarely ended. They continued, seemingly forever. This was great news for the Dutch and their shopping trips or commutes to work. Not so great for me as I was no longer being prompted to think about where I was going. It could - and did - cause problems.

I had been following the regional LF 4b route since leaving Arnhem and guessed that I might be following it all day as the Rijnfietsroute always appeared on the signs beside the LF 4b. Until it stopped doing so somewhere north of Wijk bij Duurstede. I was having a jolly old time admiring the view from my pothole-free cycle path at the side of the road, waving at passing canoeists on the adjacent irrigation channel and generally having a carefree cycle in the sun. I was also unwittingly cycling further and further away from the EuroVelo 15. I cannot recall what made me stop and turn around but am thankful that I did as otherwise I would have ended up in Utrecht. It would be another 12 kilometres before I re-found the signs for the Rijnfietsroute close to the centre of Wijk bij Duurstede. Cycling in the Netherlands was just too easy.

Aside from its wonderful name, Wijk bij Duurstede ticked every box on the Dutch bingo card. Smart, tidy, car-free, bicycles everywhere... but its crowning glory was to be found just beside the river (the Nederrijn that was about to turn into the Lek). Many places have drive-through restaurants or cafés. A few places even have drive-through shops. *The Japan Times* reports that in Nagano there is even a drive-through funeral home which "allows mourners to pay their respects without getting out of the car". There is, however, only one drive-through windmill, and it is in Wijk bij Duurstede. Alas, you cannot buy a bag of flour as you drive through the building. You cannot order a coffee or even pay your respects to the dead. The Rijn en Lek windmill was built on top of a gate to the town which is why you can now drive - or cycle - through it. I did and paused for coffee in the snack bar next door.

I had now cycled some 70km. It might have been nearer 60 had I been paying more attention to the signs but it was reasonable progress for 2 pm. A ferry took me across the Lek and after crossing the Amsterdam-Rijnkanaal I headed off for a very pleasant mid-afternoon cycle through open countryside, beside rivers and the fringes of small towns. There was absolutely nothing to distract me from the simple enjoyment of a nice ride on the bike. For most of the time I was managing to follow the Rijnfietsroute but, mindful that I needed to be in Rotterdam by the end of the day, on occasions I decided to take a few shortcuts. Perhaps they would compensate for my earlier directional indiscretions.

Approaching the town of Gorinchem I spotted another short-cut. It would be a little longer than the previous ones and would mean not having to take the ferry across the Waal and the ferry to Dordrecht. I would hopefully pick up the EuroVelo 15 again somewhere to the south-east of Rotterdam. My plan was almost scuppered by a police officer who had skipped the charm part of her training. With her hand resting on her gun, she told me, in no uncertain terms, to turn around as her colleagues were dealing with an accident. I initially abandoned the short-cut plan and cycled off to catch the ferry but it did not appear to be operating. A diversion had been put in place but this itself was diverted because of some heavy-duty rebuilding of the riverbank. I reverted to the short-cut plan, cycled past the police officer waving and smiling (she did not reciprocate in either way) and back to a point where I could take a parallel short-cut along a well-maintained farmer's track.

Concerned that I no longer had the security of the signs of the Rijnfietsroute to follow in what was an increasingly urban environment, I switched on Google Maps and fed in my destination: the Holiday Inn in central Rotterdam. The accommodation budget had been blown but it was, after all, my final night on the continent. I had now cycled 120km and it was 5 pm. Google estimated the distance to be 40km and my time of arrival to be 7 pm. Although their paths would cross at some fleeting point in the final two hours of the cycling day, my Google-inspired route and the Rijnfietsroute would never follow the same path. Had this been almost any other place on earth, I might have been concerned. Here in the Netherlands, I was not. As I continued my journey into the centre of the city I was given no reason whatsoever to question my decision to abandon the EuroVelo 15. Every path was smooth, every junction well-designed. Every kerb had been flattened, every incline elongated. Every bridge accessible, every underpass swept clean. I was even shielded from the noise of the motorway for the 25km where my cycle path ran adjacent to the roar of cars. Cleverly designed concave concrete walls had been erected beside the motorway to bounce the sound back to where it was coming from. At one point two motorways had been built side-by-side and I was cycling just a few metres away from 16 lanes of traffic. However, the volume of noise was only slightly higher than what I had experienced on the country roads earlier in the day. Remarkable!

With the motorway to my right, on my left were the housing estates and tower blocks of the inner suburbs of Rotterdam. This was different in so many ways from those leafy suburbs of Arnhem through which I had salivated earlier in the day. Yet in many ways, they were so similar. The houses were immaculately maintained, the streets clear of refuse, the tower blocks almost inviting. There was greenery everywhere you looked. It was a world away from many of the inner cities of Britain where poor quality housing was the norm, fly-tipping commonplace and high-rise buildings often foreboding places to avoid.

It had been the longest cycling day of my jaunt around Europe. It had, however, provided me with an excellent opportunity to judge the country from east to west in a way that had been impossible during my coastal cycle at the start of the journey in early July. I had seen the Netherlands, warts and all. Yet there were so few warts to see. No country is perfect and it would be naïve to assume that those living in the Netherlands do not have their fair share of problems with which to contend. On a visual level, however, I had found a country that had clearly invested in the wellbeing of its people like few other countries in Europe. The delightful suburbs of Arnhem had not been developed at the expense of the less affluent neighbourhoods of central Rotterdam. The quiet country towns and villages through which I had cycled had not been left to drift into terminal decay. The governments of this country - national, regional, local - had invested and had clearly kept investing over many decades. Rome was not built in a day and clearly the Netherlands had not been either. It had not even been built over the term of one parliament or the span of one politician's career. There was something endemic in this country that had resulted in decisions being taken for the long-term benefit of all, not just for those who had the power, money or influence (or those who voted for them). It was a refreshing, uplifting place to have cycled through and one from which many other countries could, indeed should, take note.

Cycling into the centre of the city brought with it yet more joy. The sun was well on its way to the horizon and the urban landscape was just beginning to benefit from the golden-hour light. After crossing the Erasmusbrug, an elegant suspension bridge with cables fanning out from its single white supporting pillar, I was only a matter of minutes away from my hotel. But then I spotted something familiar next to a building that, via large letters on its brick façade, declared itself to be the Maritime Museum. A lighthouse. Modest in size with a bright red tower and a white metal-framed cage for its lamp. This was the lighthouse that had been replicated on a slightly smaller scale and transported close to the source of the Rhine at the Oberalp Pass in Switzerland. I had told myself to look out for it when I arrived at the other end of the river. It had not taken much finding. I cycled up to the lighthouse and touched its tower. It was a sign that my journey was nearly complete, but not just beside the Rhine. The entire Grand Tour was on the cusp of returning to where it had all started at The Hook of Holland.

Day Sixty-Three: Rotterdam to The Hook Of Holland (39km) Saturday 3rd September

"The Rhine combines every quality a river can exhibit. The rapidity of the Rhône, the breadth of the Loire, the rocks of the Meuse, the sinuosity of the Seine, the translucency of the Somme, the historical reminiscences of the Tiber, the regal dignity of the Danube, the mysterious influence of the Nile, the golden sands of the glittering streams of the New World, the phantoms of some Asiatic stream."

I had been introduced to these words by Victor Hugo, the 19th-century French novelist, courtesy of an information board about the EuroVelo 15 / Rijnfietsroute shortly after crossing the border into the Netherlands a couple of days earlier. Although I bowed to Victor's greater purported knowledge of the other rivers that he mentioned, 182 years after he travelled in the Rhineland, the river remained one of rapidity, breadth, sinuosity, (occasional) translucency, historical reminiscences, regal dignity and mysterious influence. I have no evidence of golden sands or phantoms. Perhaps I had missed them by taking the trains.

A large part of me was on the edge of euphoria at being so close to completing my long European loop. Inevitably it was tinged with the slight sadness of my imminent return to home and to work. Yet after exactly two months of cycling, even the familiar surroundings of my house near Stainland and my colleagues and pupils at The Brooksbank School in Elland offered up a modicum of excitement. Everything considered, it was a very nice feeling. But I had not finished, not quite yet.

Wanda had spent the night in the underground garage of the Holiday Inn. She had performed effortlessly throughout the trip. The only small issue had been the front inner tube which was continuing to suggest that it had a very slow puncture. Being so close to the end of the journey I had been ignoring it for several days and nothing untoward had yet happened. On the opposite side of the road to the entrance to the underground garage was a large mural featuring several stylised bicycles and their riders. I stood Wanda beside one of the bikes and took her photo. Above her was written the following, in English:

ROTTERDAM
MAKE IT HAPPEN

It seemed to be an utterly appropriate message with which to start the final day of the journey.

However, making it happen was not just a case of popping down the road to the Hook of Holland. The Cicerone guidebook suggested a cycle of over 30km to the ferry terminal from the Erasmus bridge. That might have been OK if I were planning to catch the Stena Line ferry to Harwich, but I was not. I had arrived on the P&O ferry from Hull that docked rather inconveniently on the opposite bank of the Nieuwe Waterweg. To return there from the crooked sign at the Hook of Holland would add at least an extra 30km to the cycling day. Returning to the sign was one objective but I also needed to get home. I was looking at a cycle that could stretch to well over 60km.

I found some Rijnfietsroute signs close to the Erasmusbrug and was determined to keep following them come what may. Even at 9 am, Rotterdam harbour was a busy place. The Friday, Saturday and Sunday had been set aside to celebrate World Port Days - the largest annual maritime event in the Netherlands - which would see all kinds of nautical activity take place both on and off the water. I had received an email earlier in the week from P&O explaining that my ferry - the *Pride of Rotterdam* - would be taking part in a sail past in the harbour and although the departure time would not be delayed, embarkation times had changed. It seemed I would not be alone in racing to the ferry terminal later in the day: I might well notice the *Pride of Rotterdam* doing exactly the same thing.

The area just to the west of the city centre was not short of canals and it could quite easily have been mistaken for Amsterdam had I not known otherwise. For a city that was almost entirely destroyed during the Second World War[77], it was a remarkable pocket of authenticity where I assumed that the buildings had either been repaired or more likely, reconstructed from the rubble. Just a few kilometres away the centre of Rotterdam had been rebuilt with modern office blocks, wide boulevards and skyscrapers. The two neighbouring districts sat in stark contrast to each other.

The further west I cycled, the more thinned out the urban environment became until, after about 20km of cycling, I was able to rejoin the banks of the Nieuwe Maas. It would be here where I would stay for the remainder of the cycle to the Hook of Holland. At Maassluis I was back in familiar territory. It was the place from where I had caught the ferry from the

---

[77] In 1940, by the Germans and subsequently by the Allies although looking at photographs of the 1940 damage, the Germans had done most of the work. Many of the later raids were aimed at the shipyards and then in the latter stages of the war were restricted to leaflet and food drops.

southern side of the river on the first day of the journey. It was also the place to where I would need to return to catch the ferry back in the opposite direction later in the day.

I tried to remember what my thoughts had been as I had cycled this path nine weeks earlier. Everything that I now knew about the journey had been empty pockets of knowledge filled with hopes, expectations and, admittedly, some fears. I had known nothing of the people that I would encounter. I had known little about most of the places that I would visit. It was a satisfying feeling to begin to look back on events and reflect. Many of the hopes had been fulfilled: the cycle along the Avenue Verte, the uniqueness of Brittany, the beauty of the pink city, Toulouse and the jaw-dropping return to the Alps and Andermatt. Most of the expectations had been met but some had been dashed: the Canal du Midi chief amongst them. As for my fears... I had survived the ordeal. As a man in his 50s, I was still capable of cycling long distances for day after day after day. I had encountered few problems, just a handful of gripes that were, in fairness to all others and all places, chiefly as a result of my ongoing internal monologue. On a bicycle, there can sometimes be too much time to think.

I no longer needed the signs. There was only one direction. Yet again the river had been renamed - this time as the Nieuwe Waterweg - but someone, somewhere at some point in time had indeed once considered this as the Rhine. *How did I know?* The kilometre signs were back. In fairness, they had probably never gone away but as to which of the myriad of rivers they had chosen to follow on their own journey across the Netherlands, I had no idea. My research earlier in the week had told me that the last sign I would see before arriving back at my starting point on the beach would be the one for kilometre 1,031. Shortly after descending from the rather frivolous but fun climb to the Uitkijkpunt De Maeslantkering[78], I spotted the sign for 1,026km. Just 5 kilometres remained.

Bearing in mind it was a nice Saturday afternoon in very early September, the Hook of Holland was not a busy place. There were a good number of lean, Lycra-clad cyclists racing past me and a handful of much slower cyclists sauntering gently beside the river but there was no more congestion on the cycle path than there had been on that Sunday morning in early July. For much of the time it was just Wanda and me. Then, as I knew it would, the route turned slightly left, down a short bank beside a food kiosk and

---

[78] A 19-metre-high mound that was built as part of an enormous storm-surge barrier across the river and which now offers local cyclists the opportunity to add a short climb to their otherwise flat rides around The Netherlands. It even has its own segment on Strava.

took up position next to the water itself. Past the Atlantic Wall Museum on my right and that final sign - 1,031km since the bridge at Konstanz - we rolled over the concrete slabs weaving very occasionally to avoid the couples out for a walk. They knew nothing of my journey that was about to reach its climax. The scrubland to my right had now been replaced with sand, some of which had blown across the concrete, exactly how as I remembered at the start of the epic loop around the continent. Then, there it was. Memorably as wonky as it had been 62 days earlier, the sign telling me that I was 8,934km from Shanghai, 1,831km from St. Petersburg and just 26km from Rotterdam. I had somehow managed to stretch that to 39km but I was past caring. What I was here to see were the words emblazoned in large blue letters on each of the four sides of the square post:

HOEK VAN HOLLAND

My journey was complete.

Epilogue

Well, nearly…

After a few moments of thought and a few photographs, I got back on the bike and continued cycling. The sign had been my official starting point and it had now become my official finishing point. There remained, however, a long pier stretching out into the North Sea for another kilometre. Very slowly I cycled along it and joined the fishermen who were dangling their rods into the sea towards its furthest point. Here there was a metal tower on top of which was a small collection of navigation sensors and beacons. It seemed that the need for a lighthouse was redundant. Perhaps that is why they had moved the original Hook of Holland lighthouse to the Maritime Museum. Beyond the tower were some large concrete breakwater cubes. I could go no further. It was an isolated point and the fishermen ignored my presence. It was a moment to reflect on what had just happened, including the distance I had cycled.

I had been recording my journey via a cycling app. Each morning I would switch it on and each evening I would switch it off. I had just done so for the final time at the Hook of Holland sign. The summary statistics were as follows:

Distance - 4,705 kilometres
Ride time - 267 hours, 35 minutes
Ascent - 10,865 metres
Descent - 10,912 metres

The discrepancy between ascent and descent of 47 metres was not because the Hook of Holland was sinking but, I reasoned, down to the fact that I did not always start the app in exactly the same place that I had stopped it at the end of the previous ride. Over 55 days of cycling I had averaged a daily cycling distance of 85km.

Before setting off in July I had estimated the route to be some 5,500km but judging this to be too far to cycle in two months had afforded myself the lifeline of the ten trains. None of those trains had been over 100km in their point-to-point distances. Some had come close, but others had fallen far short. Andermatt to the Oberalp Pass had been a direct distance of just 7km. Overall, I estimated the trains to have accounted for 700 to 800km of the journey. If that had indeed been the case, my initial estimate of 5,500km had been remarkably accurate.

I was delighted to have completed my loop but my enthusiasm for doing much more cycling had plummeted during the kilometre-long cycle along the pier. If the *Pride of Rotterdam* had returned from its visit to the festival in Rotterdam, it was now floating in its berth just 8km away. However, I would need to cycle at least 30km back down the river to the ferry at Maassluis, cross the water and then cycle in the opposite direction towards Europort Rotterdam. It was a journey that I could not avoid so, with a dwindling amount of energy left in reserve, I set off. I did at least have time on my side. It was only midday and the ferry would not leave until 8 pm. I could probably have pushed Wanda and still arrived in good time.

It was now the fourth time that I had cycled this way and I was seizing upon any opportunity to get off the bike and procrastinate. I had already spent a good amount of time watching the world - and its ships - go by close to the Atlantic Wall Museum and by the time I arrived at the small Hook of Holland harbour I was ready for another rest. It was from here that I had caught the ferry on that first day of the journey. It had meant that I had not been required to return to the Maassluis ferry. It was not an option today as it did not have the Europort on its itinerary.

Lots of recent building work had taken place in the area adjacent to the harbour. A new metro station had been built but it was not yet operational. That was a pity, I thought. *How nice it would be to jump on a tram for the journey to Maassluis.* A new tourist information office had also been built and it was open so I popped in to pass some time.

As I browsed, the man behind the counter started chatting. He had noticed Wanda, her panniers and the tent outside the building.

"Where have you cycled from?" he asked.

"From Andermatt along the Rhine," I replied.

"In that case, you must have a certificate!" he declared.

He proceeded to find, stamp and then sign a certificate proving to anyone who should doubt it that I had indeed cycled the length of the EuroVelo 15. No actual proof was required and I made no mention of the two trains but let's not quibble: a certificate is a certificate. I promised to frame it once I arrived back home.

"It's a pity the station is not open yet," I commented, gesturing in the vague direction of the building behind the tourist office.

"No, but you can use the old station - it's just over there," he explained pointing in the opposite direction. "You can take your bike on the metro and it will take you to the Maassluis ferry."

This was excellent news. He had just cut my journey in two. All I now needed to do was cycle the 15 kilometres back to the ferry on the other side of the water.

"I'm sorry I don't have an envelope for the certificate. But you can have this magazine. It will keep it flat," he said, handing me a thick tourist brochure.

"I actually started my journey at the Hook of Holland two months ago and cycled around France and up the Rhône before setting off from Andermatt along the Rhine," I explained.

"Wow! That's a long trip. Sorry, but we only have certificates for the Rhine Cycle Route," he explained, apologetically. "But we have Hook of Holland T-shirts. How about one of those?"

With that, my story was complete.

I had cycled from the Hook of Holland to the Hook of Holland.

I had been there, completed the cycle and had even bought the T-shirt.

Le Grand Tour

Acknowledgements

First and foremost can I thank you, the reader. Some of you will have already read my previous books and if you are in that category, thanks for having faith in me once again. I hope I did not let you down. If you are new to my writing, thank you for having made the effort to find me. Hopefully what you have read will encourage you to stay on board.

Although my previous book, *Spain to Norway on a Bike Calle Reggie* was published via Summersdale / Hachette, *Le Grand Tour* has been self-published. There has been no big team of professionals helping me to edit, check, format and market the book. That said, building upon the experiences of self-publishing my first two books, I have hopefully avoided some of the inevitable pitfalls associated with the do-it-yourself method of publication. Chief amongst these is the quality of the text itself and I am very grateful to a small group of people who have been willing to read what I have written and give honest feedback. Travel writers Helen Moat (*A Time of Birds*, Saraband) and Steve Silk (*The Great North Road*, Summersdale) were both well-placed to make invaluable qualitative comments about the first draft of *Le Grand Tour*. It is thanks to them that you didn't have to wade through page after page of interminable prologue before I actually got going and that the palette of colours was somewhat wider than it might otherwise have been. Giles Cudmore, Brian Palmer, Piers Lesser, Tim Sanders and Craig Dodson have all been equally helpful is pointing out the factual errors, misspellings and typos. I take sole responsibility for the ones that remain.

Andy Mitchell did an excellent job in providing the striking cover artwork for the trilogy of *...on a Bike Called Reggie* books. However, it seemed appropriate to explore a new look for this first *...on a Bike Called Wanda* book and I was delighted to stumble upon the designer Ellie Way. Like Andy and me, Ellie is Yorkshire-based and she has developed a reputation for designing travel posters inspired by the 'golden age of travel'. The title of this book – *Le Grand Tour* – nods in a similar direction and after meeting Ellie at her studio in Wakefield it was immediately obvious that she shared my enthusiasm for the project. The cover that she has produced is simply stunning and I cannot express how grateful I am to her. I would encourage you to visit Ellie's website – ellieway.co.uk - to see more of her work.

I would also like to thank all those people who were involved on *Le Grand Tour* well before I sat down at my computer and started to type. The people who accommodated me: Froukje and Paul in Vlissingen, Bram, his family and friends on the co-housing project in Ostend, Mizu in Paris, Joëlle in Saint-Briac-sur-Mer, Marick in Agen, Jean-Daniel and his son Célien in Sierre (and their extended family who I joined in celebrating Jean-Daniel's father's birthday) and former colleague Janina, her husband Henning and their two children in Cologne. They were all, without exception, excellent hosts.

I am very grateful to the people who appeared on the series of podcasts that were published during the journey. Many of the voices belong to unknown people I met along the way in shops, at campsites or tourist information offices, but some agreed to be more formally interviewed: cyclists Fabian, Julian and Guillaume in Brittany, Cyril of SouriezVousPédalez.com, Geoff Husband of Breton Bikes, David and Christine Naylor along the Nantes-Brest Canal, Rich and Becca in Andermatt, Claud Butler who was an excellent guide for my first day along the Rhine Cycle Route, Ken Wynn in Liechtenstein and David Ryan in Kehl.

There were many people who advised me from afar via social media and email: of particular note are the aforementioned Tim Sanders whose campsite suggestions were much appreciated, as were those of the aforementioned David Naylor who was advising me well before we actually met in person. Cathryn Ramsden's email giving positive feedback on the podcasts was also a delight to receive. Thanks to all of them and to all the others whose names I do not know or who I have forgotten to mention.

Finally, three people who featured in my first book, *Crossing Europe on a Bike Called Reggie* and who made a cameo return for book four. Basil and Liz Ford who I was delighted to spend the day with in Pézenas and German friend Claus Blanz who drove over the border into Austria to have lunch with me beside the Bodensee. In a summer packed with unfamiliar faces, it was wonderful to see their familiar ones after so many years.

About the author

Andrew P. Sykes was born and grew up in the small town of Elland, in the foothills of the Pennines in West Yorkshire and he studied for a degree in mathematics at the University of York. Following a period of time working in London and then France, he returned to the UK in 1999 to train as a secondary school teacher of French at the University of Reading. He taught in Berkshire and Oxfordshire for 15 years before taking a career break in 2015 to learn some Spanish, cycle from Tarifa in Spain to Nordkapp in Norway and move back to live in Yorkshire. He now teaches at the same school that he attended as a pupil during the 1980s.

Since 2009 he has been travelling long distances on his bicycles: first Reggie, now Wanda (with Ronnie taking up the slack on the shorter commutes to work). This is his fourth book about travelling in Europe. Accounts of all of his journeys can be found on his website CyclingEurope.org.

Andrew also produces a podcast, *The Cycling Europe Podcast*, that can be heard across all major podcast platforms. More details at CyclingEurope.org/Podcast. He has made a number of films about his cycling journeys and they can all be watched online by visiting YouTube.com/AndrewPSykes. He is also present on social media @CyclingEurope.

Andrew regularly gives talks about his travels. If you would like him to speak at your event, please get in touch. His email address is: andrew@cyclingeurope.org

———

"This is a self-published book. There is no large, marketing operation to support my efforts: just a man with a computer. I very much appreciate the support you have shown by buying the book. If you have enjoyed it and would like to support me further, one way you can do that is by writing a short online review for the book. Thanks if you do."

Andrew

**Now you've read the book,
listen to the series of podcasts and watch the films:**

CyclingEurope.org/Podcast

CyclingEurope.org/Films

*"Andrew regretted standing in the field as the
farmer made hay bales"*
C.L. Chadwick
(Caption competition winner)

CyclingEurope.org
CYCLING | TRAVEL | ADVENTURE | PODCAST

Printed in Great Britain
by Amazon

40974035R00212